CONTENTS

CANADA
BRITISH COLUMBIA
VANCOUVER ISLAND

NOOTKA SOUND

Surveyed by Mr H.D.Parizeau, Comdr J.H.Knight and assistants, 1933-34

Published under the orders of

The Honourable The Minister of Mines and Resources of Canada.

This chart is on the Mercator Projection based on Lat. 52° N.

a Burdwood Pt Lat 49°34′36″93 N., Long 126°34′05″48 W.

All bearings are true, this 295′5′ and are given from seaward.

SOUNDINGS in FATHOMS

reduced to Lowest Normal Tides.

Natural Scale, 76,871 (Lat 49°36′N.)

Tidal Information

Place	Mean Lunitidal Intervals		Height above Datum of Soundings			
	High Water	Lower L.W.	Higher H.W. Springs	Lower H.W. Neaps	Lower L.W. Springs	Mean Level
	Hrs. Min.	Hrs. Min.	Feet	Feet	Feet	Feet
Ceepeecee	XII 00	XVIII 20	12 to 12½	9	4 to ⁻2¼	7⁴
Friendly Cove	XII 00	XVIII 20	11½ .. 12½	8¼	⁻⁴ .. ⁻2¼	6⁶
Riley Cove	XII 04	XVIII 26	11¼ .. 13	8¼	⁻⁴ .. ⁻2¼	7⁶
Hayden Pass	For High Water Slack add 52 min. and for Low Water Slack add 29 min. to the times of high and low water at Ceepeecee, the duration of the slack averages 15 minutes.					

The tide is moderately declinational. For the time of higher high water and lower low water the intervals are applied to the moons upper transit in north declination and to the lower transit in south declination.

For more detailed information concerning tides see Tide Tables for the Pacific Coast of Canada published annually by the Hydrographic and Map Service, Department of Mines and Resources, Ottawa. Price 25 cents.

Bench Marks

The datum of this chart at Friendly Cove is 6.35 feet below a bench mark, the top of a ringbolt, the most northerly of three bolts below high water mark, 48 feet distant from the angle formed by the Union Oil Companys wharf and the Government wharf.

The datum of this chart at Ceepeecee is 61 feet below a bench mark, the top of a brass plug set in the rocky foreshore, below high water mark, on the inside of the westerly point of the bay, 75 feet west of the north-west boundary stake of the Canadian Packing Companys property.

Conuma Pt

MUCHALAT INLET

PIERCE

VARIATION 24° 45′ E. (1940)

VANCOUVER ISLAND'S **WEST COAST**

A wise nation fosters national pride and love of country by references to the past.

JOSEPH HOWE

VANCOUVER ISLAND'S

West Coast

1762-1962

by George Nicholson

George Nicholson
Victoria, B.C.

WITH ILLUSTRATIONS, MAP AND LIST OF SHIPWRECKS

DESIGNED AND PRINTED BY THE
MORRISS PRINTING COMPANY LTD., VICTORIA, BRITISH COLUMBIA.

The text is set in 11 point Baskerville.

First printing September 1962.
Second printing April 1963.
Third printing October 1964.
Fourth printing October 1966.
Fifth printing March 1968.

INTRODUCTION

THE HISTORY of British Columbia begins at Nootka.

Presented in a series of short stories, primarily for easy reading, the narratives here cover practically every event of historic value since the first Spaniard sailed along our coast in 1774; Captain Cook's landing at Nootka in 1778, when he thus became the first European to land on these shores, the fur traders who came shortly afterwards, the occupation of Nootka by the Spaniards, an incident which nearly led to war between England and Spain, and the naming of Vancouver Island by Captain George Vancouver, are but a few.

Fortunately, the journals of these early explorers and some of the fur traders have been preserved, and with them hundreds of priceless exhibits in the form of documents, charts, logs and letters written in their own handwriting. Much of this material, either the originals or authentic copies, can be found in our provincial archives, the British Museum, the Washington State University Library and other repositories of natural, scientific and literary curiosities.

It is conceded that no writer could attempt to present in detail the complete history of the west coast of Vancouver Island in one volume. Books by the score, most of which can be found on the shelves of our provincial and public libraries, have been written on the subject. But in general each treats the episodes of one man, group or period, and because of distance, time and other circumstances, their availability to students of history and the reading public in general is restricted.

From this mass of material the writer, in direct language without "frills", has condensed the bare facts of the more noteworthy events of historic and educational value into a single volume. No attempt has been made to delve into Indian history; such is for the anthropologists. But throughout will be found a great deal about the ways, customs and superstitions of these people, the names of the different tribes, the principal chiefs and where they resided, tribal wars, plus a vivid account of their first meeting with the white man and how they reacted.

Narrated also, are the experiences of early missionaries and pioneer settlers, the establishment of the first trading posts and about the schooners which brought supplies: shipwrecks which occurred on this part of the coast, tales of heroism associated with these and in some instances the graphic details. Events are not all in chronological order, and repetitions occur, but avoidance would change the context of the story. And only here and there do we leave the West Coast.

As it was my privilege to reside in this area for over thirty years, when the nature of my livelihood took me to every part, local knowledge made the task that much easier, and in some instances, verification of the facts more complete. Personal acquaintance with most of the older Indians also proved helpful, for events of interest which now fill our history books have been handed down, by word of mouth, through several generations. Gain the confidence of these people, have patience, and soon their stories are revealed.

I have quoted freely from Captain John T. Walbran's book *British Columbia Coast Names,* published in 1909 by the Geographic Board of Canada, and the memoirs of Rev. A. J. Brabant, the first missionary on the West Coast (1874-1908). Among others who have contributed liberally to material which appears in these pages are Rev. Charles Moser, the priest who succeeded Father Brabant, sealing schooner skippers, ship captains, fur buyers, pioneer settlers, lighthouse-keepers and others familiar with the West Coast and its history.

In many instances the story not only narrates early happenings of historical interest, but describes subsequent development of that particular locality in which the incident occurred, the object being to present a picture of the West Coast of Vancouver Island as we find it today, featuring its now populated areas, industries and improved means of communication, together with personal sketches of certain individuals who were responsible for bringing this about. Also briefly described are some of the area's scenic attractions, a few of the writer's personal experiences, phenomena peculiar to the waters of the West Coast and strange happenings of human interest.

With the historical events which occurred in the eighteenth and early nineteenth centuries duly chronicled, let us bear in mind that history was also being made on the West Coast in the years to follow; by lone traders, early missionaries, schooner captains and pioneer settlers. These men have all passed away and multi-million dollar industrial plants today stand as monuments to their courage and enterprise. But will their memory forever remain green? I think not, unless we find a niche for their names and achievements in history books of today. If we do this, present and future generations of these people can point with pride to the part their forebears played in the settling and subsequent development of so important a part of the province of British Columbia.

Pressed by friends and having accepted the challenge, it is my sincere wish that the stories will be of interest, not only to the general public, but to all who have had occasion to be associated with the west coast of Vancouver Island, its people and industries. Also, that they may recall pleasant memories to all those people who were privileged to make that never-to-be-forgotten six-day round trip on the Good Ship *Princess Maquinna*.

GEORGE NICHOLSON, Victoria, B.C.

Note: Unless otherwise stated, the term "West Coast" refers to the west coast of Vancouver Island only.

THE THREE
PRINCIPAL CHIEFS

WHEN CAPTAIN COOK and his Spanish contemporaries first landed on the shores of the west coast of Vancouver Island, the region's three principal Indian chiefs were Maquinna, Wickaninnish and Tatoosh.

Maquinna ruled the Nootka tribes and from the fact that the activities of these early explorers centred mostly around Nootka Sound, his name, spelt by different traders — Maquilla, Mokwinna, Moquina and Mocuina — appears most frequently in their journals.

Wickaninnish reigned over the Clayoquots. His principal village was at Opitis-aht, on Meares Island, opposite what is now Tofino. But he had several other homes, including a summer residence at Long Beach (proper name Wickaninnish Bay).

Tatoosh was chief of the Makahs, a tribe which inhabits the northwest tip of Washington State. His home was at Neah Bay, just inside Cape Flattery, but his authority extended along both shores of Juan de Fuca Strait.

Maquinna Point on Nootka Island's outside coast, Wickaninnish Island on Clayoquot Sound and Wickaninnish Bay, and Tatoosh Island on which Cape Flattery lighthouse stands, perpetuate their names.

The name "Maquinna" has been passed down through several generations of direct descendants to the present-day Nootka chief. However, with his two contemporaries the line has long since been broken and today there is neither a Wickaninnish nor a Tatoosh.

Cook found Maquinna very friendly and spoke highly of him in his journals. So did Captain George Vancouver who visited Nootka several years later, and the Spaniards who for eight years occupied

13

Friendly Cove. The same can be said of the early traders, even though Maquinna's men were responsible for plundering and sinking several of their ships — incidents which certain traders brought about themselves chiefly through dishonest trading and supplying the natives with rum.

The blackest mark against Wickaninnish's record, or that of a chief by the same name who succeeded him, was in 1811, when his men murdered the entire crew of the American trading ship *Tonquin,* and then set the vessel on fire. And again at Matilda Creek (Ahousat) in 1864, when one of his sub-chiefs and twelve men attacked and killed the crew of the trading sloop *Kingfisher.*

Traders never ventured ashore in the territory ruled by Tatoosh. Furs were purchased "over the side" from Indians who came out in canoes, with the ship's crew ready with loaded rifles. In 1854, United States engineers first attempted to build a lighthouse on Tatoosh Island, but the chief and his people, many of whom then lived on the island, resisted their every effort. Three years passed, with considerable bloodshed on both sides, before the light was established.

Reference to the three chiefs, with accounts of the above incidents and many others, will be found throughout these pages.

KNOW AS "OLD FAITHFUL," a Canadian Pacific Steamship Company vessel served the West Coast for many years — through fair weather and foul. Because the ship is mentioned so frequently throughout these pages, her story comes first.

". . . at 4 p.m., the Good Ship *Princess Maquinna* was at Uchucklesit, northbound." This terse message fishermen, loggers, miners, lighthouse-keepers, in fact everyone on the West Coast, heard on their radios every night at eight. Regularly at that hour, as a feature of his news broadcast, the late Earle Kelly, "Mr. Good Evening," used to announce the position of the ship that day. Of his listening audience who lived in other parts of British Columbia, few knew or cared that such a ship existed, let alone where she sailed or the places of call; but to West Coasters it meant a great deal.

Owing to weather, tides, fog and extra stops, *Maquinna*'s schedule was flexible. One never knew when she would round the corner and blow her familiar long-short-long-short whistle. At Kildonan, Kakawis or Kyuquot, she might be due one morning but not arrive till midnight or some time the following day. Persons living at isolated points had to come miles by gasboat, rowboat or canoe to meet her. There were no roads to the steamer's cannery, mine or logging camp stops. By knowing her whereabouts at 4 p.m. each day they were able to figure out her time of arrival to within a few hours, thereby saving themselves a wait and wonder about when she would come along with mail, supplies and passengers.

The *Princess Maquinna* was in every sense of the term Victoria's own ship, in fact, the only one of the Canadian Pacific Railway Company's large fleet which Victorians could really call their own.

Named after a princess, daughter of a famed West Coast Indian, Chief Maquinna of the Nootkas, the one-funnelled, single-screw *Princess Maquinna* was built at Esquimalt and launched in 1913. She was under construction at the shipbuilding yards of the B.C. Marine Railway Co. Ltd., when that firm was purchased by Yarrows Ltd. Victoria was her port of registration and the home of her crew. She underwent annual overhaul and repairs there.

An inside berth at the Belleville Street dock was the starting and finishing point of the West Coast trip she made regularly for forty years without interruption. Designed and built specially for this run, she knew no other. Promptly at 11 p.m. every tenth day, a short toot of her whistle and with perhaps a dozen people on hand to bid goodbye to friends or relatives bound up-coast, "Old Faithful" slipped her lines and silently backed out to begin the first leg of another trip to Port Alice and back. With anywhere from fifty to one hundred passengers, most for way points, but probably thirty booked for the round trip, and her holds loaded with groceries and supplies for canneries, logging camps and small settlements comprising her twenty-six scheduled northbound stopping places. During the summer months the number of round trippers might reach more than one hundred.

Then at noon on the seventh day the familiar company whistle was heard. To the average Victorian this meant just another C.P.R. ship coming in, but to the captain and crew of the *Princess Maquinna,* it was back home again.

Travelling by the *Maquinna,* one experienced the novelty and enjoyment of traditional passenger ship customs of years ago, long discontinued with the coming of the more streamlined inter-city coastal ferry steamers. The ship sailed from the dockside proper and the old-fashioned gangplank was used. Instead of street farewells, friends were permitted aboard until five minutes before sailing time.

A warning whistle was blown at all stopping places, giving those sightseeing ashore ample time to return to the ship. If a couple was left behind, the captain turned back and picked them up. Afternoon tea and midnight supper was served (free) to all passengers. A stewardess took care of the women and children. Senior officers dined with the passengers, the captain presiding at his table, first officer, chief engineer and purser at others.

The most friendly relations between passengers and crew were encouraged. Officers promoted deck games and were always on hand to point out scenic views, landmarks, local characters and the many historical spots of interest along the coast. Bridge, music and dancing was enjoyed in the evenings and often the ship's officers and passengers attended a dance ashore at some remote cannery, logging camp or settlement.

Ports of call were diversified in the extreme. First stop, the logging settlement of Port Renfrew, only five hours out from Victoria. Then Clo-oose, an Indian village where the natives came out in their dugout canoes for mail and supplies. When the weather was fine and the sea calm, stops were made at Carmanah and Pachena lighthouses, where the lightkeeper and his assistant met the ship in the station dory. Next regular stop was Bamfield. Calls were then made at canneries and logging camps on Barkley Sound. Port Alberni was usually reached late in the afternoon of the first day out.

The next day was taken up with calls at Ucluelet, Tofino, Clayoquot, Kakawis and Ahousat, then Hot Springs Cove, where Vancouver Island's only hot sulphur springs are located. An hour later anchor was dropped off Hesquiat Indian village, in the lee of Estevan Point, where again the natives came out in dugouts and gasboats.

Nootka cannery and Friendly Cove, where Cook landed in 1778, were also on the schedule. Then more canneries and fish reduction plants, logging camps, the big export mill at Tahsis, Ceepeecee, Esperanza and Zeballos, the latter a fabulous mining town where, when the mines were in operation (1938-1945), the *Maquinna* usually took on board each trip gold bricks valued at a quarter of a million dollars.

Next call Chamiss Bay where supplies for the fishing village of Kyuquot were landed. Then came the long haul around Cape Cook into scenic Quatsino Sound and before reaching Port Alice, her destination, she made stops at Winter Harbour, Quatsino village and still more canneries, mines and logging camps. A whole day was sometimes spent at Port Alice loading pulp at the local mill. Then the southbound trip back to Victoria with most of the interesting calls to be made over again *en route*.

Captain E. Gillam, the original master who occupied her bridge for twenty years, died at his post on board the *Princess Norah,* a ship that had just come out from Scotland to take the *Maquinna's* place. His acts of human kindness will always be remembered on the West Coast. Years ago, the only hospitals of the area were at Port Alberni and Port Alice, two hundred miles apart. If by reaching either place a few hours ahead of time might save the life of a seriously ill or injured person brought on board at some remote village, or to avoid converting a ship's stateroom into a maternity ward for convenience of a woman who had left the "happy event" too late, Captain Gillam thought nothing of passing up several stops. They could be made afterwards.

Succeeding him on the *Maquinna*'s bridge in turn were Captains R. (Red) and W. (Black) Thomson (no relationship) and P. L. Leslie, all now deceased, Martin MacKinnon, Leonard McDonald and R. W. Carthew.

The *Norah* never did replace the *Maquinna*. She relieved her during annual overhaul, and was used for two summers as an additional ship on the run, then placed in the Alaska trade.

After rounding out forty years faithful service to the people of the West Coast and her owners, the "Good Ship *Princess Maquinna*" finally gave up. Her boilers could no longer raise the necessary steam and in consequence her speed had already been reduced from fourteen knots to a little better than nine.

It happened one night in September 1952, when she was already loaded, passengers and mail aboard and about ready to sail. Ten minutes before sailing time, Captain Carthew, her last master, assembled his passengers in the saloon and informed them that she had made her last trip and would sail no more. They would be permitted to stay on board (many had already retired for the night) and be provided with breakfast, but must find their own way up coast as best they could.

Stripped down to the bare hull, converted into an ore carrier and re-named the *Taku,* for the next eight years — at the end of a towline — she carried concentrates from a mine in Alaska to Tacoma. But the inevitable end for this gallant old vessel has at last come and as this is written she is being cut up for her metal at a ship-breaker's yard.

In her place is a smaller vessel operated by Northland Navigation Company Ltd. out of Vancouver. Roads have since been built to many parts of the West Coast. Planes also provide passenger and mail service.

Preceding the *Princess Maquinna* in the West Coast trade were the steamers *Maude, Willapa, Queen City* and *Tees*. All maintained regular but not as frequent schedules, and before their time intermittent sailings were made by smaller vessels still. The steam schooner *Mischief* was one of them.

HISTORICAL NOOTKA

*Friendly Cove, Cook's
landing place.*

IN THE LATTER PART of the eighteenth century, Nootka was the centre of a bitter dispute between Great Britain and Spain which almost led to war. And the place got an evil reputation following the massacre there of the trading ship *Boston*'s crew by Maquinna's people early in the next century. It is one of the really historic spots on Vancouver Island's west coast.

In July 1776, aboard the barque *Resolution*, Captain James Cook, R.N., sailed from England on his third (and last) voyage of exploration around the world. In his expedition was also the ship *Discovery*, Captain Charles Clarke, R.N. Purpose was to prove whether or not the mythical "Northwest Passage" actually existed. Unsuccessful attempts had hitherto been made by many others.

Though Cook's actual sailing date was July 13, he logged it as the 12th, probably on superstitious grounds. The trip was made via the Cape of Good Hope. Cook stopped at Table Bay for awhile, then visited New Zealand for the second time. The Society Islands and several other groups were touched at and in January 1778, he (Cook) discovered the Sandwich Islands, now known as Hawaii.

Two months later the two ships set course northeast, making their first landfall off the Oregon coast. On March 29, 1778 they entered what is now known as Nootka Sound and anchored in the vicinity of Bligh Island. A few days later, Cook took the longboat and landed at Friendly Cove. Thus he became the first European to set foot on the shores of what is now known as British Columbia.

Because Cook noticed that the natives possessed coins and trinkets of Spanish origin, he knew that the Spaniards must have made contact with them somewhere along the coast, but there was no evidence of them having landed here or that they claimed sovereignty over the territory. He was also unaware that the cove was on a small island (Nootka), or that the land in the vicinity was part of another and larger island (Vancouver Island). He raised the Union Jack and claimed this part of the coast of North America for Great Britain.

The Spaniards, under Estevano Martinez, did land at Friendly Cove, on May 5, 1789, eleven years after Cook, when they seized three British merchant ships and occupied the place until March 25, 1795. The dispute as to the sovereignty of this part of the coast was in the meantime settled (in favour of the British) by arbitration and the Spanish garrison withdrawn without incident.

From the fact that his ships anchored here, Cook thus also became the discoverer of Nootka Sound, though the Spaniards mistakenly claimed priority in 1774, under the name San Lorenzo. Cook first named the inlet King George's Sound, afterwards changing the name to Nootka under the impression it was the Indian name. It is incorrect, however, to say there is no such word as *nootka* (nutka) in the Indian language. There is, in fact, such a word, and the Rev. A. J. Brabant, who resided at Hesquiat for upwards of thirty years and was thoroughly conversant with the native language, explains it thus:

"The word *nootka* is a frequentation of *nutka-sitl,* to go around or make a circuit. *Nutka-a* would be a form of imperative (accent on last 'a' being slight), go around, *nutka-aktl-nish,* we are about to go around. Some form of the word *nootka* may be applied to making a circuit of the globe, or of an island, small or large, only the affix varies according to time and place. The name, therefore, may have been given understandably by Cook who made the tour of the sound (not the island) in his small boats from the small bay known as Friendly Cove, as is recorded in his journal. He probably asked the Indians, making a comprehensive sweep of his arm, what was the name of the place. The Indians may have replied with some form of the word *nootka.* In this way the word could have been impressed on Cook's mind as the proper name."

That the Spaniards did make contact with the Indians on this part of the coast, four years before Cook, is not disputed, but it wasn't at Nootka and they never actually landed. On January 25, 1774, Juan Perez sailed from San Blas in the corvette *Santiago,* and from Monterey, Mexico, on June 6 the same year on a voyage of discovery to the northwest coast of America.

Three months later he arrived back at Monterey. Adverse winds and fog kept him well clear of the coast for most of the voyage, but his log showed that he sighted land on several occasions. Also, that he contacted the Indians at the northern tip of the Queen Charlotte Islands, and again near Estevan Point on his way south. The Indians came out in their canoes to meet him, and a little trading took place, but both times the wind suddenly sprang up and the *Santiago* had to leave without Perez or any of his crew going ashore.

Before making the Estevan Point contact, while proceeding cautiously owing to poor visibility, Perez found himself in an indentation of the sea. This he named San Lorenzo, the day being the anniversary of the festival of that saint (St. Lawrence). It afterwards transpired that the *Santiago* was off the entrance of what is now known as Nootka Sound, but there is no evidence that Perez was aware of the existence of any sound or inlet. He apparently mistook it for a big, open bay.

The Indians met near Estevan Point were Hesquiats, a sub-band of the Nootkas, and many of the small articles they received from the *Santiago*'s crew members subsequently came into the possession of Maquinna, the Nootka chief. These Cook noticed when he landed at Friendly Cove four years later. (More about Estevan Point and Perez' contact with the Indians on pages 35-41).

Nootka Island is the largest on the West Coast, 25 miles long, 16 wide and separated from Vancouver Island proper by a narrow passage navigable by vessels of any size. Its two white settlements are Hecate (H.M.S. *Hecate*) on the north coast and Nootka village on the southeast. Only a handful of people reside at each of these places, except during the summer months at Nootka, where about fifty are employed at a fish reduction plant. The plant was originally built by the late William R. Lord who pioneered the pilchard industry (see page 244). It is now operated by Canadian Fishing Company Ltd. Before that, Mr. Lord had a salmon cannery at Nootka, the third to be built on the West Coast. The other two were at Kildonan on Barkley Sound (B.C. Packers Ltd.) and at Kenfalls on Clayoquot Sound.

There are two Indian villages on the island: Nuchatlaht on the northwest coast and Friendly Cove at the south end. Near Nootka lighthouse, which stands on a rocky headland at the entrance to Friendly Cove, are two stone monuments. One, a cairn of uncut stone, a pyramid eleven feet tall, was erected by the Historical Sites and Monuments Board of Canada. Its tablet, unveiled August 13,

1924, by Walter Cameron Nichol, Lieutenant-Governor of British Columbia, bears the following inscription:

Nootka Sound, discovered by Captain Cook in March, 1778. In June, 1789, Spain took possession and established and maintained a settlement until 1795. The capture of British vessels almost led to war, which was avoided by the Nootka Convention in 1790. Vancouver and Quadra met here in August, 1792, to determine the land to be restored under the convention.

The inscription on the other reads:

Vancouver and Quadra met here in August, 1792, under the treaty between Spain and Great Britain of October, 1790. Erected by the Washington State University Historical Society, 1903.

An inscription on the cornerstone of the new Roman Catholic church at Friendly Cove, built to replace one destroyed by fire in 1955, commemorates another historic event. It reads: "A.D. 1788. Meares built on this spot the *Northwest America.*" The *Northwest America* was the first ship built on the northwest coast of America (see page 45). The site is also where the Spaniard's church stood.

After a month's stay, occupied principally with replacing spars and repairing gear, Cook sailed northwest in continuation of his mission, to find the "Northwest Passage." Ice in the Bering Sea interfered with these plans and his ships headed south for the Sandwich Islands, where it was intended to winter and head north again in the spring.

Here, at Karakakooa Bay, Owhyhee (Hawaii), Cook met his death. During the night of February 13, 1779, one of the *Discovery*'s boats was stolen by the natives. Cook, with a party of marines, landed the following day in an attempt to retrieve it. A scuffle with the natives compelled them to retreat to their boats. Cook was the last to retire and as he was nearing the beach he received a blow from behind which felled him. He arose immediately and vigorously resisted the crowds that pressed upon him, but as the boat crews were unable to render assistance he was soon overpowered.

Friendly Cove, whose Indian name is Yuquot or Youkw-aht, derived from the words *yuk-witte,* wind, and *aht,* people of village, is the ancestral home of Chief Maquinna and the Nootka Indians. The proper name of the tribe is Mo-achts or Mow-ach-ahts, "Indians of the deer," because deer *(mowach)* were plentiful in their domain. At the time of Cook's landing, Indians residing there, or thereabouts, numbered several thousand. Today, they number only a few hundred. All Indians residing at other points on the west coast of Vancouver Island are sub-bands of the Nootka. The cove's entire white population consists of a lone Roman Catholic priest, with the lighthouse-keeper, his family and the assistant light-keeper, living in the vicinity of the light. Standing in front of Chief Maquinna's house is the Governor-General's Totem, bearing a brass plate indicating that it was presented to Lord Willingdon, when governor-general of Canada.

Although friendliness of the natives is recorded in Cook's journals, it was some time after that famous navigator's death that the place was named Friendly Cove. This was bestowed upon it, obviously on account of the natives' friendliness, in 1786, by Mr. Strange, super-cargo of a trading expedition to this coast consisting of the "snows" *Captain Cook* (Captain Lawrie) and *Experiment* (Captain Guise). A snow is a vessel with two main masts and a third small mast to carry a trysail.

Friendly Cove has an extensive burial ground. Found on the graves, many now slabbed with concrete, is an unusual collection of sewing machines, gramophones, canoes and former personal belongings of the deceased, items of almost every conceivable nature, even to handbags and old corsets. On one grave is a small gasboat complete with engine and propeller. By now, maybe there are vint-age radios. Whether or not the drag-saw (see page 25) was placed on Chief Napoleon Maquinna's grave, the writer hasn't been back to learn. The practice of placing on a person's grave all of his, or her, personal effects, although discouraged by the priests, is still common among our coast Indians.

Most of the adult Nootkas are fishermen who operate their own salmon trollers and seine boats. Others find year-round employment in the logging camps and mills.

In 1908, Albert Leon, a notorious Russian counterfeiter, pur-chased an abandoned farm not far from Friendly Cove. At this secret hideout he manufactured his product and through the medium of two accomplices in the United States was soon flooding that country with spurious $20 bills. However, the United States Treasury, assisted by the British Columbia Police, finally caught up with Leon and his associates in crime. All three were convicted and sentenced to long terms in Leavenworth prison.

It was at Friendly Cove, in 1803, that the Nootkas murdered the captain and almost the entire crew of the trading ship *Boston,* then plundered, burned and sank the ship (see story page 71).

On January 16, 1865, the American barque *Iwanowna,* after drifting helplessly for several weeks, was wrecked on the outside shores of Nootka Island; six lives were lost. Two sealing schooners were wrecked on Nootka Island during a gale, January 23, 1892: the *Northern Light* at the north end, and the *Laura* at Friendly Cove. Both crews were rescued and brought to Victoria by a schooner which rode out the storm.

In January 1898, the British steamer *Commonwealth*, 6,200 tons, Kobe to Portland, Ore., in ballast, lost her propeller when 500 miles off Vancouver Island. Sails were rigged and the vessel finally anchored off entrance to Nootka Sound. Picked up by the steamer *Willapa* (Captain Foote), she was towed to Sydney Inlet and later to Victoria by the tug *Lorne*. The four-masted U.S. schooner *Kilueve*, as a derelict, found bottom-up on Bajo Reef, 10 miles west of Friendly Cove, March 1903; fate of crew unknown. Also wrecked on Bajo Reef, on December 13, 1905, was the sailing ship *King David* with the loss of seven lives.

The barge *Louisiana,* former American ship, beached and burned in Nootka Sound in 1929. The former North Vancouver Ferry *No. 2*, converted into a floating logging camp and now the property of Gibson Brothers, burned to water's edge at Tahsis Inlet, Nootka Sound, February 8, 1939. The Vancouver tug *Royal No. 2* sank in Tahsis Inlet, January 1961.

Nootka lighthouse was established in 1911, and a foghorn installed in 1928.

THE GOVERNOR-GENERAL'S TOTEM

*Ceremony at Friendly Cove has
a unique and profitable ending.*

AN AMUSING INCIDENT occurred at Friendly Cove when Governor-
General of Canada, Lord Willingdon, and the Honourable
Randolph Bruce, then Lieutenant-Governor of British Columbia,
made a trip up the West Coast aboard the new C.P.R. steamer
Princess Norah.

Napoleon Maquinna was the Nootka chief at this time and by
way of doing honour and emphasizing loyalty to the "Skookum
Chief," the governor-general, he was to present His Excellency
with a 30-foot totem pole specially carved by one of his tribesmen
for the occasion.

The vice-regal party, which had come ashore in the *Norah's*
boats and landed on the beach, was escorted to a grassy patch in
front of the village where the totem stood. Officials, ship's officers
and passengers, cannery workers from nearby Nootka and every
Indian within gasboat range gathered around. Introductions were
made through natives of the younger generation and presentation
of the totem carried out by Chief Maquinna to Lord Willingdon.

His Excellency thanked them for the gift, then a running conversation followed through an interpreter, between Lieutenant-
Governor Bruce and the chief, who at this stage appeared to make
it perfectly clear that the presentation of the totem was very definitely a potlatch — in other words, "I give, sometime you give me
something too." Realizing "he was on the spot," there was nothing
Bruce could do but ask the chief what he would like in return.
After an exchange in Chinook between the young interpreter and
Chief Maquinna, the answer was a "drag-saw" (power saw).

The next regular trip of the *Princess Maquinna* the chief received

25

his drag-saw, notwithstanding the fact such articles cost about $250. The Nootkas are recognized as handy mechanics and their fuel supply chore was no doubt a much easier one from then on.

As for the totem, the policy of the Department of Indian Affairs was to discourage as far as possible removal of totems, effigies, welcome figures and such-like Indian relics from native environments. His Excellency graciously acquiesced and his totem was allowed to remain where it stood and is there to this day. However, in a few months time a brass plate setting forth details of its presentation to Lord Willingdon arrived from Ottawa and was duly affixed to the back of the totem. Chief Napoleon Maquinna died several years later. Ambrose Maquinna is today's chief of the Nootkas.

NOOTKA SOUND

Descriptive account . . . lover's
treachery prolonged a feud.

IT WAS AT Resolution Cove, on Bligh Island, Nootka Sound, that
Captain Cook obtained new spars for his ships, H.M.S. *Resolution*
and H.M.S. *Discovery*. That was in 1778 and it can therefore be said
that the forests on Bligh Island were the first, in what is now British
Columbia, to feel the blow of a white man's axe. The cove was
named by the British Admiralty after the *Resolution*. Its Indian
name is *Kathniaktl,* meaning a place of driftwood. Discovery Point,
about five miles away at the sound's eastern entrance and immediately opposite Friendly Cove, was named after the *Discovery*.

Bligh Island is the largest of a group of islands which stand in
the entrance to the sound. It was named by Captain George H.
Richards, R.N., of H.M.S. *Hecate*, when surveying the sound in 1862
after Vice-Admiral William Bligh, who as a captain, was master of
the *Resolution* with Cook. Bligh was later known as "Breadfruit
Bligh," owing to the notoriety he gained in connection with the
mutiny in the *Bounty*. The island is uninhabited. The passage on
the east side of the island is known as Zuciarte Channel, an adaptation of the Indian name *ze-sa-at* and derived from the name of a
Nootka chief. Cook Channel, the main passage for ships, lies between Bligh Island and Nootka Island.

Muchalat Inlet, named after the Indians who live there, is
Nootka Sound's longest arm. In some places less than a mile wide,
it extends 25 miles due east. High mountains rise from the water's
edge on either side and it is navigable for ships of any size.

Gore Island, also named by Richards after Captain John Gore,
R.N., a native of Virginia who was first lieutenant in the *Resolution*,
stands in its widest part. Richards also named the passages on either
side of Gore Island after King and Williamson, second and third
lieutenants of the *Resolution*.

Gold River, one of the largest on Vancouver Island, flows in on the north side about six miles from the head of the inlet. Many of its tributaries drain out of Strathcona Park. The Spaniards named the river "Rio Del Oro," but there is no evidence of their having found any gold there. Its native name is *muchalee,* derived from the name of the Nootka Indians (Mowach-ahts, Indians of the Deer), who prior to Maquinna moving his headquarters to Friendly Cove because it was nearer the open sea, made their principal home there. The name of the village at the river mouth is "Aaminkis," meaning mouth of a river.

However, Maquinna still claimed fishing right over all waters in his domain, including Gold River, the only one which provided good year-round fishing. This the people still living at Aaminkis resented, and raiding of their river by the Nootkas caused ill-feeling and occasionally much bloodshed. The worst outbreak of violence occurred when Shiyoush, Maquinna's brother, was the Nootka chief. At a place called Ow-is, down the inlet a little way where the Aaminkis people had gone to pick berries and gather grasses, the Nootkas wiped out half the male population of the neighbouring tribe.

A maiden from Aaminkis had come to marriageable age. A young Nootka pretended to love her. The wedding was arranged and, according to custom, he invited his friends to accompany him to Ow-is and help him go through all the ceremonies usual to such occasions.

The Nootkas were careful to see that each sat next to a man from Aaminkis. At a given signal they jumped to their feet, drew knives and other weapons concealed under their clothing and murdered nearly every one of their hosts, more than forty, an eye-witness testified.

This act of treachery weighed heavily on the Aaminkis people, but as the Nootkas were a powerful tribe it would have been an act of madness to venture on an expedition of revenge. Years passed and the Nootkas began to congratulate themselves that the hatred had died out and that they and the people of Aaminkis now harboured friendly feeling towards one another. And so, one day, Chief Shiyoush and two of his men, Kenim and Tokwit, went to Aaminkis (Gold River). Their object was to offer presents to the principal men, and secure fish in exchange.

The Muchalats recognized Shiyoush and his companions as among murderers of their friends at the place called Ow-is. The three Nootkas were met by Toushkeyitim, whose son, Kikekeya, had been killed at Ow-is. He shot Shiyoush dead, shouting at the same time, "Toushkeyitim is my name, my time for revenge has come!" The other two escaped in their canoe under a hail of bullets.

On another occasion, a man at Aaminkis was stabbed to death and his wife and daughter taken as slaves to Nootka. But they were afterwards ransomed for 80 blankets and returned to their friends.

The above incidents, and scores of others, are referred to in Father Brabant's memoirs, gleaned firsthand from descendants of these people. Brabant lived amongst them for over thirty years (1875-1908) and spoke the language fluently.

Seventy years ago, before there were any canneries on the West Coast, on a site immediately across the inlet from the mouth of Gold River a group of enterprising Norwegians from Tofino put up salted salmon in barrels which they made themselves (see page 277).

In the past twelve years, on the flats adjoining Aaminkis village—now only a row of shacks — has grown the township of Muchalat, population 400. With neat rows of modern bungalows, well laid out with paved and lighted streets, ball park and other recreational facilities, it is the headquarters of the Tahsis Company's Gold River logging operations. On a site close by, the same company plans on building a $45 million 500-ton bleached kraft pulp mill.

Muchalat has road connection with Campbell River on the east coast and based there is the M.V. *Uchuck III*, which provides water transportation to all points on Nootka Sound. More than 250 men are employed at the Gold River camp, and another 100 at smaller camps farther down the sound. When the pulp mill is built, Muchalat's population will be increased by approximately 1,000.

A few Indians live in the Aaminkis houses. All are employed in the logging camp, the husbands in the woods or driving huge diesel trucks, their wives and daughters in the cookhouse. Direct descendants of the two separate tribes, they now inter-marry and live in harmony without a thought of the days when, at the slightest pretext, their respective ancestors cut one another's throats. One is Mrs. Beatrice Benedict, a direct descendant of Maquinna and daughter-in-law of Captain Jack, a Nootka sub-chief. As a student at Christie Indian Residential School near Tofino, Mrs. Benedict studied the early history of the West Coast, including Cook's landing at Nootka and the occupation of that place by the Spaniards. With the knowledge thus gained and from tales told by her grandparents and father-in-law, she can not only recite but add gruesome details to the incidents chronicled here.

Tahsis Inlet is another long and narrow arm. On Vancouver's chart, published in 1798, the inlet and village are referred to as Tahshies, and in the Admiralty chart of 1849 the channel is shown as Tasis. The bay at the head of the inlet, where the town of Tahsis now stands, was known as Macuina basin, evidently after Chief Maquinna for it was known to be one of his favourite summer homes. Not until Captain Richards surveyed the whole area between 1859 and 1862, in H.M. SHIPS *Plumper* and *Hecate* was the inlet officially named Tahsis.

The name is derived obviously from the Indian word *tashee,* meaning a way, trail or passage by land, for commencing at the head of the inlet is a trail which the Indians used to cross over the island to Nimpkish River on the east coast. This led over a divide to Woss Lake, where they made dugout canoes and travelled down the river to Nimpkish Lake and over to Alert Bay. Until comparatively recently few white men had crossed Vancouver Island via this route.

Prior to 1940, two trappers and a lone prospector comprised Tahsis Inlet's total inhabitants. In that year a logging camp (Olsen's) employing about 25 men was established. Then Gibson Brothers built a sawmill at the head of the inlet, around which has since grown the modern town of Tahsis with a population of 1,200, making it the largest town on the West Coast beyond the Albernis. The mill, now owned by the Tahsis Company Ltd., a subsidiary of East Asiatic Company Ltd., is one of the most up-to-date in British Columbia and employs 400 men. Tahsis is British Columbia's seventh largest lumber port. Ships, flying the flag of practically every nation, load there for various parts of the world, principally the United Kingdom, United States, South Africa, Australia, South America, the Orient and Europe.

Tlupana Inlet, between Muchalat and Tahsis Inlets, is twelve miles long. The name is an abbreviation of Tluplananulg, given by Eliza or Malaspina in 1791, after a Nootka sub-chief reputed to be "one of great wealth and power." Don Jose Manuel Alava, the Spanish governor at Nootka, who in 1794 visited the "inhospitable looking inlet, with its stupendous precipices and gloomy ravines," expressed his astonishment that such a country could ever have been the object of contention between the respective sovereigns of Great Britain and Spain.

On the shores of this uninhabited inlet is an old marble quarry, abandoned in 1914. Owned by a Victoria syndicate, some of the marble was used in the construction of the British Columbia legislative building. Tons of cut slabs are still there. Fishermen help themselves to it for ballast, or take it home to make garden paths.

AUTHOR'S NOTE: Muchalat: name since changed to Gold River and the townsite moved to a new site nine miles inland. Construction of the $45 million pulp mill now half completed.

THERE IS LITTLE EVIDENCE that the Spaniards during their activities on this coast in the latter part of the eighteenth century did any trading with the natives. Their purpose was primarily exploration, in which they did a very good job. Hence the frequency with which Spanish names appear on our charts.

They examined the coastline thoroughly, missing scarcely a bay or inlet between Juan de Fuca Strait and Alaska. The early fur traders and British Admiralty surveyors, who came many years afterwards, found their charts surprisingly accurate.

Remarkable also was the size of their ships. One, the schooner *Sonora,* in which Quadra made his first trip north from Mexico, was only 36 feet long at the waterline, about the size of a present-day West Coast salmon troller. Galiano's schooners *Sutil* and *Mexicana* were each about 45 tons burden. Today's seine boats and fishpackers are twice that size.

Quadra, in the *Sonora,* in 1775 made a voyage of exploration as far north as 58° latitude. On sailing southward, after sighting what is now known as the Queen Charlotte Islands, the *Sonora* kept too far off the coast for Quadra to make useful observation until below Juan de Fuca Strait. He arrived back at San Blas after eight months. On another voyage in 1779 Quadra, with the *Favourita,* accompanied by the *Princesa* commanded by Arteago, proceeded as west as the Aleutian Islands when Mt. St. Elias and Prince William Sound (named by Cook) were seen. Both vessels were small schooners.

The *Sutil,* commanded by Galiano, and the *Mexicana,* by Valdes, each mounted one swivel and four small guns, with 18 muskets, 24 pistols and 18 cutlasses for the crew; commander, lieutenant and 17 men.

Captain Vancouver met these ships when at anchor off Point Grey (Gulf of Georgia) and had breakfast with Galiano on board the *Sutil*. Vancouver notes in his journal regarding the officers' quarters: "Their apartments just allowed room for sleeping places on each side, with a table in the intermediate space at which four persons with some difficulty could sit, and were in all other respects the most ill-calculated and unfit vessels that could possibly be imagined for such an expedition. Notwithstanding this, it is pleasant to observe, in point of living they possessed many more comforts than could reasonably be expected."

In 1774, Juan Perez, in the corvette *Santiago,* made a voyage of discovery along the coast. Twice he contacted the natives — who came out in their canoes to meet him — at the extreme northwest tip of the Queen Charlotte Islands, and near Estevan Point on the west coast of Vancouver Island (see page 35). But in neither instance did Perez land. He intended doing so, but each time a westerly blew up and he had to leave hurriedly. Perez returned to Monterey under the impression that the land at both places of contact was part of the mainland. According to Indian tradition — substantiated by subsequent events — the *Santiago* was the first ship seen by the west coast of Vancouver Island Indians, or those residing on the Queen Charlotte Islands.

Cook landed at Friendly Cove, Nootka, in March 1778, and thus became the first white man to set foot on these shores, whereupon he claimed the surrounding territory for Great Britain. The whole world, including Spain, soon heard about it. Cook remained at Nootka for about two months, principally repairing his ships. He was killed shortly afterwards by natives in the Sandwich Islands (Hawaii).

Disregarding England's claims, and that British and American trading vessels were now making considerable use of Nootka harbour (Friendly Cove), in 1789, eleven years after Cook left, Don Estevan Jose Martinez, under orders from Don Manuel Flores, then viceroy of Mexico, occupied the place in the name of the King of Spain.

At this time only the Indians knew that Nootka was on an island (Nootka Island), or that what is now known as Vancouver Island was separated from the mainland by the sea. Martinez had barracks built for the garrison and a fort mounting 16 guns on a small island, where Nootka lighthouse now stands, at the entrance to

Friendly Cove, and his priests built a church. He also seized two British ships, the snow *Argonaut,* Captain James Colnett, and the sloop *Princess Royal,* Captain William Hudson, both the property of John Meares and his company, the Associated Merchants of Calcutta. The *Argonaut,* Martinez despatched under escort to Monterey. The *Princess Royal* he renamed the *Princesa Real* and despatched her, under Lieutenant Manuel Quimper, to examine the Strait of Juan de Fuca.

Meanwhile, a third vessel was seized, the schooner *Northwest America,* which Meares had only just built at Nootka. This action on the part of Martinez began the trouble between Great Britain and Spain, known in 1790 as the "Nootka Difficulty" which nearly resulted in war. It was settled, however, under the terms of the Nootka Convention dated October 28, 1790, but only after England had mobilized her Home Fleet, referred to in history as the "Spanish Armament."

Vancouver, representing Great Britain, and Quadra, Spain, met at Nootka in August 1792, to supervise the carrying out of the convention terms. Quadra was then governor at Nootka. His vessel, flying his commodore's broad pennant, was the brig *Activa,* 12 guns.

A stone monument, erected at Friendly Cove by the Washington University State Historical Society, commemorates the meeting there of these two gentlmen. Another, close by, erected by the Historical Sites and Monuments Board of Canada, records Cook's landing at the cove in March 1778.

The withdrawal of the Spanish garrison at Nootka was accomplished without incident in March 1795, under the supervision of the British and Spanish commissioners, Lieutenant Thomas Pierce of the Royal Marines, and Brigadier Don Jose Manuel Alava, Colonel of the Regiment Puelba, commander at Nootka, and the captured British ships subsequently returned to their rightful owners — with substantial indemnities.

Vancouver had arrived at Nootka with his ships *Discovery* and *Chatham* around the north end of Vancouver Island — then unnamed and for the first time circumnavigated by a white man — from his headquarters at Port Discovery, Puget Sound. Galiano and Valdes, in the schooners *Sutil* and *Mexicano,* followed a few weeks later (more about these explorers circumnavigating Vancouver Island on pages 65-68).

Alexander Malaspina, an Italian seaman in the naval service of Spain, with the corvettes *Descubierta* (Discovery), commanded by himself, and *Atrevida* (Audacious), Captain Jose Bustamente, anchored at Nootka in May 1791, after examining the Alaska coastline and the inlets on his way south. He remained in the sound several months, during which time he explored and named many of the inner channels. Although his name appears several times on the British Columbia mainland (Malaspina Inlet, Strait, Mountain, etc.), there is no evidence that Malaspina examined, or even entered the Strait of Juan de Fuca; and it is not probable that he did, because two of Eliza's ships, the snow *San Carlos* and the naval schooner *Santa Saturnina* (Saturna Island), in charge of Jose Maria Narvaez, were then engaged upon this work.

Malaspina sailed from Nootka, September 25, 1791, and after calling at Monterey, continued his voyage across the Pacific, visiting the Philippine Islands, Australia and New Zealand, returning to Europe via Cape Horn.

Eliza, with the frigate *Conception* and the sloop *Princesa Real,* the captured *Princess Royal,* was then at Nootka, where for a short period he was governor. Sub-Lieutenant Manuel Quimper, with the *Princesa Real,* he despatched to further examine the western portion of Juan de Fuca Strait, when he (Quimper) gave every place between Port San Juan (Port Renfrew) and Esquimalt their original Spanish names.

Upon completion of this task, Quimper left Neah Bay, where he had unsuccessfully attempted to establish a Spanish fort, with the intention of returning to Nootka. But stormy weather prevented him making there, so he headed for Monterey where he remained in command of the *Princesa Real* until she was returned to her British owners. On her way down the coast to Monterey the *Princesa Real (Princess Royal)* must have passed the released *Argonaut* in charge of the irate British commander James Colnett, with the order in his possession for the sloop *(Princess Royal)* to be delivered up to him at Nootka. When Colnett arrived at Nootka and found she was not in port he thought the Dons had deceived him and did not intend to give her up; of which charge, the Spaniards were innocent.

Jacinto Caamano, with the corvette *Aranzazu,* was at Nootka in June 1792, while searching along the coast for the mythical "Rio de Reyes." This strait of river, supposed to connect the Pacific to the Atlantic, was claimed to have been discovered in 1640 by Admiral Pedro Bartolome de Fonti, in command of a fleet of four vessels, his flagship being the *Holy Ghost*. Vitus Bering (or Behring), the Danish-born explorer in the service of Russia and the discoverer of the Bering Sea and Strait, in 1741 sighted the coast of what is now British Columbia, but never landed.

HISTORICAL
ESTEVAN POINT

Indians see their first ship.
Tragedy came in wake of early
explorers.

ESTEVAN POINT, the site of one of our most important lighthouses, has its name emblazoned in Canadian history. It was there that our native Indians first saw and made contact with a ship. That was in 1774, four years before Captain Cook landed at Nootka.

Then more than a century and a half later, Estevan Point again became famous; it was the only place in Canada to come under enemy shellfire in World War II, when a Japanese submarine shelled the lighthouse.

In June 1774, Captain Juan Perez sailed in the *Santiago* from Monterey with instructions from the Viceroy of Mexico to "examine the coast as far north as 60° North latitude; to take possession of the lands for Spain and to plant bottles containing the evidence."

Two Franciscan priests, Rev. Fathers Juan Crespie and Tomas de la Pena, accompanied the expedition. Together they kept a diary, which, with a translation in English, was published in 1891 by the Historical Society of Southern California.

But Perez was back in Monterey within three months. He sighted the snow-capped mountains of the coast ranges, but fog and bad weather kept him off shore and he never actually landed, although he nearly did so once. When his water supply was almost out he decided to make land and as he neared the shore several canoes loaded with Indians came out to meet him.

It was obvious that this was the first ship they had ever seen and, though they appeared to be friendly, kept a safe distance away. Several boats were lowered, contact was made in sign language and a little trading subsequently took place. But it seemed impossible to make them understand that the ship required water. Meanwhile,

35

the wind freshened and the ship began to drag her anchor. The boats were hoisted back on board, the *Santiago* hurriedly put to sea and that was the last they saw of the Indians. The two priests had in the meantime made careful note of the type of clothing they wore, made principally of skins and mattings, the design of their canoes and other observations. An exchange of notes with other explorers in years to come definitely identified these people as Nootka Indians.

Snug in the lee of Estevan Point is Hesquiat village, the home of the Hesquiats, a sub-band of the Nootkas, where the first mission on the West Coast of Vancouver Island was established. An attempt was made by the Roman Catholic Church during the occupancy of Nootka by the Spaniards, 1789-1795, to christianize the Indians, but with little apparent success. Seventy-five years later, in 1869, Bishop Charles Seghers of Victoria tried again, but not until 1875 did he show success, when a church and a residence for the priest was built at Hesquiat and the Rev. A. J. Brabant placed in charge.

That Perez' contact with the Indians occurred in the vicinity of Estevan Point is further substantiated by an entry his navigation officer, Don Esteban, made in the ship's log. This disclosed that the *Santiago* had anchored a mile off shore in latitude 49.30°, which is the approximate position of Estevan Point.

Perez named the point after his second-lieutenant, Estevan Jose Martinez. Four years later, Captain Cook, unaware of the voyage of the *Santiago,* named it "Breakers Point", but the Spanish name was restored in the Admiralty chart in 1849.

This historical incident is also confirmed in Father Brabant's own diary. The Hesquiat's account of the strange happening was told to him by direct descendants of the Indians who actually took part in it.

According to their story, the *Santiago* anchored in front of Oummis, one of their villages about three miles west of Estevan Point. They first saw the ship when it was far out to sea and thought it was an immense bird. It was watched with eager eyes and when it came closer they saw that it was no bird. Was it a big canoe coming back from the land of the dead with their bygone chiefs? No, it was a floating house, with big sails and people standing on top of the house.

So they went out in their canoes to investigate. Yes, there were people aboard, but different from themselves in colour and appearance. It was something they had never seen or heard of before. They traded a few furs and articles of clothing, for iron, knives and other odd trinkets; but the wind sprang up and the ship sailed away. Puzzled as they were, they gave the white men on board the name *manathine* (floating house), which is still the name given by west coast Indians to white men.

A few weeks previous to making his contact with the Indians at Estevan Point, Perez made a similar contact at the northwest tip of the Queen Charlotte Islands (then undiscovered), which he named Cape Santa Margarita — now Langara Point and Island. Had he gone ashore at either place, he would have been the first European to set foot on these shores. Instead, that honour fell to Captain Cook, who landed at Friendly Cove, Nootka, four years later.

The shelling of the lighthouse by a Japanese submarine on June 20, 1942, is best told by an eyewitness, E. T. Redford, then chief wireless operator at Estevan Point:

> The submarine surfaced about two miles off shore and was plainly visible. Shelling commenced at approximately 9:40 p.m. and continued for about 40 minutes. The first shells landed on the beach about 100 yards in front of the lighthouse. Mr. Lally, who was the lightkeeper at the time, immediately put out the light. The sub apparently then raised its sights, for from then on the shells went overhead.
>
> Approximately 25 shells were fired and, except for a few buildings hit by shell fragments, no damage was caused either to the lighthouse or radio station. With the exception of the men on shift, who tapped out word of the shelling to Pacific Command, all others gave a hand getting the women and children away from the settlement.
>
> The submarine pulled out on the surface and everyone could see her and hear the diesel engines quite clearly. While naturally there was some nervousness, everyone, including the women and children, took the whole incident in their stride, then spent the following day souvenir hunting.

A photograph, taken by Mr. Redford of an unexploded shell which he found on the beach in front of the light, disclosed that they were no "baby" missiles. It was of 5.9 (approximately) calibre and weighed 80 pounds. Several landed in the vicinity of Hesquiat Indian village, three miles directly behind the lighthouse. They scared the natives but did no damage.

Several months later, a Japanese submarine was sunk off the New Zealand coast. Its crew was rescued and the first thing they told their captors was that their submarine was the one that shelled a lighthouse on the Canadian west coast.

Estevan Point lighthouse was established in 1907. The wireless station has since been discontinued and the operators, with their families, moved elsewhere. Raising cattle on the Estevan peninsular was attempted by the Rev. A. J. Brabant, in 1887, and again in 1916 by the Hamilton brothers, but the land was found to be unsuitable for this or any other type of farming and the herds subsequently went wild.

The Hesquiat Indians claim to have been the first to see and make contact with a ship is conceded by all the west coast tribes, and that the vessel was the *Santiago,* there can be little doubt.

Hesquiat is an adaptation of Heish-kwi-aht, derived from the Indian word *Heish-heish-a,* meaning "to tear asunder with the teeth." Near Hesquiat village, a salt water grass (eel grass) drifts on shore in large quantities, especially at times when the herring spawn. Indians are in the habit of tearing this grass with their teeth to disengage the spawn, which is esteemed by them a great delicacy; hence the name Heish-kwi-ahts given them by neighbouring tribes.

A dangerous rock, 30 feet high and about half a mile off shore, stands a few miles west of Estevan Point, almost opposite Oum-mis village (now deserted). Formerly known as Sunday Rock, probably named on the Sabbath during an early survey, the name was changed in 1930 by the Canadian Hydrographic Survey to Perez Rock.

In the same vicinity, but a few miles farther west and about ten miles from Nootka, is Escalante Reef, where the rum-running schooner *Noble* was lost on January 5, 1928. She was blown off course in a southeast gale when returning to Vancouver after delivering her load off the California coast. Captain Kerr and one of his crew drowned; the other two crew members were rescued by the Tofino lifeboat and placed aboard the fisheries cruiser *Givenchy.*

The name is a Spanish word meaning to climb or scale. The reef, formed of rocks jutting out from the shore in a row, one rock smaller than the other, like a series of steps, until they disappear in the water, is doubtless the reason for the name given by some Spaniard. Escalante was also the name of a friar of the Franciscan Order, one of the Roman Catholic priests at Nootka during the Spanish occupation of that place.

Hesquiat Harbour, named after the village by Captain Richards, H.M.S. *Hecate,* 1861, is fully exposed and very shallow. Another hazard is Boulder Point at the western entrance. Here the boulders, acres in extent and many the size of a house, extend far out into the sea.

The sighting of the *Santiago* by the Indians, shipwrecks and other occurrences in the general area of Estevan Point — events which would have made headlines had they occurred today — have long since found their way into our history books. In many instances the details are sketchy, but thanks to men like Captain Walbran and Father Brabant we are able to fill in the gaps.

In February 1869, the barque *John Bright,* outward bound with lumber from Port Gamble to Valparaiso, was wrecked on Boulder Point during a southeast gale, when all hands perished, among them the captain's wife — a Chilean lady — their one child and a servant girl. News of the wreck was brought to Victoria in March, and from information received from Captain Christianson of the schooner *Surprise*, and others, it was surmised that the Indians had murdered all survivors who managed to reach shore, as the mangled bodies of ten men and one woman, some of them headless, were found near the wreck. H.M.S. *Sparrowhawk*, Commander H. W. Mist, was despatched from Esquimalt to investigate. Surgeon-Lieutenant Peter Comrie examined the bodies, and after they were buried, seven prisoners were brought to Victoria.

The trial of the Indians for murder took place in May, and ended in two, Anietsachist and Katkinna, being sentenced to death by Chief Justice Needham. The convicted men were taken to Hesquiat by the *Sparrowhawk* and hanged there July 29, on a gallows erected near the scene of the wreck. All the Indians in the neighbourhood were collected to witness the execution as a warning.

The Hesquiats always stoutly denied to Father Brabant, their spiritual teacher, that the shipwrecked people were murdered. They said the bodies were washed ashore and mangled by the surf dashing them among the rocks and boulders, and that all the Indians did was to remove the bodies above high-water mark so that the fish, the Indian's chief source of food, could not feed on the bodies. They also said that the executed men were the victims of an interpreter's mistake, false accusations of rival tribes, and too credulous white people.

Inscribed on the *John Bright*'s boom-board, subsequently washed ashore with other wreckage, was the motto, *Neminem time, neminem laede* (Fear none, injure none).

On the night of October 9, 1882, the American barque *Malleville,* of Freeport, Me., Captain Edward Harlow, from Shanghai to Royal Roads in ballast, was driven ashore near Sunday Rock (now Perez Rock), when all those on board perished, among them the captain's wife, their two small sons and the second mate's wife.

The bodies of Mrs. Harlow and seven of the crew were the only ones recovered. These, Father Brabant, who had been called to the scene from his mission, eight miles away by overland trail, had wrapped in canvas salvaged from the wreck and buried near where they were found.

Father Brabant goes on to relate:

> The Indian who discovered Mrs. Harlow's body and brought it ashore, had taken from her hand two diamond and gold rings — wedding and engagement rings; also two diamond earrings, a gold pin and a piece of gold chain — the watch having in all probability dropped into the sea. . . . This man afterwards gave me these articles and asked me to take them in charge. I told this good fellow, who might be given as an example to civilized people for his honesty, that we would send them to the lady's relatives.
>
> From documents washed ashore, I ascertained the vessel's identity, and from personal papers, Mrs. Harlow's home address. Two young Indians volunteered to go by canoe to Alberni, a distance of 150 miles, then overland by trail to Nanaimo, with my message carrying the news of the wreck.
>
> Word subsequently reached naval authorities at Esquimalt and on November 22, H.M.S. *Kingfisher* arrived at Hesquiat. Captain Thorn conducted his investigation and left two days later. Entrusted to him, to be mailed at Victoria, was a parcel containing Mrs. Harlow's jewellery, together with her Bible and sealskin coat, recovered afterwards, addressed to her parents who lived at Brewer, Maine.
>
> Among other pathetic finds in the wreckage washed ashore from the *Malleville,* were the letter-blocks and toys of the two little Harlow boys, and the body of their pet pig. Appropriate acknowledgement for the articles despatched to Mrs. Harlow's relatives was duly received.

In recognition of their heroic work in attempting to save the lives of the crew of the *Malleville,* and those of the women and children on board, the United States government awarded Chief Matlahaw a suitably inscribed gold medal, and $200 to be distributed among his men.

It was at the entrance to Hesquiat Harbour, in December 1874, that the American barque *Edwin,* Captain Hughes, was wrecked. She had drifted there after becoming water-logged and unmanageable caused by her lumber cargo shifting after clearing Puget Sound for Australia. The captain's two little boys were drowned and his wife was crushed to death by heavy timbers when the ship split wide open. The Chinese cook was also drowned. Mrs. Hughes' body was afterwards recovered and buried at Hesquiat. Chief Matlahaw, for his work in organizing canoe parties which resulted in saving the lives of the others on board, afterwards received from the

Canadian government a silver medal, and from the United States government a liberal cash award for himself and his men. Lumber salvaged from the *Edwin* was used to build the Hesquiat mission.

Six members of the steamer *Cleveland,* wrecked in Barkley Sound, December 1897, after drifting for three days in an open boat landed at Hesquiat and were cared for at the mission. In return for Father Brabant's hospitality while waiting for a U.S. Coastguard cutter to come and take them to Seattle, they helped build the new church. The original church had only recently been destroyed by fire.

In November 1901, the American barque *Highland Light* foundered off Estevan Point. The crew was rescued by the sealing schooner *Arilla* and brought to Victoria by the steamer *Queen City.* Old Hesquiat Indians claim that long before the Catholic priests came (1870), an unidentified ship, burned to the water's edge and still on fire, came ashore a few miles east of their village. That would be about midway between Estevan Point and the entrance to Sydney Inlet.

TRADERS FOLLOWED
COOK

Nootka, British Columbia's first seaport. Launching of the North-west America, first ship built on this coast.

WHEN COOK'S SHIPS returned to England, so fabulous were the accounts found in his journal of rich furs — mostly sea otter — obtainable on this coast, that many expeditions were fitted out, at London, Boston and Calcutta, to exploit the trade. They naturally headed for Nootka, which place Cook had indicated as the best spot a valuable cargo might be collected. Thus, Nootka, both during the occupation by the Spaniards, 1789-1795, and for many years afterwards, was a busy seaport; in fact, the most important north of Mexico.

There were no white residents at Nootka then, nor for that matter at any other place in what is now known as British Columbia; and of course, no government customs. Ships came and went as they pleased. Trade with the Indians was conducted "over the side." This, however, presented no diffiiculties, for the average vessel in those days had but little freeboard; an Indian standing in his canoe could lean over the ship's rail.

James Hanna, with the brig *Sea Otter*, 120 tons, was the first trader to buy furs at Nootka. Shortly after his arrival, in August 1785, the natives, taking advantage of the smallness of his vessel, attempted to capture her in daylight; but the attack failed and many Indians were killed. After this defeat, they traded peacefully and Hanna was successful in procuring 560 otter skins which sold at Canton for $20,000.

Thus encouraged, Hanna refitted at Macao and was back at Nootka the following year. Meanwhile, other vessels (*King George* and *Queen Charlotte*) had been there. About 50 sea otter skins was all Hanna could secure. After staying about a fortnight, he sailed

42

westward and anchored in Sea Otter Cove (name given by Hanna, retained to this day), near Cape Scott. He then visited what is now known as Queen Charlotte Sound where he examined and named several of its geographical features. Furs procured on this voyage, 100 sea otter skins and 300 slips and pieces, sold at Canton, for $8,000.

Hanna, on a visit to Clayoquot Sound, exchanged names with Chief Cleaskina, an incident which caused considerable confusion (and amusement) when the chief introduced himself to subsequent traders as "Captain Hanna." The exchanging of names by Indian chiefs with their visitors, common practice in those days, was intended as a great compliment and the traders played it up. A third voyage to this coast was planned by Hanna, but before this active seaman set out he was called to make that voyage from whence there is no return.

John Strange, trading under license from the East India Company with the snows *Captain Cook,* 300 tons, Captain Lowrie, and *Experiment,* 100 tons, Captain Guise, arrived at Nootka from Bombay in 1786. Between them, the two ships secured 300 sea otter skins at Nootka, but most of their trading was done in the Queen Charlotte Islands and along the continental shoreline. Lowrie and Guise named Cape Scott after David Scott, the Bombay merchant who assisted in fitting out this expedition. Lowrie named Queen Charlotte Sound after Queen Charlotte, wife of King George III.

John Mackay, surgeon's mate of the *Captain Cook,* at his own request — for the purpose of investigating the agriculture possibilities of Nootka should a settlement be established there — was left at Friendly Cove. Friendly relations existed between Mackay and Maquinna, whose people watched with awe as he planted rows of vegetables. But under no circumstances could they be induced to eat them. He was picked up twelve months later by Captain Barkley in the *Imperial Eagle.*

The King George's Sound (the name Cook first gave to Nootka Sound) Company sent out two vessels, the ship *King George,* 320 tons, under the command of Nathaniel Portlock, and the *Queen Charlotte,* after which the Queen Charlotte Islands were named, a snow of 200 tons, George Dixon in command. Both arrived on this coast in 1786. The voyage was most successful; furs collected, 2,552 skins, realized $54,847, in China. Thence the ships returned home with tea for the East India Company, arriving at London, September 1788.

Dixon, after whom Dixon Entrance, between the Queen Char-

lotte Islands and the south coast of Alaska was named, and Portlock (Portlock Point near Tofino), had both been on the coast
before with Cook. Dixon tells of an incident which occurred while
cruising along the west coast of the Queen Charlotte Islands where
most of the expedition's furs were obtained. He met an old Indian
"of authority" to whom he gave a light-horseman's cap. Some
weeks later, after his vessels rounded Cape St. James (named by
Dixon because he rounded this promontory on St. James's Day,
July 25, 1787), the same old Indian was met again, this time as a
person of first consequence, for he turned out to be the chief of the
Cumschewas (Cumschewa Inlet, Moresby Island). He had lost the
cap, and coming aboard showed Dixon the wounds he received in
battle defending his property. He begged for another, which was
given him, intimating at the same time he would lose this one only
with his life. Dixon further remarks that the second cap was not
bestowed in vain. The chief proved extremely useful in traffic, everything being referred to him by his followers and his ruling was final.

The 50-ton sloop *Princess Royal,* Charles Duncan, had quite an
adventurous career on the coast. She left England in September
1786, manned by 15 men, in company with the *Prince of Wales,*
James Colnett. Both arrived at Nootka, via the Horn, in July 1787.
Here they found that Captain Barkley, in the *Imperial Eagle,* had
anticipated them, and in consequence, trade was slack. Leaving
Nootka, they met up with Dixon, in the *Queen Charlotte,* who
advised them to steer for the Queen Charlotte Islands where he had
met with a good market. The vessels wintered in the Sandwich
Islands, returning to this coast in the spring. Many furs were
obtained, which later sold in China at a good profit.

Duncan sailed in the *Prince of Wales* for England, having made
a prosperous voyage in his little vessel. The *Princess Royal,* now in
charge of Captain William Hudson, returned to Nootka in company
with the *Argonaut,* Captain Colnett. On arriving there after the
Spaniards had taken possession of the place, both vessels were un-
justifiably seized in July 1789. Crew, cargo and stores were turned
out of the *Princess Royal,* and the vessel, renamed the *Princesa Real,*
placed in the Spanish naval service with Sub-Lieutenant Quimper
in command. The *Argonaut* was despatched as a prize to Monterey.

John Meares, a one-time British naval officer turned merchant,
first arrived at Nootka in 1786 with the snow *Nootka* from Calcutta,
where he had recently formed a company — the Associated Merchants — to develop the Northwest America fur trade. This expedition, however, was not very successful. Bad weather and his men

44

CHIEF MAQUINNA
Provincial Archives

CAPTAIN JAMES COOK, R.N.
Provincial Archives

Habitations at Friendly Cove when Captain Cook landed in 1778. Note cedar slab houses and racks for drying fish. *Photo from a drawing, B.C. Provincial Archives.*

Monument erected at Friendly Cove, Nootka, in 1903, by the Washington University State Historical Society bears the following inscription: "Vancouver and Quadra met here in August 1792, under the treaty between Spain and Great Britain of October 1790." NOTE: R.C. Mission Church to right of monument is on site of original church built by the Spaniards when they occupied Friendly Cove in 1789.

The schooner Santa Saturnina, Pilot Commander Jose Maria Narvaez, was at Nootka in 1791. Photo from a drawing by F. P. Thursby, courtesy Vancouver City Archives.

Fur trading ships at Friendly Cove, Nootka, 1780's.

Launching of the schooner *Northwest America*, the first ship built on this coast, at Friendly Cove, Nootka, on September 28, 1788. Note British and American ships in bay firing salvos in salute. *Photos from drawings, B.C. Provincial Archives.*

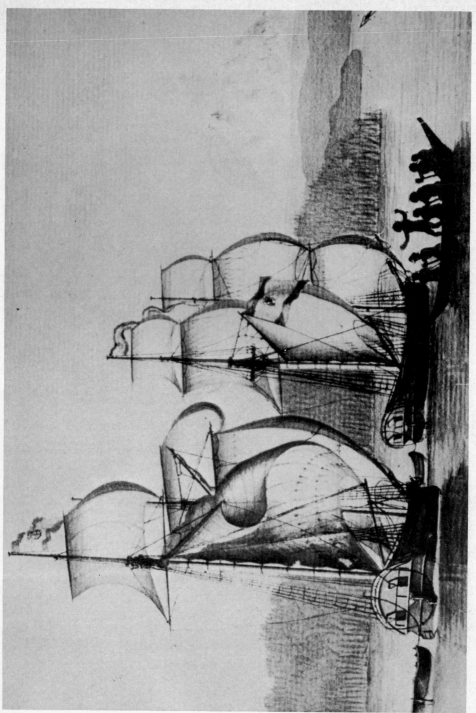

Tiny Spanish ships of exploration, *Sutil* and *Mexicana*.
Photo from a sketch, courtesy *Captain W. Cates.*

Aerial view of Estevan Point Light Station. *R.C.A.F. Photo.*

Unexploded shell found on beach in front of Estevan Point Lighthouse. One of 25 fired at the light by a Japanese submarine on June 20, 1942. *Photo by chief wireless operator E. T. Redford.*

S.S. PRINCESS MAQUINNA

Photo courtesy C. F. Timms, Vancouver, B.C.

suffering from scurvy forced him to return to Macao, now his head-quarters, with but few pelts. He returned the following year with the snows *Felice Adventurer* and *Iphigenia Nubiana* and traded at different places along the coast. He also built the 48-foot schooner *Northwest America,* the first vessel to be constructed on the north-west coast of America, which he launched at Friendly Cove on September 20, 1788 — to be seized shortly afterwards by the Spaniards and renamed the *Gertrudis.*

Meares was in China when he received word by a returning ship of the seizing of the three British vessels. He immediately took passage for London via the Indian Ocean and the Cape of Good Hope, and appeared in person before the British Parliament to protest the action of the Spaniards.

The Boston traders, John Kendrick and Robert Gray, with the ship *Columbia,* 220 tons, and sloop *Lady Washington,* 90 tons, were at Nootka during the early days of the Spanish occupation, but being American citizens, were unmolested by the Spaniards during the quarrel with Great Britain. In 1789 the two commanders traded ships, Gray taking the *Columbia* to China and thence to Boston, Kendrick remaining on this coast with the *Lady Washington.* Kendrick spent 1790 organizing a new trade in sandalwood from the Sandwich Islands to China. The next year he was back at Nootka in the *Lady Washington,* changed from a sloop to a brig.

Gray, with the *Columbia,* returned to this coast in 1792 and wintered in Clayoquot Sound. There, on Meares Island, he built a schooner named the *Adventure*, the second vessel constructed on this coast and which was later sold to Quadra for 75 choice sea otter skins. He then proceeded south and discovered the large river which he named after his ship. Gray's Harbour he named after himself.

The largest vessel to arrive at Nootka to this time was the British ship *Imperial Eagle,* Captain Charles William Barkley. Formerly the East Indiaman *Loudoun,* this full-rigged ship of 400 tons, mounting 20 guns, was at Nootka in June 1787. An excellent market was found and a large number of skins speedily purchased, principally through the agency of John Mackay, who was found living with the natives and taken on board the *Imperial Eagle.* Mackay, it will be remembered, was surgeon's mate on the snow *Captain Cook* and, at his own request, had been left behind at Friendly Cove.

On leaving Nootka, an easterly course was steered along the land till the sound now bearing Barkley's name was discovered. Con-tinuing south-eastward, Juan de Fuca Strait was passed and when off Destruction Island, below Cape Flattery, Beale, the ship's purser and super-cargo, with second mate Miller and the whole of a boat's crew, were killed by the natives. Destruction Island was named by Barkley for this tragedy. From here the *Imperial Eagle* proceeded to China where furs, 800 in number, were disposed of for $30,000 after some difficulty, the market being overstocked.

Mackay's coming aboard the *Imperial Eagle* at Nootka is described by Mrs. Barkley, who accompanied her husband on this and a later voyage, in an amusing manner:

> His dress and appearance, the same as a native, was, to say the least, disgusting . . . the surprise when he introduced himself as Dr. John Mackay to Captain Barkley and myself was great indeed.

Barkley, again accompanied by his wife, was back at Nootka in 1792 with the brig *Halcyon,* but with this small vessel he had his troubles. First, the trip met with only fair results. Then, after disposing of his furs in China, he sailed for Mauritius where the French promptly seized the brig. However, due to influential French friends whom Captain and Mrs. Barkley had made when in the *Imperial Eagle*, the vessel was restored to him. The *Halcyon* was afterwards stolen by an unprincipled scoundrel under whose command Barkley had placed her. Years later, when in England, Barkley learned that his brig was in Boston. He went there, and through the influence of the British consul, she was restored to him. Mrs. Barkley, the first white woman the Nootkas had ever seen, started her first voyage at the age of seventeen-and-a-half, immediately after their marriage, which took place at the Protestant Chapel, Ostend, on October 25, 1786. She died in 1843 and was buried at Enfield alongside her husband, who pre-deceased her in 1832.

Captain William Brown, with his three-vessel squadron, the ship *Butterworth,* which he commanded himself, the schooner *Jackal,* Captain Stewart, and the sloop *Prince Le Boo,* Captain Sharp, was buying furs at Nootka in 1793. Trading was only fair and the ships moved west. Weeks later, while sheltering at Qlawdzeet Cove, Stephens Island, Brown sighted two strange vessels in the offing and promptly despatched the *Jackal* to guide them to a safe anchorage. They turned out to be Captain George Vancouver's ships *Discovery* and *Chatham* and as they entered the cove Brown saluted Vancouver with seven guns, a courtesy duly returned with five. After this ceremony, Brown visited the *Discovery* and gave Vancouver all possible information of the neighbourhood, for which the noted explorer-navigator was very grateful.

Vancouver continued his voyage the next day, the sloop *Prince Le Boo* accompanying him, Brown having placed her at his naval friend's disposal. Vancouver speaks most favourably of this small vessel as a means of prosecuting the survey of the coast. When she returned to the *Butterworth* he regretted not having one or two vessels of 30 or 40 tons like her, calculated as well for rowing as sailing, to assist in the intricate investigation of these shores. The following summer Vancouver again met Brown, this time in command of the *Jackal*, the *Butterworth* (herself only 30 tons) at the end of the 1793 season having been despatched to England. Their next meeting was at Nootka, where Brown arrived in the *Jackal*, October 6, 1794, after procuring a rich harvest of nearly one thousand sea otter skins. Vancouver sailed for England a few days later. On January 1, 1795, Brown was killed at the Sandwich Islands by natives when attempting to capture the *Jackal*, in which they failed.

Captain John Ingraham, who had previously been on this coast as second mate of the *Columbia*, was at Nootka in 1791 with the brig *Hope*, 70 tons, out of Boston. He sold his furs in China and was back the following year. The *Hope*'s supercargo did most of the trading, while Ingraham collected information as to the geography, natural history, language, manners and customs of the natives, on which subjects his journal contains interesting details. The American brig *Hancock*, Captain Crowell, was also at Nootka in 1791, and the British brig *Venus*, Captain Shepherd, in 1792.

Trading on the coast in 1794 was the Boston schooner *Resolution*, Captain Burling. In 1795, the British ships *Ruby* and *Despatch*, Captains Charles Bishop and Elias Newberry, respectively; the schooner *Phoenix*, Captain Hugh Moore, from Bengal, the brig *Jefferson*, Captain Josiah Roberts, out of New England, and the snow *Mercury*, Captain Thomas Burnett. All were at Nootka, but most of their trading was carried on in the Queen Charlotte Islands and along the continental shore. (More about the *Resolution* and *Phoenix* on page 72.)

Richard J. Cleveland, with the American sloop *Caroline*, 50 tons, and sixteen men, made a successful trading voyage from China to this coast in 1799 — for the size of the ship, the richest: value of outward cargo, $9,000, and return cargo of furs, sold at Canton, realized $51,000.

Cleveland's description of the coast Indians was not very complimentary:

A more hideous set of beings, in the form of men and women, I had never before seen. The fantastic manner in which many of the faces of the men were painted was probably intended to give them a ferocious appearance, and some groups looked really as if they had escaped from the dominions of Satan himself. One had a perpendicular line dividing the two sides of his face, one side painted red, the other black, with the hair daubed with grease and red ochre and filled with the white down of birds.

Another had his face divided with a horizontal line and painted black and white. The visage of a third was painted in checkers. Most of them had little mirrors, before the acquisition of which they must have been dependent on each other for those correct touches of the pencil which are so much in vogue, and which daily require more time than the toilet of a Parisian belle.

The women made, if possible, a still more frightful appearance. The ornament of wood which they wear to extend an incision made beneath the under lip, so distorts the face as to take from it almost the resemblance to the human; yet the privilege of wearing this ornament is not extended to the female slaves, who are prisoners taken in war. Hence, it would seem that distinctive badges have their origin in the most crude state of society. It is difficult, however, for the imagination to conceive of more disgusting and filthy beings than these patrician dames.

The ship *Atahualpa,* Captain Oliver Porter, out of Boston, was at Nootka in the spring of 1805; also the sloop *Caroline,* under the command of Captain Sturgis. These two vessels did most of their trading farther to the west. (More about the *Atahualpa* on page 72).

It is gratifying to know that the names given by these early traders to so many of the coast's geographical features have been retained by the Geographic Board of Canada. Nearly all can be found somewhere on our charts and maps, some quite frequently.

SIX MUSKETS AND
A FLAG

For a little kingdom.

KENDRICK INLET, the smallest arm of Nootka Sound, was named in 1862 by Captain George H. Richards, R.N., after Captain John Kendrick (see page 45), a man who did some remarkable trading with the Indians. It is stated that in one instance, for some cheap chisels and other small articles worth altogether not more than $100, Kendrick and his partner, Gray, received sea otter skins to the value of $8,000.

Besides dealing in furs, Kendrick attempted to make good deals in real estate. In the summer of 1791 he purchased from Maquinna, Wickaninnish and other chiefs several large tracts of land near Nootka Sound, for which he obtained "deeds" signed by these personages and witnessed by the officers and men of the *Washington*.

The deed for one tract of land is still to be seen, filed in the Department of State at Washington, D.C., and reads as follows:

> In consideration of six muskets, some boat sails, a quantity of gunpowder and an American flag (they being articles of which we, at present, stand in need of, and are of great value), we do bargain, grant and sell unto John Kendrick of Boston, a certain harbour in said Ahasset (Ahousat), in which the brig *Washington* lay at anchor on the 5th day of August, 1791, latitude 49.50°, with all the lands, mines, minerals, rivers, bays, harbours, sounds, creeks and all islands, with the produce of the sea, being territory of 18 miles square, to have and to hold. . . . signed by Maquinna, Wickaninnish, Narry-Youk and Tarrasone.

Attempts were made by the owners of the *Washington* to sell these lands in London, England, in 1793, but no purchasers were found. The circular issued on this occasion, written in four languages and couched in vague terms, is a curious document:

49

The inhabitants of Europe are informed that, in 1787, Captain Kendrick while prosecuting an adventurous voyage with the natives for furs, purchased from them, for the owners (of the *Washington*), a tract of delightful country, comprehending four degrees of latitude, or 200 miles square, and that such as may be inclined to associate, for setting up a commonwealth on their own code of laws, on a spot on the globe nowhere surpassed in delightful and healthy climate, and fertile soil; claimed by no civilized nation, and purchased, under a sacred treaty of peace and commerce, and for a valuable consideration, of the friendly natives, may have the best opportunity of trying the result of such an enterprise.

From the circular, nothing is learned of the situation of this tract of "delightful country", except that it lies in America, and that the deeds for the land are declared to have been registered in the office of the American consul at Macao, the Portuguese trading colony in South China.

That the lands were thus sold by the savage chiefs, though their dominions did not amount to one twenty-fourth part of 200 square miles, there is no reason to doubt. Maquinna and Wickaninnish would have as readily conveyed the whole of North America for the consideration of a copper kettle.

Captain Kendrick was killed in 1793, at Karakakooa Bay, in the Sandwich Islands (Hawaii), by a ball accidentally fired by a British vessel while saluting him. Captain Cook was killed by the natives at the same place in 1779.

TAHSIS HONOURS
GALLANT SAILOR

JOHN MEARES, born in 1756, entered the navy in 1771 on board H.M.S. *Cruiser* and after serving for seven years was promoted to lieutenant. About his later turning merchantman, his subsequent exploits as a fur trader, the seizing of his ships at Nootka and how he personally appeared before the British Parliament to protest the action of the Spaniards, we have already learned.

It has been said by some that Meares was a bit of a rogue when it suited his purpose. His ships are alleged to have sometimes displayed the Portuguese flag. The propriety of his having purchased from Maquinna — for eight or ten sheets of copper and some trifles, a portion of the foreshore at Friendly Cove on which to build a storehouse and later the schooner *Northwest America*, was also questioned.

A letter written by Robert Duffin, first mate of the *Felice*, one of Meares' ships, is of interest. After being sworn to before Captain George Vancouver, to whom it was addressed, the letter was forwarded (by Vancouver) to the British Admiralty and subsequently deposited in the Records Office, London, where it still may be seen.

In part, it reads as follows:

To Captain George Vancouver, commander of His Britannic Majesty's ships *Discovery* and *Chatham,* now lying in Friendly Cove, Nootka Sound.

Sir, whereas different reports have been propagated as to Meares' conduct on Nootka Sound, I shall here state, with the candour and veracity which always influenced me on such occasions, an impartial account of Meares' proceedings at the above place.

Towards the close of 1787, a commercial expedition was undertaken by John Henry Cox, Esq. & Co., merchants, then residing at

51

Macao, who accordingly fitted out and equipped two ships for the fur trade on the northwest coast of America. The management of the expedition was reposed in John Meares Esq., as commander-in-chief and sole conductor of the voyage, and who was likewise one of the merchant proprietors.

These vessels were equipped under Portuguese colours, with a view to mitigate the heavy port charges imposed on ships of every nation (the Portuguese only excepted), which circumstance is well known to all commercial gentlemen trading in that part of the world. Under the circumstances, the vessels were fitted out in the name and under the firm of Juan Cavallo Esq., a Portuguese merchant then residing at Macao. Cavallo had no property in them whatsoever, both their cargoes being entirely British property, and the vessels navigated solely by subjects of His Britannic Majesty.

Duffin goes on to say:

On our arrival the first time at Friendly Cove, which was in May 1788, the two chiefs, Maquilla (Maquinna) and Callicum were absent. On their return, Mr. Meares, accompanied by second officer Robert Funter and myself, went ashore and treated with the same chiefs for the whole of the land that forms Friendly Cove, in His Britannic Majesty's name. He (Meares) accordingly bought it for eight or ten sheets of copper and several other trifling articles.

The natives were fully satisfied with the agreement. The chiefs, and likewise the people, did homage to Mr. Meares as their sovereign, using those formalities peculiar to themselves. The British flag was displayed on shore at the same time, not the Portuguese flag as has been insinuated by several people who were not present at the time; consequently they advanced those assertions without foundation.

The chiefs with their subjects offered to quit the cove entirely and reside at another village, and leave the place to ourselves as entire masters and owner of the cove and lands adjacent. Meares had a house built, which he left in Maquilla's (Maquinna) care when we departed. On our return in 1789, the cove was found to be occupied by subjects of His Catholic Majesty, Don Estevan Jose Martinez having arrived there in the meantime and claimed the territory for Spain.

Captain John Kendrick was also there with the ships *Columbia* and *Washington,* under the flag and protection of the United States of America. Two days after our arrival at Friendly Cove, two ships, the property of John Meares, which were lying there, were captured by Martinez. The Americans (Kendrick and Gray) were suffered to carry on trade with the natives unmolested.

Should anyone doubt the truth of this protest, I am always ready to attest it before any court of jurisdiction, or any person authorized to examine me. I have the honour to be, with the greatest esteem, (signed) Robert Duffin.

That the above was the identical truth was sworn before me this 21st day of September 1792. (signed) George Vancouver.

Here it might be pointed out that to this day, when it suits their purpose, some of our own Canadian ships, along with those of Great Britain, the United States and Greece, evade the shipping regulations of their respective governments by changing registration and flying the flags of such countries as Panama, Paraguay and Liberia, and so enjoy cheaper operating costs. It will be remembered that the *Imperial Eagle,* Captain Charles William Barkley's ship, although one hundred per cent British, was sailing quite legally under Austrian colours when that gentleman discovered and named Barkley Sound.

Meares was a renowned British seaman, and his name will forever be associated with the early history of this coast. Promoted to the rank of commander in the British navy in February 1795, after several years of retirement he died in 1809. Meares Island, the largest of Clayoquot Sound, where he also did considerable trading, was named after him.

Today, Meares would find Friendly Cove pretty well unchanged, except that the Indians now live in modern houses and use gasboats instead of canoes. And he would see big steamers, any one of which could carry his small schooners on deck, passing the cove almost daily. (Friendly Cove is a pilotage boarding station).

Only 20 miles away, at the head of Tahsis Inlet, where he often visited with Maquinna, Meares would find a modern town of 1,200 inhabitants. But what would probably please him most would be seeing the name "JOHN MEARES" emblazoned in bold letters above the main entrance to the town's high school, tangible evidence that, after 175 years, his name is still honoured. And Meares would meet Carol Macleod, the grade seven student who, after reading her history books, suggested that the school be named after him — and thereby won a prize.

Meares brought across the Pacific scores of Chinese labourers, which he employed on the construction of the *Northwest America,* dwellings and storehouses, but when the Spaniards seized his ships, he had no means of taking them back — that is if he ever intended doing so. The Spaniards then used them as slaves to till the land and raise vegetables for the garrison. Some are believed to have been employed looking for gold on Gold River. What finally happened to the Chinese is not clear. There were no women amongst them, but it is known some married Indian women.

ESPERANZA INLET

*The Spaniards called it
Esperanza
and so did Captain Cook.*

SPANISH NAMES predominate on Esperanza Inlet. The reason is obvious, for it was named by Captain Alexandro Malaspina when in these parts in 1791 with the corvettes *Descubierta* and *Atrevida,* and whose officers, Lieutenants Joseph de Espinosa and Ciriaco Cevallos, examined the inner channels.

Captain Cook had previously (in 1778) named it Hope Bay, "as with mountainous land around there was hope for a good harbour." He was not mistaken. The name given on Cook's chart was undoubtedly translated by the Spaniards and applied to the inlet in which there appeared the greatest possibility of a secure anchorage.

Catala Island, wooded and uninhabited, stands on the west side of the entrance to the inlet. It was named on Galiano's chart of 1792 as Isle de Catala, after the Rev. Magin Catala, a Franciscan monk who for 44 years was engaged on Spanish-American coast missionary work. He served 13 months (1793-1794) at Nootka, during the Spanish occupation of Friendly Cove.

The headland at the western entrance is known as Tatchu Point, the ancient Indian name for this locality and derived from the word *tatchttatcha,* to chew. There is a fine beach here, and it was a great fishing place for the Ehattisat Indians (the tribe which inhabited these parts), and much food was consumed there at feasts and entertainments (Brabant). The name was adopted by Admiralty surveyors in 1861.

Ferrer Point, originally named Ensanada de Ferrer, by Galiano and Valdez in 1792, guards the southern entrance. The R.C.A.F. maintained a radar station here during the Second World War.

The main steamer channel was named by the Hydrographic

Survey Board of Canada, after Captain E. Gillam, for twenty years master of the C.P.R. steamer *Princess Maquinna,* and the *Tees* before that.

The inlet separates the northern portion of Nootka Sound from Vancouver Island proper. Hecate Channel and Tahsis Narrows, the latter only a few hundred feet wide, connects it with Tahsis Inlet, thus forming a waterway, navigable for ships of any size, completely around Nootka Island.

Its four principal arms are Port Eliza, Espinosa Arm and Zeballos Arm, all on the Vancouver Island side, and Nuchalitz Inlet, which makes a deep indentation into Nootka Island. Port Eliza, the smallest, was named after that Spanish naval officer, Lieutenant Francisco Eliza, who was governor at Nootka for a short time and with the frigate *Conception* and snow *San Carlo,* also examined the inlets.

Two mountain peaks in this area were named after the same officer, Eliza Ears, 3,595 feet, and Eliza Dome, 2,960 feet. Prominent landmarks from far out to sea, they are used by fishermen for taking cross bearings.

Acres of native oyster beds occur at the head of the inlet, from which thousands of sacks were once shipped to Vancouver and Seattle; but with the introduction of oyster (the large species) farming nearer to the markets, the industry languished. Now they are free to anyone who wishes to gather them. Immediately inside the entrance to Port Eliza, on the starboard hand, is Queen's Cove, an important salmon trolling centre during the summer months.

Espinosa Arm, Malaspina named after Lieutenant Espinosa. Only inhabitants here are in a few small logging camps. Zeballos Arm was named after Lieutenant Cevallos. It was at the head of this arm, in 1935, that a spectacular gold rush occurred, and where a group of enterprising prospectors, most of them unemployed West Coast fishermen, made small fortunes. Prior to then, the only sign of habitation consisted of two trappers' cabins on the beach. Within a year, a prosperous town with a population of 1,500 had arisen, and by 1937 there were six producing mines, each with its own mill.

Gold to the value of $13 million was shipped during the next ten years, most of it in brick form to the mint at Ottawa. Concentrates went to the Tacoma smelter. Of the total production, approximately half came from the Privateer. The mines closed down in 1945, not because their gold reserves were exhausted, but owing to the federal government pegging the price of gold at $35 an ounce, which made further operations unprofitable.

Zeballos is now an important trading centre and the site of a big logging camp. Within four miles of the wharf is a mountain of high grade iron ore, said to be the largest deposit on the British Columbia coast.

The Japanese bulk ore carrier *Fukukawa Maru* sailed May 25, 1962, with 20,700 long tons of iron ore concentrates from the Zeballos Iron Mine. This was the first shipment in a five-year contract to supply Japanese smelters and refineries. Regular shipments have since been made every two weeks.

On the north side of Hecate Channel, eight miles from Zeballos, is Esperanza village. The Nootka Mission General Hospital is here, also a hotel. A mile further on is Ceepeecee, the settlement with a peculiar name and built around a cannery and reduction plant (since burned down). As I happened to be around these parts when the place was "christened", I know how the name originated. It is the initials "C.P.C." spelled out into one word. The three capital letters stand for Canadian Packing Corporation, a subsidiary of the California Packing Corporation, which built the reduction plant in 1926. The name was submitted to and subsequently adopted by the post office department when an office was established there.

Hecate, named after H.M. SURVEY VESSEL *Hecate,* a paddle-wheel sloop, 860 tons, five guns and brigantine rigged, is on Nootka Island, immediately across the channel from Esperanza and Ceepeecee. This was formerly a pilchard reduction plant, but the houses and sheds are now used for residential and school purposes by the Nootka Mission Hospital. Hecate was a Greek Goddess of the Moon. Because the vessel which was named after her carried out such an extensive survey of this coast, many of its geographical features were named after her. The name appears at least nine times on our charts.

Of the 26 pilchard reduction plants built on the West Coast of Vancouver Island during the period 1925-1945 when that industry flourished, five were located at different points on Esperanza Inlet. Each represented a capital outlay of up to $250,000, employed about seventy-five fishermen and a similar number of shore workers. The pilchard schools mysteriously disappeared in 1945 and there hasn't been a pilchard seen since. (For the mystery of the disappearance of the pilchards, see page 244.)

Prior to 1935 there were several dry salteries on the inlet which put up chum salmon in the fall and herring during the winter months. The plants were Japanese owned, but the fishing was done by whites and Indians. The product went to China, where the salt was extracted and the fish re-shipped to Japan. Meanwhile, the pilchard plants and salteries have all since been dismantled. However, salmon, herring and other species of fish are as plentiful as ever and provide profitable employment for several hundred fishermen, many of whom make their home on the shores of the inlet.

In the summer of 1928, the tug *Daring*, with two scows, both loaded with pilchards, in tow, and bound for Ceepeecee reduction plant, caught fire and sank off the entrance to Esperanza Inlet. Captain George MacFarlane and his three-man crew were rescued by a passing fishboat.

On October 2, 1948, the Nootka Hospital Mission boat *Messenger II,* when returning from Kyuquot with Dr. H. A. McLean and his son, Bruce, on board, was wrecked during a storm at the mouth of the inlet. The lad was drowned and the timely arrival the following morning of the fishpacker *Co-Operative No. 2,* saved his father, who had clung all night to a wave-washed rock.

CAPE OF STORMS
HONOURS
COOK'S MEMORY

IN SELECTING SUITABLE NAMES for the more important geographical features of the British Columbia coast, or adopting those already given by the early explorers, one name was almost overlooked. It was that of Captain James Cook, R.N., that famous navigator and father of British hydrography, who, after almost completing his third voyage of discovery around the world, landed at Nootka in March 1778, and thus became the first European to set foot on these shores.

But when, 82 years later, a suitable landmark was selected to perpetuate his name, the site chosen could by no means be described as a garden of paradise. That Cook's name should appear only once on the first Admiralty charts is surprising, for the names of others, British, Spanish and American, closely associated with the early history of this coast but who came long after Cook, appeared several times, also the names of their ships.

Named after Captain (then second master) George Alexander Browning, of H.M. SURVEY VESSEL *Hecate,* were two passages, an entrance, creek (small inlet), a group of small islands, a rock and a port, all on different parts of the coast. And no less than nine geographical features, after H.M.S. *Hecate* herself. A harbour, sound, bay and a small island were named after Edward Parker Bedwell, second master of the *Plumper* and later commanding the *Hecate*. Five times we find the name Moresby, for Rear-Admiral Fairfax Moresby, commander-in-chief, Pacific station, 1850-1853, and four Maynes, for Richard Charles Mayne, who served on this coast, 1855-1861, as a lieutenant and later became an admiral. H.M. SHIPS *Chatham, Thetis* and *Grappler* each was honoured four times. The Hudson's Bay Company steamers *Otter* and *Beaver* have six and seven namesakes respectively. Coast features named after Alexandro Malaspina, we read about in a previous chapter. In many instances where similar localities on different parts of the coast were identified by the name of the same man or ship, recent surveys conducted by the Canadian hydrographic survey have substituted new names and so removed these duplications.

Cape Cook is at the extreme end of Brooks Peninsular, about midway between Kyuquot and Quatsino Sounds. Cook sighted this "bold promontory", as he described it in his journal, in March 1778, a few days before making his historical landing at Friendly Cove. He named it Woody Point, and thus it appeared on his and subsequent charts until 1860, when Captain George Henry Richards, H.M. SURVEY VESSEL *Plumper,* changed it in honour of the great navigator.

Standing about a mile off the cape is Solander Island, half a mile long, 400 feet high, barren except for stunted shrubbage, the home of sea lions and a breeding place for sea birds. It was first named Split Rock, because of its shape, by Captain George Dixon, who was on this coast with Cook, and later (1787) in the *King George.* Captain Richards renamed it Solander in 1860 after Dr. Daniel Charles Solander, a distinguished Swedish botanist and member of the medical profession who accompanied Cook on his first voyage of discovery to the South Pacific. Solander was never on this coast.

The sea lion herds on Solander Island were always a source of interest to passengers on the steamer *Princess Maquinna.* That is, when the sea was sufficiently calm to permit the captain to approach near enough for a close look. A toot from the ship's whistle and the huge animals would make a mad scramble into the sea.

Brooks Peninsular was also named by Richards, after the name which Captain Charles Duncan of the trading sloop *Princess Royal* gave, in 1788, to what is now known as Klaskish, a small inlet immediately to the west, where Duncan anchored on his way south from the Queen Charlotte Islands. However, neither Richards nor Duncan identify Brooks.

This oblong-shaped land formation is approximately ten miles long and six wide, heavily wooded, with hills rising to 2,500 feet. Although it juts further out into the Pacific Ocean (in a southwesterly direction) than any other headland on the West Coast, it has no lighthouse. The only light in this vicinity is an unwatched light on Solander Island. To the west is another small inlet, Klaskino, and to the east Nasparti, Ououkinsh and Malksope Inlets. Their entrances are strewn with reefs and not one offers safe anchorage.

Without a doubt, this 60-mile stretch of coastline, with its deep indentations accounting for an additional several hundred miles, is the most desolate and God-forgotten piece of real estate in British Columbia. Mariners give it a wide berth. In bad weather, so great are the seas in this locality, the *Princess Maquinna,* one of the best sea boats the C.P.R. ever had, after leaving Quatsino Sound southbound, sometimes had to turn back, a thing she never had to do on any other part of the West Coast during the forty years she sailed between Victoria and Port Alice. Except for an occasional trapper, the entire area is totally uninhabited. In late summer, a few Kyuquot Indians visit the streams at the head of the inlets to obtain their winter supply of smoked salmon, but none actually live there.

Viewed from the deck of a passing steamer, the scene today is the same as when Cook first saw it through his telescope. Not a wisp of smoke, not a tree disturbed, and the only sign of life, the sea birds and sea lions on Solander Island. Here one is about as far from civilization on Vancouver Island as it is possible to get. Owing to the trees of the spruce forests being mostly stunted and misshaped from constant exposure to the gales which sweep in from the open Pacific, logging operations are unlikely to reach this area for many years to come. The nearest road is 80 miles away, with inaccessible mountain ranges between.

It was in a small cove on this rock-ribbed and wave-beaten stretch of coastline that in May 1930, the crew of the Ucluelet halibut boat *Manhattan I* found a lone prospector stricken with a heart attack and took him to hospital at Port Alice.

Cook Inlet in Alaska, at the head of which is the town of Anchorage, was also named after Cook. After leaving Nootka, he sheltered there before entering the Bering Sea in hopes of finding the mythical "Northwest Passage."

SHIPWRECKS: VICINITY OF CAPE COOK

On November 25, 1866, the Hawaiian barque *Mauna Kea,* Puget Sound to Honolulu with lumber, after drifting helplessly for fifteen days was wrecked in Klaskino Inlet, west of the Cape; three lives were lost, remainder of crew reached shore. Indians attempted to hold them for ransom, but two made their escape and managed to reach Fort Rupert. When word reached Victoria, H.M.S *Sparrowhawk* was despatched and rescued the others.

The barque *Thos. R. Foster* left Esquimalt, December 18, 1886, with coal for Honolulu; vessel sprang a leak off Cape Flattery and ran for Vancouver Island, Captain purposely beached her in vicinity of Cape Cook. Crew spent two months on barren coast, was subsequently brought to Victoria by the lighthouse tender *Sir James Douglas*. In February 1897, the four-masted British Ship *Glenorchy*, 2,229 tons, sailed for an Australian port from Puget Sound. Six months later, wreckage and a ship's lifebuoy with her name on it were found washed ashore in the vicinity of the cape.

On May 23, 1893, the whaling schooner *Jane Gray*, out of Seattle, foundered off Cape Cook. Of the 61 persons on board, 36 perished; survivors reached Kyuquot after being adrift for five days, were brought to Victoria by the sealing schooner *Favourite*. In October 1899, a schooner captain reported sighting an unidentified derelict off the cape. The peruvian barque *Libertad*, Chili to Victoria with nitrates for the Victoria Chemical Works; cargo ignited and vessel abandoned off Solander Island, November 6, 1899. One lifeboat with 12 crewmen aboard never heard of again. Captain and remainder of crew reached shore; picked up by a passing schooner and later brought to Victoria by steamer *Queen City*; derelict subsequently came ashore in Brooks Bay, the big bight immediately to the west.

In 1901, the barque *William Foster* was wrecked on Solander Island (of this wreck we have no further details.) Lost with all hands off Cape Cook, in 1903, was the sealing schooner *Triumph*; wreckage found near the cape. Fishboats by the score have been wrecked in this area. A dramatic sea drama occurred here in December 1939, when the fishpacker *Great Northern V* was lost. One crew member was drowned and but for the determined efforts of ground, sea and air rescue parties, the others would undoubtedly have perished (see page 261).

The M.V. *Otter*, former C.P.R. steamer, but at the time owned by Gibson Brothers, loggers, burned and beached a total loss, Malksope Inlet, March 1937; what's left of her is still there. In January 1943, H.M.C.S. *Surf* (FY24), formerly the fishpacker *Arashio*, converted for patrol duty in the Fishermen's Reserve (R.C.N.), beached on the east shore of Brooks Peninsular. Salvaged to Esquimalt where she was written off a total loss. The salvage scow *Recoverer* sank in 12 fathoms, Ououkinsh Inlet, September 1961; was raised four months later and taken to the Fraser River, now in commission again.

CAPTAIN
GEORGE VANCOUVER, R.N.

He named our Island.

CAPTAIN GEORGE VANCOUVER, of the Royal Navy, made an extensive survey of this coast in command of H.M.S. *Discovery,* accompanied by the armed tender *Chatham,* during the years 1792-1793-1794.

The two vessels sailed from Falmouth, April 1, 1791, and the *Discovery* anchored in the Shannon on her return, September 12, 1795, the *Chatham* arriving in England a few weeks afterwards. This note relating to the return of the *Discovery* appears in the Annual Register under date, September 24, 1795:

> The *Discovery,* sloop of war, Captain Vancouver, arrived at Limerick on the 13th inst., in company with the homeward bound East Indian fleet, having completely effected the object of her expedition and made some important discoveries on the northwest coast of America. She sailed from England with 150 men on board, and such was the attention of her officers as to their health, that only one man died in the course of a very fatiguing voyage of four years. They speak in the highest terms of the inhabitants of the Sandwich Islands, from whom they experienced every possible civility and attention.

Vancouver was born at King's Lynn, Norfolk, June 22, 1757, son of a customs officer of Dutch or Flemish extraction. He entered the navy as a "young gentleman of the quarter deck." There were no midshipmen in those days, and young Vancouver was rated as an A.B. Under this rating, he sailed with Cook in the *Resolution* on that navigator's second voyage of discovery, 1772-1775, and again in the *Discovery,* Commander Clerke, during Cook's third and last voyage, 1776-1780.

There's an anecdote relating to Vancouver's voyage in the *Resolution* in the *Naval Chronicle* of 1799:

Captain Vancouver used to say that he had been nearer the South Pole than any other man — for when the immortal Cook, in latitude 72°, was stopped in his progress by impenetrable mountains of ice, he (Vancouver) went to the very end of the bowsprit and, waving his hat, exclaimed, *Ne plus ultra.*

Vancouver was present at the beach fracas on the shore of Karakakooa Bay, in the Sandwich Islands, when Cook was murdered by the natives, February 14, 1779. He narrowly escaped meeting the same fate, as the day before Cook's death Vancouver was on shore with Edgar, the master of the *Discovery,* attempting to capture a native who had escaped with some plunder from that vessel. A scuffle arose with the natives regarding a canoe. Edgar and Vancouver owed their lives to the interference of a chief named Pareah.

On the return of the *Discovery,* Vancouver passed for lieutenant, his certificate dated October 19, 1780. Two months later he was posted to the sloop *Martin,* and from her moved into the *Fame,* one of the ships which sailed with Admiral Rodney for the West Indies, December 1781, and took part in Rodney's victory over the French fleet in April 1782.

The *Fame* returned to England in the summer of 1783 and the following year Vancouver was appointed to the *Europa,* a two-decked ship of 50 guns, which in 1786, under the command of Captain Vashon, went out to Jamaica with the broad pennant of Commodore (afterwards Lord) Gardner. Gardner Inlet, Devastation Channel, and Gardner Mountain, Bowen Island, Howe Sound, were both named by Vancouver in his honour.

From the *Europa,* Vancouver was paid off in September 1789, and was then, on Gardner's recommendation, appointed to go out with Captain Henry Roberts, R.N. (Point Roberts, Gulf of Georgia) as second-in-command of an exploring expedition to the South Seas, as the Pacific was then generally termed, and a new vessel, named the *Discovery,* ship rigged, 340 tons burthen, copper fastened, sheeted with plank and coppered, was selected for the purpose.

Owing to the Nootka difficulty, which took place in the summer of 1790, the voyage was postponed and the *Discovery*'s men and officers distributed in the fleet. Vancouver was appointed to the *Courageux,* commanded by Gardner. In December of the same year, he was ordered to London to attend the commands of the board of Admiralty, when he was promoted commander and given charge of the expedition which gained for him on this coast imperishable fame. The *Discovery* would be accompanied by the armed tender *Chatham,* brig rigged, 135 tons, commanded by Lieutenant-Commander William Robert Broughton, R.N. (Broughton Strait).

Vancouver's instructions were to proceed to the northwest coast of America for the purpose of acquiring a more complete knowledge of it between 30° latitude and Cook's River (inlet), Alaska. In further instructions, received in despatches brought by the storeship *Daedalus* after the two ships reached this coast, Vancouver was also to re-possess Nootka, the district and parcels of land, in terms of the Nootka convention made between England and Spain. Cook had landed at Nootka in 1778 and claimed these lands for Great Britain. Vancouver, as a junior officer with Cook had witnessed the fact. Meanwhile, the Spaniards had taken possession of Nootka.

The vessels came out by way of the Cape of Good Hope, Australia, New Zealand and the Sandwich Islands, arriving on this coast in April 1792, when surveying was commenced and carried out during 1792, 1793 and 1794, with zeal beyond praise.

While absent from England, Vancouver was advanced to post rank, August 28, 1794. After his return he devoted himself entirely to preparing his journal for publication. He had corrected the proofs of all but the last few pages, when he died at the Star and Garter Inn, Richmond Hill, Surrey, May 10, 1798, at the age of 41, and was buried in the churchyard of St. Peter's, Petersham, May 18.

His brother John, with the assistance of Captain Peter Puget, a lieutenant with Vancouver in the *Discovery* and after whom Puget Sound was named, completed the work for the press. It was dedicated to King George III and published in two editions; three volumes, with folio atlas and charts, 1798; and six volumes, with one general chart, 1801. The copper plates of the charts were stolen between the first and second publications and never recovered, the general one only being re-engraved.

Atop the main dome on the legislative buildings, Victoria, is Vancouver's statue. Made of copper and painted with gold leaf, it stands ten feet high, including the staff and flag held in Vancouver's right hand. The statue was executed by A. Gizek and fabricated at Perry and Turner's foundry, Victoria, in 1894.

In the legislative chambers is an oil painting (copy) of Captain Vancouver. The original is supposed to have been painted in 1796 by Lemuel F. Abbott, and is now in the National Gallery, London. Standing on the lawn in front of Vancouver's city hall is another statue of the famed explorer.

It is recorded that Vancouver was a strict disciplinarian, and it is true that he had men flogged. Actually, he was a typical seaman of his time. He was cruel, but the system under which he served was brutal. Its cruelties were to lead in time to the mutiny of the *Nore* and, later, to reforms in the terms of service for the lower deck. In Vancouver's time, when voyages sometimes lasted from three to four years, the master of a vessel had no backing beyond his own force of character to prevent mutiny and murder.

A midshipman in the *Discovery*, no other than the Honourable Thomas Pitt, for continued wilful disobedience and comptemptuous conduct, Vancouver punished by discharging him to the shore at the Sandwich Islands. Neither was aware at the time that the midshipman's father had died in England, and the young aristocrat was now Lord Camelford.

During his great voyage, Vancouver also charted the Sandwich Islands, made friends with their ruler, King Tamaahaah, and cleverly persuaded him to cede the islands to King George III, who would assure them immunity from all enemies. When Vancouver returned home he reported his acquisition to the British authorities. But all England was then agog with the expectation of an invasion by Napoleon. In consequence, the cession was never taken up and these beautiful islands passed first to Spain, then became for a time independent before being annexed by the United States.

VANCOUVER CIRCUMNAVIGATES THE ISLAND

After spending some time examining the Oregon and Washington coastline, when he named many of its geographical features, Vancouver rounded Cape Flattery (previously named by Cook) and sailed up the Strait of Juan de Fuca, keeping to the south shore, on April 30, 1792.

Discovery and *Chatham* anchored in a snug bay just west of the entrance to Puget Sound (then unnamed). In his journal, Vancouver speaks in glowing terms of the surrounding country:

> A picture so pleasing could not fail to call to our remembrance certain delightful and beloved situations in old England. Thus we proceeded without meeting any obstructions to our progress, which, though not rapid, brought us before noon abreast of a stream that discharges its waters from the western shore near five miles within the entrance to the harbour, which I distinguish by the name Port Discovery, after the ship. There we moored in 34 fathoms, muddy bottom, about a quarter of a mile from shore.

The following August, while at Nootka, Vancouver learned from Quadra that two Spanish ships, the *San Carlos* and *Santa Saturnina*, under Eliza and Narvaez, respectively, had previously anchored in the bay he (Vancouver) had named Port Discovery. Out of respect for the Spaniard, he changed the name to Port Quadra, and so advised the Admiralty. However, the name "Port Discovery" appeared on all subsequent charts.

It was while lying here that Vancouver named Mt. Baker, after Joseph Baker, a lieutenant in *Discovery*, who first sighted it. The mountain, it transpired later, had been previously named, in 1790, "la Gran del Carmedo," by the Spanish exploring officer Manuel Quimper. It was Vancouver, however, who first named Mt. Rainier, after Captain Peter Rainier, r.n., who later became an admiral.

From his base at Port Discovery (now United States territory), Vancouver made a careful examination of Puget Sound, proceeding as far as where the city of Tacoma now stands, and also the gulf archipelago (Gulf Islands), naming many of the islands and channels. He named Puget Sound after Peter Puget, a lieutenant in *Discovery*, for it was he who first examined the inlet. When Broughton, in charge of the *Chatham*, left with despatches for England in January 1793, Puget was placed in command of the armed tender and remained in her till the termination of her commission, October 17, 1795.

Proceeding northwest, Vancouver kept mostly to the continental shore side of the gulf (Gulf of Georgia), which he named after King George III, while his officers, using small boats, examined the inlets, passageways and adjacent islands — to all of which Vancouver gave names, most of them retained to this day.

It was in the vicinity of Point Grey, which he named after his friend and former shipmate, Captain George Grey, that Vancouver, to his astonishment and annoyance, met with the exploring vessels *Sutil*, Commander Dionicio Galiano, and *Mexicana*, Commander Cayetano Valdes, at anchor off Spanish Bank (so named in later years by Hudson's Bay Company officers, and adopted by Captain Richards, h.m.s. *Plumper*, when he surveyed the area in 1859).

The British and Spanish explorers examined Burrard Inlet about the same time. Vancouver named it Burrard's Channel after his friend, Captain Sir Henry Burrard, r.n., who was a lieutenant with him in the *Europa* in the West Indies. Galiano named it Canal de Sasamat which he understood to be the Indian name. However, Pilot Commander Don Jose Maria Narvaez, another Spaniard, with Eliza's expedition in the *Santa Saturnina* (Saturna Island) had, in the year previous, July 1, 1791 to be exact, named it Boca de Florida Blanco, having mistaken it for the main outlet of the Fraser

River. Ferguson Point, near the entrance, Narvaez named Punta de la Bodega at the same time.

Narvaez in the *Santa Saturnina,* made an exploring voyage from Nootka around the southern end of Vancouver Island (then believed to be part of the mainland) to Cape Lazo, which Narvaez named Punta de la Lazo la Vega; *Lazo*, in Spanish, means a snare; *Vega*, an ópen plain, which describes the topography thereabouts.

Keeping more or less together, Vancouver and Galiano's ships proceeded in the direction of Cape Mudge, which Vancouver named after Zachary Mudge, first lieutenant in the *Discovery*. This point on the southern tip of Quadra Island, named later by the Geographic Board of Canada to perpetuate the name of Juan Francisco de la Bodega y Quadra, was known by the Spaniards as Punta de Magellanes. Mudge later returned to England with despatches from Vancouver. He left Nootka in the small Portuguese brig *Fenis and San Josef,* Captain Juande Barros Andrede, September 30, 1792, and on arrival in China took passage on the East Indiaman *Lord Macartney*, arriving at London nine months later. Mudge described the trip to China in the Portuguese brig as most unpleasant, the accommodation and food of the meanest description.

Boats from the two explorers' ships frequently met in the inlets and channels when their officers exchanged notes. In the vicinity of Texada Island, so named by Narvaez, but mentioned by Vancouver under the name Favada, Vancouver had Galiano and Valdes to dinner on board the *Discovery*. Valdes, who could understand the native language, told Vancouver the Indians had said that from Cape Mudge the sea flowed northward through a channel to the open ocean; but Vancouver, knowing the Indian character, and still not aware that the land on his port bow (Vancouver Island) was an island, did not attach much credence to the report.

Vancouver decided to make his own observations and accordingly he despatched two boat parties to investigate. They returned eight days later and reported having experienced the ocean swells at what later proved to be Queen Charlotte Sound. The boats travelled both ways via the waterways to the east of Cortes and Sonora Islands, but they noted that the greatest body of water flowed west of Quadra Island, the channel which the Indians had told the Spaniards led to the open sea (Discovery Passage).

Now convinced, Vancouver had *Discovery* and *Chatham* up anchor and proceed through this passageway, which he named after the *Discovery*. They navigated Seymour Narrows (named later after Admiral the Honourable Sir George Francis Seymour,

Commander-in-Chief, Pacific station, 1844-1848), without incident, passed through Johnstone Strait (named by Vancouver after Lieutenant James Johnstone, the officer who was in charge of the two boat parties and the actual discoverer of this important waterway) and finally reached Queen Charlotte Strait. While here, the Spaniards caught up with Vancouver and the four ships spent several weeks in the area, sending out boats to examine the inlets on the continental shore. It was here that Vancouver met the British fur-trading brig *Venus*, Captain Shepherd, and learned that H.M. STORESHIP *Daedalus* was at Nootka awaiting his arrival.

Meanwhile, Galiano had also informed Vancouver that Quadra had reached Nootka in May and was anticipating his early arrival, and as it was now August 10th, he (Vancouver) called off his examination for the time being and headed for that place. Count de Revillagigedo, Viceroy of Mexico, on behalf of the King of Spain, had selected Quadra to meet Vancouver at Nootka and arrange for the occupied territory to be restored to Great Britain under the terms of the "Nootka Convention."

As the ships approached Queen Charlotte Sound, the two explorers parted company. The Spaniards gave as an excuse for the separation that the powers possessed by their miserable ships were unequal to co-operation with the British, and were apprehensive that their attendance might retard them. Vancouver was of the opinion that the real cause was Spanish pride.

Galiano continued northward to complete his examination — the last made by the Spaniards on this coast — passing out to sea through Goletas Channel, which he named after his schooners (*goletas*) *Sutil* and *Mexicana,* naming at the same time the south point at the western entrance after the former, and the northern after the latter. Six weeks later these two ships arrived at Nootka, whence they had sailed in May. Thus Galiano and Valdes also made a complete circumnavigation of Vancouver Island.

VANCOUVER NAMES THE ISLAND

The most cordial relations existed between Quadra and Vancouver. Both were also on exceedingly friendly terms with Chief Maquinna, whom they frequently visited at his summer home at the head of Tahshies (Tahsis) Inlet. In a despatch to the Admiralty, dated at Nootka, September 5, 1792, Vancouver says:

. . . in the course of a conversation which passed this afternoon, Sigr. Quadra requested that in the course of my further exploring this country I would name some port or island after both of us, in commemoration of our meeting and the friendly intercourse that on that occasion had taken place. This I promised I would do and, conceiving no place more eligible than the place of our meeting, I have therefore named this island "The Island of Quadra and Vancouver" (now Vancouver Island), which compliment he was exceedingly pleased with, as also by retaining the name of Port Quadra to that which in May last I had called Port Discovery, but finding it had been formerly explored and named by this officer (actually two of his subordinates, Eliza and Narvaez), I have since adopted the name.

However, Vancouver and Quadra, in their deliberations, failed to find agreement on all points under which the terms of the Nootka Convention were to be carried out. They met again some months later at Monterey, and still being unable to resolve their differences, referred the whole matter back to their respective governments.

Finally, at Nootka, on March 28, 1795, in the presence of the British and Spanish commissioners, Lieutenant Thomas Pierce of the Royal Marines, and Brigadier-General Don Jose Manuel Alava, the British flag was hoisted in token of possession and General Alava gave orders for Spanish troops to embark.

Quadra and Vancouver left Monterey together, January 15, 1793, the former for San Blas and the latter for the Sandwich Islands, where he wintered. On the 18th, when the little squadron separated, Vancouver gave a parting dinner on board *Discovery* for his friend Quadra. They never met again, for Quadra died in March of the following year at San Blas.

Back in the spring, Vancouver continued his examination of the remaining inlets as far west as the Aleutian Islands. Lynn Canal, Alaska, he named after his birthplace in England; Point Bridget and Berners Bay, both in Lynn Canal, after his mother.

The remarks Vancouver made in his journal while examining this broken and intricate coastline respecting the description of the shore, rocks and shoals, are excellent. The names he bestowed along the coast of what is now the State of Washington, British Columbia and Alaska, are an enduring mark of his faithful work. Long Spanish names he abbreviated, and changes were necessary where duplication occurred. Most of the Indian names he either adopted or used in translation. But it can be said that throughout Vancouver was most generous in retaining, as far as possible, the original names, whether bestowed by Indian, Spaniard, American or Britisher.

He was not, however, over-enthusiastic about some of our inlets. Following is his impression of Desolation Sound, hence the name:

Our residence here was truly forlorn; an awful silence pervaded the gloomy forests, whilst animated nature seemed to have deserted the neighbouring country, whose soil afforded only a few onions (native onions), some samphire and here and there bushes bearing a scanty crop of indifferent berries. Nor was the sea more favourable to our wants; the steep rocky shores prevented use of the seine, and not a fish at the bottom could be tempted to take the hook.

Vancouver's chart, prepared during his stay on this coast, was considered a masterpiece of accuracy and comprehensiveness and is still referred to by cartographers as the "Great Chart." That the four biggest rivers in these parts, Columbia, Fraser, Skeena and Nass, are not shown might seem strange, but it must be remembered that Vancouver was charting salt water, not fresh. However, his journal discloses that he did discuss with Galiano and Valdes a "large river" which flowed into what is now known as the Gulf of Georgia. This undoubtedly was the Fraser.

The Spaniards never claimed to have discovered the river, but Narvaez, through reports of its existence by the Indians — who called it "Tacoutchi" — in 1791 named it "Rio Blanca," after the then prime minister of Spain, Count Florida Blanca. The present name was given by officers of the North West Company, before coalition of that company with the Hudson's Bay Company in 1821, after Simon Fraser, superintendent of the District of New Caledonia, 1805-1809.

Vancouver missed, by two weeks, meeting with Alexander MacKenzie (afterwards Sir Alexander). After crossing Canada on foot, MacKenzie arrived at Bella Coola on July 20, 1793, then set out by canoe for the open sea. He reached a point on Dean Channel where his party spent the night. Upon learning from the friendly Bella Coola Indians that the natives who resided farther down the sound were hostile, and not being provided with sufficient arms to offer any resistance should his party be attacked, MacKenzie turned back and retraced his course to Lake Athabaska. But before doing so, he mixed some fish oil and red ochre and wrote these words on the face of a rock: "Alexander MacKenzie, from Canada overland, July 22, 1793." The Historic Sites and Monument Board of Canada, in 1926, erected a suitably inscribed 14-foot-high stone cairn at this spot. Vancouver had examined Dean Channel — which he named after the Reverend James King, D.D., Dean of Raphoe, Ireland — and adjacent inlets, only two weeks previous.

MURDER LURKED
ALONG THE COAST

THE EARLY TRADERS found the coast Indians friendly and anxious to trade, but, unfortunately, the "good" whites were followed by some who not only drove their bargains in a harsh and arbitrary manner, but treated the Indians, especially their chiefs, with contempt. When a tribe was thus insulted, the news was quickly communicated to others, and soon all trading vessels were tarred with the same brush. At least six that we know of were set on fire and the crews murdered. Others were attacked, but managed to drive the invaders off, killing many.

Another type of trader, fortunately in the minority, supplied the Indians with liquor. This not only brought trouble on themselves, and those who were innocent of the practice, but created untold harm among the native population.

In March 1803, the Nootkas captured the trading ship *Boston* and massacred the crew with the exception of two men. In a dispute over a gun which he had presented to Chief Maquinna, Captain Salter is said to have called the chief a liar and used other opprobrious language towards him. This, the great Maquinna, who had previously been lavishly entertained by both Spanish and British officers, deeply resented. He also knew enough English to understand the meaning of the captain's insulting terms.

Revenge was planned, and when the opportunity arrived, Maquinna, with his men, killed the captain of the *Boston*. Two men only were allowed to live, and they were made slaves. One was the armourer, John R. Jewitt, of Hull, England, the other, John Thompson, of Philadelphia, sailmaker.

After two year's captivity, they obtained their freedom when, on

71

July 19, 1805, the brig *Lydia*, Captain Samuel Hill, arrived in Nootka harbour. Jewitt found several neighbouring chiefs were willing to assist him and his companion to escape by undertaking to deliver a letter to any vessel they might meet. He sent out several and one was received by the *Lydia*.

The *Boston*, after being stripped, was burned and sunk in Friendly Cove. A full account of the *Boston* tragedy, and the experiences of the two men while held captive, is contained in *Narrative of John R. Jewitt*, published in 1816.

In 1805, the ship *Atahualpa* was attacked while lying at anchor in Sturgis Cove, Millbank Sound, but managed to escape after Captain Oliver Porter and ten crew members were murdered. In this instance there is no reason to believe that the Indians had in any way been provoked, nor was liquor involved. More than likely it was a straight case of looting. Captain Sturgis, with the trading vessel *Caroline*, was in the vicinity a week previous and reported no trouble with these people.

In July 1794, at Cumshewa Inlet, on the east coast of the Queen Charlotte Islands, the Haidas overpowered and killed Captain Burling of the schooner *Resolution,* out of Boston, and all but one of his eleven-man crew, then plundered and burned the ship. Shortly after this act of savagery, the Haidas attacked the trading vessel *Phoenix*, Captain Hugh Moore, from Bengal, killing one sailor. After the atttackers were driven off the vessel moved closer to shore and opened fire on the natives. To Captain Moore's surprise they answered with cannon. He was forced to withdraw. It was surmised the cannon was among the loot taken from the *Resolution*. The sole survivor of the *Resolution,* a sailor named Bears, was made a slave by the Haidas. Twelve months later he was freed from bondage by the trading vessels *Despatch* and *Mercury*.

Near Village Island, Clayoquot Sound, in June 1811, Indians attacked the Boston ship *Tonquin* and killed Captain Jonathan Thorn and all but one of his crew. The full facts of the tragedy can never be correctly known, as the only survivor was an Indian interpreter who joined the vessel at the Columbia river.

According to the survivor's story, told on his return to Astoria several months later, the *Tonquin* anchored in a small bay near Lennard Island (where the lighthouse now stands). Trading went well for the first few days, but Thorn's harsh and arbitrary manner greatly exasperated the Indians. He also treated their chief with contempt, much against the advice of Alexander McKay, his super-cargo, who had been on the coast before and was fully aware of the

Indians' savage nature. McKay was with Alexander MacKenzie when he crossed Canada on foot, arriving at Bella Coola on July 20, 1793.

The interpreter, while on shore with the Clayoquots, grew to suspect that all was not well for the *Tonquin*, and through McKay, warned Captain Thorn. But the advice went unheeded. A few days later, the natives attacked the ship, killed the captain and nearly the whole crew. Five survivors managed to clear the ship of Indians, and after nightfall attempted, with the exception of one man who was badly wounded, to make their escape in a boat.

The next day the Indians crowded on board the apparently deserted ship and, when the decks were filled with them, she blew up with a tremendous explosion. The interpreter, who had been taken ashore the previous day by the Indians, stated that the bay presented an awful spectacle after the catastrophe. The ship had disappeared, but the bay was covered with fragments of the vessel, shattered canoes and Indians swimming for their lives or struggling in the agonies of death.

The wounded man left on board is believed to have been Mr. Lewis, the ship's clerk. It is thought he somehow managed to crawl below and rather than be murdered in cold blood by the savages, put a torch to the *Tonquin*'s powder magazine. The five men who escaped in the boat were ultimately captured and killed.

The blowing up of the *Tonquin* was long remembered in and around Clayoquot Sound. Writing about it in his diary, Father Brabant recollects how the old Indians spoke of the disaster in terms of awe. They told him that after the explosion the bay was strewn with blankets, which because of their excellence, were long afterwards greatly treasured. They were looked upon as different and superior to all others, and spoken of as *Claokwahitske*.

The *Tonquin* was owned by John Jacob Astor. She still lies somewhere on the bottom of the sea in the vicinity of Village Island, a few miles from Tofino. Several expeditions have endeavoured to locate her and recover the seven brass cannon she is known to have carried, but without success.

A man named Barney, who sailed from Victoria in the sloop *Trader*, was murdered by the Kyuquot Indians in 1854, and his vessel plundered and burned. His companion, an Indian boy who belonged to a neighbouring tribe, was also killed, the Indians fearing he might implicate them. Word of this deed reached Victoria ten years later. It was reported by Captain Walter, of the schooner *Rose Newman*, who declared the west coast of Vancouver Island from Clayoquot Sound and beyond to be unsafe for traders. He said the Indians asserted they cared nothing for men-of-war, or Governor Douglas, or anyone else, and that they still boasted of having killed trader Barney.

In 1863, the north-bound schooner *Thorndike* was attacked by the Indians when passing through Johnstone Strait. Two crewmen were shot dead. Captain Frank, the only survivor, was wounded, but in the exchange of shots he managed to kill several of the attackers. Only the timely arrival of the schooner *Nanaimo Packet* saved Frank and his vessel. The *Nanaimo Packet* towed the *Thorndike* to Fort Rupert, where the seamen, James Freeman and Charles Brown, were buried.

So numerous were reports being received by the authorities at Victoria of vessels supplying up-coast Indians with liquor, that in April 1863, H.M. PADDLE SLOOP *Devastation*, Commander John William Pike, was despatched to investigate. Liquor was seized at various places and the *Devastation* returned towing behind her the trading schooners *Langley* and *Petrel*, and the sloop *Kingfisher*, caught red-handed. The masters of the two former vessels were convicted and fined $500 each at New Westminster, and the master of the latter $250. Court ordered forfeiture of the vessels and cargoes.

The *Kingfisher* met with a tragic fate in August the following year. While anchored in Matilda Creek (now inlet), Flores Island, a party of Ahousat Indians consisting of Chief Cap-chap and twelve men attacked her. Captain Joseph Stevenson and his three-man crew were murdered, their bodies sunk with stones and the vessel pillaged and burnt. News of the outrage reached Victoria, by canoe, on September 10, when H.M.S. *Sutlej*, with Rear-Admiral the Honourable Joseph Denman (Denman Island), Commander-in-Chief Pacific station, 1864-1865, and Mrs. Denman on board, was despatched from Esquimalt, accompanied by H.M.S. *Devastation*, to capture and punish the murderers.

In those days the Ahousats had several villages. These were shelled and many houses and canoes destroyed, and about fifteen Indians, said to include three of the culprits, killed. Eleven prisoners were brought to Victoria for trial, but all were acquitted for lack of evidence. Chief Cap-chap was never captured. It is said that he lived in a secret hiding place for many years afterwards.

Shells (solid) fired by the *Sutlej* and *Devastation* on this expedition still are found buried where the old villages stood. One, which came into the possession of the writer, was recently donated to the British Columbia Maritime Museum at Esquimalt.

On a similar mission, in 1865, H.M. CORVETTE *Clio*, Captain Nicholas E. B. Turnour, cruised along the coast as far north as Port Simpson. On the way, *Clio* raided suspected Indian villages and destroyed gallons of liquor. From Metlakatla a special trip was made to Kitimat and back to Port Simpson, an alarming rumour reaching the *Clio* that the Kitimat Indians had killed and devoured an Indian boy. The rumour could not be verified, but several Indians were arrested for illicit practices.

Three small vessels were caught in the vicinity of Port Simpson — not exactly red-handed — in the whisky traffic. Evidence was enough to satisfy William Duncan Esq., J.P., who presided at the court held on board the *Clio* at Port Simpson. He convicted the captain and mate of the schooner *Nonpareil*, fining the former £800, or eight years' imprisonment, and the latter £200, or two years; and Captain Jack Knight, of the sloop *Eagle*, £500, or five years, and his mate and cook £100 each, or in default one year in prison.

These exceptionally severe sentences were appealed and the result was that on the prisoners being brought before Mr. Justice Matthew Begbie, at New Westminster, they were released on their own recognizances of £100 each.

The general effect of these legal proceedings on the Indians was harmful, for they could not reconcile the harshness of the punishments at Port Simpson with the leniency of the appeal judgment at New Westminster. The result was to indirectly foster the illegal traffic. Three years later, in 1868, the Oweekayno Indians murdered the same Jack Knight, along with two other men, then plundered and burnt his sloop.

About this time the coasting trade was carried on nearly exclusively by small sloops and schooners. The crews often experienced on their lonely voyages hair-breadth escapes from Indian attacks. At other times the attacks were lamentably successful. These trading vessels mostly sailed out of Victoria, which was then the principal shipping centre for the whole coast. Many afterwards engaged in the sealing trade, their names, and those of their masters, well known along the coast.

Notably absent among the schooners which traded on the west coast of Vancouver Island were those of the Hudson's Bay Company. That company confined its activities to the continental shore and the island's east coast, principally Nanaimo and Fort Rupert.

Bamfield, Ucluelet, Clayoquot, and Nootka each had its own

independent trading post, most operated by schooner owners. Fur seal skins, obtained by the Indians off the west coast, and oils, were their principal trade. The men who ran these stores were then the only white residents on the west coast of Vancouver Island. One was Frederick Christian Thornberg, a Dane, who ran the Clayoquot post. He married an Indian woman from Ahousat. Frederick, the youngest, is the only survivor of their five children. Now in his seventies and still living at Clayoquot, he is the last link between those lone traders of one hundred years ago and today.

Another was W. E. Banfield, who in 1846 came out to this coast as ship's carpenter in H.M.S. *Constance*. He left the service in 1849 and for several years traded with the Barkley Sound Indians. Banfield, after whom the settlement was named, lost his life under mysterious circumstances on October 20, 1862. He was first reported by an Indian to have been accidentally drowned from a canoe when going out to meet a schooner for supplies. Later it was reported that he was killed by an Indian on shore. An Ohiat Indian, charged with the murder, was tried at Victoria and acquitted for lack of evidence. When the Indian returned to Barkley Sound he openly boasted that he had killed Banfield.

Attacks and other outrages committed by the Indians continued at different places on the coast, but it is impossible to list them all. In 1859, the brig *Swiss Boy*, Port Orchard to San Francisco with lumber, put into Barkley Sound to stop a leak. Indians swarmed aboard her in great numbers, drove the captain and crew to the forecastle and stripped the vessel, including masts, rigging and sails; then set her on fire. Captain Weldon and his crew, who were later picked up and brought to Victoria by the schooner *Morning Star*, attributed the preservation of their lives to the timely intervention of the Indian chief. H.M.S. *Satellite* was despatched to punish the miscreants; several were arrested and brought to Victoria, where they were jailed for six months and then released.

The Na-kwawk-to Indians, on June 13, 1868, attacked the sloop *Thornton*, 29 tons, Captain James Warren, when she lay becalmed in Queen Charlotte Sound, but were defeated by the gallant action of the captain and his five-man crew. At least fifteen Indians lost their lives and many were wounded. The chief of the party, a noted old scoundrel and long a terror on the coast, was the first to lose his life, being shot through the head as he attempted to climb over the side. The rapid fire of a Henry repeating rifle was the factor in the white men's victory. Warren was wounded in the breast, and Steadman, the mate, in his head and side, the Indians firing buckshot, bullets and slugs. Captain Warren was the head of a well-known Victoria family of seamen.

Notwithstanding the boastfulness of the Indians after killing traders Barney and Banfield, the hanging of several, imprisonment of others and the shelling of their villages, in time had its effect. Missions were now established at different places along the coast, sawmills and salmon salteries were built, and around them small white settlements began to make their appearance. The presence in these settlements of police officers, Indian Agents and other government officials, was helpful in putting a stop to the barbarism.

LAST BATTLE
FOUGHT BETWEEN
WEST COAST TRIBES

UNTIL ABOUT THE MIDDLE of the last century Indian wars on British Columbia's coast were frequent. And the west coast of Vancouver Island was no exception to the rule of raid and plunder, murder and enslavement of captives. It was a history of savagery.

People of the Bela Kula (Bella Coola) tribe, who inhabited the head of Burke Channel, were raided so frequently by the Bella Bellas, who lived nearer the open sea, that they seldom ventured beyond the recognized boundaries of their domain. The Haidas, in their huge war canoes, crossed Queen Charlotte Sound and attacked villages on the British Columbia mainland, the northern shores of Vancouver Island and as far south as Cowichan. They raided the Nootkas, the Nitinats and other tribes on the West Coast, travelling as far south as Tatoosh Island (Cape Flattery), approximately 600 miles from their homes at Massett and Skidegate.

Neither were the Haidas strangers to Victoria, where long before the city was incorporated (1862) profitable trading and social intercourse with their Songhees (name of the local tribe) cousins attracted them in such great numbers that one hundred Haida canoes could be counted in the harbour at one time. They caused so much trouble on the waterfront that every now and then the police would round them up and pack them off home. Homeward-bound they continued their raiding of villages and finally the authorities saw that a gunboat convoyed them part way.

The Clallams and the Makahs crossed the Strait of Juan de Fuca and almost annihilated both the Sooke and Becher Bay tribes, and they frequently raided the Nitinats. The remains of the stockades, behind which the Nitinats defended themselves from attacks by these people, can still be seen at Whyack, a village situated where Nitinat Lake flows into the sea, about a mile west of Clo-oose.

From bits and pieces told by actual participants or their immediate descendants to Reverend A. J. Brabant, who established a mission at Hesquiat in 1874, and Captain Peter Francis of the schooner *Surprise* who hired West Coast Indians as hunters and boat steerers for his sealing expeditions to the Bering Sea, we learn the story of the war of the Clayoquots and other tribes against the Kyuquots.

The year 1855 seems to have been a season of extraordinary restlessness and crime on the part of the Clayoquots. After killing Trader Barney, and afterwards the Kyuquot chief Tlaninitla, they found soon afterwards a pretext for going to war against the whole Kyuquot tribe. A young woman, half Kyuquot and half Clayoquot, had been killed by a Kyuquot who later confessed to the crime. Having a deeply-rooted feeling of enmity against the Kyuquots, the Clayoquots at once put the blame on the whole tribe. The occasion for war was at hand and generally welcomed.

In order to make sure a success of the expedition, Sitakanim, the leader, after maturely considering the matter, proposed to his warriors that the services of several other tribes unfriendly to the Kyuquots be enlisted. Messengers were accordingly sent to Hesquiat, Mo-achat (Nootka), Ehattisaht and Chiklisaht with orders to the chiefs of those tribes to have their men ready when the Clayoquots arrived so that they could join forces and by common attack crush forever the power of the Kyuquots, then the most numerous tribe on the coast.

The attackers assembled on a small island adjacent to the two on which the Kyuquot villages stood. When all had arrived, plans were arranged and men left behind to stand guard by the canoes and have them in readiness for a speedy retreat. Cautiously and noiselessly they proceeded and it was midnight — the time selected — when they arrived at their destination. The time element had another significance. The assembly island and the two on which the Kyuquot people lived were joined by a sandspit which was dry at low water. This the attackers had to cross on foot and be back before the tide came in. High water would seriously delay any organized counter-attack by those of the Kyuquots who might have escaped, for Sitakanim, the Clayoquot chief and master-strategist in making his plans, had detailed certain men to destroy the enemy canoes. By next low water, the attackers would have reached their canoes and be well on their way home.

79

The Kyuquots were to be killed in their sleep. Each warrior had an assistant whose duty it was to bring the cut-off heads of the slain back to the canoes. Others were detailed to kill yelping dogs and to set the houses on fire. Indian houses then had no door that could be bolted or locked. A cedar mat which could easily and without causing any noise be pushed aside, hung over the entrance of each house. Before the Kyuquots realized what was going on, many had already been killed, and when others commenced to defend themselves with fierce valour, the Clayoquots, with their allies, hastily made their retreat, setting fire to the village as they fled in the darkness.

When Sitakanim returned with his warriors to Clayoquot, there was wild rejoicing by the whole tribe. The heads of the slain Kyuquots were placed on long poles and these were planted as trophies along the sandspit on Stubbs Island. Reverend Brabant estimates that at least 70 Kyuquots were murdered on that tragic night and Clayoquots boasted the taking of 20 slaves, most of them women. Among the attackers, losses appear to have been comparatively few: the Chiklisahts lost 12 men, the Clayoquots 8, the Ehattisahts 3; the Hesquiats had 1 man wounded and the Nootkas suffered no casualties.

Hans Hansen, a sealer, who went ashore at Kyuquot a few years after the battle, reported half the houses in the village destroyed. He also saw evidence of the comparative recent disposal — in shallow graves or boxes placed in trees — of at least sixty dead. Hansen, who afterwards lived on the island with a Kyuquot for a wife, later lost his life in a canoe upset while staking timber claims with a Victoria man named Jack Donohue. Donohue's life was saved by the quick action of a native woman he afterwards married.

Amos Ellis, also a former sealer, lived on Village Island where he operated the trading post originally established there in the early 1880's by Captain Spring. Married to the daughter of a Kyuquot chief, Ellis probably knew more about the massacre of the Kyuquots by the Clayoquots than any other white man, and in substance his story is the same.

Early in this century when the writer visited the island, an old Indian, who was a child at the time and whose father was among those murdered, not only told me the story but showed me the resting places of the slain. By this time most of the boxes placed in trees had disintegrated and the shallow graves had all been uncovered, probably by scrounging dogs and wild animals. The result: human bones, bleached white, literally covered the ground — grim evidence of the battle between the Clayoquots and the Kyuquots fought over half a century ago.

Scalps of the victims which the Clayoquots placed on poles and planted along the sandspit on Stubbs Island, also remained as evidence for many years afterwards. They were seen by sealing schooner crews, who, it is alleged, took some for souvenirs, and a few were still there when Fred Thornberg ran the trading post at Clayoquot (on Stubbs Island). Reverend Brabant saw that the last ones were done away with, but even today, when heavy seas change the shape of the spit, the odd one makes its appearance. I remember in 1926, when a group of Japanese children playing in the sand, found three and brought them to the Clayoquot school teacher.

This was the last tribal war on the west coast of Vancouver Island. The influence of the missionaries who arrived soon afterwards, cooled the Indians' lust for revenge. However, many years passed before sealing schooner captains could sign on Kyuquot Indians as hunters and boat steerers, for they still feared the Clayoquots might attack them again.

H.M.S. FORWARD

A busy little ship

SHIPS ON THE Esquimalt station in the early days added many colourful pages to British Columbia's history There were frequent clashes between Indians and whites, often enough bloody and violent.

One of the smallest and most active ships was H.M. GUNBOAT *Forward*, two guns, 253 tons. Accompanied by the *Grappler*, also a gunboat, only smaller — three guns, 237 tons — she arrived from England at Esquimalt on July 12, 1860, under the command of Lieutenant Charles Rufus Robson, R.N. Both were convoyed out by H.M.S. *Termagant,* 25 guns, 1,547 tons. Robson died at Victoria, November 5, of the following year, from the effects of a fall from a horse. He was succeeded by Lieutenant the Honourable Horace Lascelles, who remained in command until 1865, when he was relieved by Lieutenant D'Arcy Anthony Denny, who in turn was succeeded by Lieutenant Thomas H. Larcom.

During her long commission on this station, approximately ten years, the *Forward* was frequently called upon by the colonial authorities for assistance in saving shipwrecked life and property, and to arrest and punish Indians for deeds of pillage and plunder. These missions took the little vessel to every part of the British Columbia coast, hence her name and those of her officers appearing so frequently on our charts.

In January 1861, the *Forward,* under Robson, was despatched to Nootka, where the Peruvian brigantine *Florencia* had drifted after becoming unmanageable shortly after leaving Juan de Fuca Strait, bound for Callao with lumber. News of the vessel's misfortune had been brought to Victoria by Charles E. Barrett-Lennard on his return from a cruise around Vancouver Island in the cutter-yacht *Templar,* which he had brought out with him from England on the deck of the ship *Athelstan* the previous year. Barrett-Lennard was accompanied on the cruise by Captain Napoleon Fitz Stubbs, North Gloucestershire Regiment, who had come out with him on the *Athelstan.*

On arrival at Nootka and hearing through the Indians that the American brig *Consort* had been wrecked the previous October at San Josef Bay, near Cape Scott, and that her crew and several passengers were on the beach, Robson proceeded there and took on board the shipwrecked people. The *Forward* then returned to Nootka and took the *Florencia* in tow for Victoria, but owing to boiler trouble had to cut her charge adrift, with the unfortunate result the vessel went ashore on a small island — hence the name Florencia Bay and Island — about five miles west of Amphitrite Point, Ucluelet, where she became a total wreck. Prior to 1930, Florencia Bay was known as Wreck Bay from this fact.

Forward's boiler trouble was soon overcome, but unfortunately with loss of steam pressure. The weather broke, and not being able to buck the heavy seas, she was forced to return around the north end of Vancouver Island to Esquimalt, where she arrived two months later after having been given up for lost. Meanwhile the surveying vessels *Hecate* and *Plumper* had unsuccessfully searched for her on the west coast.

The *Forward,* under the command of Robson, in May 1861, made an attack near Cape Mudge on a large encampment of marauding Haida Indians who were on their way home in about thirty canoes, laden with goods stolen from the homes of settlers on Salt Spring Island, the schooner *Laurel* and other vessels.

Robson had to open fire on the encampment before the Haidas would come to terms regarding restitution of the stolen property, treating all overtures made them with contemptuous insolence. The Indians returned the ship's fire and a seaman on the *Forward* was wounded. Only after numerous Indians had been killed or wounded, were five Haida chiefs secured (by a landing party) as prisoners, and much of the stolen property given up.

The plunder consisted of goods of all descriptions, many articles not being the slightest use to the thieves, such as a quadrant, theo-dolite, hydrometer and writing case. There were saws, planes, ham-mers and other tools, and a quantity of rum, flour, calico, blankets, cotton and silk.

It must be recorded, however, that the rascality was not exclusively on the side of the Haidas, because the excuse given by their principal chief, "Captain Jefferson," of Skidegate, when charged at Victoria for the attack on the *Laurel*, was that whisky sold to him and his friends had been adulterated with salt water.

At Saturna Island, in November 1862, the Lamalchi Indians, a band of the Cowichans, murdered Frederick Marks and his young married daughter, Caroline Harvey. When word reached Victoria, the *Forward* and three other warships were immediately despatched to the scene. Their combined action, in which the *Forward,* now under the command of Lascelles, played a prominent part, resulted in the arrest and bringing to Victoria for trial of eleven men and six women.

Anticipating the arrival of warships, the Indians had scattered to different islands, with the result that several of their villages had to be destroyed before the culprits were rounded up. *Forward* suffered one casualty, when a seaman was shot dead by an Indian from the shore. Lieutenant Lascelles then let loose with grape, canister and shell, firing over 300 rounds altogether, completely destroying a village, every canoe in sight, and killing several Indians. Of the 17 Indians brought to Victoria, 4 were sentenced to death by His Honour Chief Justice Cameron, and later hanged.

In the year 1862, the number of northern Indians, mostly Haidas, congregated at Victoria had grown to such proportions, and become, through intemperance, crime and disease, such an intolerable nuisance, that the authorities decided to deport them to their homes. The *Forward* was instructed to convoy them for part of the journey. While the canoes, in tow of the gunboat, were passing between two islands, the Cowichans fired at the Haidas from shore, some of the shots passing unpleasantly close to the gunboat. Lascelles stopped his vessel, cast off the canoes, sent an armed boat's crew ashore, who captured the rascals and brought them on board the gunboat. They received three dozen lashes each. It is recorded that this flogging exercised a very wholesome influence on other tribes along the coast, to whom the news was soon communicated.

In April 1863, news arrived at Victoria that a man named Brady had been murdered by Indians on one of the Gulf Islands. Lascelles, with the *Forward,* was despatched to investigate, and returned with one woman and three men prisoners. Tried and convicted at Victoria, the men were hanged and the woman got penal servitude.

The *Forward* was sold by public auction at Esquimalt, September 28, 1869, for $7,000, to Messrs. Millard and Beedy, agents for the Mexican government. A revolution occurring a short time afterwards, she was seized by the rebels and subsequently burned. Lascelles, in the meantime, had returned to England. Retired from the navy, he came back to live in Victoria where he invested in real estate. He had an interest in the Harewood mine (Nanaimo), named after his father, the Earl of Harewood. Lascelles died June 15, 1869; he and Governor Seymour were buried in the Esquimalt Naval Cemetery the same day.

The *Columbia* anchored in Clayoquot Sound. The *Adventure* ready for launching, 1791 (see page 86).
Photo from a sketch done on glass by George Davidson, artist on the Columbia.
Courtesy Massachusetts Historical Society, Boston, Mass.

CLAYOQUOT SOUND

THIS SOUND is almost as closely associated with the early history of British Columbia as Nootka. The name is derived from the Indian words *Tla-o*, or *Cla-o*, meaning another, or different; *aht* means people or place. There is a tradition that the inhabitants here were originally quiet and peaceful, but later became quarrelsome and treacherous; hence they were called by their neighbours *Cla-o-quahts*. Different traders dating from 1785 spelt it Cliquatt, Clayocuat, Klooquat and Klaoquaht. The number of Indians residing on the sound in 1788 is estimated at 3,000; now the number is reduced to about 1,000 or even less, divided between the principal villages of Ahousat and Opitisaht. In 1787, Captain Barkley of the *Imperial Eagle* named it Wickaninnish Sound, after the hereditary name of the principal chief residing there. It was named Clayoquot Sound by Captain Richards, H.M.S. *Hecate*, who surveyed these waters in 1861.

Its three principal arms are Tofino Inlet, Bedwell Sound and Herbert Inlet, which vary in length from 15 to 20 miles. All are connected by navigable passages. In the middle of the sound is Meares Island, also named by Richards, after John Meares, that British naval officer who afterwards engaged in trading between this coast and China and whose name is frequently mentioned in previous pages.

At the close of 1791, the American vessel *Columbia*, Captain Gray (Gray's Harbour, Washington), wintered in Clayoquot Sound. On Meares Island, to protect his crew from the Indians, Gray built a fort. He also built a small schooner named the *Adventure*, the second vessel to be constructed on this coast north of Mexico. The first, the *Northwest America*, Meares built at Nootka in 1788. In the spring of 1792, Gray proceeded southward in the *Columbia* and discovered the large river which he named after his ship. The *Adventure* went from Clayoquot to the Queen Charlotte Islands in charge of Mr. Haswell, the *Columbia*'s mate, and as we have already learned (page 45) was there sold to Quadra for 70 choice sea otter skins.

Flores Island, which lies between the sound and Sydney Inlet, was named in 1791 by Lieutenant Eliza, after Don Manuel Antonio Flores, Knight of the Order of Calatrava, Viceroy of Mexico 1787-1789. It was Flores who, in February 1789, despatched the expedition under Lieutenant Estevan Jose Martinez (the man after whom Estevan Point was named) to Nootka, which led to the dispute between Great Britain and Spain regarding their respective rights on this coast.

The trading schooner *Alpha*, 58 tons, built at Nanaimo in 1859—the first vessel to be constructed there — was wrecked on Flores Island, November 27, 1868. She had sailed from Victoria, bound for Hawaii with lumber. Nothing was saved but a few blankets and a little flour, and after spending nine days on the exposed coast, the shipwrecked crew induced the Ahousat Indians to take them by canoe to Alberni, whence they walked to Nanaimo. Three other vessels are known to have been wrecked on Flores Island, all in the vicinity of Rafael Point: the British barque *Lord Weston,* in 1854; the small steamer *Transport,* Victoria to San Francisco, engines not yet installed and under sail, 1866, and the U.S. schooner-type halibut vessel *Mololo,* in 1920. Crews of the *Lord Weston* and *Transport* were rescued by Ahousat Indians. Halibut fishermen were taken off beach by partner vessel. Lost off Rafael Point in October 1950 was the speedboat-cruiser *Maureen R.,* when Reece Riley her master-owner was drowned (see page 260), and in July 1955 the salmon troller *Maidie H.,* with her two crew members, Ian C. McLeod and Kenneth Wilson. In June 1930, the fishpacker *Anchorite* went ashore and broke up on the southeast end of Flores Island.

Ahousat (proper name Mak-to-sis), an Indian village inhabited by the Ah-ous-aht tribe, which at present numbers about four hundred, is on Matilda Inlet, at the southeast end of Flores Island. The Indian meaning of the word *Ah-ous-aht* is "people living with their backs to the land and mountains," because their original home was on the island's outside shores. Mak-to-sis, where their village is now, was once their principal burying ground. The word is derived from *Mak-yak-sats*, a coffin, or *Mak-yak-wilt*, to bury.

Matilda Inlet was named after a British schooner engaged in trading along this coast in the 1860's. It was here that the sloop *Kingfisher* was attacked by the Ahousat Indians. Adjoining the Indian village is a United Church of Canada mission and school, established in 1896 by the Presbyterian Church. John Telford Ross, ninety-six and now residing at Alberni, was the school's first principal. Also on Matilda Creek is the white settlement of Ahousat, comprising about ten families.

Herbert Inlet, where Strathcona Park reaches tidewater on the west coast — at the mouth of the Moyeha River — is in this area. Several hundred gold claims were staked here during the years 1934-1940. Two mines came into production, but little ore was shipped. Some of the properties, however, are still in good standing.

On Matilda, Shelter and Sydney Inlets, which together with Herbert Inlet form the western portion of Clayoquot Sound, when the pilchard industry flourished (see page 244), were six reduction plants. Also on Sydney Inlet was a copper mine, in operation — on and off — for about ten years. Today, there are no buildings or other sign of habitation at any of these sites.

Lennard Island lighthouse, established in 1904, guards the main entrance to Clayoquot Sound; the island was named after Captain Barrett-Lennard, and nearby Templar Channel (ship's entrance), after his yacht. Wickaninnish Island (formerly Village Island), immediately on the port bow going in, is where, in 1811, the Boston ship *Tonquin* was attacked (see page 72). Father Charles Channel, named after Reverend Charles Moser, the priest who succeeded Reverend A. J. Brabant, separates Wickaninnish Island from Vargas Island, the third largest island on the sound. Galiano, who with Valdes in the vessels *Sutil* and *Mexicana* explored these waters in 1792, named it "Isle de Vargas," after the noted Spanish governor of that name who re-conquered the province of Mexico. Shortly before the First Great War, about twenty British immigrants settled on this island, but at the outbreak of hostilities, the majority of menfolk enlisted. The few that returned subsequently found that the land was unsuitable for farming. Now, a handful of Indians, residing at the village of Kilsimat, are the island's only inhabitants.

West of Vargas Island is another entrance to the sound. It has a deep-water channel, but owing to obstructing islets and shoals is seldom used. It leads to Cypress Bay (on Bedwell Sound), which is marked on charts as an Admiralty Anchorage. H.M. ships of the British West Indies station visiting this coast years ago used it extensively. They rendezvoused there to repaint and tidy up before entering Esquimalt harbour after the long haul around the Horn. R.C.N. vessels still use the anchorage while exercising off the West Coast.

Prior to the First Great War, there was a gold mine (Ptarmigan) on Ursus (Bear) River at the head of Bedwell Sound. The employees, who were all Britishers, when news was received that war had broken out, to a man packed up and trekked overland to Sproat Lake; then on to Alberni, whence they proceeded to England. Not one man ever came back. The camp was left intact, even dishes used for their last meal, still on the table. In time, mice and moths destroyed blankets and clothing. Everything else, including the mine machinery, was looted and carried away. About twenty-five years later, the claims were re-staked and other discoveries made by local prospectors. At least one man struck it rich. He sold his property, which afterwards came into production, but little ore of value was shipped. At this writing, the same mine is again being brought into production.

We have referred to three mining areas on the Sound, but during the past seventy-five years, gold or copper claims had been located in the hills at the head of almost every inlet. Some of the properties were partly developed, but most, merely "holes in the ground." The same can be said of the Island's entire west coast. The area is known to be highly mineralized and assays have been encouraging, but so far the Zeballos gold strike in 1935 was the only one that really paid off.

Tofino, an organized village municipality with a population of about 500, is the Sound's largest settlement. Its chief industries are fishing, logging, crab canning and oyster culture. It takes its name from the inlet, already named by Galiano and Valdes in 1792. Tofino is the western terminus of the Trans-Canada Highway. One of the West Coast's two lifeboats is based here; the other at Bamfield. The waterfront presents an animated scene during the summer months, when each evening up to one hundred salmon trollers land their day's catch at four fish-buying camps moored in the bay. Tofino is also noted for its geese and duck shooting. The inlet is smack in the centre of one of the flyways which these birds use when migrating south, but an estimated ten thousand winter on the tidal flats.

Clayoquot settlement and post office, on Stubbs Island, across the bay from Tofino, is the oldest settlement on the West Coast, though other communities have since been established and outgrown it both in population and industry. The island was named after Captain Napoleon Fitz Stubbs (see page 83). The first trading store on the West Coast was at Clayoquot. About 1875, a Captain Pinney landed there with a shipload of goods, consisting chiefly of anchors, chains and other ship chandlery. Ports where such supplies could be obtained were few and far between in those days and Pinney conceived the idea that schooners would call there from time to time to refit. There was no Lennard Island lighthouse then and to attract the schooners he built one of his own at the end of the sandspit, where it could be seen from far off shore. The light consisted of an iron framework, upon which he piled driftwood and set fire to it every night.

However, few schooners came and as there were only a handful of white settlers in the area, and the Indians had little or no money, his venture failed. Thomas Earle of Victoria took over the store, scrapped the makeshift lighthouse, sold the rusting anchors and chains for junk and a few years afterwards sold out to Stockham and Dawley, also from Victoria, and who in the meantime had a store and hotel on a small island adjacent to Opitisaht Indian village, a mile away. A Methodist mission (long since abandoned), with Rev. Sam Stone in charge, shared the same island.

It was 1890 when Thomas Stockham and Walter T. Dawley first landed there. Most of the lumber used to build store and hotel they salvaged (from shipwrecked vessels) at Long Beach and rafted it ten miles down the inlet. Sealing was now in full swing and early in the spring the schooners (they owned two themselves) from Victoria called in for their Indian hunters and boat steerers. The Indians now had money and business was brisk.

In the meantime white settlers came to live at Tofino; prospectors were rushing into the hills in search of gold and timber cruisers began to make their appearance along the coast. The two partners also opened up trading posts at Ahousat, Nootka and Neuchatlitz. Stockham disposed of his interests shortly afterwards and W. T. Dawley conducted the business until he retired in 1937. He was J.P. and postmaster, and also the first mining recorder on the West Coast. Mr. Dawley died at Victoria in 1956.

The original Clayoquot store was rather unique. Indians were not permitted inside. Instead, they had to make their purchases (mostly in trade) through a small wicket, handy to which the storekeeper kept a loaded rifle. At times, when the Indians found the store closed, they displayed their wrath by firing buckshot at the closed porthole. The store manager during this period was Frederick Christian Thornberg, a Dane married to an Indian woman from

Ahousat, and who afterwards had a store of his own at Ahousat village. His son, Freddy, the sole survivor of the couple's six children and now in his seventies, still lives at Clayoquot.

Clarence Dawley followed his brother to Clayoquot in 1900 and until prohibition came along operated the hotel there. He had the job of tearing down the original store building when he found the heavy timbers riddled with buckshot. Clarence afterwards staked and became part owner of the Rose Marie gold mine on Kennedy River. The buildings still stand between the river and the new Alberni-Tofino road. The old steam boiler and hoists were buried by bulldozers when the road was under construction.

Clayoquot is an ideal vacation spot, with its broad sandy beaches, where sea shells of every kind may be found, and lupin-covered sand dunes seldom found anywhere else on the coast. Thousands of black brant winter there every year, and if one is quick enough with a shovel, gouey-duck (huge clams) may be dug at low tide. There is a good hotel at Clayoquot. (More about Clayoquot Sound's early settlers on page 276.)

On the shores of Meares Island and facing Tofino is the Indian village of Opitisaht, the principal home of the Clayoquots, present population about 300. Also on the shores of Meares Island, at the foot of Lone Cone Mountain, one of the Sound's most prominent landmarks, is Christie Indian Residential School. A Roman Catholic institution, which can accommodate 150 boarders, it was established in 1899 by the Right Reverend A. Christie, Bishop of Victoria. Kakawis, the name of the locality and its post office, means "many berries."

In November 1899, the three-masted U.S. schooner *Hera*, Puget Sound to Honolulu with a cargo of lime, caught fire shortly after leaving Juan de Fuca Strait; the vessel managed to reach Clayoquot Sound where she burned and sank off Round Island. A lone woman on board, said to be the captain's wife, was the hero of the ordeal.

Following is the captain's account of the wreck of the barque *Atlanta* in December 1890:

> The tug *Tyee* cut us adrift on the 8th. All went well until I set sail off Cape Flattery, when the vessel began taking water; but being lumber laden I did not think it necessary to turn back. The sails all blew away on the night of the 13th, and soon after the heavy deck-load of 80-foot timbers broke adrift. On the morning of the 14th, the foremast and mainmast went by the board, one smashing the long-boat, destroying our only means of leaving the ship. Seas were now breaking over us fore and aft and the deck was awash, preventing anyone from going below. About noon the vessel commenced to

break up, and at 3 p.m. she parted just aft of the main hatch, leaving fourteen of us on the after house. Night began to set in, and night in the month of December off Vancouver Island's west coast is a long one, even when one is comfortably situated. The mizzenmast went shortly after daylight and took with it nearly half of our limited raft. Later, this broke in two and on these pieces of floating wreckage, in the clothes we stood up in, drenched to the skin and with nothing to eat or drink, we drifted 170 miles in four days and nights. Miraculously, we kept in sight of one another and finally drifted ashore in Clayoquot Sound, where some Indians took care of us.

Later, the shipwrecked men were brought to Victoria by the schooner *Katherine*. Fate of the other members of the *Atlanta*'s crew, on the forward part when the vessel broke in two, was never known.

On March 16, 1894, the British barque *Archer* sailed from Victoria in ballast for Portland, Oregon; encountered a gale off Flattery, ballast shifted and she was thrown on her beam ends drowning three crewmen. Captain John Dawson and the remainder of crew hung to poop rail for several hours before a boat could be launched; finally escaped and were picked up by the ship *John C. Porter*, Nanaimo to San Francisco. Months later, the derelict vessel was found by the steamer *Maude* and towed into Clayoquot Sound. There she was righted and tug *Pioneer* towed her to Victoria, where she was repaired, and later sold.

In July 1923, the American halibut schooner *Pioneer III* was wrecked near the entrance to Clayoquot Sound; crew rescued by Indians and later taken to Seattle by another fishboat. December 13, 1961, the American dragger *Roberta* burned and sank ten miles west of Lennard Island; her four-man crew rescued by partner fishboat *Kokiak*.

CAPTAIN GEORGE VANCOUVER, R.N.
Vancouver City Archives Photo

Vancouver's ships H.M.S. *Discovery* and H.M.S. *Chatham*.
*Photo from a painting by F. P. Thursby for the late Mrs. J. S. Matthews. Courtesy Major
J. S. Matthews,* V.D., *Vancouver City Archivist.*

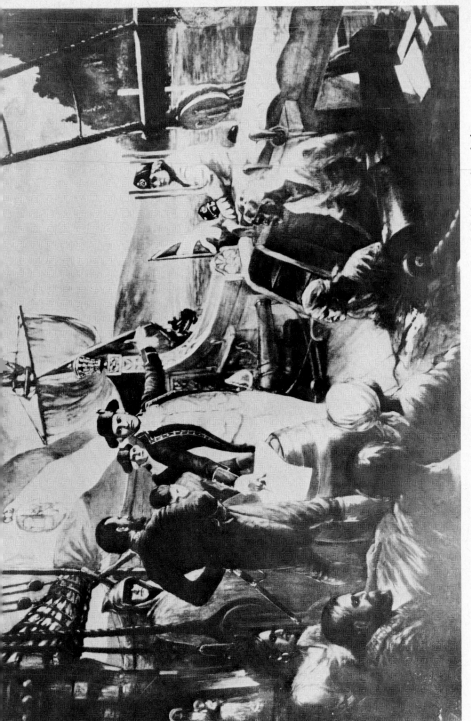

Vancouver meets Spaniards off Point Grey and welcomes Galiano and Valdes on board the *Discovery. Photo from a sketch; courtesy Vancouver City Archives.*

Photo of the *Carelmapu* taken from the *Princess Maquinna*. Note the two sets of distress flags flying from her yardarms. A few hours after this picture was taken the *Carelmapu* was dashed to pieces on the rocks with the loss of 19 lives. Only five men and the ship's dog survived. *Photo taken by H. H. Tanner, a mining engineer and passenger on the* MAQUINNA.

WRECK OF THE
CARELMAPU

ON NOVEMBER 23, 1915, the treacherous West Coast claimed the lives of 19 seamen and their stout ship. During a howling gale, with her canvas torn to ribbons and anchors dragging, the Chilean ship *Carelmapu* was wrecked at the western extremity of Long Beach. Only 5 of her crew of 24, and the ship's dog, survived. To this day, forty-six years later, the remains of her rusting steel frames may still be seen at extreme low tide.

Remembered also, is the thrilling part played in this drama of the sea by Captain E. Gillam of the *Princess Maquinna* who, with a heavy passenger list and a valuable cargo, went to her assistance. Though frustrated by a 40-mile-an-hour gale and mountainous seas, his courageous attempt to save the ship and her 24 seamen will go down in the history of ships and iron men.

The *Carelmapu* was inbound to Puget Sound for lumber. Displaying signals for a tug, which in those days were always on the lookout for sailing ships arriving off Cape Flattery, and with her canvas close-hauled, for days she tacked back and forth to seaward off the entrance to the Strait of Juan de Fuca. But owing to a succession of storms no tug ventured out. Suddenly a violent storm whipped up from the southeast and being in ballast and difficult to handle, she drifted towards Vancouver Island.

At dawn on the fateful day Captain Fernando Desolmes found himself only a mile or two from land. With scarcely any canvas left and only 20 fathoms of water under her keel, he had no option but to drop anchor. Still drifting, he dropped another but not until the vessel was within a few cable's lengths of the rocks did they take hold.

93

Shortly after noon the *Maquinna* came out from Clayoquot Sound southbound and to quote Captain Gillam's own words, "Never in all my long experience in the West Coast service have I been called upon to nurse a ship through such terrible seas." Actually he was just debating with the officer of the watch whether to turn around and go back, when he sighted the *Carelmapu* between himself and the land flying two sets of distress signals.

These "upside-down" flags meant much to Captain Gillam, who could see with his own eyes that the ship was doomed. His only thought was to try to save the crew. So ordering everything moveable lashed down, a full head of steam, passengers to remain below and all seamen on deck, he eased the *Maquinna* stern first towards the stricken vessel. He also ordered his two anchors dropped and the mate, Captain Kenny, paid out the long anchor chains. This assisted the engines in keeping her bow to the seas.

Oil pumped overboard broke the seas a little. An upturned lifeboat was seen with hats and oars floating on the surface, but no sign of survivors. Its crew had apparently all perished soon after the boat was launched.

At one time the *Maquinna* came to within 150 yards of the ship and, though men could still be seen on board, communication by voice was impossible. Captain Gillam then tried drifting a line down-wind, with its end fastened to a water breaker, but this failed. Then a big sea hit the *Maquinna* and the strain on the anchors broke the winch. It split the shafts and supports, stripped the cog-wheels and tore the machinery out of the steel deck. Rather than risk having his bow damaged he ordered the chains cut with a hacksaw and lost both anchors and 60 fathoms of chain.

A crew volunteered to man one of the *Maquinna*'s lifeboats, but the captain considered the situation hopeless and refused. About this time the *Carelmapu* lowered a second lifeboat and, although it succeeded in getting clear of the ship, it capsized and drowned seven more of her crew. As far as could be seen there were now only six men still aboard.

Another huge sea carried the vessel right over the reefs. There was nothing more the *Maquinna* could do, so Captain Gillam reluctantly headed for Ucluelet and sent word to the Tofino lifeboat. A few hours later the *Carelmapu* broke in two. Her forepart sank, but her stern held fast on the rocks. Then, as the tide receded, one by one the five survivors made their way ashore. All were cut and badly bruised by floating wreckage and jagged rocks.

It was dark, but four managed to find an Indian shack. Having no matches they spent a miserable night. In the morning the fifth man showed up. He had spent all night in the woods and was almost out of his mind. The others had difficulty in restraining him from jumping into the sea. The survivors were Captain Desolmes, three seamen and a nineteen-year-old Chilean student on his way to school at Seattle, and a dog.

It was after dark when word reached Tofino but it was impossible for the lifeboat (which at that time had no power) to put out with such a sea running, so her crew proceeded overland. With only meagre details as to where the wreck occurred, they had to search the entire shoreline from Tofino to Long Beach and it was not till after daybreak the following morning that they arrived at the scene on foot. Meanwhile, two independent parties, one from Clayoquot headed by the local Provincial police constable (Bevan), and the other from Tofino, had found the survivors.

They were taken to Long Beach, where the lone settler and his wife cared for them. They adopted the ship's dog, which enjoyed a comfortable home at Long Beach for many years afterwards. Later in the day the survivors were taken to the Clayoquot hotel by the Tofino lifeboat, where they waited for the next southbound trip of the *Maquinna*. Six bodies were subsequently recovered and buried near the scene of the wreck.

When the weather moderated the Tofino lifeboat proceeded to the scene and recovered a considerable portion of the survivors' personal belongings, the ship's papers and numerous other articles from the afterpart of the wreck, which at extreme low water was high and dry. Two years later, a quantity of steel was salvaged to be manufactured into munitions of war. The *Carelmapu* was formerly the British ship *Kinross*, out of Liverpool. Exact location of the wreck was at Shelter Bay, half a mile east of Portland Point, between Wickaninnish Bay (Long Beach) and Clayoquot Sound.

FATHER BRABANT was born in West Flanders and educated at the University of Louvain. He came to the Roman Catholic diocese of Victoria in the early 1870's, was one who refused to be discouraged where weaker men would have given up. Many were his disappointments, but he went on and fought through the years and today's relations between our native Indians and their fellow Canadians are due, in no small measure, to what he did so long ago. His published memoirs, long since out of circulation, vividly record a priest's life among the (then) far from civilized Indians of the west coast of Vancouver Island. We quote from its pages a few of his experiences, but first,

A NIGHTMARE JOURNEY FOR BISHOP AND PRIEST
MASS WAS THANKSGIVING

Travel isn't always easy on Vancouver Island's west coast today. But it's a little better than it was in 1874, when two venturesome Roman Catholic priests tested the transportation facilities. The journey north from Victoria was made in different stages by sealing schooner, canoe and a British warship. Coming back proved more adventurous still. Six times they changed canoes, provided in turn by chiefs of the different tribes visited. And, twice they had to walk overland, following wild animal trails through dense forests.

At Ucluelet there was no vessel on which they might take passage to Victoria, or one due for many months. And as one of the priests was now too weak to make the long voyage by canoe, the last leg of their return journey was made by the east coast. Crossing from Alberni to Qualicum on foot — for there were no roads then — they made their way by canoe to Nanaimo, arriving there on a Sunday, and, quoting from one of their diaries, "in time to hear the Protestant bells ring for evening service."

On the morning of Whit Sunday, 1874, the Right Reverend Charles J. Seghers, D.D., Bishop of Victoria, accompanied by Reverend A. J. Brabant, set out from Victoria in the schooner *Surprise*, Captain Peter Francis, for the West Coast. Their purpose was twofold: to get acquainted with the Indians and to choose a site amongst them for a mission.

The Indian village of Hesquiat, just inside Estevan Point, was considered the most suitable, and the following year the mission, which consisted of a small church and a residence for the priest, was established. Father Brabant was placed in charge and continued to administer his church until 1910, when he was succeeded by Reverend Charles Moser, O.S.B., from Mt. Angel, Oregon.

The *Surprise* took them as far as Clayoquot Sound. From there to Nootka, they made their way by canoe. While Captain Francis carried on his trading business — and also during periods when the schooner had to remain at anchor owing to adverse winds and fog— they made their acquaintance with the Indians with the aid of an interpreter who was a crew member of the *Surprise*. He explained who they were and the purpose of the visit.

Not since the occupation of Nootka by the Spaniards, 1789-1795, when a church was built at Friendly Cove by priests of the Franciscan Order from Mexico, had the Indians seen "white men wearing skirts," their way of referring to the priests' cassocks.

At some of the villages they received a somewhat mixed reception; at others an attentive hearing. Altogether the two priests baptized several hundred children, and married scores of young people. Promises were also received from many of the older Indians that they would henceforth give up their pagan customs and beliefs, especially the manner in which they treated their dying and dead.

Fortunately, they didn't have to spend many nights ashore except at the trading posts, where they were always made most comfortable. A night spent with the Indians at Port Renfrew is typical of what they had to put up with. There they shared a house with five different families, a blind horse, several dogs and dozens of chickens.

On arriving, soaked to the skin, at another village, they were permitted to lie down and "take some rest". In the morning, Father Brabant's memory was clear on all the events of the night:

> I heard the crying of Indian children, and the coaxing and singing of their mothers to get them to sleep again. An old couple had a

row in the middle of the night. A dozen mangy dogs constantly growled, barked, fought, ran in and out of the building, got into trouble with the cats, and only stopped their uproar when someone threw a piece of cordwood at them. Then, in a few minutes, their yelling and barking would start all over again. And, long before daybreak, the roosters, which slept on the cross-pieces overhead, started crowing.

All this time the Bishop thought I was fast asleep (on bare boards) alongside him under one blanket. But I knew that he was not, for he was continually turning about and now and then would give a determined scratch of his lower limbs. In the morning he told me the cause of his troubles — fleas.

The Indian population then comprised eighteen different tribes, numbering in all approximately 3,000 people. They formed, in effect, one nation, the Nootkas. All spoke the same language and as their manners, habits and mode of living were so much alike, to know one tribe was to know them all.

The women did wear calico dresses, at least many of them, but the menfolk practically nothing, except a blanket or bearskin wrapped around their bodies. The villages were separated by inlets or arms of the sea. In consequence, intercourse between the different tribes was impossible except by canoe. Five trading posts, each with one white man in charge, had, however, been established at widely separated points. Besides these five white men, there were absolutely no settlers to be found on this extensive coast of nearly 300 miles.

Means of communication were almost non-existent, except for an occasional man-of-war, and sealing schooners which made periodical calls for the purpose of supplying the trading posts with goods and provisions, or to pick up their Indian hunters.

H.M.S. *Boxer* came into Friendly Cove just as the two priests were preparing to leave for Kyuquot by canoe. Lieutenant-Commander William Collins invited them to take passage in her, and in a few hours they arrived. He also offered to wait one day and then take them back to Victoria, but as the Bishop had promised to make several calls on his way south at villages missed coming north, the invitation was reluctantly declined.

Father Brabant describes the journey back to Victoria:

Our mission completed in that area, and there being no other means of transportation available, we started out on the return journey by canoe, hoping, eventually, to find the *Surprise*, or some other schooner, at Ucluelet. Eleven Kyuquot warriors took us as far as Nootka in one of their biggest canoes. The trip was made in sheltered waters (behind Nootka Island) and except for having to spend two uncomfortable nights sleeping in Indian houses, it passed more or less pleasantly.

After another night sleeping on hard boards, we left Friendly Cove, this time with a Nootka chief and eight of his men handling the canoe. We were now on the open ocean. When off Sunday Rock (since re-named Perez Rock) near Estevan Point, we met a Hesquiat canoe crowded with young men who were on the lookout for our expected arrival. As soon as they recognized us they put about, intending to precede us and warn the tribe.

However, the Nootkas took to the paddles and a regular race between the two crews took place. There was no wind, but the seas ran mountains high. We would lose sight of the Hesquiat canoe for several minutes, then see it again on the crest of a huge wave, whilst we were, as it were, in the abyss of the ocean.

We stayed two days at Hesquiat, finalizing plans for the erection of the mission, when the chief and his son took us to Ahousat, stopping enroute at the hot springs (*Hot Springs Cove*, see page 251) to take a much-needed bath, the first for over a month. Spent another two nights among the chickens and dogs, when another canoe, manned by local Indians, conveyed us to Clayoquot. Here we met Fred Thornberg who kept the trading post. He was a Dane and had taken an Indian woman for a wife. Together they made us most comfortable.

At nearby Opitisaht village we called on Chief Shiyous, and here it is recorded that His Lordship, the Bishop of Vancouver Island, and one of his priests (*Brabant*), had to cool their heels outside the house while the chief finished his breakfast. Those dreary hours we spent at the chief's house are painful to remember, the smoke and the stench inside cannot be imagined; besides, the house was so low and the abundance of salmon hanging on the rafters to dry (and be smoked), so great, that we could not move except in a stooped position, nor could we put down a foot except on or over dissected salmon or salmon roe.

The next morning we begged for help that we might continue our journey. Old Shiyous was very obliging and, accompanied by his son and a slave, took us up an arm of the sea which is now known as Tofino Inlet. Although raining cats and dogs, it was a nice trip and I remember seeing thousands of ducks and geese on the mud flats.

A short trail from the head of the inlet brought us to Long Beach. From here to Ucluelet, a distance of 20 miles, we had to walk. Shiyous ordered his slave to accompany us, to carry our tent and satchels, and we set out, for the first few miles, owing to the tide being out, along the beach. That part of the journey was comparatively easy going, notwithstanding the rain which continued to pour down in torrents, accompanied by a gale of wind.

When the beach petered out we were compelled to follow wild animal trails through dense forest, which, as usual, lead to nowhere. Often, on hands and knees, and sometimes our bellies, we had to force our way through tangled underbrush which the sea coast is noted for. To make matters worse, we became lost and had to spend a most uncomfortable night under the wet trees. We did manage to light a fire, but it was of little use, except to boil water to make some tea. We had no provisions.

Cold, wet and hungry, bones aching and feet sore, we started off at daylight. Had travelled only a short distance, when the Bishop began to take fainting spells, mainly from exhaustion, lack of food and a wet skin day and night. However, we continued on slowly and headed for the shoreline, which was indicated by the thundering surf. We finally reached a small cove, where the slave gathered for us some mussels, and we ourselves, salal berries. These we ate with great relish, but unfortunately the raw shellfish didn't agree with the Bishop's stomach, for he was immediately seized with vomiting spells. That night we pitched our tent behind the drift logs, and reached Ucluelet the following morning, having taken two days and nights to walk 20 miles.

Two pitiful objects we must have looked. Clothing reduced to rags, bodies cut and bruised from falls on the sharp rocks and struggling through devil-club thickets, Mr. Francis at the trading store hardly recognized us. He immediately provided us with new clothing and nourishing food, made us comfortable and insisted we stay with him for several days. We were grateful for his hospitality and glad of the opportunity to recuperate before continuing any further.

Finding no schooner at Ucluelet, or the likelihood of one coming soon and the Bishop in no shape to make the long journey to Victoria by canoe, we decided to go by way of Alberni. The Bishop's condition soon improved, an Indian offered to take us to Alberni, and we started out, this time with a big, fat klootchman sitting in the stern, steering. Stops were made at different villages, where we again slept among the dogs and chickens, and the 40-mile trip occupied two days.

From Alberni we walked over the new wagon road which had just been built between there and Cameron Lake, crossed the lake by canoe and walked the trail to Qualicum. Here we pitched our tent and on the following morning, by chance found a canoe in the bush, and with paddles, and a sail made with our tent, travelled at great speed to Nanaimo.

We arrived at Nanaimo on a Sunday, in time to hear the Protestant bells ringing for evening service. It happened that the steamer *Emma* was to leave the next day for Victoria and in her we booked passage, arriving early Tuesday morning. We went ashore at once and astonished everyone by arriving in time for Mass, which for both of us was a Mass of Thanksgiving.

For the purpose of getting construction started on the church and mission, I returned to Hesquiat a few months later, again taking passage on the *Surprise*. Most of the material the schooner brought, but we were fortunate in obtaining additional supplies of lumber which had come ashore from the barque *Edwin,* wrecked in front of the village some months previous (see page 40).

As many men would be required to salvage and carry this lumber to the site, I deemed it wise to instruct the carpenter in charge, whom the Bishop had engaged at Victoria and who accompanied me in the *Surprise,* to hire certain able-bodied relatives of the chief. The frameworks were soon up and I returned to Victoria to receive from the Bishop his blessings and final instruction for the work ahead of me.

On my third trip up coast, to take charge of the mission, we sailed in the sloop *Thornton,* Captain George Brown, leaving Victoria on May 6, 1875. Good weather was encountered and the voyage to Hesquiat took only five days including a stop at Barkley Sound. I took a bull and several heifers along, which formed the nucleus of a herd of cattle that roamed the Estevan Peninsular for many years and provided us with fresh meat.

At that time, except for the lighthouse keeper at Cape Beale and the lone traders at Bamfield, Ucluelet, Clayoquot and Nootka, there were no other white people on the outside West Coast. Means of transportation were almost non-existent, except for two trading schooners that came about every six months. Sealing schooners called in for their Indian hunters, but often I went months without seeing another white man's face. When news of the death of Pius IX reached me, Leo XII had already been two months on the Papal throne. As a matter of fact, it was close to five months since I had received a newspaper, letter or a word of news of the civilized world.

All the Indians of this mission live on the sea coast and inter-course between the different tribes is impossible except by means of canoes. No two tribes can visit each other on foot, as their villages are separated by inlets or arms of the ocean. Opportunities for visiting are limited, especially during the fall and winter months, for no canoe could live in the incessant, heavy and indescribable gales which rage on this open coast. When travelling, I have many times been compelled to camp on the open beaches and wait for days before being able to continue my journey.

For years there was not an Indian within fifty miles who could understand a word of English and not till I taught myself Chinook, could I converse freely with my wards. I later found an Indian at Clayoquot who spoke good English. He served me faithfully, but I was soon to learn that he had murdered a man at Pedder Bay, near Victoria, and had been hiding at Clayoquot. In time his conscience got the better of him and he asked me to take him to the authorities at Victoria, which I did. All this time I had been conducting classes in English among the younger and more intelligent Hesquiats, both men and women, and soon the language difficulty on both sides was overcome. I was now able to take with me an interpreter when visiting other parts of the coast.

Word was received that a large number of Nootka Indians were sick and several had died. The report said the sickness was smallpox; that the whole tribe was wild with excitement and would come to Hesquiat and kill as many of the tribe as had died of the disease. I spurned the threat and persuaded them not to be uneasy.

A short time afterwards the wife of Chief Matlahaw died rather suddenly and I suspected everything was not right. I assembled all the Indians on a hill and told those who were living in the chief's house to quit. At first they were mad, but later acquiesced. Then a man came and told me his father and sister were dying. Both were dead the following morning and upon investigating I made up my mind that all three had died of smallpox.

Now came the task of burying them and none of their relatives would touch the bodies. With the help of two Cape Flattery Indians (Makahs), who were visiting, I dug the graves, hauled a canoe into the house and placed one of the corpses therein.

The scene in the death house was ghastly — as is always the case with smallpox — and before anyone would help me they insisted that I give them medicine. As I had none, I boiled water and broke some biscuits in it; then sweetened it with sugar and insisted this would be the very best preventative in the world against smallpox.

After this and further persuasion, ten Indians volunteered to help and never was such a funeral seen by mortal man. I led the procession, then came the ten Indians with their faces blackened and their heads covered with Indian charms. They all wanted to take the very end of the 40-foot rope with which we hauled the canoe to the grave. We took the old man first and in a like manner buried all three, using the same canoe. It was a ghastly sight; blood and bloody matter oozed out of the old man's mouth and covered his face. Friends had covered the women's bodies with blankets.

After the burial, an awful spectacle occurred. The ten Indians all came to my house, but not before they had all rushed into the river praying and shouting. Having thrown away their blankets, which were their only covering, in they came as naked as the day they were born. However, a thoughtful woman brought a supply of blankets, and then the spectacle became rather more decent and respectable.

Now another scene was enacted. While burying the dead, the Indians noticed that I was chewing tobacco. They insisted upon doing the same and not being accustomed to that polite practice, swallowed the tobacco juice. Some of them in consequence came near dying and it took hours before they got over their vomiting.

The next day I buried Chief Matlahaw's daughter, who had also died of smallpox. Her father and another old Indian helped bury her. The sight of the corpse was simply horrible and as we left the shanty in which she had died swarms of flies surrounded us all.

At this time, Chief Matlahaw, Charley, a sub-chief, and two other Indians, had obtained permission to sleep in the Indian room of my house. In return for the privilege, the chief promised and gave me all the strip of land between the river and beach. I passed most of the time vaccinating the Indians and trying to cheer them up, for fear and discouragement in some cases were altogether alarming. Matlahaw and Charley would sit for hours telling me of the importance of their lives and insisting upon my using all possible means to preserve them from the disease. Charley had been vaccinated successfully, but on Matlahaw the vaccine had no effect. This seemed to increase his fear and he now became morose and avoided the company of his friends.

Rising early one morning and looking through my window, I observed Matlahaw sitting alongside his father apparently engaged with him in secret conversation. On October 27 (1875), he shot some bluejays on my potato patch, and the rest of the time he stood outside obviously watching my movements, and from time to time exchanging a few words with the Indians who were constantly about my house.

That evening, after visiting a sick woman, upon entering my house and about to ring the bell for Mass, Matlahaw asked me for the loan of my gun, which upon handing to him I stated to be unloaded. He simply remarked that he had powder and shot in his shanty, which was made with a few planks and which with my permission he had constructed behind my little barn.

All the Indians of the tribe, save the old woman who had smallpox, and Matlahaw and his father, were at Mass. The old man was missed at once, and afterwards it was found out that he had crossed the bay with his little grandchild and gone up Sydney Inlet, where his wife had gone before him. There she died of smallpox, as also her female slave; and the old man, in a fit of passion, took a stone and with it killed the husband and slave.

Mass over, and just as I was finishing my breakfast, Charley came running into my room and said, "Lookout! *Leplet*! (priest), Matlahaw is sick; you had better take your gun from him." I made one or two enquiries, and after saying a few words jokingly, to give heart and encouragement to Charley, who looked alarmingly excited or downhearted, I went out, pipe in my mouth, and found the would-be patient squatting before a small fire in his shanty. He had on the chief's cap and coat which had been presented to him by the superintendent of Indian affairs.

Behind him against the wall, stood my double-barrelled gun and a musket. I asked what the matter was, when smilingly, he looked up, and, pulling skin from his legs, answered, "*memeloust*" (smallpox). I reassured him, saying that I would give him medicine and that by evening he would be all right. Again he looked up, his face pale and the sinews of his cheeks trembling, and, pulling the skin of his throat he repeated "*memeloust*". Once more I repeated that I would give him medicine and that he would be well before evening.

Then I asked him to hand me over my gun, which he took without getting up; then, pointing it towards me he explained, as I understood, that one of the barrels was not loaded. The fact of the muzzle being pointed straight at my face, and noticing caps on both nipples and the cocks pulled up, caused me instinctively to turn away my head, when lo! the explosion took place and I noticed blood spurting from my hand. The smoke was so thick that I could not see my would-be murderer and, thinking the whole affair to be an accident, after calmly remarking that I was shot in the hand, I walked down to the creek where I bowed down to bathe my wounds. Just then he shot again, this time hitting me in the right shoulder and all over my back.

I now knew the man wanted to kill me and I ran off to my house, where I found no one. Thence I ran to the village and was met by nearly all the men of the tribe. Some pretended that Mowachat (Nootka) Indians had done the shooting, but after my stating again and again that it was Matlahaw they became convinced that he indeed was the guilty party.

After a few moments a film came over my eyes and, thinking that I would not survive, I knelt down and said my acts of faith, hope, charity and contrition. Then I got up, went to my house and wrote on a piece of paper the name of the man who had shot me, put the paper in my bureau, locked it and put the key in my pocket. By this time the noise and alarm outside was deafening; loyal men of the tribe were there with axes and guns to kill the chief, but he had run away into the bush, not having been seen after the shooting, save by an old woman.

Meanwhile I had been divested by some of the savages of my coat and underclothing. Upon noticing the blood, they lost courage and one after another walking out of the room, announced to their friends that I was dying. This was also my own opinion, although I felt no pain whatever either in my hand or back. Then I lay down and ordered cold dressings to be placed over my wounds. I noticed very little of what was going on, thinking that the best thing I could do was to pray and prepare myself to die.

Early next morning two canoes fully manned left Hesquiat. One went to Refuge Cove (now Hot Springs Cove), Sydney Inlet, where Matlahaw's sister was residing with her husband. The Indians, excited over the doings of her brother, the chief, had decided to bring her home and in due course the girl was brought back and landed on the beach before my house. Left there alone and crying, she knew not that the Indians were plotting her death in expiation of what her brother had done to me. Such, however, was the case. When the plan was well prepared an elderly man came rushing into my house where I lay on my bed expecting that my days were numbered. He wanted my opinion; the Indians were about to kill the girl. As the savage spoke his hair stood on end, froth was on his lips and his body trembled with excitement. I gave orders to have the woman moved to a place of safety, to have her taken proper care of and appointed one of the chiefs, a relative of hers, to act as guardian during the time of unusual excitement.

The other canoe came back next day. It had gone to Clayoquot where a man named Thornberg (see page 284) had charge of a trading post. When the Indians arrived with my message he met them with rifle in hand and would not allow them inside until fully convinced that his visitors were from Hesquiat. As his neighbours, the Clayoquots, were not to be trusted, he advised them to avail themselves of the darkness of the night to return to their homes and, with his compliments and condolence sent a number of yards of calico to be used as a shroud for my "corpse."

A few days later a deputation of Indians excitedly told me they were going to send a canoe with the news of my state to Victoria, and report to the Bishop and the police. I told them quietly to please themselves, and as they were determined to leave at once, gave them a paper on which I had every morning written a few words.

Extracts from scribbled messages:

My Lord — sad news — I am shot in the right hand and in the back. Please get a priest at once. I may get well if a doctor comes at once to extract the shot.

My Lord — I am dying. *Adieu*. Pray for me.

My Lord — inflammation is setting in my hand. The Indians are very kind. The whole tribe is crying night and day. At least three are taking care of me. Do not blame them. Praise for their kindness, and may another priest be soon here to take my place — is the wish of Your Lordship's dying servant.

The diary continues:

Meanwhile, the Indians tended me day and night, but notwithstanding, as the hours and days advanced the swellings increased and inflammation was rapidly gaining. Although the Indians kept up a good fire, I trembled with cold.

At last, on Tuesday, November 9, just as it was getting dark, an Indian, out of breath, ran into my house and shouted that a man-of-war was entering the harbour. It was H.M.S. *Rocket*, Captain Harris, and I cannot describe my feelings and those of the poor Indians who were in my room and acted as nurses. On board the *Rocket* was Bishop Seghers himself, Dr. W. W. Walkem, who had volunteered to come to my aid, and Superintendent Todd of the police.

Within an hour Dr. Walkem was at my bedside, and after examining my hand expressed the opinion that it could not be saved and that I would have to submit to amputation. By this time Bishop Seghers, God bless him, had also come in. I can see him now, a picture of sadness. With tears in his eyes he told me how happy he felt at finding me alive. I could hardly utter a word; my strength was gone, for I had not tasted food or drink for several days. The Bishop opened a bottle of port wine and gave me a full dose of the medicine — as he called it — in the presence of the natives, and my strength and courage came back almost at once. I then told him full details of the situation. The navy doctor (Surgeon Lieut. Thomas Redfern) also thoroughly examined my wounds and it was decided that nothing could be done at present. That I would have to go to hospital at Victoria. Food was brought, but I could only take a few mouthfuls.

Next morning Captain Harris came ashore and proposed to have the would-be murderer arrested. In fact, he stated that it was part of his object in coming to Hesquiat. But just then an Indian came into my house with news of new cases of smallpox, and expressing his uneasiness, and that of the other Indians, to be left alone with the dread disease in the village. Happily, Captain Harris did not understand the messenger and so we urged upon him the necessity of returning to Victoria, as the doctors insisted that my wounds would have to be attended to without further delay. Besides, I told him that the man who had shot me had run away into the bush, and as he had not been seen since might be now in the mountains.

An arrangement was then made with the principal men of the tribe to take Chief Matlahaw — when he showed up — to Victoria, where he would be arrested, and that the police would pay them for their trouble the sum of $100, and a supply of provisions.

I was placed in one of the ship's boats and was soon on board the *Rocket*. We arrived at Victoria the next morning. There was an immense crowd on the wharf. The city was indeed in great excitement, for news had just reached the people that the steamer *Pacific* with 260 passengers — quite a number from Victoria — had foundered at sea and that thus far only one passenger had reached shore alive. As we came from the very coast where the mishap occurred, and as it happened just the day before, the people were all in hopes that the *Rocket* might have picked up a number at sea. We had seen nothing of the wreck, and the crowd, looking for friends and good news, were doomed to return home disappointed. (For *Pacific* tragedy see page 128).

The same bluejackets who had placed me safely on board the *Rocket*, now carried me on their shoulders to the Bishop's residence, and then landed me on the table in the dining room. That room where I had passed so many pleasant hours with Bishop Demers and Bishop Seghers, his successor, and my colleagues, the priests of the diocese and especially the Cathedral, now looked gloomy. Everyone wanted to have a look and say a good word. The Sisters of St. Ann were there with linen, towels, warm water and other necessities, and soon the doctors, four in number, began to talk business.

They were going to amputate the hand! Yes, perhaps it would do to amputate only the first two fingers! Such and other remarks I heard them make. However, I was not going to part with those necessary members of a priest's body to allow him to say Mass, without an objection. And object I did! And asked them to allow me to die rather than have me become a useless man in the world, such as a priest would be if he cannot say Mass. Protestants as they were, the doctors at first did not understand my reiterated pleadings to be allowed to keep my hand and fingers. However, they concluded to wait a couple of days and for the time being agreed among themselves to cut open the main ulcers, remove the broken bones and cut out pieces of lead and other foreign matter.

They left me with the full expectation of returning later to perform the amputation, but prayer had the best of them. Two days later one of the doctors made his usual call, and seeing that the blood had begun again to circulate he could not conceal his astonishment and went away wondering how this unexpected change could have occurred.

I was in the doctor's hands for nearly five months. I then heard that a schooner was sailing for the West Coast, and foreseeing that no other opportunity to return to my mission would offer for the next six months, I asked for passage. We sailed on March 23, 1876, and arrived at Hesquiat April 5, bad weather and having to make several calls en route accounting for the longer than usual voyage.

My house was in the state I had left it, my own dried blood on the floor; water, dressings etc. still there. Everything reminded me of the sad days and sleepless nights. It all had a tendency to make me feel downhearted, but the Indians were then so happy to see me back that I put aside all other thoughts, and after a few days cleaning, settling down again, recommenced my work where, so abruptly, I had left off.

FIRST RITES — STRANGE FUNERALS

The first funeral according to the rites of the Catholic Church took place at Hesquiat June 28, 1875. A funeral is never a very funny affair, still this one seems to be an exception. The Indian died about midnight; as was customary he was put in the box or trunk at once, a fact of which I had been warned by a messenger. I got up at once and told the messenger that the funeral could not take place before morning; however, there was no objection to having the corpse put outside the Indian house.

About three o'clock I was aroused again and once more told the messenger to have patience till Mass time. At four, there were quite a number of Indians outside my house. I got up again and this time the primitive coffin was in evidence at the church door. Still I thought it rather unusual to bury the dead at four o'clock in the morning, and by five there was no use putting it off any longer. Mass over, I solemnly headed the funeral procession; when looking behind me I noticed that the savages had taken another route with the corpse; in fact they had put it into a canoe and were paddling across the small bay around which I was walking. Still, we arrived ultimately at the same spot, but to my dismay there was no grave dug. Shovel and pick were sent for, I took off my surplice, began digging, got an Indian to continue and went home and had breakfast. When everything was ready I went back and blessed the grave and the first Christian of this region was laid to rest in consecrated ground, *R.I.P.*

The Indians up to this time had never buried their dead under ground. When it was time to remove the corpse, usually immediately upon the person being pronounced dead, they made an opening in the side of the house. They never took a corpse through a door, especially on account of the children who, as the savages thought, would die if they passed through any passage used by people carrying a corpse. The body was taken through this opening, made by removing a few boards. Then they walked, if possible, along the beach below high-water mark. If the body was placed in a canoe, that canoe was afterwards destroyed. The bodies were removed to only a small distance from the village and placed in a prominent place on the limbs of trees ten to twenty feet from the ground. There they were fastened with strong cords made of cedar bark. They were afterwards covered with blankets and a display made by hanging baskets all round. In some instances, the dead were placed in caves, usually along the shoreline.

While this was going on, the people in the house, especially the old women, gathered everything that had belonged to the dead man or woman, made a fire outside, threw all the relics into it and destroyed what was not inflammable.

And now you could hear them in the houses cry and lament and utter the most unearthly wailings that one can listen to. When men of importance die, the mourning is general and the scenes that are enacted go beyond the limits. Those of lower rank are mourned by only their relatives and nearest friends.

My efforts to discourage the placing of corpses in trees or caves in time bore fruit, and except in rare instances, mostly in remote places which I seldom visited, all burials are now in the ground. The practice of destroying by fire the deceased's personal effects, however, continues, but as it in no way conflicts with the Christian teachings of these people, I refrained from offering any objection. Some tribes still do it. Others place the articles on the grave.

Many instances are narrated where Indians have been buried alive. Thornberg, the Clayoquot trader, told me that a man, supposed to be dead, was put in a box and placed on his island (Stubbs Island). During the night somebody rapped at his door; he got up and there stood a naked Indian, the man who had been buried the day before. He lived for two years after his supposed death. The strange part of this story is that the Indians who had buried him still maintained that the man was dead, and that a bad spirit now occupied his corpse.

A young married woman had given birth to her first child. She took convulsions and fainted away. No time was lost in putting her in a box and removing her to a cave close to the village. Next morning a man went bathing in the neighbourhood and heard the poor woman cry for pity. She was alive . . . and, horrible to relate, was left to die in her misery. Her new-born baby soon followed her in death, having starved for the want of food. This happened at Nootka.

Another case came to my notice as reported by an eye-witness: A middle-aged man was cutting down a tree; it fell unexpectedly and crushed one of his legs very badly. He was carried home, bled a great deal and at last was pronounced dead by the "medicine-men", although every other witness knew he was only in a faint. Next morning as my informant was walking along the beach he noticed that one leg stuck through the square box into which the body had been placed, an evident sign that the man had been buried alive, and that in attempting to free himself he had used the sound leg to break through the side of the box, the injured one having been too far destroyed or too painful to be used for this purpose.

I know of a man whose son, the father of a small family, took suddenly sick through exposure. After four or five days the old man ordered a box to be made and asked the services of three men — they narrated this to me themselves with delight — to force the sick

Kyuquot Indian Village, where last tribal war on the West Coast was fought.
Provincial Archives Photo

H.M.S. FORWARD
Provincial Archives Photo

Clayoquot on Stubbs Island. Dawley's store left; building at far right was the jail. *Provincial Archives Photo.*

Trader bartering with Indians on the sand at Clayoquot. *Provincial Archives Photo.*

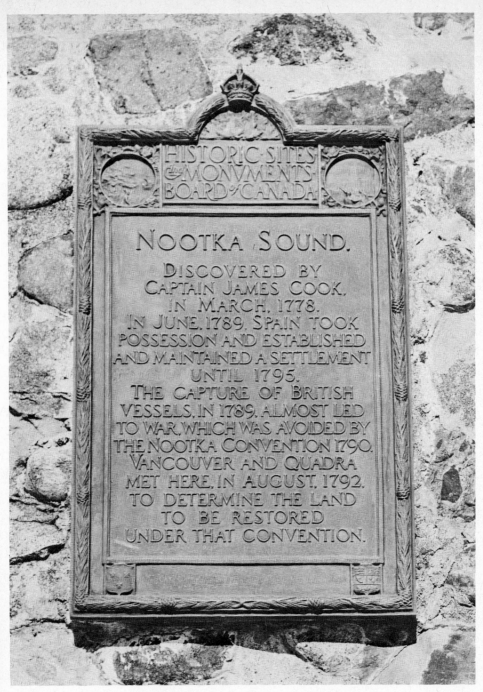

Tablet on cairn erected at Friendly Cove by the Historic Sites and Monument Board of Canada.
B.C. Government Travel Bureau Photo

Commander Phillip J. Hankin, R.N., with Surgeon-Lieutenant Charles B. Wood, R.N., made historic trek across Vancouver Island in 1862. *Provincial Archives Photo*.

son into the box; they tied his hands and feet, and having him well secured, did as they were told by the heartless father and took him out into the bush to perish of misery. During all this transaction, the unfortunate fellow groaned and seemed to ask them to have pity on him. They were inclined to comply with his wishes, but were told: "Never mind, do as I tell you; my son is dead, the bad spirit has hold of him and makes all this resistance."

In Tlimeghka, Hesquiat's deaf and dumb cripple, we have living proof of this wicked practice. Different versions exist as to how this man came to be so treated; however, none of these I can vouch for, because it happened before my time. Two old Indians, at least, declared to me that they were eye-witnesses. Others learned it second-hand. Details are therefore sketchy, but all agree that the man, when quite young, was either presumed dead by his relatives, or pronounced so by medicine-men. Then, to "fit" the corpse into a small box, both legs were broken in several places and doubled-up. The "remains" were then placed either in a tree or cave.

Several days later, the "dead man" was found creeping back towards the village on his hands, dragging his broken limbs. How it came about that the medicine-men didn't insist on the "corpse" being forthwith placed back in the box and left to its fate, I never did learn; or how he came to be deaf and dumb. He might have been born that way, hence the reason why he was so treated in the first place. Anyway, although a helpless cripple, hobbling along the ground like an animal and making noises like a dog, he thereafter led an otherwise active life and lived to a ripe old age.

(Tlimeghka died shortly before Father Brabant left Hesquiat, when he was given a Christian burial.)

Instances have also been reported to me where medicine-men have ordered bodies purposely mutilated even after positive death, such as drownings etc., in order that evil spirits might not enter and revitalize the corpse.

Since the abolition of medicine-men and women, free recourse is had to me for medicines and medical treatment. Day and night calls are made for remedies for old and young; they want medicine for any and every complaint, often only a mild attack of everyday diarrhoea; there is no end to it. Strong, burning medicines are preferred; in fact mild remedies are discarded. Since last year I must have applied yards of blistering mustard plasters to the aching limbs and bodies of my parishioners. I hope this habit of calling for help for even the most trivial ailments will cease; if not, I have a hard and busy time before me.

ONE OF THE earliest recorded treks made by white man across
Vancouver Island was accomplished in June 1862, from Kyuquot
Sound on the West Coast, to the mouth of Nimpkish River on the
eastern side. It was undertaken by Lieut. Phillip James Hankin, R.N.,
and Surgeon-Lieutenant Charles Bedingfield Wood, R.N., of H.M.S.
Hecate, on instructions from Capt. George H. Richards, R.N., then
engaged in making a survey of the coast.

The trip completed, Captain Richards had this to say in the
opening remarks of a report submitted by him to His Excellency
Governor Douglas:

> It has been my desire and practice, whenever the more immediate
> duties of the maritime survey would permit, to gather as much
> information as possible of the interior of this island, as well as the
> adjacent continent, and with this in view, parties have from time
> to time been equipped and dispatched from the *Hecate*.
>
> I am fully aware that the limited time I have been able to devote
> to these objects, the physical difficulties of the country, and the
> obstructions always incident to first explorations, will deprive such
> attempts of much of the value which at first sight might seem to
> attach to them, and that results can only be considered commensu-
> rate with the labour and risk frequently attendant on their accom-
> plishments. Yet I believe such preliminary explorations will serve
> materially to aid further research.

The difficulties in this instance involved the uncertainty of Indians
hired to act as guides and carry supplies, flooded rivers which had to
be crossed and re-crossed several times, lack of game which the
party relied on for food, and having to build log rafts to reach the
opposite shore of every lake encountered.

Accompanied by four Indians, the two officers left the *Hecate* at Queens Cove, Esperanza Inlet on May 25, and the following day arrived at Kyuquot, where they hoped to find enough men to carry their provisions, instruments and other equipment. They were met by Chief Kai-ne-nitt, a young man about twenty-two or twenty-three. Hankin was familiar with the language of the Ohiats, for he had spent many months on Barkley Sound. The Kyuquots spoke the same dialect, but the expressions were different. However, he soon made himself understood, and in due course seven men were engaged to make the trip. For their services, each was to receive a small sum of money, three blankets and a shirt.

Hankin's comments on the Kyuquot Indians are interesting:

We found the natives here most civil and obliging. I had afterwards occasion to remain with these people several days, and although they had both temptation and opportunity, it is worthy to remark that not the smallest trifle was stolen from us. On one occasion I lost a meerschaum pipe, which was afterwards found and returned to me.

With the exception of occasional visits from trading schooners, they had seen but little of the whites. But two of them had visited Victoria and had returned with such wonderful accounts that others were eager to go. And their desire to see the *Hecate* was intense. Some of the younger women wore calico dresses, and a few of the young men, trousers. But the elder men and women were clothed principally in a blanket and cape made of either deer or bearskin, or from the bark of the cypress (cedar). A few wool blankets seen were prize possessions of the chief's family. From the cypress tree they also manufactured canoes and paddles, and from its bark or fibre, hats which shed the rain (the Nootka hat), matting, fishing nets, twine and stout rope used for whale fishing.

One of their favourite games was a trial of strength. Fifty or sixty men, with naked bodies and faces daubed in red or black paint, would seize a long pole, using it as a battering ram, and with tremendous yells, looking more like demons than men, charge against some hundred and fifty others, who, with their united strength, would endeavour to rout the invaders.

A quieter game was to stick a feather in the ground, when an Indian standing on one foot would stoop down and without touching the ground with his hand, extract the feather with his teeth. This feat I tried several times and generally tumbled, my embarrassment causing a hearty laugh all round. I showed them some of our games, leaping, jumping, racing, etc., in which they appeared to be both interested and amused.

We endeavoured to discover if the Indians had any religious ceremonies or impressions, or if they held any one day more sacred than another, but they appear to be perfect heathens, worshipping neither the sun, moon or stars, nor having any idea of a Supreme Being.

The day of departure having arrived, the two officers were up at the crack of dawn and soon had their blankets, tents, provisions, instruments, and Dr. Wood's collecting material packed. But there was no sign of the Indian bearers, who failed to appreciate the necessity of such an early start. However, Hankin relates, the seven men were soon rounded up, and with misgivings as to whether their combined effects would be more than the Indians could carry, in addition to baskets of dried halibut for their own use, a start was finally made.

After six hours' paddling, they were at the mouth of Tahsish River, some 14 miles up Kyuquot Sound, and spent the night in Indian houses occupied only during the salmon fishing season. Tahsish River, Kyuquot Sound, is not to be confused with Tahsis River on Nootka Sound. Both names originate from the same Indian word *tashee*, meaning a trail or passage. Trails along both rivers were used by West Coast Indians as a means of crossing the island to the Nimpkish River.

It had been raining hard for two days, and with the river in flood, only four miles' progress was made the next day. From here the river was no longer navigable by canoe, and in order to follow the animal trails, waist-deep crossings would be required from time to time. With heavy packs and the river still rising, for the rain continued to pour down in torrents, this the Indians objected to, and refused to proceed any further. There was nothing the two officers could do about it and the following day they were back at Kyuquot.

Fearing the whole expedition had failed, Hankin had almost made up his mind to remain at Kyuquot until the arrival of the *Hecate* in two or three weeks, when the unexpected happened. An intelligent Indian outlined for them on the sand the trail across the island to Nimpkish, putting in the lakes and rivers and telling them their native names. Six volunteered their services as guides and both men were amused to see them dispute respective distances marked on the sand.

If another start was made immediately, it would still be possible to cross the island in time to meet the *Hecate* at Fort Rupert on the 15th. Hankin upped the pay from three blankets to five, plus a shirt, and in return received a promise, made before the chief, that regardless of what might first appear to be insurmountable obstacles encountered on the way, once started there would be no turning back. In addition, when the *Hecate* arrived back at Kyuquot, one blanket was to be given each member of the tribe.

To lighten their burden, Dr. Wood was reluctantly obliged to leave behind his collecting gear and that feature of the expedition had to be abandoned. The original plan called for stopping here and there to examine more minutely the features of the country and to collect specimens. Now the party must push on, diverging neither to the right nor left, stopping only to eat and sleep.

The rains had ceased and, with the rivers back to normal, hopeful of success this time, a start was made the following morning. By 5 p.m. they made camp four miles up the Tahsish River, the point reached on their first attempt. Morning broke, the canoe hidden in the bush and, thankful for another fine day, preparations were made to continue on foot. It was here that stock was taken of their food supplies. After disappointment at having to retrace their steps, and not counting on making a second start, they had been too lavish with their provisions and given Chief Kai-ne-nitt, in return for his kindness, both flour and meat.

It was now June 3 and, with the journey hardly begun, all that remained was 15 pounds of flour, a few beans and a small quantity of preserved meat. However, Hankin had his gun and a good supply of powder and shot and, with game plentiful — according to the Indians — this gave them no cause for alarm.

Tracks indicated the presence of elk and deer in great numbers. In fact, it was well-beaten elk trails that they were following. But not a single animal was seen throughout the trip. A grouse shot on the shores of a lake was all they had to supplement their meagre rations. The elk trails were quite good, except for windfalls and devilclub thickets. The river had to be crossed and re-crossed many times, often waist-deep, but as elk usually select a gravel bar when they cross a stream, that made it less difficult. Waterfalls were numerous and steep bluffs had to be climbed to avoid them. The compass was relied on when taking short cuts through heavily timbered country.

Hankin records that only once did the Indians threaten to turn back. A treacherous crossing was necessary immediately above a 30-foot waterfall. They told him an Indian had been drowned here the previous year. He had lost his footing and was swept over the falls. After a heated argument and a two-hour delay they compromised by crossing farther upstream. It rained all day on the sixth and, with the river again in flood, the next crossing, this time breast-deep, was accomplished by all holding to a long pole, all hands supporting one another. This method was resorted to on several occasions.

Hankin noted the size of the trees but, being a sailor, was more impressed with the spars, the most beautiful he had ever seen, averaging 170 to 180 feet in length. Atluk, Hooston and Anutz Lakes, crossed in that order, Hankin was amazed to find exactly as the Indian had marked them on the sand at Kyuquot. At each one, a raft of sufficient size and buoyancy to carry eight men and their dunnage across to the other side had to be constructed. Trees were felled and lashed together with strips of cedar bark, but with only one axe — a second one was lost while crossing a river — the task held up progress more than anything else.

The stream connecting Hooston (Huston on present-day maps) and Anutz Lakes, Hankin named Famine River, for now a meal consisted of tea and "damper", with the Indians reduced to eating roots and fern. Soon Lake Karmutzen was reached and the first sign of habitation — fishing weirs along the shore and deserted shacks which the Nimpkish Indians occupy during the salmon season. Seventeen miles long and now known as Nimpkish Lake, this is the largest lake in the northern portion of Vancouver Island.

Here the party hoped to find a canoe, but instead a large log found on the beach improvised for a raft, and on board it they packed their traps and themselves. They had paddled only a short distance when it commenced to roll and threatened to capsize them into the lake. Returning to the beach, they lashed spars to form an outrigger, and aboard this strange craft, with a blanket for a sail and by paddling, they managed to negotiate the full length of the lake.

The lake empties into Broughton Strait (named by Vancouver in 1792, after Lieut.-Commander W. R. Broughton, H.M.S. *Chatham*) via the Nimpkish River, but as the stream was too rapid to venture down except by canoe, the party again took to the trail. Several deserted fishing villages were passed and soon the snow-capped mountains (the Coast Range on the mainland) came into view. Finally they arrived at Cheslakee (Nimpkish) Indian village. A canoe was hired, and that evening Hankin and Wood were at Fort Rupert where they were most hospitably entertained by Hamilton Moffat of the Hudson's Bay Company. Two days later the *Hecate* arrived.

Retiring from the navy, Hankin held several offices in the colonial service under Governor Douglas, 1864-1866, one as Superintendent of Police. On the union of the colonies of Vancouver Island and British Columbia, he returned to England and shortly afterwards was appointed Colonial Secretary in British Honduras. Back in British Columbia, he became Colonial Secretary of the new province,

1869-1871, when confederation with Canada took place. Subsequently reinstated in the British navy, he retired with the rank of commander. Hankin Range in the Nimpkish district, and Hankin Point, Quatsino Sound, were both named after him. Wood Mountain and Wood Islands, both Clayoquot Sound, and Wood Bay on Raymond Channel, were named after Doctor Wood.

INTERNATIONAL in character, with the boundary line between Canada and the United States running smack down the centre, Juan de Fuca Strait is the most used inland waterway on this part of the coast. Eighty-five miles long and varying in width from 10 to 20 miles, it separates Vancouver Island from the northwest part of the State of Washington. An average of thirty deep sea ships, flying the flag of practically every major trading nation, passes through it every day in or outward bound to or from British Columbia or Puget Sound ports. It is used by warships, coastal freighters, tugs, private yachts and thousands of fishing vessels.

Two lighthouses, at Cape Flattery on the American side and Carmanah Point on Vancouver Island, guard the entrance. In 1909, the U.S. Coast Guard established a lightship on Swiftsure Bank, which lies about ten miles off the entrance and an equal distance between the two shores. The vessel served as a further aid to navigation in this area till 1961, when it was moved to a new position off the Washington coast (see page 232). A line drawn from Bonilla Point, 12 miles west of Port Renfrew, to Cape Flattery, officially defines the western boundary. Net fishing for salmon, by vessels of either country, is not permitted west of this line.

Who discovered the strait has long been a matter of controversy. Juan de Fuca claims he did, in 1592, but some historians tell us that his name appears nowhere in either the Spanish or Mexican archives, and as much as call him a liar . . . that his name is only a myth. Spanish pride somewhat explains this, for Juan de Fuca was a Greek in the service of Spain. His real name was Apostolos Valerianos, a native of Cephalonia.

From other sources, one is *Purchas, his Pilgrimes*, published in 1625, we learn that in the year 1592 the Viceroy of Mexico sent a pilot named Juan de Fuca on a voyage of discovery to the Northwest. De Fuca, in his direction, followed the coastline until he came to the latitude of 47° and there found that a broad inlet trended to the eastward between latitudes 47° and 48°. As he rounded the headland (Cape Flattery) he noted the presence of a flat-topped island, and particularly, a pinnacle or spired rock — 150 feet high — standing in solitary grandeur about two miles to the southeast. He sailed up this inland navigation for more than twenty days when he found many small islands and also a broad sea, much broader than at the entrance.

The strait was named, or rather re-named, by Captain Charles William Barkley of the fur-trading ship *Imperial Eagle*, who was off the entrance in July 1787 and recognized it — from the accurate description given by the Greek of its geographical features at its approach — as the long-lost Strait of Juan de Fuca. In the journals of some of the other traders who were in these waters about the same time as Barkley, reference is made to their having seen the flat-topped island and spired rock reported by Juan de Fuca. Years afterwards, the islands referred to by Juan de Fuca were definitely identified as the Gulf Islands, the broad sea, the Gulf of Georgia and the flat-topped island he saw as he entered the strait, Tatoosh Island (on which Cape Flattery lighthouse now stands). The spired rock has since been officially named "De Fuca's Pillar" by the United States Coast and Geodetic Survey. It can be assumed that considerable research must have been undertaken by the governments of both Great Britain and the United States before adopting officially the names: "Juan de Fuca" for the strait and "De Fuca's Pillar" for the spired rock. Thus added weight is given to the general belief that Juan de Fuca was the original discoverer of the strait.

Owing to bad weather, Cook missed the strait when bound from the Hawaiian Islands to subsequently discover and land at Nootka in 1778. But he did name Cape Flattery — which he thought was merely a point jutting out on an uninterrupted coastline — in token of the prospect of an improvement in the weather.

Manuel Quimper, commanding the *Princess Royal*, then in the service of the Spanish navy under the name *Princesa Real*, was in the strait in 1790. The *Princess Royal*, it is recalled, was (by rights) the property of John Meares; she was one of the three British ships seized by the Spaniards at Nootka two years previously, but which were subsequently released to their rightful owners. Francisco Eliza, in command of the *San Carlos,* accompanied by the schooner *Santa Saturnina* in charge of Jose Maria Narvaez, was also in the strait in 1790. Galiano and Valdes came two years later in schooners *Sutil* and *Mexicana.* Vancouver, with the ships *Discovery* and *Chatham* (Lieut.-Commander Broughton), also sailed up the strait in 1792.

These early explorers all made partial surveys of the strait and adjacent waters. But not until the arrival on this coast, between 1857 and 1870, of H.M. SURVEY SHIPS *Herald, Plumper, Hecate, Egeria* and the hired vessel *Beaver,* was a detailed job undertaken. After the turn of the century, the Hydrographic Survey Board of Canada took over the survey of the coast of British Columbia and the work still goes on. Waters on the American side are charted by the United States Coast and Geodetic Survey.

In 1836, the Hudson's Bay Company steamer *Beaver* sailed up the strait for the first time. Other company vessels already here were *Drysdale, Nereid, Llama* and *Cadboro*; also several ships of the United States Exploration Expedition. In 1844, H.M. CORVETTE *Modeste,* based at Fort Vancouver on the Columbia River — to look after British interests there — entered the strait and used Port Discovery, she being the first British man-of-war to do so since Captain Vancouver's visit. The same year, the paddle-sloop *Cormorant,* first of H.M. ships to do duty on this station, sailed up the strait. Esquimalt Harbour was surveyed in 1847 by Lieut. James Wood, R.N., in H.M. SURVEYING BRIG *Pandora* which, accompanied by the *Herald,* had arrived from England the previous year.

The first thing Quimper did on entering the strait was to claim for his king all the land between Cape Flattery and Puget Sound, now United States territory, but then inhabited only by Indians. He then made a careful examination of the north shore (the Vancouver Island side) as far as Esquimalt, which he named Puerto de Cordova after the 46th viceroy of Mexico. Indian name for Esquimalt is *Is-whoy-malt.*

Royal Roads, Quimper named Rada de Valdez y Bazan. Noting that British warships anchored there during his survey of the area in the *Herald,* 1846, Captain Henry Kellett gave it its present name. Merchant ships in the old days also anchored there while "waiting for orders"; an occasional freighter still does. During the height of a southeast gale on the night of April 14, 1883, four sailing ships, *Connaught, Tiger, Gettysberg* and *Southern Chief,* were driven ashore there. *Tiger* freed herself on the next high tide. *Gettysberg* and *Southern Chief* remained there for months and were finally refloated — both in damaged condition — after they had been sold at auction. *Connaught* became a total wreck. Eleven years later, in December 1894, the *Southern Chief*, bound for Australia with lumber, sprung a leak and was abandoned off Cape Flattery, the crew rescued and taken to Port Townsend by tug *Sea Lion* and vessel itself subsequently picked up and towed to Port Townsend. But damage to her hull was found to be so extensive she was written off as a total loss.

During her visit to Victoria, Her Royal Highness Princess Margaret reviewed eighteen ships of the Royal Canadian Navy, one British man-of-war, a United States aircraft carrier and three other United States ships, and five Canadian government service vessels at Royal Roads.

Albert Head, close by, was named after H.R.H. Prince Albert of Saxe-Coburg, Queen Victoria's husband. The name Albert was given by Captain Kellett, H.M. SURVEY VESSEL *Herald*, to this headland because the name of the Queen had been given to the town (Victoria) on the opposite side of the roadstead (Royal Roads). A lighthouse was established here in 1930 after the *Empress of Canada* ran aground on the far side of the point, October 13, 1929 (refloated on the 15th). The U.S. motorship *Coolcha* went ashore near Albert Head on February 15, 1923, was subsequently salvaged, but with a broken back, and taken to Esquimalt.

Quimper named Bonilla Point because of its appearance. The word in Spanish means high or bold. Port San Juan (Port Renfrew is the name of the settlement, not the harbour) he named Puerto de San Juan de Narvaez, for Jose Maria Narvaez, master of the *Santa Saturnina*, one of Eliza's ships. It was here that the longboat of the *Felice* (Meares' ship), in charge of Mr. Duffin, the first mate, was furiously attacked by the natives and nearly captured in July 1788. Duffin, it is recalled, is the man who testified before Captain Vancouver as to John Meares' good character.

Sombrio Point (and river), 12 miles east of Port San Juan, Quimper also named, from "its dark and shady appearance." The word in Spanish means a shady place. Prior to the First Great War, alluvial gold was recovered here, but not in worthwhile quantity. Remains of the flumes and sluice boxes are still there. Wrecked between Port San Juan and Sombrio in November 1860, was the schooner *Dance*; and between Sombrio and Jordan River, the schooner *D. L. Clinch,* 1860, and the sailing vessel *Ciro,* 1882.

Quimper named Jordan River after Alexandro Jordan, one of the Franciscan priests at Friendly Cove, and Sooke Inlet (harbour),

Puerto de Revillo Gigedo, after the (then) viceroy of Mexico. According to John Muir, who resided at Sooke in 1850, the correct spelling is Soke, the name of the local Indians. The present spelling was adopted by Captain Kellett. (more about Sooke on page 193). The schooner *Surprise* was wrecked near Sooke in November 1874, the *Garlie*, also a schooner, in 1904 and the tug *Doreen* on January 8, 1928. Wrecked at Otter Point, four miles to the west, on March 24, 1897, was the small auxiliary schooner *Spinster*. Captain and owner Arthur Scroggs drowned. Currently (1962), skin divers are attempting to identify a sunken wreck just inside the entrance to Sooke Inlet. It could be any one of the aforesaid vessels.

Kellett also re-named Sheringham Point after Commander William Louis Sheringham, R.N., an able and talented surveying officer, changing it from Punta de San Eusevio, the one given by Quimper. A lighthouse was established here in 1912. The barque *Anna Barnard*, San Francisco to Sooke for a cargo of lumber and piling, was wrecked in this vicinity February 26, 1862, with the loss of two lives. The British motorship *Iossifoglu* went ashore there but was later refloated, August 25, 1928.

Beechey Head, Becher Bay, Church Island and Point, all between Sooke and Race Rocks, Kellett also named after surveying officers: Captain Frederick Beechey, a noted Arctic navigator and geographer, Commander Alexander Bridport Becher, R.N., and Lieutenant William Harvey Church, R.N.

Race Rocks was named by officers of the Hudson's Bay Company and adopted by the Admiralty on the recommendation of Captain Kellett who states in his journals: "This dangerous group is appropriately named, for the tide makes a perfect race around it." The lighthouse was built by the British government in 1860, five years after those at Cape Flattery and New Dungeness were established.

Fisgard lighthouse which stands at the western entrance to Esquimalt harbour was built at the same time. The granite blocks used in their construction, and bricks for the dwelling houses, were brought out from England in sailing ships. London born George Davies was British Columbia's first lighthouse keeper. He came with the equipment for these two lights, helped install it and lit both for the first time, Fisgard on November 16, 1860 and Race Rocks, on February 7, 1861.

On Christmas Eve, 1865, Davies watched helplessly as his sister, her husband and three friends drowned within a stone's throw of the landing place at Race Rocks when the sailboat in which they had journeyed from Victoria to spend Christmas at the light, capsized and drifted away with the tide. The station rowboat had been washed away in a storm only a few days previously. Davies never recovered from the shock. He died two years later at Race Rocks.

A little to the southwest of Race Rocks is Rosedale Reef, named after the British ship *Rosedale* which ran aground there on December 12, 1862. The vessel got off without assistance, but found to be leaking badly was beached at Ross Bay. There her cargo was discharged to several vessels which came to her assistance and she was subsequently towed to Esquimalt. A buoy, placed there in 1900, now marks this reef.

The vicinity is known as a "boarding station," where the pilot boards all ships inbound for British Columbia ports. Just inside Race Rocks is William Head, formerly a quarantine station, but now an "open" penitentiary. Nearby Bentinck Island was until recently a leper colony. The island was named after Henry Bentinck, holder of the ducal title of the House of Portland.

Kellett described Race Rocks as "this dangerous group." He stressed the tide rips and dangerous currents, but overlooked another hazard — fog. In October 1925, the lighthouse experienced 494 hours of fog, including one continuous run of 292 hours.

We know the names of at least thirty-five vessels which met with disaster in the immediate vicinity. That is, those which sank, went ashore and subsequently broke up or were later towed off in damaged condition. Scores of others, the number will never be known, after grounding temporarily (mostly during fog), refloated themselves and continued on their way.

On Race Rocks: The American ship *Morning Glory*, Puget Sound to San Francisco with lumber, aground May 31, 1859; later salvaged to Esquimalt in leaking condition. December 23, 1860, British barque *Nanette*, total wreck. These two mishaps occurred before the light was first lit. January 19, 1872, U.S. ship *Lookout*, ashore in fog, refloated badly holed and towed to Port Townsend. 1875, ship *Nicholas Biddle,* Nanaimo to San Francisco with coal, ashore but later pulled off. 1884, U.S. steam collier *Umatilla*, ashore; two years later same vessel struck a rock near Cape Flattery, freed herself and in sinking condition was towed by the steam collier *Wellington* into Esquimalt harbour where she sank. November 29, 1889, U.S. steamer *Idaho*, ashore, total loss.

On September 15, 1918, calm and dense fog, the four-masted schooner *Rosamond* ran aground only 300 feet from the lighthouse, and ten days later the British barque *Harold* in the same place. Steamer *Alaskan* failed in attempt to pull *Rosamond* free; next day, tug *Qualicum* pulled her off with the steamer *Tees* standing by. The *Harold* was also towed free. Both bottoms badly damaged.

Ashore and later refloated with the aid of tugs or salvage vessels: freighter *Albion Star*, November 22, 1928; American steamer *James Griffiths*, March 3, 1931, refloated a few days later by tug *Salvage King*; and the fishpacker *Harriett E.*, September 1, 1933. The tug *Storm King*, on March 19, 1939 and the fishpacker *Nahmint,* June 4, 1939. The fishpacker *Western Ranger,* September 10, 1951 and the *Western Pilot*, also a fishpacker, on October 4, 1959. The steamer *Robert Adamson* and the ship *Bylton Castle* are both said to have run aground on Race Rocks, the former about 1898, but neither mishap can be confirmed. The freighter *Atlantic City*, grounded during fog two miles west of Race Rocks, August 25, 1936, freed herself next high tide, but a bad leak put engines out of commission. Picked up later by *Salvage King* and *Salvage Queen* and towed to Esquimalt drydock. On October 28, 1936, the passenger liner *Manunalei* collided with the freighter *Temple Moat* in fog near Race Rocks. *Temple Moat* suffered extensive damage, tugs escorted her to Seattle; damage to *Manunalei* slight.

Bentinck Island: November 21, 1886, steam collier *Barnard Castle*, Nanaimo to San Francisco, beached after striking Rosedale Reef; remained there for several months before breaking up. Meanwhile nearby settlers helped themselves liberally to the coal. Freighter *Siberian Prince*, aground July 29, 1923; refloated by tugs August 13.

The Dutch freighter *Eemdyk* went aground on Bentinck Island during dense fog October 15, 1925, was refloated week later after cargo removed by lighters. During salvage operations, longshoremen travelled back and forth from Victoria every day on the tug *Hope*. On October 17, the *Hope*, with twenty-eight of them on board and her six crew members, fouled one of the *Eemdyk*'s mooring cables, causing her to capsize and sink. Six men were drowned. One of the survivors clung to a log and drifted with the tide halfway to Jordan River before being picked up. On November 2, 1929, the steamer *Gogovale* went aground on Bentinck Island, but was later towed free.

The Canadian Pacific Navigation Company steamer *Otter*, after 37 years of useful work on this coast — the last few as a coal hulk — ended her days on Bentinck Island, where, in 1890, she was burnt for the metal in her. The *Otter* was the second historical steamer on this coast; built in 1852, at Blackwall, London, for the Hudson's Bay Company, she was brought out to assist the *Beaver* and afterwards sold to Canadian Pacific Navigation Company.

At Pedder Bay, to the east of Race Rocks, the tug *Tyee* sank on December 29, 1923, with the loss of three lives, and at Parry Bay, farther to the east, on November 1, 1929, the American freighter *Sutorpco* went ashore, to be refloated some days later by the *Salvage King*.

As far back as 1860, a small sailing vessel named either *Sparrow* or *Swallow,* was wrecked on Beechey Head, and the British ship *Swordfish*, San Francisco to Hastings Mill in ballast, on November 6, 1877. The small shelter-deck steamer *Sechelt*, Vancouver to Jordan River with men and material for the hydro power station then under construction there, capsized off Beechey Head on March 25, 1911, when all 48 persons aboard her were drowned. The tragedy was witnessed by the Becher Bay Indians, who were unable to render assistance owing to rough seas.

The m.v. *Pacific* went ashore, owing to fog, on Beechey Head, August 22, 1920, but was later towed free. Fog also caused the small rum-runner *Miowera* to hit Church Island, September 24, 1926, and the four-masted schooner *C. S. Holmes,* on September 23, 1928. The rum-runner was subsequently beached at Becher Bay for repairs. The *C. S. Holmes,* towed free several days later by the Victoria tug *J.W.P.* On August 5, 1946, the freighter *Sapperton Park* ran aground on Secretary Island, two miles west of Beechey Head; pulled free by the tug *Salvage Chieftain* she was taken to Esquimalt drydock where it was found that her forefoot had been torn off and carried away.

During fog, August 13, 1947, the U.S. freighter *Diamond Knot*, with salmon from canneries in Alaska, collided not far from Race Rocks with the steamer *Fenn Victory*, outward bound. *Diamond Knot* beached near Crescent Bay, west of Port Angeles; part of cargo salvaged, vessel a total loss. *Fenn Victory* suffered only slight damage. Wrecked during a violent snowstorm, November 28, 1923, on the American side of the strait almost directly across from Race Rocks, the small rum-runner *Clam,* out of Victoria. A month later and without the U.S. Coastguard knowing anything about it, vessel was refloated and brought back.

In 1853, the Hudson's Bay Company brigantine *Una,* while sheltering at Neah Bay, dragged her anchors and went ashore; crew rescued by Indians, who then, in spite of the strenuous efforts of Captain Mitchell to prevent it, stripped vessel of her copper and other valuables, then burnt her. In August, 1861, H.M. SURVEY VESSEL *Hecate*, during fog, grounded on a reef two miles east of Cape Flattery; refloated with the assistance of an American steam schooner (no record of name) which by chance was handy and though leaking badly managed to reach Esquimalt. Damage proved to be extensive, was temporarily repaired and vessel dispatched to San Francisco for dry-docking, accompanied part way by the sloop *Mutine*. It is interesting to note that the following winter, *Hecate*, anchored in James Bay, Victoria harbour, was frozen fast in the ice.

Scores of other ships met with mishap in the strait, or cleared Cape Flattery and were never heard from again. Some we have record of, others none, and those we do know of, details in many instances are sketchy. In the fall of 1855, the brig *Hodgdon* sailed from Victoria for San Francisco and was never heard from again, though construction men building Cape Flattery lighthouse at the time reported a vessel answering her description was wrecked near Tatoosh Island. On November 10, 1856, the American barque *W. A. Banks* was wrecked near Clallam Bay.

The brig *Persevere*, San Francisco to Victoria with merchandise for Chinese storekeepers, was abandoned when she sprang a leak and sank off Cape Flattery, September 15, 1861; passing vessel brought crew and her three passengers to Victoria. August 23, 1864, German barque *Armin*, Royal Roads to China with lumber, wrecked between Sooke and Port San Juan (Port Renfrew); crew escaped in boats and arrived back at Victoria, vessel total loss. American barque *Ocean Bird* (in company the barque *Rival*) sailed from Puget Sound March 19, 1864; gale encountered after clearing Flattery, lumber cargo shifted and vessel capsized; crew, after staying with upturned ship for two days, rescued by steamer *Panama*. December 1866, American ship *Ellen Foster*, Callao to Puget Sound in ballast, wrecked just inside Cape Flattery; crew reached shore, vessel total loss. In September 1867, American barque *Lizzie Boggs*, San Francisco to Port Townsend, ashore in dense fog on Cape Flattery; crew escaped in boats and brought to Victoria by barque *Ava*. Schooner *W. H. Meyer*, after discharging cargo at Victoria loaded lumber on Puget Sound; out for San Francisco was wrecked three miles west of Port Angeles, May 24, 1872, total loss.

The schooner *Eliza*, last reported off Flattery January 24, 1874; in March, vessel found floating upside down off Port San Juan, crew presumed to have drowned, H.M.S. *Boxer* tried to sink her with gunfire, but failed. Derelict later towed to Esquimalt by steamers *Grappler* and *Isabel*. On January 19, 1875, the Nicaraguan barque *Pelican*, Callao to Port Townsend in ballast, wrecked near Cape Flattery; crew reached shore, vessel total loss. The American ship *Washington Libby*, wrecked west of Port Angeles July 23, 1879,

Reverend A. J. Brabant, missionary on west coast of Vancouver Island from 1875 to 1908.

Right Reverend Charles J. Seghers, Bishop of Victoria, 1874, *Provincial Archives Photos.*

and on November 8, of the same year, ship *Marmion,* Nanaimo to San Francisco with coal, sprang a leak and was abandoned off the entrance to the strait; crew rescued by *Tam O'Shanter* and taken to San Francisco. On December 10, 1881, the Chilean barque *Twenty-First-of-May* (formerly the *Camelia*), Valparaiso to Royal Roads, wrecked on Bentinck Island.

In February 1883, the American barquentine *C. L. Taylor*, Puget Sound to San Francisco with lumber, on her beam ends off Flattery, captain's wife and son drowned; righted herself after crew cut away masts, captain and two men stayed with ship and subsequently taken off by passing vessel, meanwhile remainder of crew took to boats and reached west coast of Vancouver Island.

In 1886, at least twelve vessels are known to have met with disaster in the strait or its approaches. Five are reported in previous pages; following are the names of the other seven: The brig *North Star* sailed from Puget Sound on April 8, with lumber for San Diego; lost with all hands after clearing Flattery, later found bottom-up near Clayoquot Sound. On September 19, the American barque *Sierra Nevada* sailed from Puget Sound to San Francisco with coal. Never heard from again, she is believed to have foundered off Cape Flattery.

On November 10, the British barque *Webfoot* sailed from Port Townsend with lumber for Callao, sprang a leak after clearing Cape Flattery, put back and headed for Royal Roads; meanwhile vessel caught fire and was abandoned in the strait, crew picked up by tug *Pilot* and brought to Victoria. The derelict subsequently came ashore near Clo-oose. The Chilean barque *Lillie Grace* left Puget Sound December 2, with lumber for Valparaiso; caught in a storm off Flattery, cargo shifted, she sprang a leak and was abandoned, though crew reached shore. American ship *Harvey Mills*, Seattle to San Francisco with coal, foundered off Flattery December 14; eight men found on a raft picked up by ship *Majestic*. Remainder of her twenty-six-man crew perished. On December 16, the barque *Ella S. Thayer* sailed from Nanaimo with coal for San Francisco, and was abandoned in leaking condition off Flattery; after ten days at sea in boats, crew picked up by barque *Von Moltke* and brought to Esquimalt. Also in December, the Bolivian barque *Irene*, Puget Sound to Fiji with lumber, was abandoned off Flattery and crew picked up by the ship *Iroquois* and taken to Port Townsend.

Storms off the entrance claimed five sailing vessels in 1887: On January 21, U.S. ship *Austria*, San Francisco to Nanaimo in ballast, wrecked on Flattery Rocks. In March, the U.S. collier ships

Eldorado and *St. Vincent*, Comox to San Francisco. *Eldorado*, all hands lost; *St. Vincent*, two survivors picked up and brought to Port Townsend. In February, the Victoria sealing schooner *Active* disappeared after clearing the strait; found later ashore 30 miles below Flattery, all on board, a crew of three and twenty West Coast Indians, had apparently drowned. Fifth vessel was the U.S. ship *St. Stephens*, Nanaimo to San Francisco with coal, lost in April; all those on board, including captain's wife and three children, perished. Identified wreckage was found washed up on the west coast of Vancouver Island.

In March 1890, barque *Nellie May*, Nanaimo to San Francisco with coal, lost off entrance, fate of crew unknown (probably drowned); nameboard and other wreckage picked up off Flattery by tug *Lorne*. Vessel's lifeboat and identified wreckage washed ashore Clayoquot Sound. *Andrada*, British ship, last reported off Columbia River, September 1892; same winter Clayoquot Indians sighted a ship on its beam-ends some miles off shore. Vessel's nameboard and wreckage found on beach near Clo-oose. On October 4, 1893, Chilean barque *Leonore* wrecked near Flattery, all hands saved. In September 1894, U.S. ship *Ivanhoe* (collier) disappeared after clearing the cape, all hands lost; only trace, wreckage and a lifebelt "Ship Ivanhoe San Francisco" washed ashore near Clo-oose village. December 1894, two U.S. colliers, *Montserrat* and *Keweenah*, Nanaimo to Alaska, last reported by Cape Flattery lightkeeper about ten miles out, storm raging at the time, believed to have foundered; identified wreckage found near Cape Scott; nameboard "Keweenah" brought to Victoria by schooner.

May 12, 1895, the Victoria tug *Mogul* collided with the barque *Darra*, which she had just towed to sea and freed off Flattery; *Darra* undamaged, *Mogul*, in sinking condition beached at Neah Bay, crew saved, vessel total loss. The former Union Steamship Company steamer *St. Denis*, Vancouver to Salina Cruz for delivery to her new owners, believed lost somewhere off Cape Flattery, December 1910. Identified wreckage found on beach near Cape Scott at north end of Vancouver Island; vessel was said to have been overloaded with coal. November 1922, U.S. schooner *Henry T. Scott*, was sunk off the entrance after colliding in fog with the steamer *Harry Luckenbach*; crew picked up. February 14, 1923, small U.S. steamer *Nika* on fire off Flattery, crew taken off by coastguard cutter *Snohomish* and taken to Port Angeles; still burning, vessel drifted and finally sank off Ucluelet. Also burned and abandoned off the Cape, Canadian schooner (rum-runner) *Speedway*, February 1925, crew saved.

Fisgard Lighthouse. Its light first shone on November 16, 1860.

Race Rocks Lighthouse, constructed from granite blocks brought out from England, was lit for the first time on February 7, 1861. *Department of Transport Photos.*

Hesquiat Mission Church, established in 1876, destroyed by fire ten years later and since rebuilt.

H.M.S. *Boxer*. Bishop and priest were passengers. *Provincial Archives Photo.*

In 1944, the Victoria-built coal-burning steamer *Fort Camosun*, loaded with plywood, zinc, lead and other materials for the manufacture of war munitions, sailed down the strait on her maiden voyage and when about 100 miles southwest of Cape Flattery was hit amidships by a torpedo fired by a Japanese submarine. However, owing to the buoyancy of the plywood, which comprised the bulk of her cargo, the vessel remained afloat and, head down, managed to reach the vicinity of Neah Bay where she was beached. With the assistance of salvage tugs, the vessel was refloated and brought to Victoria where her cargo, in which fragments of the torpedo were found, was unloaded at Ogden Point pier. Vessel was then taken to Esquimalt and after damage repair by Yarrows Ltd., reloaded and sailed again. So far as this writer can learn, the torpedoing of the *Fort Camosun* and the sinking, about the same time, of an American oil tanker off the lower California coast were the only marine casualties suffered on this coast as a result of operations by Japanese submarines during the Second World War.

On the night of November 4, 1949, steamer *Andalusia* on fire and beached American side of strait, fire observed from Canadian shore; Victoria salvage tugs responded, but found U.S. coastguard cutters already standing by, vessel total loss. The Vancouver fishboat *Chuckwalla* burned and sunk in the strait, October 16, 1961; its two crew members picked up by U.S. coastguard and taken to Port Angeles. Names of other vessels which became unmanageable or were abandoned in the vicinity of the entrance to the strait and subsequently drifted ashore on the west coast of Vancouver Island will be found on pages dealing with the particular area.

In 1901, the ship *Abby Palmer*, formerly the *Blairmore*, collided during fog with the *Empress of Japan* in Juan de Fuca Strait; both vessels suffered only slight damage. In 1903, was dismasted during a gale off Cape Flattery and towed to Esquimalt by the steamer *Vermont*. Later became the *Star of England* and ran between San Francisco and Alaska with cannery supplies. In 1935, purchased by Island Tug and Barge Co. and converted into a log barge. Now (1962) being broken up for scrap at Victoria. Most of her fittings are destined for the San Francisco Maritime Museum.

STEAMER PACIFIC SINKS

ONE OF THE greatest marine casualties to occur in the Strait of Juan
de Fuca was the sinking of the passenger steamer *Pacific*, when
at least 250 men, women and children were drowned. The vessel
steamed out of Victoria harbour on the morning of November 4,
1875, bound for San Francisco. About 9 o'clock that night, when
she should have been about off Cape Flattery, tragedy struck. Out
of the darkness came the sailing ship *Orpheus*, its bow crashing into
the starboard side of the *Pacific*. What happened during the awful
moments which followed could only be pieced together by two
men — the sole survivors, Neil Henley, the ship's quartermaster, and
H. F. Kelly, a passenger. Both were picked up later on floating
wreckage. The *Pacific* sunk within minutes of being struck. Ironically, the following day, the *Orpheus* piled up near Cape Beale on
the west coast of Vancouver Island, a total loss.

H.M.S. CONDOR LOST

ON DECEMBER 2, 1901, H.M.S. *Condor*, Captain Clifton Schlater,
left Esquimalt for Honolulu and the South Pacific and was never
heard from again, all hands, 130, lost. Vessel is believed to have
foundered after being caught in a terrific gale which was raging off
Cape Flattery at the time. It is also possible she might have been in
collision with the steam collier *Matteawan*, which cleared (Nanaimo
to San Francisco) Cape Flattery the same night and also was never
heard from again. A dinghy, a lifeboat and other wreckage identified
as having come from the *Condor* was found shortly afterwards at
different places along Vancouver Island's west coast. Forty-eight
years later, in May 1949, an old binnacle was hauled up by the
crew of the Seattle trawler *Blanco* when fishing about forty miles
northwest of Cape Flattery. Binnacle bore maker's name, Kelvin
and James White Ltd., Glasgow, the firm that supplied same piece
of equipment to the *Condor*.

H.M.S. CONDOR
Provincial Archives Photo

S.S. PACIFIC
Provincial Archives Photo

BARKLEY SOUND

THIS SOUND was discovered and named in 1787 by Captain Charles William Barkley of the British trading vessel *Imperial Eagle*. The entrance, about 15 miles wide and studded with small uninhabited islands, comprises three main channels of navigation, each of which Barkley also named: the west channel, Loudoun, the former name of his ship, the middle channel, Imperial Eagle and the one to the east, Trevor, his wife's maiden name. Trevor channel permits clear sailing up to Port Alberni and is the one used by deep-sea ships.

Two lighthouses guard the entrance, Cape Beale (established in 1874) to the east, and Amphitrite Point (1905) to the west. The latter also guards the entrance to Ucluelet Inlet, on which stands Ucluelet settlement, whose inhabitants (approximately 700) engage mostly in fishing and logging (see page 279).

Amphitrite Point was named in 1859 by Captain Richards, H.M. SURVEY VESSEL *Plumper*, after H.M. FRIGATE *Amphitrite*, 24 guns, 1064 tons, on this station 1851-1857. In Greek mythology, Amphitrite was the wife of Poseidon (Neptune) and as such was Goddess of the Seas. Here the name is appropriate, for the passage is treacherous and difficult to navigate in bad weather, and it often requires more than a stout heart and a good engine to bring the little fishing boats safely home.

Cape Beale was named by Barkley after John Beale, his purser, who with Miller, the *Imperial Eagle*'s second mate and the whole of a boat's crew, were killed by the natives after going ashore near Destruction Island, south of Cape Flattery. The island was so named by Barkley from this fact.

Banfield Inlet (not spelt with an "*m*"), named after W. E. Banfield (see page 76), is about five miles inside the sound from Cape Beale. Prior to the coast being resurveyed in 1932 it was known as

Banfield Creek. The "*m*" was erroneously used when a post office was established there some years before. In 1900 J. B. McKay, who had previously settled on an adjacent island, built a cabin at the head of the inlet and thus became Bamfield's pioneer resident. He married Annie, daughter of Emmanuel Cox, the lightkeeper at Cape Beale. Construction of the Bamfield cable station (see page 136) commenced the following year and its employees formed the nucleus of the now thriving settlement.

The settlement, which straddles the inlet, is a fishing community with a population of about 250, the site of a Red Cross outpost hospital, and one of two life-saving stations maintained on the West Coast by the Department of Transport. The other is at Tofino. Each has a six-man-crew 40-foot lifeboat capable of standing any weather and ready to put to sea at any hour of the day or night. In past years these little boats have rendered valuable assistance to fishermen and saved many lives. Bamfield is also the terminus of the transpacific cable.

As this is written, Bamfield has no road connection with the out-side. However, a system of private logging roads already extends from Port Alberni along the east shores of Barkley Sound to Pachena Bay, four miles south of Cape Beale. This will eventually reach Bamfield and be made available to the public. Vacation seekers will then have within easy reach another Vancouver Island area, with broad sandy beaches — all facing the open ocean, sheltered coves, weird rock formations, scenic trails to two lighthouses (Cape Beale and Pachena Point), and fishing — both fresh and salt water, its chief attractions. Meanwhile, transportation is provided from Port Alberni by the Barkley Sound mail boat.

Grappler Inlet (formerly Creek) an arm of Banfield Inlet, was named after H.M. GUNBOAT *Grappler*, three guns, 237 tons, which arrived at Esquimalt, July 1860. Withdrawn from service eight years later, she was sold by public auction to Captain Frain for $2,400 and subsequently placed in the local coasting trade.

On the night of April 29, 1883, the *Grappler*, Captain John F. Jagers, was destroyed by fire near Seymour Narrows. About 72 passengers, principally Chinese on their way to up-coast canneries, lost their lives.

For a time during the earlier period of the First World War, when this coast depended on Japan for its protection, one of that country's cruisers was based at Grappler Inlet, in readiness should one of the three German cruisers, then roaming the Pacific sea lanes, show up in these waters.

The Barkley Sound Indians, except for the Ucluelets and several other bands who adopted the name of the locality in which they reside, are known as the Ohy-ahts, or Ohiats. All are sub-bands of the Nootkas. One of their principal villages was at Dodger's Cove, on Diana Island, across the channel from Banfield Inlet. The cove was named by Captain Richards in 1861. Today's Ohiat chief is ninety-year-old Louis Nookomis.

Returning to Victoria with Captain E. H. King, who had been despatched by the governor to investigate the wreck of the *Florencia* which occurred a few miles west of Ucluelet, the small schooner *Saucy Lass* put into a cove on Barkley Sound and lay there for several weeks "dodging the weather." During this time Captain Pamphlett, in the schooner *Meg Merrilies*, the supply boat for the Alberni sawmill, on two occasions supplied the *Saucy Lass* with provisions. While lying there, Captain King was killed by the accidental discharge of his rifle while deer hunting.

Shown a sketch of the place, a passage between two islands — Diana and King Edward — by the master of the *Meg Merrilies*, with the remark, "it is a fine place to dodge the weather in," Richards replied: "That is so, and it will for ever be known as Dodger's Cove."

Diana Island was named after the steam tug *Diana*, 87 tons, purchased in San Francisco by Captain Stamp and used for towing sailing vessels arriving and leaving Barkley Sound, to and from his sawmill at Alberni. She afterwards carried mail between Victoria, the San Juan Islands and the mainland. Old-time Victorians used to describe her as the "largest small steamer," or the "smallest large steamer" that ever ran in these waters.

Two large inlets, both uninhabited, extend deep into the mountains on the west side of the sound. One is Effingham, named by Captain John Meares, in the trading vessel *Felice*, July 1788, in honour of the Right Honourable Thomas Howard, third Earl of Effingham and deputy marshall of England. Meares anchored here while on one of his trading expeditions. The other is Pipestem, obviously named from its shape. It was in this inlet, in 1927, that the minesweeper H.M.C.S. *Armentieres* struck an uncharted rock and sunk, not far from where her sister ship, H.M.C.S. *Thiepval*, sank five years later. *Armentieres* was subsequently refloated. *Thiepval* is still there.

It is said that at the time the *Armentieres* was playing a hide-and-seek game with a suspected rum-runner. The navy never admitted this, but it was known that Barkley Sound, with its inlets and hundreds of small islands, provided a haven for the rum-running schooners. Our minesweepers were often employed on customs preventative duty. Liquor cargoes were sometimes cached there. Occasionally one was found by the authorities and confiscated. The first whaling station on the West Coast was at Sechart, near the entrance to Pipestem Inlet. It was abandoned fifty years ago when these mammals became scarce.

Uchucklesit, the name of a small inlet on the west side, near where the sound narrows to about half a mile in width to form Alberni Inlet, is derived from the Indian word *how-chuck-les-aht*, meaning "people who live by a spring situated on or at the end of a deep inlet." Kildonan cannery and cold storage plant on Uchucklesit Inlet, was one of the first on the West Coast.

Henderson Lake, which drains into the inlet, was named by Dr. Robert Brown, PH.D., M.A., F.L.S., commander of the Vancouver Island Exploring Expedition, 1863-1864, after Captain John Henderson who, in 1860, brought out to this coast from England the composite barquentine *Woodpecker*. She had nine passengers, which brought the population of Alberni up to forty. In her hold was the machinery for the Alberni Sawmill Company. The *Woodpecker*, the property of the company, was afterwards wrecked at the mouth of the Columbia River. She was a total loss, but the crew was saved. Captain Henderson then took command of the 78-foot schooner *Alberni*, built by the sawmill company at Alberni in 1862. She was later sold to Hawaiian interests and converted into a whaler.

The annual rainfall at Henderson Lake is 263 inches, the highest recorded anywhere in Canada, and probably the North American continent. Records were kept by the superintendent of a fish hatchery which the department of fisheries maintained there for 25 years. It was closed down in 1932, along with several other hatcheries.

Alberni Inlet, until recently known as Alberni Canal, was named in 1791 by Lieut. Francisco Eliza, after Don Pedro Alberni, a Spanish infantry brigade captain who was in charge of the soldiers in Eliza's expedition, sent by the viceroy of Mexico to occupy this part of the coast, with headquarters at Nootka. It is interesting to note that, in the winter of 1861-1862, the inlet was frozen solid from Pocohontas Point, its narrowest part, to Alberni, a distance of approximately twenty-three miles. This hasn't occurred since.

Together, sound and inlet, they form by far the greatest body of inland water on the West Coast, almost cutting Vancouver Island in two and leaving only an eleven-mile strip of land between Alberni and Qualicum.

Somass, the Indian name of the river which flows into the sea at Alberni, means "a creek flowing over or down an embankment." The name is appropriate to its upper reaches, where there are numerous falls. One is Stamp Falls, on Stamp River, a tributary of the Somass and named after Captain Edward Stamp, who in 1860 established and managed a sawmill at the head of Alberni Inlet. The site of the mill was at the foot of what is now Argyle Street, Port Alberni, then standing timber country with the Indian village of Tom-a-muk-is on the waterfront. The mill was destroyed by fire in 1869, but in the intervening years lumber and spars had been shipped to different parts of the world. Out of nearly one hundred ships which took these cargoes, only one was a steamer, the Japanese tramp *Fushi Yama*, 994 tons, destined for Shanghai.

Extending for miles along Port Alberni's waterfront, and on reclaimed land at the mouth of the Somass, today stand some of British Columbia's largest and most modern lumber, pulp, paper and plywood mills, with wharfage for half a dozen deep sea freighters at one time. Together, these plants represent a capital outlay of hundreds of millions of dollars, and employ over 1,000 men and women.

Sproat Lake, one of the sources of the Somass, was named by Doctor Brown after Gilbert Malcolm Sproat, who succeeded Stamp as manager of the sawmill and was later appointed government agent, customs officer, justice of the peace and coroner at Alberni by Governor Douglas. The Indian name for Sproat Lake is *Kleecoot*, meaning "like the head of a salmon split open and spread out."

Doctor Brown also named Franklin River, which flows into Alberni Inlet on the east side about ten miles from Port Alberni, after Selim Franklin, a Victoria auctioneer and chairman of the committee (in British Columbia) which sponsored the Vancouver Island Exploring Expedition.

Nahmint Lake, and the river of the same name which connects it with the inlet, about five miles below Franklin River on the west side, were named by John Buttle (Buttle Lake, Strathcona Park), the expedition's naturalist, after the Nah-mint Indians who resided in that neighbourhood. Nahmint River is famous for its steelhead fishing, and the bay at its mouth, for tyee salmon.

Barkley Sound forests provide most of the logs for the Alberni mills, whose products are shipped by both rail and water. An average of six ships leave the Sound every week for world ports. The pilot is picked up or dropped off Cape Beale. Logging operations in the area have been so extensive during the past seventy years that today, viewed from the air, the network of grades looks like a great spider's web. There is an operation on practically every inlet and these extend far up the valleys, but the principal camps are at Franklin River and Sarita Bay. Sarita Bay is on Trevor Channel, about eight miles east of Bamfield.

British Columbia's first paper mill was on the Somass River, about a mile upstream from Alberni. It was built in 1891 by a syndicate headed by Henry Carmichael. Its product was not made from wood as might be supposed, for no method for making ground-wood pulp had yet been invented, but from rags and waste paper, which had all to be brought in by ship. Bracken fern and straw was tried, but without success. The enterprise folded in 1895. The original millstones, which were brought out from England, today stand as a monument to this early history on the site where fifty years later the McMillan, Stewart and Welsh Company Ltd. (now McMillan, Bloedel and Powell River Co. Ltd.) built the first unit of its multi-million-dollar pulp, paper and plywood plant.

A fleet of 500 trollers, seiners and gillnetters, based principally at Port Alberni, Ucluelet and Bamfield, fish the Sound and adjacent waters for salmon. Between 1925 and 1944, when pilchards were plentiful on the West Coast, there were no less than six reduction plants on the Sound; now there is only one at Port Albion on Ucluelet Inlet, and it processes herring. The Sound, like all the others on the West Coast, for years also had its share of canneries and salteries, but now the fish are taken to Vancouver and New Westminster to be processed.

Gold, copper and iron is found in the mountain ranges on both sides of the sound. Scores of properties have been worked during the past 75 years, but only one brought into worthwhile production. That was in May 1962, when Noranda Mines Ltd., from its Maggie Lake iron ore deposits near Ucluelet, shipped 26,400 tons of con-centrates to Japan. The mine, an open-pit operation, is now making regular shipments.

Regular mail and passenger service between Port Alberni, Bam-field, Ucluelet and way points was started in 1913 by Sam Stone, a former missionary at Clayoquot, and his two sons, Stuart and Chet.; first with the 35-foot M.V. *Tofino*, and later the former North Arm (Vancouver) ferry *Roche Point*. Both vessels were gas-engined. The *Tofino* was wrecked at the entrance to Ucluelet Harbour, 1917. The *Roche Point*, later converted into a fish-packer, was lost off Cape Beale in 1920.

The brothers, E. Douglas and Percy F. Stone, took over the run in 1920 and with their fleet of "Victory" boats maintained it for the next sixteen years, when Barkley Sound Transportation Co. Ltd., using the M.V. *Uchuck II* and later the *Uchuck III*, was awarded the contract. In 1960 that company withdrew its ships in favour of the M.V. *Lady Rose* (Alberni Marine Transportation Co.) which now maintains the service. Stone Brothers' *Victory V*, formerly the Howe Sound ferry *Marine Express*, burned and sunk, Alberni Inlet, 1938.

REVEREND
MELVIN SWARTOUT

BASED AT Bamfield is the United Church of Canada's mission boat *Melvin Swartout*, which serves the more isolated communities between Barkley Sound and Kyuquot. The vessel was named after the Rev. Melvin Swartout, who between 1894 and 1904, when he was accidentally drowned, not only preached the Gospel and taught school, but acted as advisor, counsel and friend to the Barkley Sound Indians.

The mission was established in 1890 at Ucluelet by the Presbyterian Church. Reverend Swartout, teacher and missionary, and Dr. Charles McLean, appointed by the Department of Indian Affairs, medical officer, with their families, both lived close by. To reach the scattered Indian villages, most of them on small islands, Mr. Swartout used a sailboat and on one of these missionary trips, made on July 11, 1904, he failed to return. The weather was stormy and it was thought he might have sought shelter on one of the small islands at the entrance to Ucluelet Inlet. Search was made and wreckage found identified as from his boat. Weeks later, Mr. Swartout's body was found washed ashore at Wreck Bay (now Florencia Bay), five miles west of Ucluelet. He was buried behind the mission.

To EVERYONE who made the West Coast round trip on the *Princess Maquinna* and *Princess Norah,* when those vessels were on the run, Bamfield will always be remembered as one of the most interesting places. It was usually about noon on the first day out from Victoria that the steamer called there and the first chance the passengers had of stretching legs ashore. But the chief attraction was a visit to the cable station where the ship tied up.

The station is situated on the top of a hill, from which a wonderful panorama is obtained of Bamfield settlement across the inlet and the picturesque island-studded entrance to Barkley Sound in the distance.

The staff, which comprised mostly Australians and New Zealanders, made the visitors welcome and, in addition to showing them around the station itself, were always willing to explain the delicate instruments which can send a message completely around the world in less time than it takes to type one out. For their special benefit, an operator would sometimes send a short message of greetings to Sydney, which might read as follows: "Hello Australia, how's the weather down there this morning." In an instant back would come the reply: "Cheerio Canada, its a nice moonlight night over here." Though the two messages were sent and received within a few seconds of one another, one would be timed as noon at Bamfield, and the reply about midnight Sydney. The Sydney message would also be a day out according to the calendar, for the international dateline lies between.

The installations were built in 1902 and comprised powerhouse, office quarters, staffhouse for single employees, superintendent's residence and bungalows for married men. The submarine cable between Bamfield and Australia is approximately 7,000 miles long, with sub-stations at Fanning Island, Suva, Fiji and Norfolk Island. In places it lies 3,000 fathoms deep on the bottom of the sea.

This was once known as the "All Red Cable Route" between England and Australia. But at that time "red" had a different significance than is commonly applied to the same word today. The term originated because all British possessions were then shown in every atlas and map in red and the cable touched only at these countries and islands.

Because of its strategic importance, the Bamfield plant was closely guarded during both First and Second World Wars. In addition to a detachment of infantry, anti-submarine guns covered the harbour entrance and barbed-wire entanglements completely surrounded the station.

The Fanning Island station was indeed surprised by the German raider *Emden* in the First World War. A landing party cut the cable and destroyed (as it thought) the instruments and equipment. However, what the raiders didn't know was that the staff, on sighting the *Emden*, had dismantled and buried the instruments, and in their place, installed a discarded set which had been kept on hand in anticipation of just such an emergency. The raid was over in a few hours. *Emden* had scarcely disappeared over the horizon, when the cable ends (fortunately it had been severed in shallow water) were re-spliced, the obsolete instruments thrown back on the junk heap, the real ones dug-up and replaced, and the station was back in operation. *Emden* never returned, and for a very good reason; a few months later the Australian cruiser *Sydney* sent her to the bottom.

Prior to 1956, 45 persons, including 24 operators, were employed at Bamfield. The reason why most of the senior staff were either Australians or New Zealanders is because the station was originally administered from the system's headquarters at Sydney and the practice was to transfer them from one station to another on a rotation basis.

Now, owing to the introduction of more modern world-wide communication system methods, the station is completely automatic and the staff reduced to five, a watchman and four maintenance men. On a round-the-clock, three-shift basis; this means one man on duty at all times. The main cables (there are two) still end at Bamfield, but the messages are automatically relayed, via a smaller submarine cable system, to Alberni, another relay station which is remotely controlled from Vancouver, where the operators are now stationed.

EARLY DAYS AT
CAPE BEALE LIGHTHOUSE

EIGHTY-FIVE YEARS AGO, the paddle-wheel tug *Alexander* left Victoria with the barque *Brierly Hill,* outward bound with a cargo of lumber, for San Francisco. She turned the ship loose off Cape Flattery and proceeded to Barkley Sound to land a new lightkeeper, Emmanuel Cox, at Cape Beale. Also aboard the tug were Mrs. Cox, their three daughters, Frances (the eldest), Annie and Pattie, and two sons, Charles Augustus (Gus) and Ernest Ruxton.

Cox originally came from County Cork, Ireland, and brought his family to Victoria on a sailing ship in the early seventies. Prior to being transfered to Cape Beale, he was lightkeeper on Berens Island at the entrance to Victoria harbour, long since replaced with an automatic light and electric bell.

Mr. Cox died while at the lighthouse, and his wife some years after she had moved to Alberni. Gus died after serving for many years as a provincial policeman and later as Indian agent at Alberni. Ruxton, the youngest of the family, later became telegraph agent at Hazelton. He is now retired and lives at White Rock, British Columbia.

Prior to going to Cape Beale, Frances and Gus were pupils at the old Craigflower school, Victoria, the first public school in British Columbia. The other children were still under school age.

Frances (Mrs. R. M. Morrison) and Pattie (Mrs. P. A. Haslam), both widows, now reside at Victoria. Annie (Mrs. J. B. McKay) died at Bamfield in 1956. Her husband had been linesman and telegraph operator there for many years. They first met when he helped build the telephone line and life-saving trail from Victoria to Cape Beale in 1890.

The landing of the Cox family at Cape Beale was quite an experience, especially for a mother with five young children. The *Alexander* had landed them at an Indian village at Dodger's Cove on Diana Island a few miles inside the entrance to Barkley Sound. From there the Indians were to transfer them to the lighthouse by canoe.

Bad weather kept them at Dodger's Cove for nearly a week and they were finally landed on the beach in front of the lighthouse. The six-mile trip was made in five canoes, each manned by two Indians and a klootchman. The girls relate being somewhat terrified by a school of blackfish (killer whales) which came (as they thought) dangerously close to the canoes; but this was compensated for by the thrill they received afterwards when carried ashore on the Indians' backs.

"Whisky Charlie" was the name of the Indian who carried Pattie. She recalls that he was a very good-looking Indian. Only five at the time, she remembers him shouting to her "Hang on, hang on," which she could hardly do for laughing. It took two Indians to carry her father who weighed more than two hundred pounds.

In spite of a heavy surf breaking on the pebble beach, all were landed without getting wet. The Indians then carried all their belongings up the steep cliff to the lighthouse.

Annie and Pattie were afterwards sent to Victoria, where they attended the Bishop Cridge private school. Later, the mother assisted them with their education, as she did with the three other children who remained at home.

As her husband's assistant — permitted in those days — Mrs. Cox was in charge of the light during his temporary absence from the station at any time. On one occasion, when he was in Victoria on business, the revolving mechanism failed. One of the lightkeeper's most important duties is to see that the revolving apparatus synchronizes to a split second with the timing of the flashes. As it now had to be turned by hand, someone had to be up in the tower all night. This the different members of the family did by taking turns. The girls took the early shifts, with the mother and Gus dividing the time from midnight on. Ruxton was too young and wasn't allowed up the tower. They continued to do this until the father returned ten days later.

There were no telephones in those days; nor were there any gasboats. All transportation was by canoe. Indians living at Dodger's Cove brought the mail and supplies from the steamer which came only two or three times every year. To call the Indians, a Union

Jack was displayed at the light station and an old Indian named John Mack was the one that usually responded to the signal. For this and for being available at any other time, should his services be required, the government paid him $5 per month.

Immediately the light was found to be out of order, Mrs. Cox hoisted the flag and over came John Mack. She gave him some food and a letter to the marine agent, and he set out alone for Victoria. The 85-mile canoe trip down the coast and around Race Rocks took him two days and nights and he duly delivered the letter. The necessary parts were obtained and the lighthouse tender *Sir James Douglas* was dispatched. It brought back Mr. Cox, John Mack and his canoe. Like the *Alexander*, the *Sir James Douglas* has long since been scrapped, but the name of the famous old vessel is perpetuated in a new tender which works the British Columbia coast.

John Mack had always proved a faithful friend of the Cox family. More so in time of death, when several years later Mr. Cox died of a heart attack. Gus and the two elder sisters had in the meantime married and were living at Alberni. A telephone line had just been built expressly for life-saving purposes along the coast from Victoria to Cape Beale. Pattie, now the only daughter at home, was the operator. But the line was down owing to high winds and she was unable to get a message through notifying the marine agent of her father's death.

The mother was also anxious to notify her married children. So up went the flag and over came John Mack, this time accompanied by his aged father, Nespus. Mrs. Cox gave the Indians a letter and they paddled all night the 40 miles to Alberni. How they found her elder daughter, Mrs. Morrison, is a mystery, for she then lived three miles up the Alberni valley. The Indians arrived at the house at 2 a.m., when Mrs. Morrison and her two children accompanied the Indians back to Cape Beale. Gus and his other married sister followed in another canoe.

Pattie afterwards managed to get a message through to Victoria, when the lighthouse tender *Quadra,* which in the meantime had replaced the *Sir James Douglas*, came and took the father's body to Alberni where he was buried. Mrs. Morrison relates how John Mack steadfastly refused to take any money for the canoe trip to Alberni and back. In fact, she further recalls, he became so offended at being offered *chickamin* (money) for what he considered his last act and deed for an old friend, that he sulked for weeks afterwards. "*Kahta-mika-tum-tum*", meaning "How do you feel," was all they could get out of him.

Mrs. Cox left Cape Beale soon after her husband's death and came to live with Mrs. Morrison. There were scarcely a dozen families living in the Alberni valley then and only a few Indians where Port Alberni now stands. Mrs. Morrison was employed at the Alberni paper mill on the Somass River, then the first and only paper mill in British Columbia. She recalls working alongside Alfred Carmichael, who also worked at the mill and later became a Victoria real estate agent.

Mrs. Haslam (Pattie) was the government telegraph agent and operator at Alberni for forty-five years and for five years at Cape Beale before that. In recognition of her long and faithful service, in 1935 she was awarded the King George V Diamond Jubilee medal. This and another medal, received for services during the First Great War, she is very proud of and wears on special occasions.

Of their life at Cape Beale, the sisters have many fond memories and interesting stories. One concerns Pattie and how she saved a ship from possible destruction. Telegraph operator at the lighthouse when the full-rigged ship *Old Kensington* became becalmed off Cape Beale and drifted dangerously near the rocks, she wired Victoria for a tug, but none would come unless they received a guarantee of $500, and the vessel had no agent there.

As time meant everything and there was no way of contacting the ship, Pattie, who had that much money in her savings account, took it upon herself to guarantee the amount. A tug arrived the following day and towed the vessel to sea. The captain collected his fee and, unknown to Pattie, he told the ship's captain who had guaranteed it.

Six months later, Pattie received a letter from China, where the *Old Kensington* had in the meantime arrived safely. The captain thanked her profusely for sending for the tug and in return for her kindness, sent her a silk shawl, five pounds of tea and a photograph of the ship under full canvas. The family drank the tea, but the shawl and the photograph are still among Pattie's proud possessions.

On one of his sealing expeditions to the Bering Sea in the schooner *Minnie*, Captain Victor Jacobson brought his wife to Cape Beale to stay with the Cox family while he was away. When he called there on his return, Annie and Pattie accepted Mrs. Jacobson's invitation to accompany her to Victoria. This wasn't the first time the girls had taken passage on a sealing schooner. They always enjoyed these short voyages and the stories told by the seal hunters; tough, rough fellows, but always most respectful and kind.

They spent a pleasant holiday in the city, but as the tender was then temporarily out of commission and they might have to wait months for a steamer or schooner, they decided to go back home by canoe with Gaelic Dick and his wife, an Indian couple who were returning from hop-picking in the States. Indifferent weather was experienced and the 85-mile journey occupied four days. Each night, after helping haul the canoe out, the girls built a fire, made tea and prepared a meal from what scant provisions they had brought along, or cooked a fish if they had been lucky enough to catch one that day; then wrapped themselves in blankets and settled down for the night under the trees.

The only time they were really afraid was the night on the beach at the mouth of the Nitinat river. Here, Dick warned them to keep perfectly quiet and if any Indians should come near, not to show their faces. *"Delate mesth-chie tillikum"*, meaning very wicked friends, he kept repeating. The girls had little sleep that night and neither did Dick, who admitted that he slept with one eye open. They didn't bother about breakfast and were thankful to be on their way again as the Indian quietly slid the canoe into the water long before dawn.

Dick then told them that he was on unfriendly terms with the Nitinats. His wife was one of them and he didn't even trust her, they also learned. He had taken her without the chief's consent and also feared that they might kill them all if they knew he was carrying white people in his canoe. They had killed a friend of his for doing that very same thing, he said.

The girls took turns at the paddles and when the wind was favourable a small sail was hoisted. Each was thoroughly at home in a canoe, for they had several of their own and often went fishing or visited Bamfield and nearby islands.

Pattie was a good marksman and kept the family well supplied with deer meat. Four cougars also fell to her rifle. With one in particular she had rather an exciting time. Pattie had surprised the cougar while walking along a trail, but instead of taking to the woods, it attacked her dog. The dog naturally ran to its mistress and the two animals became mixed up between her feet. During the scramble that took place, Pattie fell to the ground, but she managed to kill the cougar with one shot before it seriously injured the dog. Her father was so proud of his daughter's achievement and saving the family dog's life, that he had a gold brooch made from two of the cougar's claws, suitably inscribed "Pattie from her father, October 31, 1890."

Mrs. Morrison recalls the time when the captain of the sailing ship *Dunbarton* mistook Barkley Sound for the Strait of Juan de Fuca and went sailing merrily on until he found himself among a group of small islands. Realizing his mistake and not daring to turn his ship around, he dropped anchor, just in time. Some Indians came out in their canoes from a nearby village and he asked them to take him to Cape Beale lighthouse, to seek the lightkeeper's advice. They agreed and their chief accompanied him.

Mr. Cox told the captain that he might have to remain there for weeks before a tug could come from Victoria and tow him to sea. Also, that if the weather broke in the meantime, he might find himself in difficulties and probably lose his ship. Through Mr. Cox, who acted as interpreter, the chief offered to take the ship safely out to sea, but only on one condition — that the captain give him complete charge and undertake not to interfere with him in any way while he (the chief) navigated the ship.

According to Mrs. Morrison's narrative, Mr. Cox had further to explain the reason for the chief's extraordinary demands. Many years before when the captain of an American trading schooner had found himself in the same predicament, he asked the Indians to show him the safest passage out. About twenty climbed on board, most of them merely for the novelty of a ride on a big ship and to do some further trading.

Two fairways loomed up and the Indian chief chose the one which he knew was free of hidden rocks. The captain insisted on the other and the schooner piled up. The crew threw the Indians overboard without their canoes and two were drowned. When the schooner commenced to break up, the crew took to the boats, headed for the open sea and were never seen again. The Indians looted the wreck.

At first the captain of the *Dunbarton* demurred, but after listening to Mr. Cox and realizing the precariousness of his position, finally concurred. He returned to his ship and the following day, the wind having shifted to a moderate off-shore breeze, the Cox family witnessed a sight unique in marine history: a full-rigged three-masted ship sailing out of the island-studded Sound, with all her canvas spread and an Indian chief at her helm. The Indians took the *Dunbarton* far out into the ocean and returned home in their canoes. Duly rewarded and proud of his achievement, the chief gave himself a new name, *Hyas ship tyee*, meaning big ship chief.

On July 27, 1879, the sailing ship *Bechardass Ambiadass* was abandoned after striking a reef three miles east of the lighthouse. Some of the survivors were taken care of by the Cox family until the schooner *Favourite* came and took them to Esquimalt. The sisters well remember this wreck; not only on account of the sailors inability to speak English, but amongst the wreckage washed ashore were many casks of excellent wine, which they salvaged.

On December 8, 1880, the barque *Glen Fruin* came to grief on Danger Rock (now known as Hornby Rock) at the entrance to Barkley Sound, after her master had made the same mistake as the *Dunbarton*. Frances (Mrs. Morrison) was the first to sight the wreck and noticing the crew leaving the scene in the ship's lifeboats, knew they were safe. They landed at Village (Effingham) Island, where all they had to eat for several days was dried fish found in an Indian smokehouse and some goats that belonged to a priest. The Indians and the priest were away, so the sailors helped themselves.

The men subsequently reached the lighthouse where they stayed for two weeks. In gratitude for the sanctuary offered them by the Cox family, they split a whole winter's supply of wood, did the station chores, mended, carpentered, painted and polished. One of the sailors made Mrs. Morrison a rag mat which she still keeps beside her bed. Its centre pattern is the St. George Cross insignia. Finally, the sealing schooner *Favourite* was hailed and Captain Spring took the shipwrecked men to Victoria.

Prior to coming to Victoria, in 1955, Mrs. Morrison and Mrs. Haslam lived together at Alberni in a house they occupied for over sixty years. There they kept themselves busy in the garden during the summer months, and with needlework, crocheting and rug-making while confined indoors in winter. Both took an active interest in church and other social activities, but what pleased them most was to have some old West-Coaster drop in for a cup of tea and talk over their pioneering days and life in a lighthouse.

Mrs. Morrison is a life member of the Ladies' Guild of All Saints' Church, Alberni, which, with hammer and saw, she helped build. Before leaving to come to live in Victoria, the members tendered her a party in the Church hall, the occasion being her ninetieth birthday. Thomas E. Morrison, her son, also spent most of his life in the lighthouse service. He joined the lighthouse tender *Quadra* as mess-boy, subsequently became chief engineer on the new and larger tender *Estevan,* and later, marine agent at Victoria, a position he held until his retirement in 1954. Tom well remembers the time when his grandfather died and that canoe trip he and his mother made from Alberni to Cape Beale with the two Indians.

The sisters still enjoy good health and seldom miss their afternoon walk through Victoria's Beacon Hill park.

IN THE DAYS OF SAIL, and for steamers also before the advent of radio, radar and other modern aids to navigation, the west coast of Vancouver Island was a death trap for the weather-blinded. Wherever sailormen gathered in the crowded fo'c'sles, they spoke in unholy words of the "Graveyard of the Pacific," referring to these rocky shores. Masters of sailing vessels especially feared this area, and always breathed more easily once their ships were inside Juan de Fuca Strait. The prevailing currents are to the north, and a sailing vessel in the throes of a fresh southeasterly, if she missed Cape Flattery, was always in jeopardy of being carried ashore somewhere on Vancouver Island.

In addition to those mentioned in preceding pages, we know of the following ships which also came to grief in the immediate vicinity of Barkley Sound: In 1870, the American sealing schooner *Elsie*, wrecked entrance to Ucluelet Harbour; crew reached shore, taken by Indians to Captain Spring's trading post at Spring Cove. The fulled-rigged ship *Orpheus*, San Francisco to Puget Sound in ballast, on November 5, 1875, made the same mistake as the *Dunbarton* (mistook Barkley Sound for Juan de Fuca Strait) and was wrecked on one of the small islands which stud the entrance, crew reached shore, vessel a total loss. Only the day previously, off Cape Flattery, the *Orpheus* collided with the steamer *Pacific*, sending her to the bottom with the loss of 250 lives (see page 128).

On November 20, 1886, the barque *Charles B. Kinney* sailed from Port Townsend with lumber for Australia and never reached her destination. Late in December, the lightkeeper at Cape Beale reported that an unidentified vessel, with no sign of life on board and all the appearance of having been abandoned at sea, had drifted ashore near the cape. Big seas were running and ship broke up the same night, when most of the wreckage drifted away. Among pieces found was part of a nameboard with the letters "Charles V (or B) . . . ." November 1891, the sealing schooner *Lillie* sunk in Dodger's Cove. November 19, 1892, the American ship *Ericsson*, 1,568 tons, wrecked Entrance Island; crew brought to Victoria by tug *Lorne*.

On June 27, 1898, the stern-wheel river steamer *Marquis of Dufferin*, San Francisco to Alaska (for use on the Yukon River) in convoy with the steamer *Progress*, broke up under stress of heavy weather and sank off the entrance to the Sound; passengers and crew transferred to *Progress*. In April 1902, the schooner *Amethyst*, water-logged and derelict after having been abandoned by her crew, drifted into the Sound; looted by Indians but later salvaged. In 1904, the full-rigged ship *Lamora*, was wrecked on Starlight Reef; all hands lost.

During Christmas night, 1905, the steel four-masted British ship *Pass of Melfort*, 2,200 tons, Panama to Port Townsend, was driven ashore in heavy southeast gale a short distance from Amphitrite Point, with the loss of all hands. Three American halibut schooners were wrecked in the same vicinity, fortunately with no loss of life, while attempting to reach the shelter of Ucluelet Harbour during stormy weather: the *Agnes* in 1917, *Eagle* on September 11, 1918 and the *Mary* in 1921. In August 1920, the halibut vessel *Lief E*, burned and sank off Cape Beale. Her seven-man crew took to the dory and after spending two days and a night on stormy seas finally reached Hot Springs Cove, then known as Refuge Cove.

February 15, 1923, the freighter *Tuscan Prince*, wrecked on Village Island, later broken up for scrap. February 26, 1924, the freighter *Tatjauna*, also wrecked on Village Island; was later salvaged and brought to Victoria for repairs. The Victoria-built four-masted auxiliary schooner *Malahat*, in the rum-running trade after making several trips to Australia with lumber, and now converted into a log barge, ended her career when she was beached in Uchucklesit Inlet after having been swamped off Cape Beale, 1944. The fishpacker *Kodiak*, loaded with 120 tons of herring, sank off Amphitrite Point, January 20, 1959; crew reached shore in dinghy. During fog on night of January 1, 1962, the Greek freighter *Glafkos*, Japan to Vancouver in ballast, ran aground on a small island off Amphitrite Point; crew taken off by helicopter. Vessel later pulled free by tugs *Sudbury I* and *Island Challenger*; leaking badly, with engine room and holds flooded, was towed to Esquimalt. Damage so extensive, was subsequently sold for scrap.

MINNIE PATERSON

British Columbia's
Grace Darling

ON DECEMBER 6, 1906, Captain J. Allison and nine crew members of the barque *Coloma* were saved from a watery grave off Cape Beale by the lighthouse tender *Quadra*, Captain Hackett, minutes before the vessel was dashed to pieces on the rocks. The *Coloma*, an old wooden vessel of 850 tons, San Francisco-owned and outward bound from Puget Sound with lumber for Australia, ran into a southeast gale shortly after clearing Cape Flattery. Springing a leak she quickly filled and, with decks awash, partially dismasted and her lifeboats carried away, drifted helplessly before the storm.

Fortunately she was sighted when dangerously near the rocks, by Thomas Paterson, the lightkeeper at Cape Beale (1895-1908), with her flag flying upside-down (the international distress signal) from what was left of a mast. There was only one chance of saving those on board, and that rested with the *Quadra*, which Paterson knew was at the time sheltering at Bamfield, six miles away. But the telephone line to Bamfield, along with the one to Victoria, was out of commission. Trees uprooted by the same storm, it transpired afterwards, had cut both in a hundred places.

Paterson couldn't leave his foghorn by day, or the light by night, so his wife insisted on going. Donning heavy clothing, with a lantern in her hand for it was now dark, and accompanied by her dog, Minnie Paterson set out. Her path led part way along the rock-strewn shoreline and then through the bush. Exhausted, drenched through and her clothing torn, she finally reached the home of an old friend, Mrs. McKay, the daughter (Annie) of Emmanuel Cox, lightkeeper at Cape Beale in 1878. (Mrs. McKay died at Bamfield in 1956).

James McKay, the husband, was away at the time helping to repair the broken line. But that didn't daunt his wife, who without waiting even to offer Mrs. Paterson a cup of tea or a change of clothing, took the family boat and the two women rowed out to the *Quadra*, anchored in the stream. Mrs. Paterson told Captain Hackett of the distressed ship's plight and within a very short time the *Quadra* was proceeding at full speed in the direction of Cape Beale.

The derelict vessel was sighted shortly after rounding the lighthouse. The gale had somewhat subsided by this time, but heavy seas prevented Captain Hackett from approaching close. A ship's boat, manned by second officer McDonald and a picked crew, was lowered over the side and soon had a line on her, and one by one the crew was taken off. They had scarcely reached the *Quadra* when the already doomed vessel hit the outside reef and that was the end of the *Coloma*.

Meanwhile, Minnie Paterson walked the trail back to the lighthouse and her family. Owing to poor visibility, the rescue operation was not observed from the lighthouse and it was a week later, when the telephone line was repaired, that she first learned that her mission had not been in vain. Hailed as British Columbia's Grace Darling, Mrs. Paterson, the mother of five children, never recovered from the effects of her heroic mission. She died five years later.

Thomas Paterson, lighthouse keeper at Cape Beale, 1895-1908, with Mrs. Paterson and family. For her part in saving the lives of the crew of the barque *Coloma*, wrecked off Cape Beale, December 1906, Mrs. "Minnie" Paterson was heralded "British Columbia's Grace Darling." Children, left to right: May (Mrs. F. G. Andrews, Southport, Australia), Agnes (Mrs. George Cruickshank, Clayburn, B.C.), Thomas (Alberni), George (deceased), and Violet (Mrs. Wm. McKay (Alberni).

Bamfield, a picturesque setlement on the West Coast, with the *Princess Norah* at dock and Barkley Sound islands in distance. Photo taken from cable station. *B.C. Government Travel*

CABLE STATION AT BAMFIELD
B.C. Government Travel Bureau Photo

CAPE BEALE LIGHTHOUSE
Department of Marine Photo

One hundred years ago. Vessels loading lumber at Port Alberni. *Provincial Archives Photo.*

British Columbia's first paper mill, on the Somass River, Alberni. *Provincial Archives Photo.*

FORTY WRECKS,
ONE FOR EVERY MILE

THE COAST BETWEEN Port San Juan (Port Renfrew) and Barkley Sound offers no shelter for ships, big or small, in any weather. Its only indentations, a few small bays, are exposed to the winds from every direction. Is it any wonder then, that over forty major shipwrecks — one for every mile of its rugged shoreline — occurred in this area, most of them during the winter months. Scores of fishboats and other small craft, the actual number will never be known, have also been lost in the same locality.

Clo-oose, about midway between, is the only settlement. It once had a population of about two hundred, but since its only industry, a cannery on nearby Nitinat Lake, ceased operations 35 years ago, one by one the residents drifted away and now there is only a score left. Carmanah Point (lighthouse established there in 1891) is six miles east of Clo-oose village, and Bonilla Point, which marks the western boundary (on the Vancouver Island side) of Juan de Fuca Strait, two miles farther to the east.

Seventeen of the forty known wrecks — nearly all sailing vessels— occurred in the Port San Juan, Bonilla Point, Carmanah Point area. On December 23, 1858, the brig *Cyrus*, Puget Sound to San Francisco with lumber, lost with all hands. On November 10, 1860, the ship *John Marshall*, San Francisco to Puget Sound in ballast, ashore as a derelict after having apparently been abandoned at sea; fate of crew unknown. Also in November 1860, the schooner *Morning Star*, wrecked. December 23, 1865, U.S. ship *William Tell*, inbound in ballast to load spars for the French government; crew picked up by schooner *Surprise* and brought to Victoria. July 1870, American barque *Gem of the Ocean*, Seattle to San Francisco with coal.

September 9, 1883, U.S. barque *Revere*, inbound from Honolulu, crew and passengers brought to Victoria by Indians. February 21, 1884, U.S. barque *Lizzie Marshall*, also inbound from Hawaii. November 29, 1886, American ship *Belvidere*, inbound to Nanaimo for coal; ashore Bonilla Point, pulled free by tug *Tyee*; leaking badly and later sunk, crew saved by *Tyee* and brought to Victoria. October 11, 1887, four-masted iron British ship *Duchess of Argyle*, ashore, total loss. December 23, 1890, the schooner *Dare* and in April 1895, the schooner *Dart*, both a total loss on Bonilla Point. On August 9, 1895, the passenger steamer *Warrimoo*, inbound from Australia, ran aground (in fog) four miles west of Carmanah Point, refloated herself next high tide and steamed on to Victoria. November 13, 1896, the four-masted auxiliary schooner *Puritan*, total loss.

In November 1899, the U.S. barque *Colusa*, Honolulu to Puget Sound, freed herself after running aground on Bonilla Point, then drifted west in leaking condition and was abandoned off Barkley Sound; crew reached shore in boats. October 28, 1903, the ship *Wempe Bros.*, and in October 1905, the schooner *Fawn*, ashore in same locality and both a total loss.

Wrecked almost in front of Clo-oose village: on October 26, 1906, the schooner *Skagit*, with the loss of three lives. February 15, 1923, the *Santa Rita*, and January 16, 1925, the *Rita Papipe,* both steam schooners in the coastal trade. Also three small sailing vessels, believed to have been sloops, back in the 1880's; but all we have is their names, *Persian, Continental* and *Woodrich*, supplied by an old time resident of Clo-oose. The *Santa Rita* went aground in a snowstorm, her 32-man crew reached shore by means of a breeches buoy and were afterwards taken care of by the villagers. Next storm broke the vessel in two and her rusting plates are still there.

Nitinat Lake is joined to the ocean by a short and treacherous tidal waterway a mile west of Clo-oose. The Nitinats (Nittin-ahts or Dinnin-ahts), once a powerful tribe with whom it did not do to be off one's guard, had a high reputation as hunters, whalers, fishers and warriors. Why-ack, or Why-aht, at the seaward entrance to the lake was (and still is for the few that are left) their principal village. Because of frequent raids made by the Makah Indians from Neah Bay, across the Strait of Juan de Fuca, and the Ohiats from Barkley Sound, it was once well fortified. Traces of these fortifications can still be seen.

No vessel larger than a medium-sized tugboat or fishpacker can cross the Nitinat bar, and then only if the captain is thoroughly familiar with it. Few skippers even try. More boats have been capsized in the attempt, some with considerable loss of life, than at any other passage of its kind on the British Columbia coast. Supplies for logging camps on the lake are now taken in by road (to the head of the lake) from Cowichan Lake, and the logs are brought out in "bundle booms" designed specially to negotiate the bar.

In 1887, the schooners *Rustler* and *Champion* both capsized when attempting to cross the Nitinat bar. On April 12, 1912, the 52-foot cabin cruiser *Inlet Queen* filled and sank after hitting the bar, the cannery tender *Renfrew* in November 1918 and the tug *Beryl*, in 1920. Thirteen persons lost their lives with the sinking of the *Renfrew*, most of them cannery employees on their way home to Vancouver. The other thirteen persons on board owed their lives to the prompt action of the residents of Clo-oose.

For years, prior to and since 1880, the remains of an unidentified gunboat lay on the beach approximately four miles west of the Nitinat, about where Tsusiat Falls (see page 154) spill into the sea. Two other wrecks occurred at almost the identical spot: the three-masted auxiliary schooner *Vesta*, on December 10, 1897, and the American barquentine *Uncle John*, October 7, 1899.

Known wrecks which occurred on, or in the vicinity of Pachena Point: On New Year's Day, 1854, the brig *William*, San Francisco to Victoria, drove ashore about four miles to the east. Captain and cook drowned. Remainder of those on board, fourteen in number, made shore and were fed and housed by the Indians, who later took them by canoe to Sooke. One of the survivors was William Thomson, who later settled at Mt. Newton, Saanich.

The barque *Maria J. Smith*, November 1869; lumber laden, vessel cleared Cape Flattery on the 8th, ran into a gale, sails blew away and she sprung a leak, came up on a reef about five miles east of Pachena Point, crew abandoned ship, reached shore, lived in the bush for three days when they were taken off by schooner *Surprise* and brought to Victoria. Weeks later, wreck refloated itself and with decks awash drifted 400 miles north into Millbank Sound, where it again went ashore and subsequently broke up.

On March 12, 1888, the small Sooke-built steamer *Woodside*, Victoria to Barkley Sound with four passengers and general cargo, lost her rudder and piled up about the same place, no lives lost, vessel total loss. In March 1891, the schooner *Laura Pike*. November 8, 1891, the British barque *Sarah*, Manilla to Royal Roads in ballast, two lives lost. January 20, 1893, steamer *Michigan* wrecked at the mouth of a creek which now bears her name. December 31, 1895, four-masted British barque *Janet Cowan*, with the loss of seven lives (see story on page 165). February 23, 1923, auxiliary schooner *Robert E. Lewers*, Port Angeles to Hawaii with lumber, lost with all hands.

On April 30, 1943, the 10,000-ton Russian supply ship *Uzbekistan*, Portland, Oregon to Seattle to load lend-lease supplies for Vladivostok, went ashore just west of the mouth of Darling Creek, two-and-a-half miles east of Pachena Point. Lighthouses on the West Coast were blacked out at the time. First at the scene was the lighthouse tender *Estevan*, but her captain, upon observing that the vessel was armed, notified Esquimalt and the navy took charge. Crew of over forty, which included several women, reached shore safely, most of them without even getting their feet wet. Escorted by naval personnel, they then walked the 12-mile trail to Bamfield. With her back broken, vessel remained on rocks for several months, during which time she was thoroughly looted by all and sundry.

Several other vessels met with mishap on the West Coast during World War Two, but for security reasons names and particulars were never released. One was an American freighter that ran ashore close to Pachena Point. The lighthouse tender *Estevan*, again the first Canadian vessel at the scene, sighted her shortly after leaving Barkley Sound. Lighthouses were all blacked out and radios silent. As *Estevan* approached, two American tugs and a coastguard cutter were seen to be standing by. They signalled *Estevan*'s master that they had the situation in hand and the tender proceeded on its way. The stranded vessel, which was said to be loaded with munitions of war, was subsequently pulled free.

Wrecked between Pachena Point and Cape Beale: July, 1879, the barque *Bechardass Ambiadass* (see page 143) on a reef in Pachena Bay. On Seabird Islands, better described as a barren reef, the four-masted American schooner *Soquel*, January 22, 1909; except for the captain's wife who was killed when a mast fell on her as the ship heeled over after striking the reef, all on board were saved, vessel a total loss. On January 2, 1923, the same Seabird Island claimed the lives of 11 Victoria men, the entire crew of the small coastal freighter *Alaskan*, which had sailed from Victoria on New Year's Day with salt for Barkley Sound herring salteries. On August 8, 1937, the Greek freighter *Nereus* crashed ashore in heavy fog about a mile east of Cape Beale, crew of 34 taken off, but vessel declared total loss within 48 hours; Capital Iron Works of Victoria salvaged 100 tons of equipment before ship broke in two and sank.

The rusting plates of a few of the iron wrecks can still be seen. Also what remains of the telephone line (single wire strung from tree to tree) and trail built along this stretch of coastline in 1890 especially for life-saving purposes with a cabin every few miles, each with a telephone and instructions as to its use printed in several different languages, medical supplies, blankets, canned food, matches and dry firewood. Some of the cabins are still there, together with foot bridges which the linesmen built across the numerous streams and the bucket cables used for crossing the wider gulches. Some of the bridges were well-built suspension affairs, secured by strong cables, others merely a handy log, with or without handrail, felled across the stream. Those still in good condition are used by the few people who now pass that way.

In addition to the regular linesmen, extra men were employed in winter to make special patrols. Thus the lives of many shipwrecked sailors who might otherwise have died from injuries or exposure were saved. When shipwrecks became less frequent, chiefly owing to the introduction of wireless and direction-finding apparatus, the cabins were abandoned — the line also when radio telephone was introduced.

TSUSIAT FALLS

Hidden wonders at Clo-oose.

FOR COMBINED BEAUTY and grandeur, Tsusiat Falls might well be described as the finest natural water cascade on the Island. They originate in a stream which empties out of a small lake by the same name and pour over an 80-foot sheer cliff down to the beach.

The 100-foot-wide mass of white water is clearly visible from far out at sea and fishermen use this as a landmark to locate their favourite fishing spots. The captain of the *Princess Maquinna* often nosed the ship close in towards shore to enable his passengers to have a closer look and take pictures. At times when high tide and heavy swells coincide, a huge breaker will sometimes momentarily almost envelope the falls completely, which re-appear in all their grandeur as the wave recedes. But unfortunately this thrilling sight is only witnessed by a few Indians, or the crew of a fishboat well outside the breakers who usually have more important things to attend to than take in the scenery.

The area in which the falls are located was years ago set aside by the federal government as a tidewater park site, but nothing has ever been done in the way of developing it. Seen at their best during heavy rains, when the lake level is high and the stream in flood, the falls would not be the park's only attraction, for nearby are other sights equally unique.

Two miles east is a phenomenon known locally as "The Hole-in-the-Wall." It was created through the ages by erosion caused by the action of the seas on the sandstone formation common on this part of the coast. To look through this great round hole in a jutting promontory is a weird sight, and a stranger experience still is to sail through it in a canoe, possible at high tide when the sea is calm. Seen from either approach, it forms a landmark for small boats hugging the shore.

154

A blow-hole is merely a vent in the rocks from which compressed air — caused by the swells — escapes to create a blast or whistling sound. Such are common all along the coast, but one near the outlet from Nitinat Lake, which is also in the park area, is larger than usual and its blast can be heard for miles. When proceeding cautiously in fog, skippers of small boats sometimes mistake its blast for a foghorn, then look in vain for a lighthouse when the fog lifts. Here nature has taken a hand and precisely at the hour (high tide) when the treacherous Nitinat bar is negotiable, the blow-hole blasts full throat. Old time Clo-oose residents claim that this was relied on, but now when a tug is expected a man familiar with the bar is posted on the bluff to signal the captain when conditions for a crossing are favourable.

Caves are also numerous. One gallery, known as the "Cowchets," is probably the most extensive example of wave-worn galleries and caverns on Vancouver Island. Close by are rocks, standing alone or grouped and sculptured by nature's never wearying agencies into odd forms resembling human figures and animals.

Below Clo-oose is a series of broad sandy beaches, pounded by the merciless swells of the open Pacific during the winter months, but delightful playgrounds in summer. In 1911, a Victoria real estate firm promoted a seaside resort here, selling several hundred lots at fabulous prices. A special boat was chartered to take prospective buyers to see the property (and they all got terribly seasick) and a pier along the lines of those on the south coast of England was contemplated. But the plan was abandoned when the First Great War broke out. The special boat was the cabin cruiser *Inlet Queen* which, incidentally, was wrecked on the Nitinat bar (see page 151).

Nitinat Lake, partly salt water, is the largest of several in the proposed park area; the others, in addition to Tsusiat, are Hobitan, Squalicum, Cheewaat, Doobah and Spris. Nitinat and Klanawa are the largest rivers. There is excellent fishing in all these lakes and rivers and the scenery is equal to anything found on the island. There is no end of Indian lore and evidence of the early history of the coast. This together with the falls and other unusual sights and features here briefly described, makes the Nitinat-Clo-oose area an interesting place to explore. But the pity is, it is so inaccessible.

THE CATASTROPHE
OF THE VALENCIA

*By the late B. A. McKelvie in
the Vancouver Province.*

It was in the blackness of a winter night, lashed by a howling gale and blinded by freezing sleet, that the fine steamer *Valencia* crashed onto the jagged rocks of the west coast of Vancouver Island near Cape Beale. It was fifteen minutes before midnight on January 22, 1906. In the next forty-eight hours 117 persons perished miserably in one of the worst marine horrors known to that strip of the coast then called "The Graveyard of the Pacific." There were other shipping disasters when even more lives were lost, but never had such a catastrophe occurred under such circumstances; when rescue vessels standing off, impotent to give aid, as pounding waves hammered the doomed ship to pieces and snatched and clawed helpless men and women from the rigging to destruction; and high above the crumbling and shapeless *Valencia*, men watched helplessly as passengers and crewmen died before their eyes.

For two days, the pitiless battle between puny men and the sea went on. The steamers *Queen* and *Topeka* and the salvage tug *Salvor* had raced to the scene when rockets streaked high into the darkness of the night, and when a few individuals managed to get ashore and carry word of the terrible tragedy to the lighthouse at Cape Beale, from where a telegraphic message was carried to Victoria. Experienced and courageous men manned the rescue vessels— but bravery was not enough. The *Salvor* approached to within half a mile of the foam-beaten shore; to have gone closer would have been suicidal, for even the powerful engines of the salvage vessel could not be depended upon to resist the power of the undertow and the driving force of the seas.

Captain Ernest F. Jordan, of Victoria, recalls the hopelessness of

Captain Edward Gillam (right), for twenty years master of the steamer *Princess Maquinna*; with Captain C. D. Neroutsos, Manager B.C. Coast Steamships, Canadian Pacific Railway Co. *Photo courtesy Carl F. Timms, Vancouver, B.C.*

Photo shows Mrs. R. M. Morrison (Frances Cox) holding hands with her son, Thomas E. Morrison, former marine agent at Victoria, B.C. Also, Mrs. P. A. Haslam (Pattie Cox) who was twice honoured for long and faithful service on Vancouver Island's west coast. With their parents, the sisters went to live at Cape Beale lighthouse in 2??. B.W. H. (A. P. (?) I.

Paddle Steam Tug *Alexander* which took the Cox family to Cape Beale in 1877. *Provincial Archives Photo.*

Lighthouse Tender *Sir James Douglas* which brought supplies. *Provincial Archives Photo.*

Captain Charles William Barkley, who discovered and named the Sound in 1787. *Provincial Archives Photo.*

those who watched, for he was an officer on the *Salvor*. He explained recently:

When it was found that the vessel could not approach close enough to shoot a line aboard the wreck, I offered to try and get closer in a lifeboat, to, if possible, float a line down to the *Valencia*. I was not permitteed to make the attempt, which even at the time I realized offered but a hundred-to-one chance of success.

It was terrible to stand off there and watch the wreck break up, and see the people who were in the rigging drop off into the boiling sea. All we could do was to wait in hope that we might be of some assistance to those who might miraculously get away from the *Valencia*. There were a few of the 94 passengers — 14 I believe — saved; while 23 of the 60 officers and crew managed to make shore, only 37 out of a total of 154.

We did manage to help a bit, for the *Topeka* picked up one raft loaded with survivors, while we on the *Salvor* picked up another four or five that had landed on Turret Island, Barkley Sound and managed to make their way to an Indian village. They told us that two of those on the raft had become delirious and had jumped into the sea; another, a chap named Long, was in bad shape, while still another named Frank Connors had imagined that he had seen a lighthouse and had wandered into the woods. I took a boat and went in search of the missing man and in search of the raft.

The raft I located; but there was no response to our calls along the shoreline of the little bay where the raft had beached. We made a second tour along the beach, as close to land as possible. Then, just by accident, we spied Connors hanging on to the branch of a tree. He was in bad shape and was raving mad when I reached him, and I had almost to tear him from his clutch of the tree — I suppose the poor fellow imagined he was still clinging to the rigging. We did what we could for the survivors and on arriving at Victoria sent Connors and Long to hospital, where they recovered. The particular raft — or the people on it — had been piloted by Sam Hancock, the head cook of the *Valencia*. He did a good job.

The *Valencia* was an iron vessel, constructed in 1882 — twenty-four years before — in the yards of W. Cramp & Sons, Philadelphia. She was a propellor-driven craft of 1,598 tons, with a length of 252 feet and a beam of 34 feet. She carried two pole masts, and was equipped with four bulkheads. She left San Francisco for Seattle, January 20, 1906, and had good weather up the coast as far as Cape Mendicino, when it became foggy.

In describing the voyage to the coroner, Dr. E. C. Hart at Victoria, a few days later, Timothy J. McCarthy, the boatswain, related:

Monday was thick and hazy and we kept a lookout on the forecastle head and the bridge and the whistle was kept going. Monday evening (January 22) about 5 o'clock the chief officer told me to have two leads ready at six. I went with the men and the chief officer and he used the Thompson sounding machine; got no bottom at about 250 fathoms. We continued sounding until the ship struck.

Dangerous variable currents, not at that time recognized, set in off Cape Flattery due to the action of the weather. Many ships have come to grief due to this cause. Captain Johnston of the *Valencia* did not realize that the ship was 19 miles off course. He imagined that he was still off the Washington coast, when the vessel struck at 11:45 p.m. January 22.

Continuing his straightforward but intensely dramatic narration, the boatswain said:

I was in my bunk asleep. I got up at once and went on deck. It was thick dark with sleet and blowing a stiff breeze. I could not see any light. I went back and got my clothes. By that time the passengers were getting out of their rooms and most of them had life-preservers on. At the time the engines were working, but I don't know which way. The chief officer told me to clear away the boats, which I did. The deck was crowded and it was so dark I could not tell the crew from passengers. We only carried eight sailors and four quartermasters. We had seven boats and three rafts. The davits were drop davits.

The captain shouted from the bridge to lower all boats to the saloon rail and keep them there, but the four forward boats were lowered all the way; most of them were full of passengers and there was a strain on the tackles. Of those four boats, only one, No. 2, got away from the ship's side. There was a heavy sea running; was breaking almost to the bridge, and I am doubtful if those boats could have got away even in daylight. The captain turned the search-light all around. I saw No. 2 boat off at some little distance; then someone pulled the whistle and the electric light went out.

I saw No. 1 boat smash alongside. There would be 15 or 20 people in her. I had a ladder thrown over, also some ropes and I saw one man climb aboard.

At that time the *Valencia* took a heavy list to port and No. 7 boat was lowered. I saw the firemen's mess boy in No. 6 boat. She got away from the ship's side. One raft was also put overboard. There were at that time several people in the rigging and the rest on the hurricane deck. Some rockets were fired and we could see the beach. The officers were then assuring the passengers that they would be all right. At that time the social hall and the weather side of the saloon were the only dry places on the ship.

Some of the people who had put off had made the shore, for, continued McCarthy:

. . . at daylight we could see the people on the beach right under the cliff at almost low water. They would be a hundred yards or more away. Captain Johnston ordered me to get up a five-inch line to get a line ashore. I sent a man aloft and rigged the blocks and got the Lyle gun aft on the hurricane deck. The tide was coming in and the seas were getting stronger and Captain Johnston asked me if I would go in the remaining boat and try and make a landing to take a line.

I finally got a crew and got away with *No. 5* boat; Captain Johnston was in charge of lowering it. We got away with considerable difficulty; the bow oar broke. They cheered us from the ship but it was so thick we could not see her. We kept outside the breakers but at times could not see shore; it was so thick and we could not find a place to land. I came to some rocks which I took to be the Durkin Rocks off Tatooche (Cape Flattery), and finally a heavy sea hit us and two of the men lost their oars and we had only two left. We pulled a little farther and one of the men said he thought it was the Vancouver Island shore. Finally we made a landing in a place I afterwards found to be between Pachena Bay and Cape Beale.

Having landed, McCarthy and his companions stumbled along the shore until they reached Cape Beale lighthouse at 3 p.m. two hours later. It was three miles from where they had landed. Lightkeeper Paterson wired to Victoria.

Second-Officer P. E. Petterson gave Coroner Hart and jury further grim details of the shipwreck. He told of how, while McCarthy and his crew were trying to get ashore to take a line, that a rope was shot over the top of the cliff from the *Valencia* — "but" he added simply, "there was no one there to take it." He also told of how heroic Captain Johnston, in his efforts to save the lives of those entrusted to him, "burned off two of his fingers" in a mishap while firing off the rockets to attract help.

The poignant story of how hope rose and then gave way to despair was told in a few words by Petterson:

> The port side was broken up. The women refused to go into staterooms. Tuesday night we could see three steamers' lights pass by, but we had no more rockets left dry. We made a fire of bedding but they did not see us. On Wednesday morning at daylight I thought she would break up at any minute. About 8 a.m. we saw the *Queen*, afterwards another steamer (*Topeka*) and a tug (*Salvor*) came in towards us. The tug came in to about half or three-quarters of a mile. There were about 40 people in the main rigging.

The second officer explained how he came to be among those saved:

> I was in the main rigging on the port side. We launched the starboard raft. Captain Johnston wanted the women to go on it. We

then launched the port raft with much difficulty. Six or seven men got on it and the women refused to go. Some of the men also refused to leave the ship. There were 17 men on it and Captain Johnston told me that I had better go on it. I took the painter and jumped overboard and got on the raft. We got clear away and later, about 12 a.m., some of the men wanted to beach it; just as we started to do this we saw some smoke, and shortly after the s.s. *Topeka* came and picked us up. We saw nothing of the raft that left (the *Valencia*) 15 minutes before us.

Sam Hancock, the chief cook on the *Valencia*, was aboard the other raft. He told of the anguish of himself and companions when they saw both the *Queen* and *Topeka* for brief glimpses in the rain mist — only to have them disappear again. They drifted towards shore.

The terrors of that slow, inch-by-inch drift towards what seemed certain doom, was given by the cook. He told how two men, delirious as a result of their sufferings, jumped overboard and drowned; of how another was restrained, and how still another was in very bad shape. He explained:

> We struck the beach about midnight and three more went insane and died on the raft. The remaining four went into the bush until daylight, and then we walked about on the island all day Thursday. Towards evening three of us got to the beach and saw an Indian settlement about a mile away. Some Indians came and afterwards a cannery steamer took us to Toquart on Barkley Sound. In the morning the s.s *Salvor* came and took us off. They went to the island and got the raft and afterwards found Connors (the man who had wandered off).

When McCarthy reached Cape Beale lighthouse and gave the alarm, three men from Clo-oose, Dave Logan, Phil Daykin and Joe Martin, started for the scene with ropes and provisions. They reached there on Wednesday — just twenty-five on the port rigging and thirty people on the poop. There were others in the starboard rigging, but it was impossible to reach them from the top of the cliff. It was awful, they later explained, when the perishing people saw them on top of the high land and sent up a cheer. They (the three Clo-oose men) had picked up the line that was still over the edge of the land and gave it a pull — but it parted in the surf. No further attempt to use the Lyle gun was made (probably no further cartridges), and soon after the sea completed its conquest.

When word reached Victoria of the plight of the *Valencia*, her crew and passengers — and there were a number of Victoria people aboard — Mayor Morley chartered the tug *Lorne*, Captain Butler, to take a picked naval crew to supplement the efforts of the officers and crews of the three vessels already there, — but no one could do more than had been done. The worst and most ghastly story of a shipwreck on the disaster-studded West Coast was complete.

THIS WRITER'S NOTE: Where the *Valencia* went ashore is about three miles east of Pachena Point. A lighthouse was established on the point the following year.

CARMANAH IS AN adaptation by local navigators, and adopted by Admiralty surveyors in 1860, of the name (Qua-ma-doa) of an Indian village which once was situated under the eastern bluff of the promontory. Its inhabitants belonged to the Nitinat tribe. The lighthouse stands, an alert sentinel, overlooking an area of the sea where scores of ships and men have perished. But its beam has guided countless others to sanctuary.

Only fifty-five miles from Victoria, if you measure the distance by dividers, the station is one of the most inaccessible on the British Columbia coast. Supplies for the light and bulk goods for families of the lightkeeper and his assistant are brought in every few months by the lighthouse tender, but owing to the exposed nature of the site, weeks sometimes pass before that vessel's workboat can effect a landing. Anything needed between times, such as fresh meat, fruit and vegetables — plus incidentals — must be back-packed in from Clo-oose. And it isn't just a matter of slogging over eight miles of rough bush trail and ordering the stuff over the counter. It has to be ordered from Victoria weeks ahead. The freight comes by the regular steamer and is landed on the beach by the Indians in their canoes; and as there is no place to store it, and no place for perishables, one has to be there when the steamer arrives. Often if weather interferes with a landing at Clo-oose, mail and freight is put ashore at Port Renfrew, from which point an Indian fishboat brings it when the seas moderate.

To vote, the lightkeeper and his assistant must also walk the trail to Clo-oose. The round trip takes the best part of a day, and as one or the other must be on duty at all times, elections come and go with one or the other not exercising his franchise. And as the trail is too rugged for the average housewife, their wives never vote.

When the telephone line (abandoned with the introduction of radio telephone) was in operation, linesmen kept open the Clo-oose trail, and also the twelve-mile stretch between the lighthouse and Port Renfrew, but now both are overgrown with brush and the foot bridges out of repair. The linesman is no longer a constant visitor. Now the only callers are the crew members of the tender, an occasional timber cruiser and wandering Indians.

But now and then the sea brings an unwilling visitor — as in the case of the lone American fisherman, in October 1955. Vigilance is a vital part of a lightkeeper's routine and on that score his wife is usually just as conscientious. On that October morning, keeper Wellard observed a fishboat drifting about half a mile off shore. That was nothing unusual he thought, for often he had seen the same thing happen; its engine had probably "conked" and it would soon be on its way again. Shortly afterwards, through her telescope, always kept handy, Mrs. Wellard noticed the boat wallowing helplessly in the breakers and its lone occupant frantically waving what appeared to be his shirt.

The boat was now filled and bumping heavily on the bottom. Any minute it might break up, which it eventually did. If a life was to be saved, no time must be lost. The station skiff would be useless in those breakers, even if it could be launched. Wellard waded into the surf, fought the undertow and finally reached the fishboat. He managed to get a rope around the fisherman's waist, pulled him after him through the sea and got him safely ashore. Injured slightly and suffering from shock, the man was taken care of at the lighthouse. Two days later he was picked up by a United States Coastguard helicopter and taken to Port Angeles. For this exploit, His Honour Lieutenant-Governor Frank M. Ross, at a special investiture held at Government House, presented Gerald David Wellard with the parchment award of the Royal Humane Association of Canada for saving life.

The year following, another American fishboat, this time with two men on board, was wrecked during the night not far from the lighthouse. Both men, however, managed to reach shore and guided by the light's beam, found their own way to the station. The next day, they also were picked up by a United States Coastguard helicopter and taken to Port Angeles.

In case of sickness or other emergency, the tender will make a special call at Carmanah, but as landing in front of the light is possible only when the sea is comparatively calm — which during the winter months is seldom — some other means of bringing help has to be resorted to. The flat sandstone formation, peculiar to this part of the coast, fortunately provides ideal landing space for helicopters. Lightkeeper Wellard (since transferred to Pachena Point) and his assistant, when suddenly stricken with serious illness (on different occasions) were both brought to hospital at Victoria by helicopter, as were the shipwrecked American fishermen to Port Angeles. Currently (1961), the Department of Transport is building special platforms on which helicopters can land at most up-coast lighthouses. Nature built the one at Carmanah.

Compared with other light stations, Carmanah is somewhat favoured, inasmuch as it has sheltered space, and the necessary soil, for a fair sized vegetable and flower garden. And in spite of the prowling cougar and mink — and the swooping hawks — both the lightkeeper and his assistant raise chickens. Station library shelves are well stocked, each mail brings a bundle of magazines and now the womenfolk can talk to their friends over the radio telephone. At least, that is the way of things at Carmanah.

Most lightkeepers and their families enjoy the life. Possibly, the most isolated stations on the British Columbia coast are Langara and Cape St. James, respectively at the extreme north and south end of the Queen Charlotte Islands. However, seniority counts and the lightkeepers at these isolated and inaccessible places will in time be transferred to stations nearer civilization.

WRECK OF THE
JANET COWAN

*Sixty years after, son sees cabin
which sheltered his father.*

ON DECEMBER 31, 1895, the four-masted iron barque *Janet Cowan*,
2,497 tons, registered at Greenock, Scotland, was wrecked about
four miles east of Pachena Point when 108 days out of Capetown.
Bound for Royal Roads, whence, after discharging ballast, she was
to proceed to Hastings Mill to load a return cargo of lumber for
South Africa, she arrived off Cape Flattery on December 28.

There was a terrific storm off the Cape and the vessel stood off
for two days before trying to come in. Then she was driven quickly
northward by a strong southeast wind and sought the shelter of
Barkley Sound. Caught by the inshore current, she was forced ashore
on the exposed coast in the vicinity of Pachena Point, within a mile
of where the barque *Sarah* was lost, November 1891, the schooner
Laura Pike in March 1891, and the *Valencia* on January 22, 1906.

The seas were too rough to launch a boat, but a volunteer seaman
defied them and swam to the shore with a line. A breeches-buoy was
rigged and soon the entire twenty-nine-man crew reached the safety
of the land. However, seven of their number, including the ship's
master, perished while waiting ten days for help to come.

Finding a telephone wire, strung from tree to tree, seven men
followed it and came to a cabin about a mile to the west. It was
one of several built at intervals along this stretch of coast especially
for just such an emergency, and stocked with provisions and dry
wood. A notice on the wall read: "Shipwrecked sailors help your-
selves," so they decided to stay there. There was a telephone, but
the line was down. Actually, the storm had broken the line in many
places and the linesmen at both ends, Cape Beale and Carmanah,
were doing their best to repair it. But no sooner was one break

repaired, when another occurred and it was weeks before they came upon the wreck.

Certain that sooner or later some vessel would come to their rescue, and fearing if no one was on hand at the scene of the wreck its captain might presume that all hands were lost, or taken off by another vessel, and sail away again, the remainder of the crew elected to stay where they were. The stronger men must remain there anyway, to care for those unable to walk even a short distance along that rugged shoreline. Daily communication, however, was maintained between the two parties, and the supplies at the cabin shared.

During those ten days, Captain Thompson, two able seamen and the ship's cook died from exposure, while a third seaman went out of his mind and subsequently died. During an attempt to board the stricken vessel — fast on the rocks a short distance from shore but still upright — to obtain further provisions, blankets and medical supplies for their sick and injured comrades, another seaman and two apprentices were drowned, and the second mate broke his leg.

Finally, the Seattle tug *Tyee*, which had just freed an outward bound sailing ship off Cape Flattery, sighted the wreck and within a few hours had the fifteen survivors safe on board and took them to Port Townsend. The seven men at the cabin preferred to wait for a Canadian ship. One came the following day and took them to Victoria. The bodies of those who died, and two of the drowned men, were recovered some months later, taken to Victoria and buried in Ross Bay cemetery.

One of the seven seaman who occupied the cabin was a twenty-year-old named William A. Walker, who hailed from Hull, but had signed on at Barry Dock, Wales. Given his discharge by the wreck commissioner at Victoria, he subsequently returned to England, married and raised a family.

To his children he often related his experiences as a sailor on the *Janet Cowan* which ended so tragically in the winter of 1895-1896. Long after ex-seaman Walker died, his son, William Edward, now married with two children, went to live at La Mesa, California. He determined at the first opportunity to visit the scene of the wreck, if it could be reached, and the emergency cabin — if it were still there. It had afforded shelter to his father and possibly saved him from death by exposure.

In June 1958, a little better than sixty-three years after the *Janet Cowan* tragedy, Mr. Walker, accompanied by his wife and their two children, arrived at Victoria in the family station wagon. His immediate objective was Pachena Point lighthouse, but the problem was how to get there, for there is no road to that part of the West Coast, only logging grades. Officials of the logging company, when approached, proved most coöperative. Permission to use these grades was granted and that night the family camped at Pachena Bay, on the ocean front about three miles south of Cape Beale.

From here, Mrs. Walker takes up the story of the hospitality they received at the lighthouse, and the culmination of her husband's cherished wish:

Up at 4 a.m. and after a breakfast prepared the previous evening, we set out to walk to Pachena Point. The seven-mile trail led through dense vegetation almost like jungle, with trees, head-high ferns and everything overgrown with moss and creepers. Wild flowers carpeted the clear spaces and the walk was very pleasant, with views of ocean here and there.

This was to be our first visit to a lighthouse and we had visions of the lightkeeper being a "nice old man" who probably wouldn't object to the children being left to play around his lighthouse while Johnnie (my husband's nickname) and I went on alone, for the scene of the wreck — we had been informed — was four miles farther on. We had lunch with us. Failing this, I was to stay with the children and Johnnie would go on by himself.

Soon the light tower showed up, and to our surprise it was surrounded by numerous freshly painted buildings, in fact a small settlement (Until recently, Pachena Point was also an important wireless and weather-reporting station, hence the extra dwelling houses formerly occupied by the operators and their families, office and power plant).

Then a sleepy feminine voice called out across from one of the houses, "Welcome, strangers." This was our introduction to "Mary", the wife of Gerald "Gerry" Wellard, the lightkeeper at Pachena Point. It was now 7 a.m. and Gerry and Mary had only just risen, but they insisted we join them at breakfast, and I must say that after that long walk, a second one was appreciated. It also fortified us for the hike still ahead.

I was agreeably surprised to find such a pleasant and comfortably furnished home, very different to the quarters I had imagined a lighthouse keeper to have. Canada takes care of these very important people. Another surprise was to learn that Mary was born at Harrogate, England, the town where I was born; that Clarence, one of the assistant lightkeepers, came from Hull, the birthplace of Johnnie's father. This made our visit that much more interesting.

Gerry knew where the *Janet Cowan* went ashore, on a reef a short distance from shore about four miles east of the point. He had it marked on a large map, along with other shipwrecks which had occurred in that vicinity. As the sea was calm and the day quite warm, he suggested taking us out in the station boat, that we might have a look at the place from the sea.

Nothing could have appealed to us more. Accordingly, the boat

167

was lowered into the sea by the station hoist, and we followed in the same manner. This was an exciting experience; getting into the bonnet sling on the cliff, and then dropping through the air, over the sea, to the boat 100 feet below.

The sling is used for hoisting supplies out of the lighthouse tender's workboat. It consists of heavy canvas with short lengths of rope attached to an iron ring. Goods are loaded into the sling in the bottom of the boat. The hoist on top of the cliff lowers a big hook. On the cable immediately above the hook is a 75-pound weight (to bring it down). The hook is fitted into the ring and the load goes up.

We were informed that during this operation, especially when big seas are running, split-second timing with the rise and fall of the swells is required of both the boat's crew and the hoistman on the cliff, lest someone (in the boat) gets hits on the head with the heavy hook.

Persons riding in the sling sit back to back, facing outwards. As the sling lifts, it folds up, thus you ride in a doubled-up position with legs dangling in the air; not very graceful, especially for women, but its safe. All land in a heap.

We saw the reef on which the *Janet Cowan* came to grief. Gerry told us that the west coast of Vancouver Island was once known to mariners as the "Graveyard of the Pacific"; that forty ships, mostly sailing vessels, had been wrecked on the stretch of coast we were looking at (between Pachena Point and Bonilla Point), one for every mile. Also, that the rusting plates of some of the iron ships can still be seen at low tide. We also saw, partly hidden in the trees, the cabin, but a landing was impossible owing to the ground swells.

On our way back, the fin of a monster shark suddenly appeared on the surface only a short distance away. Gerry, a man completely without fear, thought it would be fun to ride the boat over the shark's back, which he promptly did. I wonder how many people would appreciate Gerry's idea of fun. He explained later that it was a basking shark, common in these waters, quite harmless and too lazy even to get out of a boat's way. This one he estimated to be over 20 feet long.

The next few moments had the quality of a nightmare. The shark dived and there was a tail at least four feet across silhouetted against the sky. Then the tail came slap down on the sea quite near us as if Mr. Shark was saying, "Take that." The boat rocked violently and all were drenched with the splash. I must admit that all the way back to the station I kept casting glances over my shoulder, dreading to see more fins surfacing, and it was quite a relief to get back onto dry land. Notwithstanding Gerry's assurances, the idea of providing a breakfast for a shark didn't appeal to us one little bit.

After a wonderful lunch which Mary had ready, the children were left to explore the mysteries of the lighthouse, while Johnnie and I set out for the cabin. The now abandoned trail was so overgrown with brush, we took to the beach. It was very rocky, littered with driftwood and wreckage, and in places piled high with slimy kelp, but we found it the easiest way. Searching among the debris I was lucky enough to find a large green glass ball, the kind Japanese fishermen use for floats. It had floated all the way across the Pacific. I brought this home with me as a souvenir. Later we found two smaller ones, which the children will keep. Finally we reached the cabin, which, though shored-up, was in a surprisingly good state of repair. On the wall was an ancient telephone, with, for the convenience of shipwrecked sailors, instructions how to use it printed in several different languages. There were moth-eaten blankets, matches, dry wood, medical supplies and canned goods, or what was left of them.

We took several pictures, and only then did I notice that my husband's eyes were moist, and I knew that he was remembering what his father had gone through on that tragic night of December 31, 1895, and the ten days which followed.

There were lots of bears around, really big brutes judging by their tracks, so we hurried to get back to the lighthouse before dark, where a welcome dinner awaited us. Our hosts had previously insisted that we stay overnight, and I must say that we hadn't protested very much at the idea. From somewhere pyjama jackets were found for the children, a pyjama suit for Johnnie and a glamorous nightie and housecoat for me. This was sheer and unexpected luxury, in a lighthouse, of all places. So was the welcome hot bath.

Awoke to a wet day. Our hosts did their best to persuade us to stay another night, but our time was limited. We left with pleasant memories of the wonderful hospitality extended four complete strangers by a Canadian lighthouse keeper and his wife.

GLASS BALLS THAT
CROSS THE OCEAN

GLASS BALLS are one of the most popular souvenirs picked up on the exposed beaches of the west coast of Vancouver Island — particularly after a bad storm. They are used as house ornaments or for decorative effect in the front garden. Occasionally, they are displayed in city stores and passers-by often ask the question, "What are they?"

They are fish-net floats, broken adrift from fishermen's nets off the Japanese coast and drifted across the Pacific to be finally cast up on our shores. Their colour scheme covers a wide range, varying from dark green, the most common, to a bluish-purple and in some cases crystal clear. In size they vary from four to eighteen inches in diameter.

They are invariably clean and shiny when found, though occasionally one turns up covered with a mass of grasses and small barnacles, indicating a sea voyage of perhaps several years. How long they usually take crossing the Pacific, one can only guess. But at that we have a fair idea. Bottle messages are found indicating that they had been dropped overboard from some Japanese hydrographic survey vessel somewhere off the coast of Japan and requesting the finder to notify the nearest Japanese consul of the locality and date of its finding. While checks between the date dropped overboard and when recovered usually varied over a range of from one to several years, one bottle picked up near Kyuquot showed that its long journey had occupied only a little over six months.

The same would apply to the glass balls. The throwing overboard of the bottles with messages inside is for the purpose of tracing ocean currents and drifts. This is common practice with all maritime countries and a $1.00 reward is usually paid the finder.

Sealed earthenware jugs, vase-like in shape, no two exactly alike and some with handles, are also found washed up on our beaches. Their origin is a mystery, though the design is definitely Oriental. Bamboo poles, practically unobtainable in this country, are what fishermen like to pick up. Found in all lengths and from one to four inches in diameter, they serve many useful purposes on a fishing vessel. Because of their extreme buoyancy, with a string of corks attached to help, they are used extensively by halibut fishermen as floating markers for their set lines, with a small coloured flag atop which identifies the owner of the gear. Our salmon fishermen use either cork, cedarwood or plastic floats to hold up their nets. Herring fishermen, the same, but as the latter often find several hundred tons of fish in their net at one time, inflated leather bags placed at intervals along the corkline are used to supplement the floats.

The deadly floating mines of World War II have also been found on this coast. Fortunately no vessel encountered one, though for years they were a menace to shipping. The mines disposal section of the Royal Canadian Navy has performed a remarkably good job in destroying most of those sighted and all that were washed ashore (most of them on the west coast of Vancouver Island), but not without injury and loss of life to several of its personnel.

S.S. QUADRA

*Ran the gamut from champagne
to rum.*

A LITTLE BEFORE MIDNIGHT, a schooner-rigged vessel hove round
the coast into Esquimalt harbour; her whistle pouring forth notes of
gladness in her arrival in what will, in future, be her home.

The above news item is from the files of the Victoria *Daily
Colonist*, dated January 6, 1892.

She was the new lighthouse tender *Quadra*, fresh from the
builder's yards at Paisley, Scotland, and destined to become one of
the best-known ships that ever sailed British Columbia waters. She
had left Greenock on the Firth of Clyde on October 15, of the
previous year. The sixty-nine-day voyage by way of the Strait of
Magellan was uneventful. To save coal, she had her canvas spread
most of the way out.

The *Quadra* was named after Capitan de navio Juan Francisco
de la Bodega y Quadra, a Spanish naval officer who explored this
coast between 1775 and 1793, and was at one time governor of
Nootka. Built at Paisley by Fleming and Ferguson, she was a single-
screw steel ship of 573 tons; length 175 feet, 31-foot beam and
with 120 h.p. quadruple engines. Her speed was 12 knots.

She was specially designed as a lighthouse tender to replace the
small wooden vessel *Sir James Douglas* and was fitted with heavy
lifting gear. Captain John T. Walbran brought her out and continued to command her till 1908. The other deck officers, the chief
engineer and guarantee officer, all returned to Scotland immediately
after she was handed over. Upon being commissioned, the following,
in addition to Captain Walbran, took over: Chief Officer W. G.
Owen and Second Officer Charles Barnes, who afterwards became
master of both the lighthouse tenders *Newington* and *Estevan*. Chief

Engineer was Gordon F. Grant and Second, W. J. Cullum, who later became steamship inspector at Victoria.

In those days, there were no lighthouses north of Nanaimo on the east coast, and Cape Beale on the west coast of Vancouver Island; only buoys marking the entrance to harbours and some of the channels. And there was no Prince Rupert. Port Simpson was then the principal settlement on the northern British Columbia coast. The Hudson's Bay Company had a trading post there and it was also the site of what few government agencies there were in those days.

The *Quadra* had to take care of the whole coast. Now there are five lighthouse tenders. Also about this time, the big gas buoys were being installed and this job called for a much larger ship than the *Sir James Douglas*. Lighthouses then had steam engines to operate the air compressors for the foghorns. These consumed coal which had to be landed by workboat and then carried up to the light in sacks. This called for extra work on the part of the tender's crew and it sometimes took days to land one station's supplies. Now the compressors are run by gas or diesel engines, and each station has a hoist.

As there were no fisheries patrol vessels, the *Quadra* had to double-up in that capacity. Inlets had to be watched during the salmon runs, halibut fishing in Hecate Strait supervised and off-shore patrols made to enforce the fur-sealing regulations. Brushes with sealing schooners were common.

Law enforcement agencies were few and far between and the *Quadra*'s master had to be a fisheries inspector and magistrate. Wages and price disputes had to be settled to the satisfaction of all concerned and when trouble occurred among the fishermen, or a boat was found poaching, the case was tried there and then on board.

Except for naval vessels stationed at Esquimalt and not available for non-naval tasks, the *Quadra* was the only government boat of any size on the coast and in addition to her regular duties was frequently called upon to make special trips and take departmental officials from place to place. She took the post office, customs and public works department inspectors on their annual tours of inspection and often made a hurried trip to some trouble spot with the police, or a doctor in an outbreak of smallpox or other emergency.

One memorable trip was in 1900, when the *Quadra* took His Excellency the Governor-General Earl Minto and Lady Minto from Victoria to Skagway. From Skagway the party travelled to Whitehorse via the White Pass and Yukon Railway, and then by the river steamer *Canadian*, to Dawson. The *Quadra* waited at Skagway and then brought them back to Victoria, the round trip occupying six weeks. The governor-general's party consisted of six and included his own chef, for whose convenience a special galley was erected on deck. T. E. Morrison, retired marine agent at Victoria, who was messboy on the *Quadra* and one of its only two surviving crew members of that time, recalls one of the mouth-watering specialties this cook served — roast turkey basted with champagne. The other crew member still living is J. E. McDonald, also of Victoria. Mr. McDonald, then an able-bodied seaman, subsequently became her chief officer.

Another vice-regal trip the *Quadra* made was when Earl Grey was governor-general. In addition to Grey and his two daughters, the party included Lord Lascelles, who afterwards became the husband of Princess Mary. This time a leisurely cruise was made up the coast as far as Alaska and the male members of the party did considerable hunting and fishing at the head of the numerous inlets visited.

When the Grand Trunk Pacific Railway was seeking a suitable site for its western terminus, the *Quadra* took President Charles M. Hayes, who later lost his life in the *Titanic* disaster, and ten company officials, on a very hush-hush trip up north. Not a man in the *Quadra*'s crew had the faintest inkling of its purpose. The party in turn visited Quatsino Sound, Kitimat, Port Essington, Metlakatla, Port Simpson and several other places. When they went ashore they took the ship's steam launch and had their own man to run it. The site where Prince Rupert now stands was subsequently selected, but the *Quadra*'s crew didn't know they had even been there. The G.T.P. subsequently became the C.N.R.

As more lighthouses were built and other navigation aids installed, the *Newington* was purchased in 1909 to assist the *Quadra*, and in 1913 the *Estevan* was built. Soon it became necessary to establish a separate agency at Prince Rupert, to take care of all lighthouses and aids to navigation between the northern tip of Vancouver Island and Alaska, and on both coasts of the Queen Charlotte Islands. In turn, the following tenders operated out of Prince Rupert: *Catherine B*, *Birnie*, *Alberni* and *Alexander Mackenzie*.

For years, the small tender *Berens*, based at Victoria, serviced the Gulf of Georgia and adjacent waters. She has since been replaced by the new tender *Sir James Douglas*, which also alternates with the *Estevan*. The department's newest tenders are the combined ice-breaker and tender *Camsell* and *Simon Fraser*, both $3-million ships. Bigger ones still are now being built.

On February 26, 1917, the *Quadra* was in collision with the C.P.R. steamer *Charmer* at the entrance to Nanaimo harbour, at 3:30 p.m. in fog. The *Quadra* was beached to prevent her from sinking in deep water. Only a portion of her funnel and masts were visible at high tide. That ended her career as a lighthouse tender. She was later refloated and sold to Britannia Mines, who used her to carry ore concentrates from Howe Sound to the Tacoma smelter.

The *Quadra* afterwards became a rum-runner and after making several very successful trips, on October 24, 1924, was seized by the United States Coastguard cutter *Shawnee* while discharging liquor to a speedboat off the California coast, and towed in to San Francisco. Ship and her cargo valued at $1 million on the San Francisco market were confiscated and her captain fined $1,000 and given two years in jail. Twelve other defendants (mostly her crew) were also fined and given jail sentences, but all jumped bail and returned to Canada. Litigation over the seizure lasted several years, during which time most of the cargo "evaporated". As the ship itself hadn't been dry-docked for several years she suffered considerable deterioration. She was subsequently sold at public auction by the United States Marshall for the sum of $1,625, and broken up for scrap.

CAPTAIN JOHN T. WALBRAN

Master of the Quadra.

CAPTAIN WALBRAN was born at Ripon, Yorkshire, on March 23, 1848, and educated at the local grammar school. At fourteen, he was a cadet on H.M. SCHOOL FRIGATE *Conway*, passing out on July 1864 with an "extra" certificate endorsed "conduct excellent and ability good." His first ship was the *Bedfordshire*, owned by Boult & Company, and by 1881 he had received his master mariner's certificate, issued at the Port of Liverpool. In 1888 he joined the Canadian Pacific Navigation Company as First Officer of the *Islander* and in 1890 had charge of the s.s. *Danube*, which was afterwards purchased by the B.C. Salvage Company and renamed the *Salvor*.

Captain Walbran joined the Canadian marine and fisheries service in 1891 and attended the building of the *Quadra* at Paisley, Scotland; commanded her on the passage out and was in charge of her from 1891 to 1908 — engaged in the lighthouse, buoy and fisheries service on the British Columbia coast.

Under his command, the *Quadra* was run man-of-war fashion. Although her crew members were all signed on as civilian seamen, they wore sailor-rig uniforms. Captain Walbran wore a frock-coat and "shipped" a long sword. He had twelve Martini-Henry rifles on board and the crew were trained in their use. He held church service and roll-call on deck every Sunday morning. He was also a stipendiary magistrate.

His book, *British Columbia Coast Names*, which was written after his retirement and published by the Geographic Board of Canada, is today a standard reference on the subject. Captain Walbran died at Victoria on March 31, 1913. His home, on Dallas Road at Menzies, still stands.

The *Quadra*'s Master, Captain John T. Walbran. He ran his ship man-of-war style, with church service on deck every Sunday morning. *Provincial Archives Photo.*

s.s. *Santa Rita* ashore near Clo-oose. Crew reached shore and vessel subsequently broke up. *Photo courtesy Alex Chisholm.*

Treacherous entrance to Nitinat Lake, where many ships came to grief while attempting to cross the bar. *W. H. Gold Photo.*

Six miles west of Nitinat Lake outlet, Tsusiat Falls pour directly onto beach over 80-foot cliff. *W. H. Gold Photo.*

Steamer *Valencia*, San Francisco to Victoria, wrecked on Pachena Point, January 23, 1906, with the loss of 117 lives. *Provincial Archives Photo.*

Grim relic of yet another sea tragedy. Boiler of the steamer *Michigan*, wrecked near Pachena Point in 1893. *Photo courtesy Alex Chisholm.*

Photo shows armed Russian supply ship *Uzbekistan* broken in two after running aground near Pachena Point, April 30, 1943. The crew, including several women, reached shore. *Photo by J. Logvinoff, Bamfield.*

Author with fishermen's glass ball floats picked up on a West Coast beach. These drift across the ocean from Japan. *Lorraine Murdoch Photo.*

Lighthouse Tender *Quadra*, which ran the gamut from champagne to rum. *Provincial Archives Photo.*

Carmanah Point Lighthouse, the scene of many shipwrecks. *Department of Marine Photo.*

BREAKERS BEACH, NEAR BAMFIELD
B.C. Government Travel Bureau Photo

THE NORTH END
OF THE ISLAND

QUATSINO SOUND, which with its numerous arms, has more than seventy miles of navigable inland waters, is the last of a series of deep indentations into Vancouver Island's west coast. Rupert Arm, at the far end and barely seven miles across to tidewater on the east coast, almost severs that part of the island lying to the northwest (Cape Scott) from the island proper.

The name is an adaptation of the word "Koskimo", the name of the once numerous and powerful tribe of Indians who resided there. Koskimo, their principal village, was just inside the Sound on the south shore. On Galiano's chart, and also Vancouver's, the Sound is shown without a name. On the Admiralty chart of 1849, it is named Quatsinough Harbour. The Sound was surveyed by Captain Richards in H.M. SHIPS *Plumper* and *Hecate,* 1860-1862.

A lighthouse on Kairns Island, formerly Entrance Island, guards the entrance on the north side. It was established in 1907. Gillam Islands, a small group in the middle of the steamer channel, were named after Captain E. Gillam, long-time master of the *Princess Maquinna.* Winter Harbour on Forward Inlet (named after H.M. GUNBOAT *Forward*), immediately inside the light, can rightfully claim to be Vancouver Island's farthest west settlement and post office. Its population comprises about fifty families, principally engaged in fishing and logging.

Twenty miles inside the Sound, on the northern shore, is Quatsino village, the oldest white settlement on this part of the coast, whose original settlers were all of Scandinavian descent. Extending from here southeast is Neroutsos Inlet, named after Captain C. D. Neroutsos, at one time manager of B.C. Coast Steamships (C.P.R.).

It was formerly known as Alice Arm, the name being changed so not to conflict with a similar one on the northern British Columbia coast.

At the head of the inlet is a pulp mill and the town of Port Alice with a population of about five hundred. For years, this was the terminus of the West Coast steamer run from Victoria. The seven-day round trip was maintained for over thirty years by the *Princess Maquinna* and *Princess Norah*, each with accommodation for 200 passengers. Many considered it equal to the Alaska trip scenically. The steamer usually remained at Port Alice for twenty-four hours loading pulp, allowing the passengers ample time to stretch their legs, take in the sights, or fish in nearby Victoria Lake. And there was always a dance in the local hall. Quatsino village, where fresh fruit from the well-kept orchards of the local residents could be purchased, was another favourite port of call.

Interesting stopping places like these are now past history, for no longer do passenger steamers serve Quatsino Sound. All travel in and out of the Sound now goes overland by road from Coal Harbour to Port Hardy on the east coast, where connection is made by airplane or steamer. Nor is there a freight boat from Victoria anymore (the *Maquinna* carried both freight and passengers). Supplies are brought in by steamer and barges out of Vancouver via the north end of the island.

Passing through scenic Quatsino Narrows, one enters Holberg Inlet which is thirty miles long and lies due east and west. Across from the narrows is Stephens Bay, named after Sir Phillip Stephens, secretary to the Admiralty. Known locally (and on land maps) as Coal Harbour, which is also the name of its post office, this is the commencement point of the eleven-mile road which crosses the island to Port Hardy. In the same bay, on the site of a former seaplane base, used by the R.C.A.F. during the Second World War, is a whaling station, the only one on this coast.

At the western end of Holberg Inlet is Holberg settlement and post office, headquarters of a big logging camp. Nearby is an R.C.A.F. installation. A road once led from Holberg to within a few miles of Cape Scott at the extreme tip of the island. Late in the 1890's, about fifty settlers homesteaded in this area, but finding it too costly to bring in supplies, and the market too far away for their products, one by one they moved away. Now there are none. The road is overgrown with trees, and the bridges in a state of disrepair.

The coast between Quatsino Sound and Cape Scott is desolate indeed. Entirely devoid of habitation, it offers no shelter for ships, big or small. Fishing vessels sometimes anchor in San Josef Bay, but only when the seas are calm, which is seldom. Then, if the truth were known, the excellent goose shooting to be had there is the attraction. In San Josef Bay, the American brig *Consort*, Honolulu to Puget Sound, was wrecked during a gale on November 15, 1860. Passengers and crew, 22 in all, reached shore safely and were subsequently taken to Victoria by H.M. GUNBOAT *Forward* (see page 83). Wrecked in San Josef Bay, March 24, 1892, the schooner *Henry Dennis*; crew saved, vessel total loss.

Cape Scott was named in 1786 by Captains Lawrie and Guise, of the snows *Captain Cook* and *Experiment*, after David Scott, the Bombay merchant who assisted in fitting out their trading expedition from that port. In 1910, a lighthouse was erected atop Triangle Island, 25 miles due west, but was abandoned ten years later (see page 186). A wireless station, maintained in conjunction with the lighthouse but operated by a separate staff, was dismantled at the same time and re-established at Bull Harbour. Not until 1960 was a lighthouse established at Cape Scott itself.

The inhospitable Scott Islands lie between Cape Scott and Triangle Island. These have had several different names. Captain Hanna in the *Sea Otter*, 1786, named the group Lance's Islands, at the same time naming the easternmost one Cox Island after John Henry Cox, a merchant residing in China who assisted in fitting out his expedition. Captain George Dixon in the *Queen Charlotte*, 1787, named them Beresford's Islands after his clerk and supercargo, William Beresford. Meares adopted Hanna's name, calling the group Lancie's Islands. In Galiano's large Spanish chart, the group is named impartially, the eastern portion being designated Lanz Islands and the western, Beresford Islands. On Vancouver's chart, published in 1798, they are named Scott's Islands, from their situation off Cape Scott. As the channels between are strewn with partially submerged reefs, they are used only by small coastal steamers and fishing boats — and then only in good weather.

It was in one of these channels in 1899 that the sloop *Floyborg*, used by the Cape Scott settlers to bring their supplies from Shushartie Bay, hit a rock and was afterwards beached — a total loss — in Erasmus Bay, near where the schooner *Louisa Downs* was lost with all hands in March 1868. The whaling barque *Hermit* was lost in the same vicinity, March 1892.

Also in 1892, wreckage postively identified (by another schooner captain) as that from the sealing schooner *Maggie Mac*, was found in a small cove just below Cape Scott. The vessel sailed from Vic-

179

toria in January and is believed to have been wrecked among the Scott Islands; not a trace of her crew ever found and the last word, a letter from her captain to her owners, was written and dated, Clayoquot, in March. In 1923, the tug *Quinitsa*, Vancouver to Port Alice with a scow load of machinery in tow, met with bad weather after rounding Cape Scott and when putting into Sea Otter Cove for shelter, piled up on a reef. She was salvaged later, when her hull was found to have suffered little damage. *Quinitsa* was Island Tug and Barge Company's first and only tugboat; name changed later to *Island Planet*. On January 16, 1943, the steamer *Northolm*, Port Alice to Vancouver with pulp, was swamped by heavy seas while attempting to round Cape Scott, fifteen of her seventeen-man crew drowned.

The extreme north coastline of Vancouver Island faces Queen Charlotte Sound, named in 1786 after Queen Charlotte, wife of King George III. First shelter of any kind is at Bull Harbour on Hope Island, 25 miles to the east, where there is a wireless station and a small settlement, the headquarters of a large fishing fleet during the summer months.

Bull Harbour was known by this name to officers of the Hudson's Bay Company and was probably named at an earlier date from the number of fierce sea lions (bulls), to be found in the neighbourhood. Sir George Simpson mentioned the harbour in 1841, and the sea lion population. Hope Island was named in 1864 by Captain Richards, after Vice-Admiral Sir James Hope, K.C.B., commander-in-chief, North America and West Indies station, 1864-1867. Bute Passage, named after John Stuart, third Earl of Bute, separates Hope Island from Nigei Island, immediately to the east and which, until 1900, was known as Galiano Island. It was changed to Nigei by the Geographic Board of Canada to avoid duplication (Galiano Island in the Strait of Georgia). Nigei is the hereditary name of the principal chief of the Nahwitti Indians, a tribe which years ago held undisputed sway on the northern shores of Vancouver Island.

Goletas Channel separates these two islands from Vancouver Island proper. It was named by Galiano and Valdes during their exploring voyage in 1792 around what is now known as Vancouver Island, after the schooners (in Spanish *Goletas*) *Sutil* and *Mexicana*; naming at the same time the south point of the western entrance after the former, and the northern after the latter. The vessels passed out to sea by this channel on their way to Nootka. On the Vancouver Island side of the channel is Shushartie Bay, another fishing settlement and post office. The name is an adaptation of

"Zuzanda", the old Indian name of the bay meaning in Kwakwala language a "place possessing cockles." There is an extensive tidal flat at the head of Shushartie Bay where shellfish abound. The name was adopted by officers of the Hudson's Bay Company in 1838. Shushartie Saddle, a double-topped mountain, is named from its association with the bay.

A few miles to the southeast is Port Hardy, the terminus of the road from Coal Harbour on Quatsino Sound. Thus we make a complete circuit of the northern end of Vancouver Island.

GEORGE NORDSTROM, Justice of the Peace and Coroner at Quatsino, is the oldest living member of that district's original pioneer settlers. His father, Chris Nordstrom, together with his brother Frederick and nine others, all of Scandinavian descent, arrived there in October 1894. George was then a lad of twelve.

The group comprised, in addition to the two Nordstroms, Halvar O. Bergh, Edjus Evensen, Halvor Norby, Harald Strandwold, Swan Lendin, Bernard Lukken, Ole Sherberg, A. Flot and E. Skideen. Two were bachelors, the others married, most with families who accompanied them. They came from Fargo, North Dakota, making the journey to the coast by rail.

At Victoria they learned about the wonderful possibilities which Quatsino Sound then offered, both for industry and mixed farming. It was to be the terminal port for transpacific liners; compared with Victoria and Vancouver, this meant a day's steaming time nearer the Orient. Docks were already planned and the Grand Trunk Pacific Railway would terminate there (Prince Rupert was later chosen). Settlers were already taking up land in the Cape Scott area. Extensive iron and copper discoveries had been made.

The steam schooner *Mischief*, Captain Foote, which then made intermittent trips up the West Coast with passengers, mail and freight, was chartered and the party duly arrived at Coal Harbour, on the West Arm. There they wintered, occupying vacant cabins of an abandoned coal mine. The coal mining operation had been initiated in 1881 by a San Francisco syndicate. The caretaker, who was still there, not only welcomed the new arrivals, but proved most helpful in his knowledge of the district.

Next spring, after having explored the area for homesites, the settlers chose a site for the village, where Quatsino now stands. Chris Nordstrom then went to Victoria to consult the lands office. He subsequently obtained a Colony Charter and in due course a government survey party arrived. The limits of the land grant were defined, houses soon sprang up and that was the origin of Quatsino village. Men, women and children, the population numbered about thirty.

Long before the arrival of Quatsino's first settlers, Ned Frigon, a French-Canadian from Quebec, had established himself as a fur trader at Koprino Harbour. After the newcomers arrived, he moved to Quiet Cove on Limestone Island, not far from the village, and built a combined store, hotel and saloon, where he did business for several years. Finally taking up a new homestead on the southeast arm, now Neroutsos Inlet, he lived with "Long-headed Lucy," his common-law wife, an Indian, and died there at the age of ninety-two.

Frigon, prior to coming to Quatsino Sound, had led a colourful career. In 1849, he walked across the Isthmus of Panama to join the gold rush into California. With no luck in the gold fields, he came to Victoria, stayed there a few years then chartered a schooner to take him, with lumber and supplies, to Hope Island, where he established a fur trading business.

The Indians, not long after he settled there, planned his murder to get his stock of trade goods. A young squaw who was living with him warned him of the plot and Frigon, after having loaded six Hudson's Bay muskets with buckshot, made secure all doors and windows that night. However, the night passed without his being molested; discovery that all means of ingress had been securely barred, indicated to the Indians that Frigon had been forewarned.

Frigon then had a trusty Indian take a letter to Fort Rupert. It was addressed to the law enforcement authorities at Victoria and months later a gunboat arrived at Hope Island. Its commander gave the Indians a severe reprimand, telling them that if any harm came to Frigon or his common-law wife on their account, he would return and lay the village low by cannon bombardment. Thereafter, Frigon never left his trading post without an escort of faithful Indians.

In 1903, Thomas Ildstad, with his family, arrived at Quatsino Sound from Leonard, Minnesota; stayed some months at Winter Harbour, where J. L. Leeson had a crab cannery, then joined the settlers at Quatsino village. The twenty-five mile voyage was undertaken in a large Indian canoe. The weather had been unsettled for days and the Indians who were to move the family of five and its belongings, were wary about going. But Ildstad told them the night before that he would petition the Good Lord for a safe passage. Next morning early, he informed them all would be well, that *Sycalee Tyee* had promised fine weather. Having studied meteorological conditions, he felt safe in this Heavenly forecast.

Household effects were loaded into the canoe, which, large as it was, soon appeared inadequate for the passengers and cargo. The Indians protested, declaring *"white man halo komtocks, mam-ook uotlamatla"* — meaning "white man not understand, makes crazy." Nevertheless, with two husky Indians as oarsmen, and a big fat klootchman, squatting in the stern and acting as steersman, the family set out in the top-heavy craft.

Clear of the sheltered harbour, the canoe was now riding moderate swells. One of the Indians then stood up, wetted his finger, held it aloft and with great satisfaction promptly announced *"Kloosh, Jesus potlatch wind."* Sure enough, soon a stiff sailing breeze was sweeping in from seaward. Up went the huge balloon-like sail and in a smother of foam the canoe went careening up sound at about eight knots. Water slopped in at every other broadside roll. This necessitated constant bailing and the family pots and pans came in handy. There were times when only a hairbreadth balance of stability stood between safety and disaster. However, within a few hours the canoe reached its destination.

Mr. Ildstad, who for years was a customs preventative officer, took a leading part in all local activities. He died in 1942. His widow, now (1962) ninety-eight and residing at Victoria, vividly remembers that nightmare canoe trip — one incident in particular.

She had set bread dough to rise the previous night, and with true economy placed the pan carefully into the canoe that morning. The rolling motion of the craft caused the batter to spill and everything in the bottom of the canoe, already thoroughly soaked, turned a milky white.

Brought along in a gunnysack was the family cat, a big black tom, which also occupied a place in the bottom of the canoe. The cat was taken ashore first, meowing angrily and water pouring from the sack. When released — now white instead of black — it headed for the woods, to show up several days later none the worse for the experience.

It was three of Quatsino's original settlers, Chris Nordstrom, Bergh and Evensen, who, in 1897, located the Yreka group of mineral claims on Quatsino Sound. They built a trail up the mountain to the 1,200-foot level and hauled all the machinery by horses to where the camp was built. A 16-foot Pelton wheel was installed to run the air compressor. About 800 feet of tunnel was run into the mountain and three shipments of copper ore made to the Tacoma smelter. The enterprise was abandoned after two successive dry summers when it was found there was insufficient water in the creek to operate the compressors. The property has changed hands many times since and is now being brought into production on a big scale.

The settlers also located the Jeune copper claims near Alice Lake. Development reached the stage where steel rails were brought in to build a tramway to the mine, but they were never laid. Jeune Landing is the headquarters of a big logging operation. A group of Quatsino prospectors, some of whom were the sons of the original pioneers, initiated the development of the Zeballos gold mine camp, 1935-1936.

There is no road connection between Quatsino Sound and Vancouver Island's highway system. This can be expected when the road is extended north from Kelsey Bay. None of Quatsino's pioneer settlers lived long enough to see it, but some of their children might.

BLIND LIGHT OF
TRIANGLE ISLAND

THE BIRDS in their sanctuary on Triangle Island cry a shrill dirge for their departed. They are alone there, and unmolested, except for the savage storms. The rare, crested puffins make their nests and guard their eggs without fear of inquisitive strangers.

The place is wild, rugged and silent — except for the perpetual murmur of the sea and the notes of the wind in the rock crevices, and the ceaseless conversation of the birds.

But it wasn't always so . . .

In 1910, Chance Bros. of Birmingham, England, a firm which has built lighthouses all over the world, set up the highest light on British Columbia's battered coast. Atop its fortress-like tower, the great Triangle light threw its beams from an elevation of 700 feet above the sea — 500 feet higher than Pachena Point, now the highest on the coast, and dwarfing Estevan's 125-foot lighthouse, Race Rock's 118, Point Atkinson's 108 and Albert Head's 88-footer.

Triangle Island was an all-round light, visible, that is, from every direction. The only trouble was that for days at a time it wasn't visible at all. Fog would shroud it, or would lie between it and the sea so that the light was lost to worried mariners hunting for its loom.

The island heaves itself like a hump or mountain out of the sea at the end of an irregular chain of islets, rocks and reefs known as the Scott group. From Cape Scott, on the northwest tip of Vancouver Island, these murderous teeth project some 25 miles. The sea, in a gale, pounds over them in frightening fury. The tides are weird and wicked there.

It would seem the logical place for a light because of the traffic to Prince Rupert, to Alaska and upper British Columbia ports, fishing boats which work in the vicinity, and transpacific ships looking for a landfall. It would have been, except for the fog. But the light was built, a wireless station established and a crew settled in. The authorities forgot to install a foghorn or, if it was considered, it was thought impractical. A foghorn should be close to sea level; and sea level at Triangle was 1,000 steps down the steep rock from the lighthouse. It would be a difficult thing for a lightkeeper to attend to. Anyway, it wasn't installed.

The fact is that Triangle's lighthouse was one of those white elephants which the best-intentioned sometimes buy. At the very times it was most needed it was out of sight — in the fog. So ten years after it was built — at great cost — it was abandoned. But not before it had driven its crew to distraction, and a tender, after landing supplies there, sailed away and was never seen again, or her crew of twenty-seven men and one woman passenger.

The glassed-in top of the lighthouse, which housed the lamp and reflectors, painted red and still intact — even to the weather-vane — today stands at the Department of Transport ship depot on Victoria's inner harbour. The wireless station was also dismantled and moved to Bull Harbour, 45 miles away round Cape Scott.

Triangle Island, named for its shape, is about five miles in circumference. Bare of everything but stunted and queerly warped vegetation, for the winds blow into flat distortion the seedlings which root there, it is the nesting place for countless sea birds and the home of sea lions.

Incredible is the velocity of the winds which sweeps the island. The wireless buildings had to be braced on all sides and further secured by guy wires, like a ship's mast stays anchored in the rock. In spite of these precautions, a hurricane in 1912 blew the towers and rigging over the cliff edge, lifted the office building off its concrete foundations and lodged it against the squat engine-room building. Only the weight of its two full water tanks kept it from following the aerials over the cliff.

On another occasion, the roof of the bachelor wireless operators' dwelling was partly blown off, windows broken and doors torn from their hinges. Out through to open spaces went most of the men's blankets, clothing and other personal belongings. Many of the articles were never recovered.

Even the huge lantern, which is the business part of a lighthouse, had to have special steel bracing built inside to prevent the heavy plate glass panes being blown out of their iron frames. It wasn't safe for the lightkeeper's children, or anyone else for that matter, to go outside in a gale. All walks between buildings had guard rails like the deck of a ship. And the houses rocked so in the high winds that their occupants were frequently seasick.

It was bleak and dreary, too, and the people who were stationed on the rock hated it. Some of the younger wireless operators claimed they were "shanghaied" to the station. The fact was, some were told they were going on relief duty for a week or so, and ended up with a suitcase full of clothes to last them twelve months.

Supplies and mail came at infrequent intervals, often two months between. The nearest safe anchorage was at Bull Harbour, 45 miles away around Cape Scott where the tender frequently had to wait for days before approaching the Triangle beaches where materials were lightered ashore or landed by breeches buoy, frequently in dangerous surf.

Men who were stationed there said the isolation was hard to bear. But the weather in winter was an even worse affliction. In summer, men might fish when off duty, watch the wheeling and nesting birds or the seals which sunned themselves on the rocks below the station. But in winter they were house-bound. Not even food relieved the monotony for there were seldom fresh vegetables, fruit or meat, and every meal had a sameness.

The first lightkeeper was James W. Davies, who first shipped aboard the tenders *Sir James Douglas* and *Quadra*, and then kept light at Scarlett Point, Egg Island, Carmanah and Pachena. The son of George Davies, British Columbia's first lightkeeper (see page 120), he retired in 1930 after 38 years with the department.

The freighter *Leebro*, temporarily chartered as a tender, took Davies, his wife and three daughters, Violet, Ella and Mona, to the rock in 1910. The girls were all of school age, but because there was no such thing as a correspondence course in those days, their tuition fell to the bachelor wireless men. These young gentlemen were delighted. And they were excellent teachers.

Mr. Davies predeceased his wife. Mrs. Davies died in Victoria in 1954, but her daughters are living: Violet, Mrs. A. Allan, agent-operator for the B.C. Telephone Company at Port Renfrew; Ella is Mrs. Edward Harris of Vancouver, and Mona, the wife of T. E. Morrison, former marine agent at Victoria.

Thomas Watkins succeeded Davies, transferred to Triple Island and died there. Then came Alec Dingwell and finally Captain Daniel O'Brien. He went to Yellow (or Chrome) Island when Triangle station was closed down; his wife was drowned there, in

Baynes Channel between Denman Island and Vancouver Island, when a rowboat in which she was a passenger capsized in the surf. Captain O'Brien himself died at Victoria some years later.

The men who served the light lived a hard life. But the men who manned the ships, the tenders which supplied the lights, lived even more precariously. It was in November, 1918, that the fisheries patrol vessel *Galiano*, doing double duty as a lighthouse tender, called at Triangle Island with supplies. She was scheduled to pick up two passengers, a Miss Brunton, who had been housekeeper for the bachelor wireless men for a year, and Sidney Elliott, one of the operators. Elliott's baggage was on the strip of beach and the first of the lighthouse freight was coming ashore when a message cancelled the operator's departure. Dejectedly he climbed the thousand steps back to the station.

Then with a suddenness which is often as terrifying as the height of a gale, a storm struck. Seamen dumped the last of the freight on the beach, snatched Miss Brunton into the work boat and headed out to the *Galiano*, which was lying uncomfortably close inshore. The work boat reached the *Galiano* safely and was hoisted aboard, and the little ship left hurriedly, steaming north for Ikeda Head wireless station in the Queen Charlottes.

That was the last anyone saw of her, her complement of 26, or Miss Brunton. The last word from the doomed ship, which probably foundered in the heavy seas, was relayed from her master, Captain Pope, by her wireless operator, Michael Neary, whose brother Jack, at Triangle, picked up the message.

"We are sinking . . ."

That was all. And that was nearly all for Triangle Island station. Two years later it was abandoned to the birds and sea lions.

ESTEVAN KEEPS
WEST COAST SAFE

WHEN ONE READS that familiar advertisement "Notice to Mariners," warning all shipping that a certain beacon is not burning, or a spar buoy out of position, it means a job for the *Estevan* on its next trip out, or a special one if the light is important.

Approaching fifty years of faithful service, by far the longest of any lighthouse tender on the British Columbia coast, the *Estevan* is still carrying on, totally oblivious to the glamour associated with ships engaged in the passenger trade, the coming and going of rusty old freighters, or the trim R.C.M.P. and Fisheries cruisers. Her business is to help keep the coast clear for all ships, from luxury liners with thousands of souls aboard down to small one-man fishing boats.

The veteran steamer still has several years of useful service ahead yet, but when the time for her retirement comes she will probably be missed, especially on the west coast of Vancouver Island, more than any boat, for tending its lighthouses and taking care of a score of gas and whistling buoys at the mouth of harbours and inlets, has always been her main task.

In between, there are innumerable blinker lights (ashore) whose gas cylinders have to be replaced from time to time, and the numerous spars and beacons which mark the channels and sandbars have to be overhauled or placed back in position after being fouled by a passing boom of logs. Aids to navigation north of Vancouver Island are taken care of by tenders based at Prince Rupert, and those between the island and the mainland by smaller vessels.

Not so much now, but in the days when there were no hospitals on the West Coast (now there are three), and no other vessel was available, *Estevan*'s captain frequently responded to an urgent call to take some sick or badly injured West Coast resident to Port Alberni.

Estevan is already missed at Union Bay, for up till 1958 she still burned coal and bunkered there regularly. Now converted to use oil, she was one of the last coal burners on the coast.

A twin-screw steel ship of 1,150 tons, *Estevan* carries a complement of eight officers (deck and engine-room) and a crew of thirty-two. Built on Lake Huron, she came out to this coast via the Panama Canal and was commissioned in May 1913. She has steam winches and is fitted with an unusually heavy foremast and boom with a safe-lifting load of 30 tons. This is for lifting the huge buoys, with their five-ton concrete anchor blocks, chains just as heavy, and the accumulation of seaweed and barnacles growing on them.

The buoys have to be overhauled every few years and one or two are usually replaced every trip. As they are all in exposed waters, the ship sometimes has to wait for days in the nearest harbour before completing the job. They are brought to Victoria where barnacles and other marine growth is removed, then repainted and the mechanism which operates the automatic light and whistling apparatus overhauled.

The very location of the lighthouse makes the landing of supplies extremely hazardous, and for this purpose *Estevan* has two strongly-built work boats. Double-enders, 25 feet long, with a ten-foot beam, and powered by 50-h.p. gas engines, they can carry a load of three tons. The landing party consists of an officer and six men.

Nearly all light stations are equipped with a cable and hoist, which enables the stores to be lifted by bonnet sling directly out of the boat. These mainly consist of coal, oil, lumber, groceries and often the personal effects of the lightkeeper and his assistant. The most difficult part of the operation is timing the securing of the sling loads with the crest of the swells, at the same time preventing the boat from being dashed upon the rocks. But awkward as the task is, *Estevan*'s officers claim that the only item ever lost overboard was a piano; though they admit that flour and sugar often gets a good soaking.

Throughout the years, *Estevan* has never missed the Christmas trip and no lightkeeper or his family has ever gone without their turkey dinner; nor have the children's toys arrived too late for Santa Claus.

Estevan's first master was Charles Barnes, followed in turn by three whose first christian names were, by coincidence, "Harry": Harry R. Bilton, Harry S. Hughes and Harry A. Ormiston. Captain

Bilton served the longest; presiding over her bridge from October 1922, till June 1944, with ten years' service prior to that as mate in the *Newington*, the *Estevan*'s predecessor. Captain Bilton served his apprenticeship in the well-known barque *Thermopylae*, which carried Canadian flour to China and brought back rice for the Victoria rice mills. Captain J. Peterson assumed command when Captain Ormiston retired in 1957, and in the past few years *Estevan* has had several different masters. As this is written Captain R. D. Engelson is her master and C. Milton, chief engineer.

FROM A LAND MAP, Sooke Inlet appears to be a splendid harbour. And the wonder is, why is not better use made of it? Look at a marine chart and you have the answer.

It is divided into two parts, inner and outer basins, of which the former is by far the larger. This body of water, about three miles long, with an average width of a mile and a half, is sheltered from all winds and deep enough for the world's largest ships.

On the other hand, the outer basin, on the northwest shore of which stands the settlement of Sooke, is nothing but mud flats, exposed at extreme low tide but with a narrow winding channel leading to the government wharf. Marked with a maze of spar buoys and piling, deep enough for fishboats at any time and small tankers at high water only, the channel presents hazards day or night.

It has often been suggested that a deep-water channel be dredged to provide access to the inner basin, but this has been found impracticable. It would require four miles of dredging, and owing to silt brought down by freshets in the Sooke River, necessitate a dredger being kept in almost constant use. Another drawback is the rock-strewn entrance to the harbour proper.

It is not generally known that early in the nineteenth century the British Admiralty coveted Sooke Harbour as a possible naval base in this part of the world, but subsequently abandoned the idea in favour of Esquimalt. By the same token, officers of the Hudson's Bay Company are said to have given serious consideration to Sooke when looking for a site for a trading post on the lower end of Vancouver Island, but eventually they choose Victoria. Had Sooke's outer basin been deeper, and either or both plans materialized, the capital of British Columbia today might have been 20 miles farther west.

According to John Muir, who resided at Sooke in the 1850's, the correct spelling of the name of the inlet was Soke. It was named by officers of the Hudson's Bay Company after the Indians who lived there and who thus pronounced the name. The tribe took the name from a small fish, commonly known as the stickleback — because of tiny spines all over its body — which were once plentiful in the river. Dr. William F. Tolmie, an authority on Indian names, also asserted that the correct pronunciation of the name was Soke.

The inlet was first surveyed and the present spelling adopted in 1846 by Captain Henry Kellett, of H.M. SURVEY VESSEL *Herald*, who gave the name of his officers to its geographical features. Goodridge Peninsular, which forms Cooper's Cove — a local name — on the north shore of the inner basin, he named after John Octavius Goodridge, R.N., the *Herald*'s surgeon.

Billings Point, actually a sandspit, at the mouth of Sooke River, was named after William Thomas Billings, R.N., assistant surgeon. Locally known as Jackson's Spit, after a colourful waterfront character who lived there for many years, this was once a favourite weekend place for Victoria duck hunters. If extended a few hundred feet farther out, the point would make a lake of the inner basin.

Whiffin Spit, which forms a natural breakwater protecting the harbour proper, was named after John William Whiffin, R.N., the *Herald*'s clerk. Mt. Maguire which towers above East Sooke and is the site of an abandoned copper mine, bears the name of First-Lieutenant Rochfort Maguire, R.N. Pim Head, on the inner basin's south shore, and Roche Cove, into which Matheson Lake drains, were also named after Kellet's officers.

Milnes Landing, on the tidal portion of Sooke River, was named later after Edward Milne, postmaster and storekeeper there for over fifty years. The "landing" part of the name originates from the fact that this might be described as the port of entry for Leech River, where gold had been found. As there was no road from Victoria, the early prospectors landed their packhorses and supplies there by boat.

Leech River, a tributary of the Sooke River, was named after Peter John Leech, lieutenant astronomer of the Vancouver Island Exploring Expedition and who years later was city engineer at Victoria. Gold was discovered in Leech River by the expedition and during the latter part of 1864 and in 1865 it is said upwards of

$100,000 worth was taken from the stream. The excitement in connection with the discovery was intense around Victoria and a number of embryo towns, with stores and hotels, sprang up in the district. "Pay dirt" may still be found in the stream, and, for that matter, anywhere in the Sooke River, but not in worthwhile quantities. Almost every vestige of the original workings and buildings has disappeared and today Leechtown is a small logging settlement, reached from Victoria by road.

Most Indian place names are descriptive of the locality's characteristics. "A sunny mountainside sloping gently down to the sea" is the appropriate Indian translation for Saseenos, a popular residential district extending two miles along picturesque waterfront facing Sooke Harbour's inner basin, from Goodridge Peninsular to Milnes Landing. To Sophie George, a Sooke Indian girl in her teens, and her seventy-year-old grandmother, Mary George, who was affectionately known among the residents of Sooke, whites and Indians alike, as "Old Lady George," went the honour of selecting the name. And with the selection went a $50 cash prize, which the two shared.

That was back in 1920 when Alfred Carmichael of Victoria, who subdivided the property, was seeking a suitable name for the townsite. In response to an open competition, over one hundred names were submitted, but none suited Mr. Carmichael. Having lunch one day at the Sooke Harbour Hotel — burned down in 1932 — and waited on by a charming Indian girl, he chanced to enquire if she knew the name of the locality in question. She informed him that she didn't, but that her grandmother might.

With Sophie interpreting, the grandmother was duly interviewed at her home on the reservation where she was born and lived all her life, on the bank of the Sooke River immediately adjoining and actually part of the area for which a suitable name was being sought; it was thought that the old lady would remember the name by which her people knew it.

Although able to speak but a few words in English, the friendly old grandmother proved to be most coöperative and with the assistance of the charming young interpreter, her interviewers (Mr. Carmichael and this writer) soon learned that the locality was named for its warm, sunny aspect, at the base of a moderately high mountain — Mt. Shepherd, 1,805 feet — which slopes gently down to the sea.

From grandmother's long descriptive explanation, expressed in entirely unpronounceable syllables of her native tongue, considerable difficulty was experienced in translating it down to one easily articulated word. However, with patience and much repetition plus a gradual process of elimination and the application of phonetics, the much abbreviated word "Saseenos" was finally coined.

The old lady agreed that the new word was as near as one would ever come to making an English-sounding name out of the long-drawn-out Indian way of expressing its meaning. In this, other local Indians concurred and the name was subsequently adopted. It should be pronounced very slowly with particular emphasis on the second syllable, "Sa-*seen*-os". Sophie died while still in her teens; Grandmother George in 1957. Both are buried in Milnes Landing cemetery.

In the intervening years, Saseenos has become a popular residential area, boasting over two hundred prettily landscaped homes, dotted either along the extensive waterfront or upon its sunny slopes. The majority of the homeowners are retired and live there permanently, though many Victorians have summer homes there.

The Sooke Indians are said to have originally lived at Becher Bay, more commonly spelled Beecher Bay, and journeyed to Sooke River every fall for the salmon run. Finally they moved there altogether, chasing out a small band of Indians from the American side — it was all one country to them — in doing so. They built a village of their own and claimed full possession of the river.

The tribe, now nearly extinct, is also said to have been a hardy and warlike race. None of the large tribes on the coast would attack them unaided. But about 1820, the Clallams — from across the strait — and the Nitinats combined, attacked the Sooke people and nearly annihilated them. As evidence that this probably did happen, the history of the west coast of Vancouver Island as chronicled by early explorers, refers to the Sooke Indians as numbering about 500; whereas for the past one hundred and fifty years their numbers have never exceeded fifty.

What happened to the others? There is no record of them having been wiped out by smallpox or any other epidemic. As late as 1900, human skeletons in great numbers, bleached by the sun and lying obviously where their former owners had met with sudden death, or died of wounds, were to be found in the hills immediately behind the Becher Bay reservation. Scattered somewhat by foraging animals and inquisitive white men, the remains bore no evidence whatever of having been either buried or placed in trees. This supports the belief that these people, along with the Sooke Indians, had been massacred in cold blood.

Grandmother George's Indian name was Ts-eae-mee, which is a

girl's first name and is handed down from one generation to another according to custom. Her husband was a fur seal hunter and was drowned when the Victoria sealing schooner *Walter Earl* was lost with all hands in 1895. Perhaps a story told by her father and which, shortly before her death, the old lady related to the writer, might throw further light on the great massacre of the Sooke people:

In order to get repossession of the coveted Sooke River fishing, and the rich clam beds in the harbour, the Clallams came across the strait one night and practically wiped out the Sookes, who then numbered about three hundred. They killed or maimed all but three, a mother, her son and a niece, who managed to escape to the hills.

The son declared he would avenge this outrage and after calling on the sacred Thunderbird to possess both himself and his mother with great powers, together they laid their plans. Meanwhile, most of the Clallams returned to their homes across the strait, leaving a few of their number behind to gather up the spoils and guard their new possessions. They camped on Whiffin Spit, which lies across the harbour entrance. The mother was to make her way through the bush to the land end of the spit (where Sooke Harbour House now stands) and wait. As she would have to move by stealth, it would take her a day or two to get there. The son was to travel by way of East Sooke to the nearest point across the water from the outer end of the spit.

When the son arrived there he was to signal his mother by hooting like an owl three times. Then he would cross the narrow channel by canoe, if he could find one, or raft, and upon landing on the spit end, give out one long hoot. This would be in the dead of night, when the unsuspecting Clallams would be asleep, but even if a few were awake they would pay no attention to an owl hooting. At this signal, the mother started from one end of the spit, and her son, the other. Each armed with a club, they killed or seriously maimed every Clallam.

The story might sound fantastic, but it is vouched for by Old Lady George's surviving sons, all mature men in their late sixties and seventies and solid citizens of Sooke. Each recollects, as young men, old Indians telling them the same story, which to this day is handed down among the Sooke Indians as the true story of the fate of their ancestors.

The Sooke Indians held their last big festival gathering in the summer of 1921, when Chief Lazzar entertained visiting tribes from Clallam and Neah Bay, across the Strait of Juan de Fuca, the West Coast, the Songhees and the Cowichans; ironically, their former enemies. The pageant, one of the most spectacular ever staged on southern Vancouver Island, was held at their village on the banks of the Sooke River and lasted nearly a week.

Sooke's first white settler was Captain W. Colquhoun Grant, of the Royal Scots Greys, who came out from England in 1849 and took up one hundred acres where the settlement now stands. In addition to farming, he also built a sawmill. The only other mill on lower Vancouver Island was at Langford. All communication with Sooke was then by sea, Indian canoes being the principal means of transportation. It was Grant who introduced Scotch broom, a shrub which now grows wild all over lower Vancouver Island. Its golden blooms in the month of May and June are a feature in Victoria's Beacon Hill Park. Grant also found the soil ideal for growing swede turnips. To this day this is the district's number one garden product. A road in the village and a nearby mountain commemorate his name.

John Muir, a Scotsman from Airdale, was another pioneer settler. With his wife, daughter and four sons, Andrew, Robert, John and Michael, he arrived at Victoria in 1849, coming out via the Horn in the ship *Harpooner*. After being employed for several years by the Hudson's Bay Company at Fort Rupert and Nanaimo, in 1854 he took over the Grant holdings at Sooke, increased them, subsequently owned 580 acres and had his own flour mill. The sawmill he extended and exported lumber, piling and ships' spars, mostly to San Francisco and Hawaii. He also established shipbuilding yards and at least half a dozen vessels were built at Sooke, among them, the small steamer *Woodside* (wrecked ten years later near the Nitinat), and the schooners *Ann Taylor* and *Favourite*. John Muir was elected to the first Assembly of Vancouver Island, 1856-1861, as representative for Sooke. Several of the district's geographical features, Muir Creek, mountain and point, were named after him.

About the same time, Captain Hugh McKay and Captain Spring operated a cooperage and made barrels for the fishing industry. Both later established trading posts on the West Coast. Another early settler was Jonas Throup, who came there in 1868, about the same time as John Murray, for years Sooke's justice of the peace. John Mugford, a Newfoundlander, came to Sooke in 1886 and died there in 1941. With his schooner *Kilminnie*, he was the last man to carry freight by sail between Sooke and Victoria.

In 1853, the barque *Lord Raglan*, Sooke to England with six passengers and a cargo of lumber and spars, foundered off Cape Flattery; wreckage washed ashore on the West Coast told of her fate. The schooner *May Belle* sailed out of Sooke Harbour in 1893, bound for the sealing grounds, and was never heard from again. Lost with Captain Edward Sheilds and his three white crew members were twenty-two Becher Bay Indians, practically the entire male population of that sub-tribe.

For over sixty years Sooke enjoyed the distinction of having the only salmon traps on the British Columbia coast; now trollers, purse seine and gillnet boats have taken their place. There is an oyster farm on the inner basin, clams are dug commercially and the tidal flats provide excellent crab fishing. Today, apart from being an ideal residential area, with half the population retired people, Sooke is also an important fishing centre, with farming and logging secondary industries.

FISHERIES PATROL VESSEL GIVENCHY

Ship of many services.

IT WOULD BE HARD to find a bay or inlet on the entire British Columbia coastline, including the Queen Charlotte Islands and Vancouver Island, that at one time or another wasn't visited by that veteran old steamer, C.G.S. *Givenchy*, better known to naval personnel with the prefix H.M.C.S. before her name.

After service on the Atlantic as a minesweeper during the First Great War she was commissioned in the fisheries protection services on this coast, serving from August 1919, until turned back to the navy in 1938. During the Second World War she was based at Esquimalt and utilized first as a training ship and later on harbour examination duty. Subsequently she was disposed of to private interests and later scrapped.

Flying the blue ensign, her primary role in the fisheries service was that of off-shore patrol, prevention of poaching and general enforcement of the fisheries regulations. The three-mile limit, inside which foreign vessels are forbidden to fish, was one of her master's biggest headaches. In dirty weather this line is difficult to define and when salmon, halibut or cod happened to be more plentiful inside than out, alien boats would slip into illegal waters. When apprehended, offenders were escorted to the nearest customs port and brought before the courts.

In the case of flagrant infractions, both vessel and catch were often confiscated and the crews fined in addition. The *Givenchy's* captain, however, being invested with discretionary powers, in borderline cases the offending boat would be escorted offshore and its master cautioned.

One of the greatest handicaps in this work was the fact she was a coal burner, one of the few left on this coast. Through no fault of the department or her officers, who would have preferred oil, Ottawa insisted on coal in deference to pressure from politicians wishing to appease Vancouver Island's coal mining industry. The result: her smoke could be seen over the horizon while still hull down, permitting ample time for any poacher to up-gear and escape. American fishermen as a whole respected the line, but certain boats made a practice of fishing inside at every opportunity. The identity of such vessels, however, soon became known and little mercy was shown them by the captain if subsequently caught.

In conjunction with her fishery duties, *Givenchy* had a host of other chores. Prior to other departments acquiring their own boats and flying became commonplace, she was frequently called upon to carry various officials to out-of-the-way places. One trip she made every year was to take the post office inspector, custom's inspector and the chief engineer of the public works department to every point of habitation outside the larger cities. Another chore took A. W. Neill, then M.P. for Comox-Alberni, completely round his vast constituency once every year. In Canadian politics this trip was unique and was a special dispensation on Ottawa's part. Except for the road system between Campbell River and Alberni, scarcely a road existed in the whole area, embracing over 1,000 miles of coastline, not counting bays and inlets. Distribution and later collecting ballot boxes was another job when the Dominion elections rolled around.

In the spring, the fur seal herds had to be shepherded safely past the west coast of Vancouver Island during their annual migration to the Pribiloff Islands breeding grounds in the Bering Sea. When clear of the Queen Charlottes the U.S. Coastguard took over, in accordance with the Pegalic Sealing Treaty between the two countries. During summer, another lot of seals had to be attended to, but this time instead of protection it became a case of destruction. The breeding grounds of the sea lions on Virgin Rock, Queen Charlotte Sound, and other places, were visited and thousands of these predatory sea monsters slaughtered by rifle and machine gun fire, sea lions being one of the greatest menaces to the salmon fisheries. Of no commercial value, neither carcass nor skin is salvaged.

Enforcement of the international halibut treaty, under the terms of which the seasonal catch in different areas is strictly regulated, also called for thousands of steaming miles between Cape Flattery and the Alaskan boundary. Reporting weather conditions and warn-

Steam Schooner *Mischief,* which brought pioneer settlers to Quatsino in 1894. *Provincial Archives Photo.*

Mr. and Mrs. Thomas W. Ildstad, who came from Minnesota and were among Quatsino Sound's pioneer settlers. *Family Album Photo.*

Lighthouse Tender *Estevan*, familiar and welcome sight along **West Coast.** *Photo courtesy Captain H. Hughes, former master on* ESTEVAN. *Note*: Water tower shown in photo is a shore installation.

Men and muscle powered Tofino's first lifeboat. *W. C. Hamilton Photo.*

ing of approaching storms was a regular job for her wireless operator.

During the rum-running days in the early twenties, *Givenchy* was assigned yet another chore. Custom's preventative service required her officers to be ever on the alert for evasive small boats slipping in under cover of darkness or fog with contraband liquor from the big ocean-going rum-runners lying far out at sea. These steamers brought shipments of liquor direct from the British Isles or Hong Kong and provided they remained a reasonable distance beyond United States or Canadian shores were immune from interference. While practically their entire cargoes were destined for consumption south of the line, small consignments managed to find their way into Canada without paying duty. It was for boats bringing in these loads that customs officials were on the lookout.

Liquor seizures were frequently made, not only from a boat caught red-handed, but from some secret cache at an isolated cove or uninhabited island. Such findings were usually from a tip-off. It is said that hunting down rum-runners was never popular with *Givenchy*'s crew members, but when several hundred cases (packed in gunnysacks) of good Scotch whisky was confiscated, many hands made light work bringing it aboard.

For years during the winter months, along with H.M.C.S. *Thiepval* and H.M.C.S. *Armentieres*, both vessels of her same class, *Givenchy* also served on life-saving duty. Month about in turn, one would be stationed at Bamfield and required to stand by day and night, ready to proceed to any call from a ship in distress. With the introduction of radio direction finding installations at Pachena, Estevan and other lighthouses, this service was subsequently withdrawn.

Speedboats lurking in the Strait of Juan de Fuca, watching for an opportunity to pick up narcotics dropped overboard (in rubber containers) from liners inbound from the Orient, also had to be watched for and if possible intercepted, though the *Givenchy* could only make 11 knots. All in all, *Givenchy*'s officers had to keep a watchful eye at all times for any suspected infractions of the customs regulation. *Givenchy*'s last master was the late Captain A. M. Henderson, with over thirty year's service.

Old *Givenchy* and her equally well-known master will long be remembered by all residing at those more isolated points along the West Coast during the years she was engaged on patrol. When regular means of transportation were less frequent and in many cases non-existent, if the ship happened to be anywhere within reasonable distance, Captain Henderson never hesitated to leave his patrol and proceed immediately to any call for help. Whether it be someone stricken with illness, or an accident to a lonely settler or one of his family, a fisherman, logger or prospector, if no other means of getting them comfortably to a doctor or hospital was available, *Givenchy* would, and did. Hospitals then being few and far between, such mercy trips might require 100 miles or more steaming time before the stricken one received aid. But this was considered all in the day's work and any extra time on shift to get another knot out of her was never begrudged by her crew.

Alternating with *Givenchy* was the *Malaspina*, a vessel of the same tonnage, but of a different type and faster. Her last master was Captain Walter Redford, now retired. *Givenchy* and *Malaspina* were years ago replaced by smaller vessels carrying crews of twelve.

Captain A. M. Henderson,
the *Givenchy*'s master.
Family Album Photos.

FISHERIES PATROL VESSEL GIVENCHY

Mrs. Mary George, Sooke's Grand Old Lady. Her ancestors exacted bitter toll.
Family Album Photo

RESCUE SHIPS

Small but efficient.

STATIONED AT Tofino and Bamfield respectively, are two highly efficient small boats playing an inconspicuous but important role in Canada's little-publicized coastguard service, the Tofino and Bamfield lifeboats. They were built and launched in 1951 by Chantier Marine de St. Laurent, Isle of Orleans, Quebec, to specifications of the latest type of lifeboat in use by the United States Coastguard. Each 40 feet in length and powered by 110-h.p. G.M. diesel engines, they are the last word in seaworthiness. Their builders claim that if turned completely upside down, they will right themselves immediately without a drop of water remaining inboard. There is no record, however, of this ever having been demonstrated.

Equipment includes a radio-telephone, direction finder, line-throwing rocket gun, powerful searchlight and first-aid kit. Both maintain communication with nearby radio stations and lighthouses on a 24-hour basis: Tofino with Estevan Point and Lennard Island, and the Bamfield boat with Cape Beale and Pachena. Thus they may be described as the "ears and eyes" on this part of the coast for the R.C.A.F. Rescue Co-ordination Centre in Vancouver, which is tied-in with the R.C.N., Fisheries Service, R.C.M.P., Hydrographic Survey, B.C. Pilotage Authority, the weather ship on Station Papa and the Department of Transport.

The Tofino and Bamfield life-saving stations have now been in existence for fifty years, during which time on hundreds of occasions these two small boats — or their predecessors — have been called upon to rescue the crew from some stranded vessel; or if the ship was not actually wrecked, to stand by until tug or salvage boat came to its assistance.

In the days of sailing ships and with steamers, too, prior to the introduction of radio and direction finding, scarcely a winter passed without several coming to grief along this dreaded section of the West Coast. In spite of the proverb "never send a boy on a man's errand," the stout crews of these little boats never hesitated to put to sea, day or night, and in any weather. Department of Transport records credit the saving of many lives and much valuable shipping tonnage to their prompt action, courage and seamanship.

But while calls for assistance from ocean-going vessels in trouble nowadays are comparatively few, an all-year-round job is keeping a watchful eye on the thousands of smaller craft, principally Canadian and American fishboats that frequent West Coast waters. A message received by radio, phone or other means, advising of a vessel in trouble, is immediately responded to by whichever of the two boats is handiest. Many such calls result in some fisherman being rescued from his leaking or burning boat. Or a disabled one taken in tow in the nick of time and saving her from being dashed to pieces on a jagged reef.

Shipwrecked crews have been taken off storm-lashed islands, or from desolate beaches, where they would have probably died from exposure if the lifeboat hadn't found them. Disabled fishboats have been picked up after days of drifting helplessly miles off shore; while in more than one instance derelicts have been located and towed in after the fisherman has been lost. To take care of the sick and injured, one of the crew is a qualified first-aid man.

Other routine chores they are called upon to perform, that incidentally provide practical training for the crew, include tending nearby lighthouses and taking care of navigation aids, such as buoys, fixed lights and beacons. They are also frequently required to take sick or injured people from isolated points to the nearest doctor or hospital. The Department of Transport, under whose jurisdiction they operate, authorizes such mercy trips where there are no roads or other suitable boats available.

When the two stations were first established in 1910, the crews had to be rugged indeed; open surf boats then being employed, with sail and ten long sweeps their only power. The Tofino boat was first based at Spring Cove, Ucluelet, and moved 25 miles further west three years later. In 1913, gasoline powered boats were substituted, serving until the present boats were secured. Their shore establishments consist of a large boathouse, into which the boat may be hauled for repairs and overhaul; accommodation for the crew and a radiophone operator on duty day and night. Station duties also include recording the daily rainfall, reading the tide gauge and reporting other data required by the hydrographic and meteorological departments.

The section of the West Coast over which these two boats keep watch extends from Port Renfrew to Nootka Sound, a stretch of approximately one hundred miles, though the Tofino boat is occasionally called as far north as Kyuquot. With the fishing fleet operating from one to twenty-five miles off shore, this represents an area of over 1,000 square miles of ocean; from any point in which a call for assistance might be received any hour of the day or night.

THE BLUE ENSIGN, WHITE ENSIGN AND "RED DUSTER"

APPROXIMATELY 1,000 Canadian boats engage in fishing off the west coast of Vancouver Island between April and October each year. One hundred or more fish all the year round. Half of them are owned by fishermen who make their permanent homes there; the remainder move from place to place as the salmon runs occur on different parts of the coast. The logging industry employs another 200 boats, ranging in size from powerful diesel tugs to one-man boom boats.

As the men who operate these little ships go about their business, scarcely a day passes but they come up with a vessel flying either the white ensign, the blue ensign or the "red duster"; often the Stars and Stripes and occasionally the flag of some far-off country.

It is those displaying the blue ensign with which they are mostly concerned, for their presence usually has to do with one of the industries, the enforcement of our laws, or the general welfare of the inhabitants. All are painted grey and vary in size from the big lighthouse tenders and hydrographic survey ships, fisheries cruisers with crews of fifteen, to one-man-operated launches. They form part of a fleet of more than one hundred similar vessels operated along the British Columbia coast by different agencies of the federal and provincial governments.

Seventeen are based on the west coast of Vancouver Island. The Department of Indian affairs has one; R.C.M.P., four; Department of Transport, two; and B.C. Forest Service, three. The remainder are owned by the Federal Department of Fisheries, which in addition, charter numerous small craft, mostly fishing boats after salmon trolling ceases. These are used by guardians, usually the owner of the boat, who is specially employed during the fall months when salmon are ascending the streams to spawn. As a symbol of authority, each is supplied with a blue ensign.

The blue ensign also flies at the stern of the lighthouse tenders, hydrographic survey ships and other government vessels which bring in supplies for projects which the R.C.A.F. and the department of public works has in hand from time to time.

The red ensign is displayed by passenger vessels, coastal freighters, oil tankers and tugboats of British or Canadian registration, also by privately-owned yachts and pleasure cruisers which visit these parts, the number of which increases every year.

The white ensign is seen when ships of the Royal Canadian Navy carry out exercises off-shore, make familiarization trips up the inlets and friendly calls at the larger settlements. The Stars and Stripes is observed on American pleasure yachts and when that country's fishing boats put in for shelter during storms. Hundreds of United States fishermen operate off the West Coast, but they must remain beyond the three-mile limit and only in case of sickness or accident, a mechanical breakdown, or stress of weather, may they enter a Canadian port. Even then, they are not permitted to tie up at a float and instead must anchor out. Nor can they sell their fish or take on supplies, other than water.

Flags of all nations are displayed (along with the red ensign) on the ocean-going freighters which load lumber at Port Alberni and Tahsis, and those which bring in sulphur and other chemicals for the pulp mill at Port Alice.

STORY OF MILADY'S
SEALSKIN COAT

AT ANY TIME of year one of the most important possessions in a woman's wardrobe is a fur coat, be it mink, marten, muskrat, squirrel, or plain rabbit under some fancy trade name. But a few still cling to sealskin; maybe considered a little old fashioned as some fancies go, but according to those who know furs, still the best buy — except for the price — and superior in warmth and all-round durability.

Few wearing these aristocrats of milady's cold weather wraps realize that as likely as not the seals that once wore the same skins were taken off Vancouver Island's west coast, though for the purpose of being tanned and processed ready for the furrier's deft hands, hides had to travel all the way to England and back.

In 1911, under the terms of the International Pelagic Sealing Treaty made between Canada, the United States, Russia and Japan, to permit the herds on the breeding grounds to build up again after being almost depleted, all fur-sealing in Northern Pacific waters by white hunters was prohibited. The principal breeding grounds are on the United States' Pribiloff Islands in the Bering Sea, and Russia's Robben Island in the Sea of Okhotsk and Commander Islands in the Western Bering Sea. It was then that the fleet of sealing schooners, once a familiar sight in Victoria's inner harbour, dropped anchor never to go to sea again, at least in pursuit of their former missions. And Victoria lost one of its primary industries.

By recognizing hereditary rights — seal meat being one of their staple foods and the skins a source of supply for clothing — the Indians were still permitted to hunt them, but only by harpooning from canoes. Thus a profitable new industry had its birth along the west coast of Vancouver Island. Traders purchased the skins from the Indians, who in turn spent the greater part of this new-found money over the counter for supplies.

Charged with the joint responsibility of enforcing the treaty regulations, vessels of the fisheries service frequently patrolled the seas to prevent white poachers from interfering with the migration, and the natives from using firearms. Local customs officers also periodically examined the raw hides in search of tell-tale shot holes. Notwithstanding these precautions a decided up-surge in the sale (to Indians) of both shotguns and ammunition was noticed. When a handful of buckshot inadvertently fell out of a skin it was confiscated by the examining officer. Skins being an inch or so thick in blubber, it was difficult to determine whether the seal had been shot or speared. However, the Indian was usually given the benefit of the doubt. One alibi that always stood was the fact that owing to fur seals being a constant menace to the salmon trollers by biting chunks out of the fish on their lines, many carried shotguns or rifles to scare them off.

Clayoquot, Tofino and Ucluelet were the principal buying centres, though a few skins were sometimes purchased at Nootka and Bamfield. From 1912 till about 1942, between 1,000 and 1,500 were bought annually at each of the three points. Owing to market fluctuations, the price varied, $8.00 per skin being the average price paid over the thirty-year period. Then the price dropped still further and the Indians turned to more profitable occupations and, compared with former years, the number purchased was negligible.

It usually takes five skins to make a fur coat. Eight dollars per skin seems a ridiculously low price, compared with the cost of the finished article; but apart from the manufacturer's profit, and the expense of handling from the time they are purchased till the coat is on the customer's back, the spread is readily appreciated.

The raw hides must be handled with extreme care, or spoilage occurs. Odd bits of flesh have first to be removed, leaving only a thick layer of fat. The skins are then piled flat in heaps and salted down in bins. With good ventilation and re-salted from time to time, in this state they keep indefinitely. For shipping purposes they are individually rolled up in salt and packed in barrels.

In those days all raw seal skins had to be shipped to W. Rice and Company, London, England, the only firm then in possession of the secret process for dyeing them, after first being cured and plucked. (If a seal skin is not dyed it looks like the skin of a grey dog.) The skins would either be sold at Lampson's internationally-famed fur auction, or shipped back to be manufactured in Canada or the United States. In later years, Rice and Company disposed of its secret dyeing process to a United States firm in St. Louis.

Shipped back to Canada the skins were subject to duty, assessment for duty purposes arrived at by the difference in value of the raw and treated fur. The duty averaged between $14 and $20 per skin. Cost of treating, freight both ways, cold storage charges (often they were placed in cold storage for years, awaiting more favourable prices), brokers' fees, insurance and other incidental expenses, averaged approximately $35 per skin by the time they reached the manufacturer. Added to this a rough figure of $100 for making it up, lining and other accessories, the high cost of a genuine sealskin coat can readily be understood.

The four principal buyers on the West Coast were W. T. Dawley, who for nearly fifty years operated general trading stores at Nootka and Clayoquot, James Sloman at Tofino, J. H. Mitchell, also of Clayoquot and Tofino, and Edwin Lee at Ucluelet. Mr. Lee recalled the interest Lord Willingdon displayed in his seal skins when as Governor-General of Canada he made a trip up the West Coast. As these were the first seal skins in the raw he had ever seen, His Excellency not only climbed into the bins for a close examination, but had Mr. Lee explain every detail from the time they were purchased from the Indians till made into fur coats.

Twelve years ago, the concession which permitted Indians to take fur seals was withdrawn and no longer can their skins be disposed of privately. Now the killing is all done at their breeding grounds under supervision of the international commission which has its headquarters at San Francisco.

Led by the bulls, as the males are known, the seals first show up off the British Columbia coast early in March, following on through April and May, with a few stragglers even in June. The vanguard is usually first sighted in the vicinity of Swiftsure lightship and Cape Beale, then passes along the entire length of the west coast of Vancouver Island anywhere from five to twenty-five miles off shore, never taking the inside passage. United States Coastguard and Canadian Fisheries patrol vessels shepherd the entire migration. This precaution is necessary as the seals fall easy prey to poachers. For long periods during daylight they sleep on the surface, enabling them to be stalked to within gunshot range quite easily. Natural protection is provided by the fact that they avoid close formation, invariably being widely scattered — a few here and a few there — with seldom more than twenty in sight at one time. Then there are times when a boat might travel miles without seeing one.

Arriving at the Pribiloff Islands first, the bulls fight vigorously among themselves to win the favoured sites for their harem when the girls arrive. There is always a surplus of bachelor bulls, out of luck and forced to gang up and live in groups by themselves.

During summer, camps are maintained on the breeding grounds where a count is made of the herds. The increase in numbers since the taking of the last count is a guide to the quota allowed for killing. Local natives are hired to carry out the slaughter by clubbing the selected victims, mostly bachelor bulls.

All harvesting is done under the control of the Soviet government on the Robben and Commander Islands, and under the control of the United States on the Pribiloffs. During 1961, the commercial take by the U.S.S.R. was 10,882 seals, and by the U.S. 95,974 animals. An additional 10,000 (mostly females) were taken for scientific purposes.

All skins are salted on the grounds. Those taken by the United States are later shipped to San Francisco. There they are re-salted and later shipped to St. Louis for plucking, tanning, dyeing and other necessary processing in preparation for the annual fur auction. Under the terms of the convention, Canada and Japan each receives 15 per cent of the net proceeeds from the total commercial take.

The honeymoon over, survivors again take to the water, accompanied by their half-grown pups. The exact route taken has never been definitely established, however, research undertaken by scientists of the four member countries indicates a certain intermingling of the herds.

CAPTAIN GEORGE HEATER

Russians in the Bering Sea. Girls at Sydney Inlet. The Sealing Schooner Favourite.

HUNDREDS OF TALES have been told and retold of sealing schooner skippers who fought gale, tide and choking fog in an endless quest for fortune. Accounts of their exploits have filled many books. Typical is the story of Captain George Heater, which tells of his brush with a Russian patrol and the ordeals of heroism which were no more than the routine of a sailor's life in those days. Also, how towards the end of an adventurous career at sea, he established a saltery where a crew of girls from Aberdeen made a rendezvous spot of Sydney Inlet, and the fate of the Sooke-built schooner *Favourite*.

At 11:45 p.m. on July 22, 1893, when proceeding under full sail in the western portion of the Bering Sea, the Victoria sealing schooner *Ainoko* was overhauled and ordered to stop by the Russian gunboat *Joucete*. An armed boarding party came on board and Captain George Heater, master, was charged with violating the terms of an agreement which then existed between the British and Russian governments. It was alleged by the *Joucete*'s commander that the Canadian vessel was hunting seals in a 30-mile-wide zone in which all sealing was prohibited.

On behalf of his owners and crew, and in vindication of his own position, Captain Heater protested the seizure and insisted that a record should be made in writing and given to him. He claimed the commander of the *Joucete* was aware that the *Ainoko* had been driven by gales and heavy seas within what he described as "the limits," and that it was well known by the Russian naval officer that it was impossible to pursue and hunt seals in such adverse weather.

Furthermore, the commander of the Russian cruiser had full knowledge of the fact that the *Ainoko*, immediately prior to being overhauled and ordered to stop, was proceeding under full canvas in an opposite direction from the prescribed waters, unaware of the proximity of the *Joucete*.

The Russian admitted that all the facts and statements made by Captain Heater were true. But in obedience to his orders, he must take from the master of the *Ainoko* all the ship's papers and direct him to proceed to Yokohama, Japan, where he was to report to Her Britannic Majesty's consul. There was no British naval vessel then near in the prescribed zone.

Finding remonstrance in vain, Captain Heater headed his vessel for Yokohoma. The crew of the *Ainoko* consisted of Captain Heater, brother William, mate, able seamen Daniel Martin and George Linfield, and a Chinese cook. Also on board were twenty-three Indian hunters and canoemen (boat steerers) from Hesquiat on the west coast of Vancouver Island.

It was these Indians who changed Captain Heater's mind. On the voyage out and back, it was the custom with all sealing schooners for their Indian hunters to stand watch at the wheel and in consequence they were familiar with the compass. They soon noticed that the ship was heading southwest towards the Japanese coast, instead of east in the direction of Vancouver Island. They emphatically refused to go to Japan and the captain had no alternative but to change course and head for Victoria. He paid the Indians off at Hesquiat on his way down the coast and arrived at Victoria on August 28.

In due course, Captain Heater lodged a ship's protest with the collector of customs for the port of Victoria, who in the meantime had technically seized the *Ainoko* and its cargo of skins. The case was heard before Mr. Justice Crease and the vessel and its cargo subsequently released.

Captain Heater was born at Harbour Grace, Newfoundland, in 1861. His early seafaring experience was gained hunting seals on the ice floes of the North Atlantic and cod fishing on the Grand Banks. He came to this coast at thirty-one and later became one of the most successful skippers in a fleet of over sixty sealing schooners which sailed out of Victoria.

The seizure of the *Ainoko* by the Russians and the vessel's subsequent arrival at Victoria instead of Yokohoma, was only one incident in this adventurous seaman's career. Twice shipwrecked on the Atlantic coast, he came near to losing his life together with his ship and entire crew, when the 120-ton schooner *Markland*, one of the largest vessels in the fleet, was caught in a storm while also hunting seals in the Bering Sea.

The storm broke while the Indian hunters were scattered across the horizon in their cockle-shell canoes and only through Captain Heater's fine seamanship were they all picked up. The gale then worsened, and with her upper structure partly demolished and the canoes all washed overboard, the vessel finally reached Unalaska. There she was repaired, lost canvas replaced, new canoes purchased and she continued sealing. However, the *Markland*'s misfortune on that trip was more than repaid, when six weeks later she returned to Victoria with a record of 1,800 skins.

Other Victoria-based sealing schooners which Captain Heater commanded at different times were the *Sapphire, Penelope, Jessie, Rosie Olsen* and *Allie E. Alger*. The Pelagic Sealing Treaty of 1910 put the entire sealing fleet out of business and for years the vessels lay idle in the Victoria inner harbour.

Captain Heater went halibut fishing and afterwards established a herring saltery at the head of Sydney Inlet on the west coast of Vancouver Island. The processing plant was built on a log raft and his employees were accommodated in a floating camp moored alongside. For this purpose he purchased the *Favourite*, one of the idle sealing schooners. He had her masts removed, rigging dismantled, additional sleeping accommodation provided and towed her to Sydney Inlet.

This 80-ton schooner was built at Sooke in 1869 by Captain Charles Spring, for cod fishing and trading. She carried lumber between Victoria and California ports and made several trips to the Hawaiian Islands. Found to be too small for that trade, Captain Spring then used her for trading along the northwest coast and also for sealing. She was one of the first schooners to employ Indian hunters and boat steerers. About twelve of each were taken along, and sometimes a few of their wives were signed on as cooks.

It was while sailing along the coast on his way to and from the trading posts, and buying skins of seals which the Indians hunted in their canoes off the west coast of Vancouver Island, that Captain Spring induced the Indians to make better use of their specialty and hunt the seals farther afield. The Indians came from all parts of the West Coast. The schooners called for them in the early spring and landed them back a few months later, when they were paid off in gold.

Under the command of Captain Laughlan McLean, with a crew of six white men and his Indian hunters and boat steerers, the *Favourite* made many successful trips. She frequently returned with more than 2,000 skins, obtained in the Bering Sea and off the Russian and Japanese coasts.

The *Favourite* is often referred to in the memoirs of Rev. A. J. Brabant, who established a mission at Hesquiat in 1874. He frequently travelled in her when he had occasion to come to Victoria. On November 15, 1885, she arrived at Hesquiat with a load of supplies, which included several boxes of medicine. This was badly needed, for measles had ravaged the village and many of the Indians were suffering from smallpox. On another trip she brought a bell for the church, which the crew helped install. Captain McLean was given the honour of ringing the bell for the first time.

In 1888, the *Favourite* was chartered by the government to carry lumber and other building material to Indian settlements along the West Coast, the object being to improve their habitations and mode of living. Also on board was lumber and bricks to build a new church at Friendly Cove.

Among the employees at Captain Heater's herring saltery on Sydney Inlet were about twenty young women, brought out from Aberdeen, Scotland, to work in what was then a promising new industry. Whether this was the attraction, or the Chinese cook's reputation for making hotcakes, the *Favourite*, now a floating hostelry moored at the head of a sheltered inlet, was a popular rendezvous for halibut and cod fishermen who called there regularly for bait.

The raft and the saltery sheds were smashed to pieces during a violent storm which occurred after operations ceased in the winter of 1919-1920. There was no one on board the *Favourite* at the time, nor anyone in the vicinity to tell what actually happened; but loose drift logs are presumed to have damaged her hull and she sank. For a long time afterwards the wreck could be seen lying in about eight fathoms of water. No attempt was ever made to refloat her. Captain Heater, who made his home in Victoria, died in 1928. His brother, Captain William Heater, was also a sealing skipper and afterwards a whaler.

In ten fathoms of water about two miles from where the *Favourite* sank, lie the remains of a wooden sailing ship. It was found in 1957 by Dr. G. W. Cottrell, an amateur skin diver from Portland, Oregon, whose hobby is locating sunken wrecks. R.C.N. divers have since recovered one of her masts, an anchor, winch, pieces of copper sheathing and several other articles, but the vessel's identity has yet to be established, and there is no record of any shipwreck having occurred in Sydney Inlet. Naval scientists estimate her to be at least one hundred years old.

The late Captain George Heater.
Family Album Photo

Sealing schooners lying idle in Victoria harbour after pelagic sealing ended. The fleet at one time numbered 95 vessels and many came to life again when rum-running became a profitable trade. *Provincial Archives Photo.*

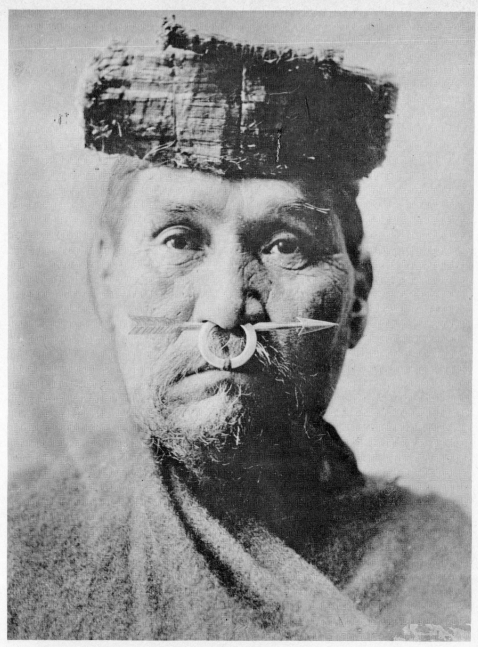

Chief Atliu, whose magic mystified the Americans. *Provincial Archives Photo.*

Raymond A. Pitre, who brought into production Zeballos' fabulously rich Privateer gold mine (see page 306). *Photo by Williams Bros., Vancouver.*

The late Walter T. Dawley, who for forty years kept store and bought seal skins at Clayoquot. *Family Album Photos.*

The late Edwin Lee, fur buyer at Ucluelet, who showed governor-general how raw seal skins are treated.

SEA OTTER
MAKES HISTORY

And survives — thanks to con-
servation measures.

THE SEA OTTER, that little animal which played such an important
role in the early history of this coast and whose fur was said to be
finer than Russian sable and much sought after by Chinese man-
darins, was so ruthlessly destroyed — for its pelts — during the
eighteenth and nineteenth centuries that it became practically
extinct.

In countless thousands, they lived in colonies at different places
on the coast between California and the Aleutian Islands. Scarcely
half a dozen pairs appeared to have survived the slaughter, then in
1911, a treaty made between the United States, Canada, Russia
and Japan, outlawed the taking of a single sea otter life. Since that
time, under the watchful eyes of United States Wild Life and Game
Authority officials, and their counterparts in the other signing
countries, slowly but surely their numbers began to increase.

As this is written, it is gratifying to learn that as a direct result
of these conservation measures, a colony of approximately 4,000
makes its home in an undisclosed area on the Alaskan coast, where
special guardians see that they are unmolested. We also have confirmation of the existence of a colony — estimated at 400 — on the
lower California coast, but here again and for very good reasons,
the exact location is a closely guarded secret. Recent sightings of
the animal, at places which they once frequented in large numbers,
have also been reported by west coast of Vancouver Island Indians,
and it is likely a few small colonies have by this time been established
on the uninhabited west coast of the Queen Charlotte Islands.

Valuable as fur seal pelts are, those of the sea otter were twenty
times as great. In China, where most of them were sold, prime pelts

fetched as high as $2,000, and as much again on the London market. It was Captain Cook's published journals that first told the world that these priceless furs were obtainable on this coast, and which brought to Nootka the early trading expeditions. Their arrival at Nootka coincided with the Spanish occupation of that place in the latter part of the eighteenth century, when three of their ships, together with their cargoes of sea otter and other valuable pelts, were promptly seized — an incident which almost led to war between England and Spain.

A true mammal, the sea otter is a first cousin to the land otter; no relation whatever to the seal. Its fur is black or dark brown, yet silvery at the base. Average length, from four to five feet — snout to tip of tail. They mate in any month and normally have only one offspring. Principal diet is crab and other crustacea. They live, feed and breed in the kelp beds close to shore where they are comparatively safe from their natural enemies — sharks and killer whales. But by the same token, this sometimes is their downfall, for they often disport themselves within harpoon range of cunning Indians concealed in nearby rocks.

Unlike the seal, sea otters never travel and because they live in water enduringly cold the fur is always prime. Having no fear of humans, a skilled Indian hunter in his canoe can approach one close enough to club it to death, or at least get within easy range for his harpoon. Pups are born in the water, but the mothers must teach them to swim. Indians purposely catch one of these helpless young, which immediately cries like a human baby; the mother responds in a frantic attempt to retrieve her offspring — a swing of the Indian's club and another dead female otter. The above are some of the factors which add up to the animal's almost complete extermination.

INDIANS AWARDED
MEDALS

Wreck of the General Cobb.

IN 1880 A GOLD MEDAL was awarded a Clayoquot chief. On its clasp is the United States motto *E Pluribus Unum* (One for All). The inscription on the medal's obverse side reads: "Presented by the President of the United States," on the other: "To Schewish, Chief of the Clayoquots. For gallant services rendered in the rescue of the American bark *General Cobb,* 1880."

The *General Cobb,* 648 tons, Captain J. L. Oliver, went ashore half a mile east of Portland Point, about midway between Long Beach and the entrance to Clayoquot Sound. On November 25, 1915, at practically the same place, the Chilean ship *Carelmapu* was wrecked with the loss of nineteen lives (see page 93). About a mile and a half farther east, at the western end of Long Beach, the British barque *Mustang,* inbound for Victoria with general merchandise, was wrecked on January 21, 1866, and the brig *Wm. G. Irwin,* after being abandoned at sea, February 1887. The *Mustang* remained upright for months before breaking up. Meanwhile, William Lyons of Victoria purchased the wreck and cargo at auction, and dispatched the schooner *Meg Merillies* to recover same; but when Captain Thomas Pamphlett arrived at Clayoquot Sound he found that the Indians had practically stripped the vessel. Little of value was recovered.

The *General Cobb* sailed from San Francisco, January 2, bound for Puget Sound in ballast. Heavy weather was experienced all the way up the coast to Cape Flattery, off which point she arrived on the 14th. Wind then veered round to SSW and weather set in thick, foggy and raining. At 8 o'clock that night the lookout reported breakers on the lee bow. Captain Oliver at once attempted to wear the ship, but owing to intense thickness of weather was unable to do so and was soon in the breakers. In a few minutes the vessel ran on to a shelving rock, with a reef dead ahead and an upright rock on either side. Finding that she was bilged and filled, Captain Oliver let go both anchors to prevent her from sliding into deep water. A spar was run out to the rock and one by one the crew slid down it and attempted to make a landing with a line. Their efforts, however, were futile, as heavy seas washed them off the rock and with great difficulty they managed to climb back on board.

Finding that no landing could be made that night, captain and crew awaited daylight with great anxiety, as the seas were breaking heavily, rendering it utterly out of the question to launch a boat. At break of day a spar was again rigged out and after much risk and hazard all hands reached the rock safely. Here they remained for two days and one night.

Fortunately the disaster was witnessed by three Indians. Unable to help, for the seas were too rough for their small canoe, they proceeded through the bush and conveyed the news to Clayoquot. On the next evening a large canoe hove in sight, much to the delight of the isolated crew who by this time had suffered severely and were prepared for the worst, knowing that any moment the ship might break over the rock on which they were imprisoned.

The canoe was manned by fourteen Indians, who, after effecting a very difficult landing, took the men ashore and conducted them to their homes (the Clayoquots' summer village) on the beach nearby. Here the castaway crew remained two days. By this time the seas had moderated and they were taken by the Indians to Clayoquot where they received every hospitality at Captain Warren's trading post, in charge of Mr. Turnbull.

Previous to this, the Indians had generously offered Captain Oliver the use of a house at their village, advising him, however, for his own benefit, to go to the trading post. Meanwhile, they had provided the shipwrecked men with blankets, mats and provisions. One of the chiefs, a son of Cedar Canim, not wishing to be outdone in generosity by Schewish, the head chief, gave the captain and crew money. They received the sum with reluctance but were forced to take it by the Indians who wished to give evidence of their good feeling.

The shipwrecked men stayed several days at the Clayoquot trading post. They then engaged two canoes, manned by twenty-one Indians, and were taken to Ucluelet. There, Captain Peter Francis' schooner *Alert* was hired to take them to Victoria.

Medals were also awarded the Hesquiat Indians by the governments of Canada and the United States respectively, for saving the crew of the barque *Edwin*, wrecked Hesquiat Harbour, December 1874, and attempting to save the lives of the crew of the barque *Malleville*, wrecked west of Estevan Point on the night of October 9, 1882 (see pages 39 and 40). Big William, born on the Ucluelet reservation and now in his late nineties, received the British Columbia Centennial Medal.

INDIANS VISIT
ST. LOUIS WORLD FAIR

IN 1904, Dr. C. F. Newcombe took seven Vancouver Island Indians, two from the east coast and five from the west coast, and all carefully chosen for their individual skills in native craftsmanship, to the St. Louis World Fair. From Nootka came Chief Atliu, who in fact was a "medicine man", and also an extraordinarily clever magician, and his daughter Annie Williams. From Opitisaht, on Clayoquot Sound, Frank Jasper, old Mrs. Curley and her son Jack. Charlie, the son of a Kwakiutl chief and another Fort Rupert man, represented the east coast Indians.

In addition to their ceremonial robes, head-dresses, face-masks, animal-skin clothing and grass rugs, they took with them a 40-foot canoe named *Heitl-hei-yachisht*, which means Sea Serpent, totem poles and house figures. Also a knocked-down Indian dwelling-house and trunks filled with baskets, beadware, matting and other articles of native art.

At the fair they re-assembled the dwelling-house, built others like it, erected the totems and house figures, and created a village typical of the British Columbia coast Indians. This was their home for the duration of the fair, where they lived and displayed their different skills. The men carved totems, both large and small, and made dugout canoes; the womenfolk: baskets, matting, beadware etc. Also built — by themselves — was an elaborately decorated communal house, in which tribal dances and other forms of entertainment were staged.

Everything made was sold, at prices unheard of on the coast, and in the end every single article they had brought with them, including the dwelling-house, totems, the sea serpent canoe and all their tribal regalia, was also sold. The proceeds, together with an admission fee charged visitors to their enclosure, not only helped defray expenses of the trip, but provided the Indians with spending money.

The showmanship of Chief Atliu was a special attraction. The Indians themselves said that his performances were "heap strong medicine." Dr. Newcombe said "they completely mystified many of the United States' most outstanding professional magicians." In one, described by Dr. Newcombe, Atliu ran a red-hot poker through the belly of an Indian (an accomplice no doubt) and had it come — still steaming hot — out of the middle of the man's back, and without his suffering any apparent discomfort.

In another, described in an American newspaper, a young negro boy was used to take the part of an Indian child, the party not having one with them. Secretly, a "double" was prepared, made of mutton and green vegetables, with a tube of bullock's blood inserted in the neck. The "act" portrayed an ancient tribal ritual, which called for the child to be sacrificed.

To satisfy themselves that he was alive, onlookers were invited to take a close look at the negro boy who had been made up to resemble an Indian child. Then, mysteriously, the two were switched, and at a given signal during the dance which accompanied the act, the live boy was spirited off-stage and the dummy thrown into a red hot oven and — amid screams from the audience — "roasted to death."

After removal from the oven, to prove that the "boy" was dead, Atliu cut off its head, when out (from the inserted tube) gushed a stream of red blood. He then invited several of his fellow Indians to cut off some portions of the roasted "child's" body (actually cooked mutton and vegetables) and eat it — which they promptly did. At this stage, women in the audience became hysterical. Some called "Police!" However, the chief managed to becalm them by declaring that he would bring the "boy" back to life. More dancing and the beating of drums, another mysterious switch and there stood the boy, bewildered, but very much alive. Handed some peanuts and bananas, and a five-dollar gold piece for his mother, the little negro boy went home quite happy. And he required no coaxing for future performances.

The secret of these illusions, of course Atliu never disclosed, but they dumbfounded the Americans. He was offered tempting vaudeville contracts, but as it was Dr. Newcombe's responsibility to bring his charges back to British Columbia, he ruled against this. At the conclusion of the exposition, Dr. Newcombe was presented with a gold medal, and Chief Atliu, one in bronze; both are now in the British Columbia Provincial Museum at Victoria.

The Indians were afterwards taken to New York, Chicago and several other big cities. They visited several of the United States' biggest museums, where what interested them more than anything else was to see exhibits from their own part of the country. One totem in particular they identified as coming from Alert Bay; in fact, Charley, the Indian from Fort Rupert, had watched his grandfather help carve it. They were also interviewed by leading United States anthropologists.

There is a special story attached to the sea serpent canoe which the Indians took to the fair — and sold. It originally belonged to the Nootkas, who in fact had on several occasions paddled it down the coast to take part — and win races with it — at Victoria's May 24th Gorge Regatta. Shortly before Dr. Newcombe's party left for St. Louis, the Nootkas planned a surprise for the Clayoquots at Opitisaht in the shape of a peaceful visit. Every precaution was taken to keep the secret; however, through the "kelpvine" the Clayoquot people learned of the expedition and were on hand with a royal welcome for their up-coast cousins. There followed one of the greatest potlatches of all time on this part of the coast, and the Nootkas, not to be outdone, gave them *Heitl-hei-yachisht*, the sea serpent canoe.

With its beautifully carved figures fore and aft, and Indian legends painted the length of its sides, the canoe was said to be one of the finest examples of native craftsmanship. Sixteen paddlers and two steerers was its normal crew, but it could carry, and often did, sixty persons or five tons of freight. Its length, over forty feet, with a beam of five foot six inches, indicates the size of the cedar tree from which it was shaped.

Known as the Louisiana Purchase Exposition, the St. Louis World Fair was held to commemorate the one-hundredth anniversary of the purchase from France by the United States of the Louisiana Territory. The United States paid the French Government sixty million francs, besides $3,750,000 in settlement of French spoilation claims.

Medals were usually carried on the owner's person, for apart from their inherent value, the Indians had good reason to know that at times they came in handy and saved them considerable embarrassment. In the days when the West Coast Indians journeyed to the State of Washington for the hop-picking season — a few still do — they often experienced difficulty in finding a suitable place to camp.

The owner of one of the gold medals recalls how on one occasion, when in search of a campsite at Tacoma, they were chased from pillar to post. In desperation, he finally produced the medal which bore the likeness of a past president of the United States. Almost immediately, the Indians were allotted a choice camping ground, with a state patrolman to watch over it.

THE COAST'S
FIRST LIGHTHOUSES

CORTES, the conqueror of Mexico, must be given credit for establishing the first lighthouse on North America's west coast. A square iron frame in which a blazing fire was lighted at nightfall, it was constructed, about the middle of the sixteenth century, outside the harbour entrance to Salina Cruz. Cortes ordered it built to guide the Spanish galleons and caravels into safe harbourage. Fuel for the braziers was difficult to obtain and it is said that the light often went unattended. When the wind blew, the blaze was hidden in billows of smoke. Coal fires were undependable for visibility, brilliant to windward but generally enveloped in smoke to leeward.

Vancouver Island also had its makeshift lighthouses, but three hundred years later. Captain Pinney, who in 1875 operated a trading store on Stubbs Island, Clayoquot Sound, when a schooner was due lit a huge bonfire at the end of the half-mile-long sandspit. Smoke by day, or flames by night, guided the vessel to his store. A modern lighthouse now stands on Lennard Island at the entrance to the Sound. Beacon fires on Whiffin Spit, lit by the families of the Indian hunters, were used to guide the sealing schooners into Sooke harbour. The lighting of bonfires was also resorted to by Indians when visiting tribes from some other part of the coast were expected, or when a canoe failed to turn up after hunting seals or whales.

The first lighthouse north of the Mexican border was built at New Archangel, Sitka, the Russian capital of Alaska, in 1837. It was incorporated with Governor Alexander Baranof's castle on Baranof Island. The governor ordered the construction of a building where he could hold grand balls and entertain foreign dignitaries.

From the top of the castle, 100 feet above the sea, a light burned as a beacon to mariners entering Sitka harbour. In the cupola, four little cups were housed. Into these, seal or whale oil was poured and wicks burned in grooves rising from them. The light was a chore for its keepers, who laboured many hours carrying the heavy containers up the stairs to the lantern; and the brass and copper reflectors had to be polished daily.

Worst of all, it had a ghost. Legend claims that the tower was haunted by a beautiful princess whose untimely death was the result of Baranof's little dictatorship. The truth of her fate is buried in conflicting tales, but the most accepted one claims that her wraith returned at six-month intervals to haunt the northwest chamber where either she had been murdered or had destroyed herself. Aware of the flaming love between the princess and one of his staff, Baranof is said to have banished the officer to Siberia and told her he had been lost at sea. By tradition, this lovely lady, daughter of a former governor, was forced to marry against her will. She mysteriously vanished from the wedding festival and later was found dead in her chamber.

For twenty years after Alaska became United States territory, the beacon continued to function, maintained by soldiers stationed at Sitka. The famous old castle was destroyed by fire in 1894; with it went the cupola that housed the light, and the apparition that haunted its keepers.

The first United States lighthouse on the Pacific coast was established in 1854, on Alcatraz Island in San Francisco Bay. It wasn't suspected then that some day the keepers would have for neighbours that country's toughest criminals. Its 90,000-candlepower light could be seen for a distance of 21 miles. The original hand-tolled fog-bell was later replaced by a 1,500-pound affair tolled by machinery.

On the California, Oregon, Washington and Alaska coasts, there are now over one hundred light stations, each with a permanent lightkeeper and one or more assistants. Cape Sarichef lighthouse, at the western end of Unimak Island in the Aleutians, is the farthest west on the North American continent. British Columbia has fifty-one, of which eleven are on the west coast of Vancouver Island. First lit was Fisgard, at the entrance to Esquimalt Harbour, on November 16, 1860, and Race Rocks, February 7, 1861. Cape Beale lighthouse was established in 1874; Cape Flattery and New Dungeness, both on the American side of Juan de Fuca Strait, in 1857.

BRIGHT STAR OF TATOOSH

*For one hundred years the light
at Flattery has guided mariners.*

JAMES SWAN, author, lawyer and pioneer of over a century ago fittingly described Cape Flattery light as a "bright star." While on a voyage in 1859, he wrote:

> The wind continuing adverse, we were obliged to beat across the entrance of the strait (Juan de Fuca) for five days without gaining anything. But every night we were cheered by the light of Tatoosh Island, which shining like a bright star amid the primeval gloom, seemed to us not only a beacon to the mariner, but as evidence of civilization and a proof that the "star of empire" had made its way westward till the waters of the Pacific had opposed a barrier to the tide of emigration. On the evening of the fifth day the wind changed and a light breeze springing up from the west we ran past the light and found ourselves in the strait.

For over one hundred years now — its light first shone in 1858 — Cape Flattery lighthouse has stood guard over the entrance to Juan de Fuca Strait, the busiest waterway on the northwest coast of the continent, and although it stands on United States territory it has close associations with the early history of British Columbia.

Situated on Tatoosh Island, about a mile off the extreme western tip of Washington State, this important aid to navigation is relied on by all ships entering the Strait, whether heading for Puget Sound or some British Columbia port. Carmanah lighthouse, immediately opposite on the Vancouver Island shore, was built thirty-three years later. During that interval, H.M. ships stationed at Esquimalt and vessels which brought (around the Horn) to British Columbia many of the early settlers, had to depend on Cape Flattery light to find the entrance to the Strait.

Tatoosh Island is also closely associated with the early history of this province. Barkley, Meares, Vancouver and other explorers, all referred to it in their journals. Owing to bad weather when in the vicinity, Cook missed the strait when bound from the Hawaiian Islands to subsequently discover and land at Nootka in 1778. But he did name Cape Flattery, which he thought was merely a point jutting out on an interrupted coastline, in token of the prospect of an improvement in the weather.

Captains Barkley and Vancouver both observed the spired rock (close by) and also the flat-top features of Tatoosh, when they sailed around it into the strait, the former in July 1787, with the East India Company fur trading ship *Imperial Eagle*, when he named, or rather re-named the strait; Vancouver, in April 1792, with his ships *Discovery* and *Chatham*.

Meares, with the sloop *Felice Adventurer*, hove to off Tatoosh on June 29, 1788. He wrote in his journal:

> The island appeared to be a barren rock, almost inaccessible and of no great extent, but its flat surface, as far as we could see, was covered with inhabitants (Indians) who were gazing at the ship. The chief, whose name was "Tatooche", did us the favour of a visit, and so surly and formidable character we had not yet seen.

Lieutenant Aemilius Simpson, of H.M.S. *Cadboro*, on the occasion of his having to anchor in a close-by bay (Neah Bay) during stormy weather in 1827, formed the same opinion of this chief. It is said that every time thereafter when he rounded Tatoosh, he would bring his ship in close, sneer at the natives for whom he bore an intense dislike, and train his six cannon in the direction of the island. Whether he fired any rounds is not recorded, but he probably did.

The decision to establish a lighthouse at Cape Flattery was made by the United States government in 1853. Construction commenced the following year, but was abandoned for over three years due to hostility of the Indians. Those in charge of the topographical survey, carried out two years earlier, termed the island unsafe for white men. Only after barricades had been built to protect the workmen, with guards posted day and night, was construction resumed.

One engineer wrote:

> Knowledge that we were always prepared for an attack, without doubt, prevented one. We built a breastwork and could fire 60 rounds without reloading. The native population numbers 150 and there have already been several unpleasant incidents.

Most of the hostile Indians belonged to northern tribes, the Haidas and the Nootkas, who came in their great war canoes to raid the Makahs, whose principal village was at Neah Bay, just inside Cape Flattery. They left for their homes in the fall, their canoes filled with loot, which included construction workers' tools, and carrying off many of the Makahs' womenfolk. The Makahs were a more peaceful tribe, perhaps because of the money most of them were now making for the first time. From them the construction crews purchased fish, game and basketware. A few were also employed, chiefly hauling supplies of firewood from the mainland and carrying the building material and equipment up from the beach.

The station was completed and in commission by December 1857, but constant fear of the Indians caused the first keepers to quit one after the other and not till late in the following year was the light in constant use. It was twenty years later before white women were permitted to live on the island.

Not only do the original light tower and dwelling stand, but the original Fresnel lens and fittings are still in use. A plate inscription at the base of the tower reads: "Fresnel light, First Order, constructed by order of Honourable the Secretary of Treasury of the United States and the Lighthouse Board. W. A. Bartlett, Lieutenant, U.S. Navy, special superintendent. Louis Sautter & Co., constructors, Paris (France), 1854." (First Order lighthouses on the British Columbia coast also use the Fresnel lens and fittings).

The 300,000-candlepower lamp at Cape Flattery is 165 feet above sea level. It is visible for nineteen miles in clear weather, but the loom of its flashes can be identified from a far greater distance over the horizon. Lard oil was the fuel first used for illuminating the light. When supplies ran short, whale oil, extracted from the huge mammals by the Indians, was substituted. Kerosene followed and in 1896 an incandescent oil lamp was installed.

The station's biggest problem was fuel for the boilers which generated steam for the foghorn and for domestic requirements. Cordwood first had to be brought from the mainland by boat, then hauled up a steep trail. This the Indians contracted to do, but when whaling and fishing was good they were conspicuous by their absence. The station staff then had to rustle what wood it could find strewn along the shore. And the beaches were not strewn with driftlogs as they are today.

Water for drinking purposes was never a problem as the roofs of the buildings are constructed to send rain down into cisterns. The annual rainfall averages 200 inches. The station is now completely electrified. It is administered by the U.S. Coast Guard. A weather reporting station was established on the island in 1883. Whereas at one time four lightkeepers maintained the station, now the island's population numbers about thirty, including the families of the coast-guard and weather bureau personnel. The Indians have long since departed, but their burial grounds and traces of the old stockades remain.

SWIFTSURE LIGHTSHIP

When a sailor gets to thinking
He is one of the best,
Let him ship out on a lightship
And take the acid test.

C. TUCKER

AN EXTRACT from *Sentinels of the North Pacific*, by James A. Gibbs:

> The most exposed aid to navigation in the world is a lightship. Brightly painted (usually red), ship-shape and infallible, it has no place to go. It rolls and pitches, heaves and strains, while huge anchors shackle it to the bottom. When all other maritime traffic takes refuge in a blow, the lightship is a target for the gale. It is at sea more than any other type of vessel, but covers less distance. When blown from station, the lightship fights back to regain position so that its lamp and foghorn might quell the fears of tempest-tossed mariners.

The world's first lightship was established at the mouth of London's Thames in 1713. The initial American lightship was in Chesapeake Bay at the mouth of Elizabeth River, 1820. Canada pioneered this type of aid to navigation on the Pacific coast, when, in 1866, a lightship was placed on station at the mouth of the Fraser River (replaced in 1957 by a steel and concrete tower).

Prior to 1961, the United States had five on its west coast; now, only one. Best known to Canadians was the Swiftsure Bank lightship, which has since been moved to a position twelve miles below Cape Flattery where it marks treacherous Umatilla Reef. The other four positions, including Swiftsure, are now marked by unwatched lights. It was originally planned to replace them with "Texas

Towers," similar to the rigs used for off-shore oil drilling, but the idea was dropped, buoys being used instead.

Established in 1909, Swiftsure lightship was moored on Swiftsure Bank, which is three-and a-half miles in extent and lies off the entrance to Juan de Fuca Strait about midway between Cape Flattery and Pachena Point. The bank was named after H.M.S *Swiftsure*, which, in 1889, reported a sounding of twenty fathoms in this position. The light vessel was used by outbound ships as a point of departure on the first leg of the Great Circle track to the Orient. It was also the point of arrival mariners sought when making in for the Strait. The vessel itself was also the turn-around point for yachts taking part in the internationally known annual Swiftsure ocean racing classic. Held in May, the race starts and finishes off the Victoria breakwater.

BLINKERS JUST USEFUL
NOT PRETTY

IMPORTANT AIDS to navigation are the little blinker lights seen at intervals along the shoreline, usually on a rock, a point jutting out into the sea, or a buoy in the harbour. They were not placed there for trigger-happy marksmen to take pot-shots at, which unfortunately happens. Instead, they were installed to assist the captain of a ship, whether ocean liner, coastal freighter, tug, fishboat or pleasure craft, to find his way through the narrow passages that lie between the myriad of small islands which dot the coast. They also help him steer clear of the dangerous reefs, shoals and sandbars, that he may reach his destination, be it one of our busiest harbours or the head of a remote inlet, without mishap.

Lighthouses guard the entrance to our main ship channels and harbours, but it is the small stationary lights and the automatically controlled "blinkers", that warn mariners of the hazards in between. Each has an official number and is named after the nearest geographical landmark on the marine chart for that area. Their exact nautical position, together with each one's individual characteristics, is also indicated in a booklet titled *List of Light and Fog Signals on the Pacific Coast and the Rivers and Lakes of British Columbia*, issued by the Department of Transport at Ottawa. Lighthouses and buoys are listed in the same publication. The buoys, usually placed off the entrance of a harbour or inlet, have an automatic light and are also equipped with bell or whistle, sounded by the motion of the buoy on the waves. Many also have a radar reflector.

Unlike our lighthouses where the tower, dwelling and other buildings are always well painted and the surroundings kept neat and tidy, these important little lights make no pretence at being ornamental. It is their usefulness that counts, not looks. They usually stand barely above highwater mark, are continually drenched by spray, and for that reason have to be sturdily built. Seagulls and cormorants mess them up a little, but this doesn't interfere with their efficiency.

These lights are all unwatched and they vary in type. The majority blink or flash every few seconds; others are fixed lights, either white or red and in some cases both, with one sector of the arc showing white and the other — to warn of a dangerous reef — red. A plain white light, flashing at regular intervals, is the most common. Where electricity is available, the light and the timing of the flashes is automatically controlled from shore. Elsewhere they are illuminated with acetylene gas, with the timing of the flashes regulated by a clockwork adjustment in the base of the lamp. It may sound strange, but kangaroo skin, the only material known to be impervious to acetylene gas, plays an important part in this delicate mechanism.

The gas cylinders are renewed periodically, a constant chore for the lighthouse tender crews. Some of the lights in remote places are supplied with sufficient gas to last over six months and the modern lights automatically turn themselves out during daylight hours. Necessity, rather than accessibility, determines where they should be placed and for that reason the majority are erected on some prominent rock at the entrance of a harbour or bay, a turn in the inlet, or near a dangerous shoal.

In construction, they consist of a short mast embedded in concrete, with the gas cylinders securely lashed to the base. To act as a daytime marker, sometimes a slatted wooden framework painted white is built a little further back on the rock and often the rock itself is painted white. Others are placed on floating platforms, a pile dolphin, at the end of a breakwater or atop a wharf shed. In some instances the light is merely a lantern suspended from a pole or the cross-arm of a mast. With each light, the timing of the flashes is definitely fixed; the character and time of light is marked on marine charts and also set out in the official list.

In addition to its 11 lighthouses, the west coast of Vancouver Island has 15 buoys and 65 blinker lights. The number increases every year, for no sooner is some industrial plant built at the head of an up-coast inlet than additional aids to navigation must be installed to assist ships to reach them. Plain spar buoys, painted either black or red, mark the channels where sandbars exist. Like the buoys, their colour denotes on which side they should be passed. They are not lighted.

THE HYDROGRAPHERS

"Slaves" plot the coast.

CAPTAIN GEORGE VANCOUVER was the first man to undertake a survey of the shores of what is now known as British Columbia. His chart, prepared during the three years (1792-1793-1794) he spent on this coast, was considered a masterpiece of accuracy and comprehensiveness, and is still referred to by cartographers as the "Great Chart." The Spanish explorers, who were here about the same time, also made charts, but only of local areas.

A more thorough examination of the coast was made by the British Admiralty during the years 1842-1900, principally by H.M. SURVEY VESSELS *Cormorant, Herald, Pandora, Plumper, Hecate, Egeria* and the hired *Beaver*. Their names and those of their masters appear frequently on previous pages and their work is reflected in the Admiralty charts of that period.

With the withdrawal of H.M. ships from this station in 1910, the work was continued by the Hydrographic Survey Board of Canada, using first the *Egeria*, which remained on the coast specially for the purpose, then the converted naval tug *Restless* and later the house-scows *Fraser* and *Somass*. The first Canadian vessel to be assigned exclusively for survey duty on this coast was the steamer *Lillooet*, which has long since been scrapped. Now there are five ships: the *Wm. J. Stewart*, largest of the fleet, *Marabell, Parry, Ehkoli* and *Richardson*, and their work is likely to continue for many years to come.

It is the *Wm. J. Stewart* which uses the "slaves" and they play a very important part in the operation of the "Decca" two-range system with which she is equipped. This is a modern installation for pin-pointing, regardless of visibility, the ship's position at sea, and it also requires the vessel to be equipped with a special 6o-foot-high aluminum lattice-work mast festooned with antenna and aerials.

The slaves are small self-contained radio stations located ashore, often on a small island or an uninhabited stretch of coastline. They comprise two prefabricated units, one to house two operators, control and receiving equipment; the other, two diesel generators. Crews are in radio telephone contact with the ship.

They must be high-level sites, free from obstructions to the radio waves carried over the sea, and located with the highest degree of accuracy, because from them measurements will be made which determine the precise position of the ship and enable charting of the exact depth of water in her location. The slave master is the chief hydrographer aboard the *Wm. J. Stewart*.

Here is how the system works: An impulse from the ship's master station triggers an answer from a pair of slave stations, whose exact positions are known. By a rather complicated comparison of frequencies, reading on two ship's dials are obtained and these are readily translated into distances. Where the arcs of the distances from the slaves intersect is the ship's position. Simultaneously, the ship's echo sounder bounces a beam wave off the sea bottom and the depth (in fathoms) is automatically recorded on a graph.

Visual signals — land or heavenly — are therefore no longer necessary and the survey of a broad expanse of water can be carried on in spite of fog, rain, snow, winds or heavy seas. The slaves take care of everything, except in the remote possibility of some freak atmospheric disturbance close by. Another advantage is that the exact position of the ship and the depth of water under it can be pin-pointed on the chart as frequently as the chief hydrographer aboard the *Wm. J. Stewart* deems necessary, and while the vessel is travelling at normal speed.

Marabell surveys the bays and smaller inlets. The *Parry* is used exclusively on tide and current survey. The field work of the hydrographers aboard her, and the readings from a score of fixed tide gauges located at different places along the coast, provide the information found in *Pacific Coast Tide and Current Tables*, published yearly by the Canadian Hydrographic Service, Surveys and Mapping Branch, Department of Mines and Technical Surveys, Ottawa. The *Ehkoli*, sister ship to the *Parry*, is engaged in oceanographic survey. The 85-foot *Richardson*, the latest addition to the fleet, was designed and built especially for work in Arctic waters and is based at Tuktoyaktuk at the mouth of the Mackenzie River. The other four vessels operate from April to October and during the winter months are tied up at Victoria, where the hydrographers co-relate their summer's work.

Referring back to Vancouver's Great Chart. At a meeting of the Victoria branch of the B.C. Historical Association held at the time of this writing, a senior officer from the Esquimalt naval base told his listeners how, for the purpose of testing the accuracy of the chart, he despatched a frigate to the head of a remote inlet on the northern British Columbia coast. The vessel was manned principally by officer cadets from H.M.C.S. *Venture*, the naval training school at Esquimalt, and her master was instructed to follow — both north and southbound — the inside passages.

On requesting his charts, the navigating officer was handed Vancouver's Great Chart, and he was further instructed that all of the ship's regular charts were to be kept in a locked and sealed drawer in the chartroom — the seal to be broken only in case of emergency. The frigate duly reached her destination and returned to Esquimalt after a successful and very interesting 1,000-mile cruise which occupied five days, and without her commanding officer having to break the seal on the locked drawer which contained the modern charts.

NOT ALL SURGICAL OPERATIONS are performed in highly specialized and spotlessly clean operating theatres. Many, by force of circumstances, have to be undertaken in places far removed from the atmosphere of a modern hospital under considerable physical stress and distress.

We frequently hear of a seaman aboard some tramp steamer on the high seas being stricken suddenly and that in response to a SOS a warship or merchant vessel in the vicinity is rushing to the scene. Then, that a doctor has been transferred by breeches-buoy or one of the ship's lifeboats — often with heavy seas running — and an operation is performed on the high seas.

Such incidents usually make headlines, but little was heard of doctors practicing in remote up-coast communities, who often had to perform a delicate operation on a kitchen table and without aid of either anæsthetist or trained nurse. In areas where there were no roads and at coastal points with infrequent steamer service, prior to airplanes becoming commonplace, many an appendectomy had to be performed or a limb amputated under these conditions. But now when we read of an R.C.A.F. or commercial pilot making a mercy flight to some isolated village or camp, it means that the patient will be operated on in a well-equipped hospital and receive all the care which modern science can provide.

These conditions didn't only apply away up in the far northern parts of British Columbia. As recently as thirty years ago, that part of the west coast of Vancouver Island between Tofino and Cape Cook was just as isolated. Steamer service was once every ten days and the only hospitals were at Port Alberni, more than one hundred miles to the south, and Port Alice, the same distance north. Neither place could be reached by road, for there were none, or via inside passages, and for days at a time during the winter the seas would be too rough for a small boat.

As there were few planes in Vancouver in those days and none on the West Coast, if a serious accident occurred between steamer days and the weather was bad, the unfortunate victim often had to be operated on there and then. The same applied if a person was suddenly stricken with serious illness.

During the summer months there was usually a fishing boat near at hand, but the trip (if the weather was favourable) might take a day-and-a-half, a long uncomfortable journey for a badly injured or very sick man. Owing to cramped quarters and limited facilities on these boats, and the fact that it was not always practical for the doctor or anyone else to accompany them, sometimes the patient died before reaching hospital.

Ship to shore communication was not as handy as it is now, but if either the lighthouse tender *Estevan* or the fisheries patrol vessels *Givenchy* or *Malaspina* chanced to be handy and could be contacted, they never failed to rush an emergency case to hospital. The public heard little or nothing about these mercy trips, but they saved many a life and untold suffering.

The Bamfield and Tofino lifeboats were often called upon for the same purpose; but these were then open boats and just as uncomfortable in rough weather as a fishboat. In later years a provincial police boat was stationed on the West Coast and it, too, was sometimes called; but it was based at Port Alberni and not always immediately available. Then by the time it did arrive it was often too late. Neither was there a road between Tofino and Ucluelet, where a person could be taken overland to a boat on Barkley Sound. This road was only completed during the Second World War.

Between 1925 and 1940 there were twelve pilchard reduction plants, several canneries and two logging camps in the Nootka-Kyuquot area alone; in all employing about 1,000 men. Each plant had its emergency kit, but the nearest first-aid station where a badly injured man could get proper care was at Ceepeecee; fortunately with a very capable man in charge, but no doctor. The only doctor on this part of the coast was at Tofino, 80 miles away by water.

Without the facilities of a hospital this lone doctor had to practice under severe handicaps. Whenever possible he sent the more serious cases out and only operated when he considered it imperative to save a life or limb. Apart from accidents, many of his emergency

CAPE FLATTERY LIGHTHOUSE ON TATOOSH ISLAND
United States Coast Guard Photo

Swiftsure Lightship, until 1961 familiar to sailormen of all nations who sailed the Pacific Northwest. Since moved to new position 15 miles farther south. *United States Coast Guard Photo.*

H.M.S. *Plumper*, Captain George Henry Richards, R.N., surveying coast in 1858. Armed with 12 cannon *Plumper* was an auxiliary steam sloop, barque rigged, 484 tons, 60 h.p.; speed under steam about six knots. *Photo from a drawing, Provincial Archives.*

HYDROGRAPHIC SURVEY VESSEL *Wm. J. Stewart*. Note lattice-work mainmast festooned with antennae and aerials. *Hydrographic Survey Photo.*

"Doll's House" Hospital at Ceepeecee which once served 1,500 people.

Kildonan, Barkley Sound. A typical West Coast reduction plant, now closed owing to the mysterious disappearance of the pilchards. *B.C. Government Travel Bureau Photo.*

cases were acute appendicitis. During a period of five years, three men had their appendixes removed on the kitchen table of the old Tofino hotel; one in a shack on a floating logging camp, at least two in private homes and those of three Indian children and a man, in a mission school. Other makeshift "operating theatres" were pressed into service wherever the patient happened to be.

Because no other doctor was available, a general anæsthetic could not be administered and a "spinal" was usually resorted to. This meant that some strong fisherman or logger had to pinion the patient's arms and prevent him from moving throughout the entire operation; an interesting experience, but an ordeal for a layman. Sometimes an ex-nurse might be available, but more often than not some housewife substituted and passed the swabs. Many a mulligan pot had to improvise as a sterilizer.

Since that time hospitals have been built at Tofino, Esperanza (Ceepeecee) and when the gold mines were in operation there was one at Zeballos. The Red Cross Society also has emergency outpost hospitals at Bamfield and Kyuquot, each with a nurse in charge.

There are also four doctors in the area instead of one and as practically every fishboat and camp now has radio-telephone, and planes are based at Zeballos, Tofino and Port Alberni, little time is lost before a doctor is at the scene. The injured or sick person reaches one of these hospitals within a few hours or, if necessary, is flown direct to one of the larger hospitals on the outside.

"DOLLS' HOUSE" HOSPITAL, better describes Ceepeecee's first-aid station referred to on page 240. Incredible as it may seem, it served the purpose of a hospital for nearly 1,500 people who lived on Nootka Sound and Kyuquot Sound. They were mostly fishermen, cannery and reduction plant workers, and loggers, their families and about 400 Indians.

Without the assistance of government grants and entirely through the generosity of fishing companies, one small logging camp and the people themselves, the little building which comprised two rooms, one with two cots, the other for examination and emergency surgery, was built, equipped and maintained.

In charge was Mr. P. B. Ashbridge, Royal Army Medical Corps-trained, with service in South Africa and later World War I, with the Canadian Field Ambulance. It made no pretence at being a hospital, nor was it possible to give the nursing care received in such institutions. If its two beds were already occupied, arrangements were made for others to be taken care of in one of the cannery bunkhouses.

The less seriously sick or injured were treated immediately and returned to their homes, to return as required for further treatment. Every effort was made to have those obviously suffering from acute illness, and those badly injured, conveyed to Port Alice or Port Alberni, either by the *Princess Maquinna*, which came every ten days, or some other vessel. If the weather was fine and the patient fit to travel by small boat, a fishing vessel would make the emergency trip, but more often than not this was impossible owing to rough seas. If handy, one of the Old Faithfuls — *Estevan*, *Givenchy* or

Malaspina — readily responded to such calls, when the patient would be conveyed to hospital in reasonable comfort.

Mr. Ashbridge continued to operate his little "hospital" till 1933, when he was appointed Indian agent and stipendiary magistrate at Port Alberni. During that time he treated practically every injury from a fractured skull to a sprained ankle. Second degree burns were common. He kept no accurate count, but during that time he also extracted about 1,000 teeth.

In addition to sitting day and night administering to some patient whose life "hung on a thread" and who couldn't possibly be moved, Mrs. Ashbridge, her husband's only assistant, sent many an anxious mother home happy after assuring her that her little boy or girl suffered nothing more serious than a sore throat or slight infection. Mrs. Ashbridge also assisted in many childbirths.

The psychological effect of having, on such an isolated part of the coast, a highly trained team like Mr. and Mrs. Ashbridge, made the lives of these people far happier. It also frequently saved them an expensive trip to the outside. The physical welfare of the native population was also taken care of, without compensation — except in very rare cases — from the Department of Indian Affairs.

Mrs. Ian Davies, a trained nurse from Vancouver, took over from Mr. Ashbridge and continued to run the little "hospital" till 1937, when the Nootka General Hospital at Esperanza, in the next bay to Ceepeecee, was built. In the meantime, the Zeballos gold rush occurred and by the time the mines came into production, that town, which two years previous had a population of about ten, now had a thirty-bed hospital. A Red Cross outpost hospital at Kyuquot, with a nurse in charge, was also built about the same time.

The little "hospital" stood across the bay from the cannery wharf, but could be reached by a short trail and was always a source of interest for passengers on the *Princess Maquinna*. No solicitation of any kind was made, but visitors frequently left behind a cheque towards its upkeep.

The Nootka Mission Hospital at Esperanza was originally sponsored by the Shantymen's Christian Association, which for the past forty years has maintained a fleet of small mission boats on the West Coast. Head of the association is Reverend Percy E. Wills, of Victoria.

243

WHERE DID THE
PILCHARDS GO?

Mystery still unsolved.

WHY DID THE PILCHARDS so mysteriously disappear? A $2 million-a-year industry was wiped out overnight and both fishermen and biological experts are still seeking the answer. Related to the mackerel family and slightly larger than a good-sized herring, this little fish with such an extraordinary high oil content, thirty-five years ago caused one of the greatest flurries in the fishing industry on the British Columbia and California coasts.

Although the species was always known to frequent local waters, prior to 1924 the schools were very small. Nootka cannery canned several thousand cases but later gave it up as the fish were not received favourably on the market. Small shipments also found their way to the fresh fish market; but they too, on account of the pilchard's high oil content, found little favour. Consequently the fishermen passed them up.

Suddenly in 1925 the waters adjacent to the west coast of Vancouver Island appeared to be literally alive with them; schools acres in extent frequently observed. For years previously the sardine industry on the California coast had been in full swing. A percentage of the catch, by U.S. law, had to be canned for human consumption, the balance processed into meal and oil. Coincidentally with an increased demand for these latter products for agriculture and manufacturing purposes, it was discovered that the pilchard found off our coast was the same fish, only considerably larger. Also, that grown to maturity, its oil content was far greater in proportion to its size than when caught farther south as a sardine.

Enterprising California manufacturers of fish reduction machinery, hearing of this, lost no time in promoting sales of their processing machinery to Canadian fishing interests; Nootka cannery and Watson Bros. at Matilda Creek (Ahousat) being the first to install the American-made oil processing and drying kilns. Other companies quickly followed suit and by 1927 there were no less than twenty-six pilchard reduction plants between Barkley Sound and Kyuquot. Many operated in conjunction with existing salmon canneries, but the majority were built specially for the purpose. Suitable sites were at a premium, requiring good penetration for pile-driving, shelter for boats and docks, and above all, a plentiful water supply. Construction crews could ask any price for their hire. Victoria and Vancouver shipyards worked night and day building seine boats and scows, while fishing companies vied with one another in a mad scramble to cash in on the bonanza. Meanwhile the pilchards continued to show up in greater bulk.

Within three years from scratch (1925) the combined plants were together employing for a four to five month season, 500 men ashore and another 500 represented in the various boat crews; 75 seine boats, 100 tugs and scout boats and 50 scows. Both the C.P.R. and Frank Waterhouse Co. diverted freighters to pack the oil and meal, and the oil companies special tankers to keep both plants and boats supplied with fuel.

During the first few years of operation fishing was confined exclusively to the inlets of Barkley, Clayoquot, Nootka and Kyuquot Sounds. The fish were conveyed to the different plants in scows. Then for some reason, known only to the fish themselves, they suddenly changed their habits and every year thereafter remained miles off-shore, only an occasional school showing up inside. The fishermen then had likewise to change their tactics. Heavy ground swells experienced out in the open ocean permitted only the larger seine boats to handle the huge nets. The flat open scows were discarded and replaced by 100-ton packers for conveying the fish to the plants.

Owing to lack of suitable boats for these changed conditions, many of the smaller plants closed down and by 1940 only ten were operating. In 1944 there was a marked decrease in the number of fish showing up, the fishermen often having to go as far south as the mouth of the Columbia River for the few they did catch. In 1946 not one showed up and there hasn't been a pilchard seen since!

The season usually lasted throughout July, August, September and well into October if weather conditions remained favourable. The fishermen then turned their attention to herring, which were also processed into meal and oil in addition to being canned. A

245

single catch (or set, in fisherman's language) by one boat usually averaged from 50 to 200 tons, but sets of 500 tons were occasionally made by one boat. In the latter case several other boats would go to her assistance, all sharing the fish. One boat's catch for the season averaged around 2,500 tons. When all twenty-five plants were in operation considerably over 100,000 tons of pilchards would be the average season's overall catch. Fishermen were paid on a tonnage basis, shared equally by the various crews, with the skippers receiving an additional bonus. With the fish in good condition, 45 gallons of oil was obtained from one ton of pilchards.

Illustrating the pilchard's high oil content: If one was placed in a bowl in the hot sun (where the cat could not reach it), in twenty-four hours only skin and backbone remained, plus a bowl of oil.

Pilchard meal (herring meal the same) has many uses, principally for fertilizers and for mixing with cattle and poultry feed. The oil was used extensively in the manufacture of most domestic products requiring an edible oil base, such as salad dressings, shortening, margarine, etc. It was also used for mixing high grade paints, and in milady's cosmetic preparations.

An interesting observation disclosed that for some unexplained reason the pilchard was seldom, if ever, observed in the waters of Juan de Fuca Strait, Puget Sound, or between Vancouver Island and the mainland. Schools occasionally showed up in Hecate Strait, but not many. Two other significant facts were also noted. They only appeared off the Island's west coast when the water temperature registered a degree or two higher than the normal summer average and when a certain form of microscopic feed made its appearance. These two points, however, appear to have little or no bearing in their subsequent disappearance, for many summers have since come and gone with both water temperature favourable and this feed showing up, but still no pilchards.

As to why they disappeared or where they went, many theories have been advanced but none substantiated. Our fishermen blamed the California sardine industry for catching every pilchard (sardine) that came their way. From San Francisco to the Gulf of California the coastline was dotted with sardine canneries, with a fleet of boats numbering in the thousands, fishing anywhere from the beaches to one hundred miles out to sea. However, one satisfaction Canadian pilchard fishermen derived out of the existing state of affairs, was that the sardine fishermen of California found themselves in the same boat.

Like the pilchards, the sardines have gone and that industry too.

The fishermen further point out that during the years they fished them, the sea would frequently be alive with pilchards and, overnight, they would disappear for weeks at a time, only to return in greater quantities than ever. They just seemed to have a habit of disappearing when they so felt inclined and reappear if and when they saw fit.

As to why they disappeared is a big question. Another theory is that they left the shores of the North American continent altogether. They have since been reported showing up in waters adjacent to New Zealand and Australia, and in the Indian Ocean. Meanwhile both United States and Canadian biologists are carrying out extensive research in an effort to find the answer, and if possible revive this valuable fishery.

But West Coast fishermen, as they ride the ocean swells in search of salmon, halibut and cod, still keep a sharp lookout for that telltale "flip", a clear indication of a school of pilchard.

Who knows? Someday they may see it again!

LONG BEACH

LONG BEACH, which lies midway between Ucluelet and Tofino, is the only place in British Columbia where the Pacific Ocean can be reached by road. A view of the ocean is obtained from other points along the coast, but only from a distance. Its broad expanse of hard white sand — ten miles long and a quarter of a mile wide — on which the surf never ceases to pound, is its chief attraction. Here, an awe-inspiring sight is presented when gale-force winds lash the coast. Mountainous white-crested seas come following one another in endless succession, only to break on the beach with a thunderous roar and cover the sands with acres of white foam. In the wake of the storm comes the ground swells, often barely perceptible a mile out, but which build up into solid walls of green water as they near shore. When they break, the earth trembles and the noise can be heard far inland.

To sit on the driftlogs strewn along high-water mark and breathe in that bracing salt air, while admiring the never-to-be-forgotten panoramic seascape, catches the most sluggish imagination. A fish boat, one minute in full view, the next, almost out of sight in the trough with only the top of its mast showing; passing ships, some hulldown on the horizon, a school of porpoise or blackfish, an occasional whale and sea lions sunning themselves on a small island, complete the picture; while an effective backdrop is created by the ever-changing colour of the clouds and their reflection in the sea.

For the treasure-seeker, Long Beach is a happy hunting ground. It is for ever coming up with something new. The rusting plates, an anchor or chain, relics of ships which came to grief on these shores, are sometimes exposed after a big storm — only to be buried again by the next. Flotsam and jetsam, brought in by tide and storm, can be picked up among the driftwood; popular finds are the glass balls which fishermen in far off Japan use for floats (see page 170). Bamboo poles, which also drift across the Pacific, are another favourite, along with shells of every kind and brightly coloured corals. Hatch-covers, wooden gratings, broken boats and other pieces of wreckage; lifebelts, empty wine casks and wicker-covered demijohns. A whale's vertebra, a sea lion's skull or the jawbone of a shark, along with similar curiosities, are eagerly sought and carried away by visitors, or to create an appropriate effect around the home of those people who live by the sea.

Visitors find no end of places to explore, among them old Indian burial grounds and abandoned villages. Also, the tumbled-down stockades and earthworks behind which the Clayoquots defended themselves against raiding tribes, principally the Makahs from Neah Bay. No Indians reside at Long Beach now. It was once the home of Wickaninnish, a famous chief who over one hundred years ago reigned supreme over this part of the coast (see page 13). Its proper name is Wickaninnish Bay, so marked on land maps and marine charts.

Monster crabs may be caught by wading in the sea, or in the shallow pools left by the receding tide, and the elusive razor clams — found only on surf-pounded beaches — may be dug. Pools in the rocks may be searched for the multi-coloured sea anemone and exotic marine plants. Schooner Cove, at the far end and separated by a rocky outcrop, is another interesting place to explore. On a cliff-face near the ruins of an Indian village are some petroglyphic carvings well worth seeing; the figures comprise seals, sea lions, halibut and several unidentified objects. It is significant that fish are plentiful in this locality, a seal rookery on nearby rocks and fur-bearing animals in the hills.

A mile east of Long Beach is Florencia Bay, named after a vessel of that name wrecked there in 1861 (see page 82). This beach is two miles long with the same exposure at low tide. Fine gold can be recovered from its sand, a pastime enjoyed by visitors. Years ago small syndicates and individual prospectors worked the sands, but returns were indifferent.

Kennedy Lake, Vancouver Island's largest, motorists see shortly before they reach Long Beach, where the road follows its east shore-line for about five miles. The lake was named after His Excellency Captain Arthur Edward Kennedy, c.b., governor of Vancouver Island from 1864 to 1866, when the mainland and the island were joined as one colony, British Columbia. Eighteen feet above sea level, it empties into Tofino Inlet at Kenfalls Rapids, where excellent trout and steelhead fishing is to be had. Kennedy and Clayoquot rivers, which both flow into the lake, also provide good fishing.

Long Beach airport, built as an operational base by the R.C.A.F. during World War II, extends from the beach back to the upper end of Tofino Inlet, where float-equipped planes land. Here boats can be launched giving visitors the whole of Tofino Inlet and Clayoquot Sound, also numerous lakes and streams, to explore. In winter, geese and ducks make Tofino Inlet a sportsman's paradise, with crab plentiful on the tidal flats.

Tofino and Ucluelet, where a fifth of British Columbia's troll-caught salmon catch is landed, are both well worth a visit; chief attraction for visitors is in the evenings when the trollers come in from the ocean and land their fish at the buying camps. There are beaches near Tofino, at Bamfield, Pachena Bay, Clo-oose and others farther up-coast. All face the open ocean and, though smaller, have the same characteristics as Long Beach.

Buried in the sand at the west end of Long Beach is the burned-out hull of a sailing vessel, about the size of a schooner and believed to have been wrecked there at least one hundred and fifty years ago. This space of time is arrived at from the fact that as far back as the 1880's, the few old Indians who still lived at Long Beach had no knowledge of it. Where it lies buried, just above normal high-water level immediately in front of the Lovekin residence, is now covered with aged driftlogs, stunted spruce and beach weeds, and few people living can pinpoint the exact spot.

Shortly before the First Great War a group of American university students spent a summer investigating the wreck, but the only tools they had to work with were picks and shovels. They did, however, manage to expose the upper part of the hull, but heavy seas which coincided with a high spring tide buried it again, and as their time was limited they were forced to abandon the project. The students took back with them, for further study, photographs, measurements, specimens of timbers, spikes and copper fastenings, but whether the vessel or its country of origin has since been identified is not known.

Known shipwrecks which occurred on or in the vicinity of Long Beach are found in previous pages.

HOT SPRINGS

In unique location.

AT THE EXTREME TIP of a wooded peninsular on what might well be described as the most exposed part of the West Coast, is a hot spring, wholly undeveloped, free for all to enjoy and worth a million if handy and accessible by road. But unfortunately it is not and perhaps never will be, at least not in our lifetime. It can only be reached, first by boat or plane, then via a one-and-a-half mile bush trail from Hot Springs Cove, an isolated fishing settlement near the entrance to Sydney Inlet.

Facing the open Pacific, with fishboats passing within a stone's throw, the location of the spring is unique, in all probability unequalled in the world. A handy patch of salal substitutes for a bathhouse and what probably catches the bather's imagination more than anything else, is to stand in that bracing fresh salt air — and get drenched with salt spray when the seas are rough — while admiring the never-to-be-forgotten panoramic seascape.

In British Columbia there are few populated areas where the spectacle of the sun disappearing over the horizon can be observed; but it does here. Stay late enough and be rewarded with a sunset that takes your breath away. Can one visualize a hot spring, of all things, in a more unique setting?

Only when the sea is calm, which is seldom, can a boat land on the rocks in front of the spring. Its origin lies about 150 feet inland and 20 feet above sea level, in dense bush. Here, at a temperature of 189°, the water flows out of the ground at approximately 100 gallons per minute, forms a short steaming stream, then over a ten-foot fall to a series of pools in the rocks below in its brief run to the sea. Temperature of the water is somewhat lowered by the time it

251

reaches the falls, but still a little too hot for a shower. Each of the pools is big enough for two or three people to bathe in at one time.

The unusual feature of the spring's location is experienced during the high spring tide period. At their peak, the swells from the open Pacific rush up a gulch and momentarily fill the pools with cold salt water, sometimes bringing with it pieces of seaweed and occasionally a fish. The bather thus has the rare experience of one minute enjoying a hot sulphur bath, and the next, cold sea water — all in the same "tub".

The water has been analyzed and found to contain, in addition to sulphur, mineral salts, iron oxides, calcium and other chemical elements, all of which afford a remedy, or at least relief, for many of our present-day ailments. West Coast residents believe it provides the "elixir of life." Many, particularly those who suffer from rheumatics in different form, visit the springs regularly. One old prospector, who lived to be ninety and credited his longevity to the curative properties of the water, made it an annual pilgrimage. He came in his rowboat and camped beside the spring. He not only bathed in the water several times a day, but drank it by the gallon; then he would return home to his cabin, forty miles away, feeling like a new man.

One can smell the sulphur fumes half a mile away and the steam can be seen by passing ships. The water is soft and lathers well; consequently, fishermen from near and far, white, Indian and Japanese alike, not only bathe there and drink it, but do their laundry as well.

The Indian name for the spring is *Mok-seh-kla-chuck*, meaning smoking water. That the water cured their many ailments was discovered long before white man came. It is a common sight to see half a dozen Indian women doing the family wash in the creek above the falls, while the menfolk bathe in the pools below. People from far away places also visit the springs regularly. A Tacoma man, partially crippled with arthritis, has been coming in his private yacht for the past twenty years. Other regular visitors come in their yachts and cabin cruisers and there is a doctor from Portland, Oregon, who comes by plane.

The trail to the springs runs through Maquinna Park. It is kept open by the Provincial Highways Department. The 35-acre park, named after the famous Nootka chief and still undeveloped, was donated to the province by Mr. and Mrs. Ivan H. Clarke of Hot Springs Cove.

The cove itself, which has a narrow entrance and is only two miles long, was formerly known as Refuge Cove because of the safe anchorage it afforded fishing vessels in bad weather. The name was changed a few years ago by the Geographic Board of Canada to avoid confusion with another Refuge Cove on the mainland coast. Its only inhabitants are about twenty white and the same number of Indian families, but transient fishermen swell the number during the summer months. Nearest settlement of importance is Tofino, twenty miles away by water.

Hot springs also occur at the head of Matilda Inlet (Ahousat), but there the water is only lukewarm and forms shallow pools. On an inaccessible rocky island off the southeast coast of the Queen Charlotte Islands is another, with the water at almost boiling point.

Long Beach, looking west from centre. *B.C. Government Travel Bureau Photo.*

A waterfall at near boiling point cascades into the sea at Hot Springs Cove; 20 miles beyond Tofino, still unexploited and free for all to enjoy. Unfortunately it cannot be reached by road, but only by boat or trail.

CHIEF JOSEPH AND
HIS "QUEEN" MARY

Maquinna and Wickaninnish each occupies a niche in West Coast history. Then came a period, between the time of the early explorers and the arrival of the first white settlers, when little was heard of those who succeeded these famous chiefs. All we know is their names and of isolated incidents — most of them unpleasant — in which they became involved with the crews of certain trading ships.

Among the tribal heads of our time, one of the best known and highly respected, among whites and Indians alike, was Chief Joseph of the Clayoquots. Joseph ruled with a firm hand and his word was law. Differences among his own people he arbitrated himself. Crime against white-man-made laws he would not countenance and he personally saw that offenders made no attempt to escape their due punishment. In that respect, his counsel was of inestimable value to the Department of Indian Affairs and the provincial police.

With his wife, "Queen Mary", a kindly old soul if ever there was one, and loved by her people, Joseph resided at Opitisaht, across the bay from Tofino. The late W. T. Dawley, who, in the days when Indians would accept nothing but gold and silver currency, operated a general store on Stubbs Island, described him as "a shrewd bargainer but an honest man". At that time Indians were not allowed inside the building. Purchases were made through a wicket, alongside which a loaded rifle was kept handy. However, the rule didn't apply to Chief Joseph and "Queen Mary". They had the run of the store.

In his younger days, Joseph's prowess as a whale killer was well known among his people. Sealing schooner captains bid high for his services as a hunter and he made many voyages to the Bering Sea. As a canoeman he had no peer, and his eight-man crew often journeyed to Victoria to take part in the May 24th Gorge Regatta.

In time, power boats replaced the canoe. Perhaps because the early model engines were hard to start, or on account of his age, Joseph was among the few Indians who never owned one. He preferred the canoe and almost every day, summer and winter, he and "Queen Mary" paddled across from Opitisaht village to Stubbs Island. There the couple would haul their canoe out on the spit and walk along the beach to the store; the purpose of their visit, more often than not, just to have a talk with Walter Dawley. To his potlatches, Joseph frequently invited the residents of Tofino and Clayoquot. He was among the distinguished guests present at the big Indian festival held at Sooke in the summer of 1921.

In 1927, on a nearby beach, members of the Tofino branch of the Canadian Legion staged "The landing, in 1778, of Captain Cook at Nootka". "Cook", wearing his tri-cornered hat, the full dress naval head-dress of that period, lace-trimmed black frocked uniform, white gloves, silk stockings and black shoes with silver buckles, was rowed ashore by twelve sailors (members of the Legion), who also were attired in uniforms of the period.

He was met by Chief Joseph, who portrayed the part of Maquinna, chief of the Nootkas, and "Queen Mary", both arrayed in their war paints, bare legged, bare armed and clothed in bearskin rugs. "Queen Mary" wore a cedar-bark wreath around her head; Chief Joseph, the traditional Nootka whaler's hat with minaret top. Their bodyguard consisted of a group of similarly-dressed Clayoquot braves. Standing on a cedar-bark mat, placed on the sand by an Indian slave to indicate that the strangers were welcome, "Cook" made a speech and an interpreter translated Maquinna's reply. The two shook hands, then to the beat of native drums and rhythmical chanting, the Indians performed their welcome dance.

A concert was held in the Legion hall that night when, still attired only in their bearskin rugs, Chief Joseph and "Queen Mary" put on a song and dance act that certainly brought the house down, and called for several encores. The following year the old couple were honoured guests at a reception tendered Governor-General Lord Willingdon by the Tofino Board of Trade.

Chief Joseph died in 1936 at the age of ninety-two. Indians from all parts of the West Coast were present at his burial. Mourning ceremonials lasted several days. "Queen Mary" died two years after her husband. Her real name was Mary. The title "Queen" is believed to have been bestowed upon her by a sealing schooner captain who for several years in succession signed her on as cook for his Indian hunters and boat steerers — one of whom was Joseph.

Chief Joseph of the Clayoquots, and his wife "Queen Mary". *F. W. Towler Photos.*

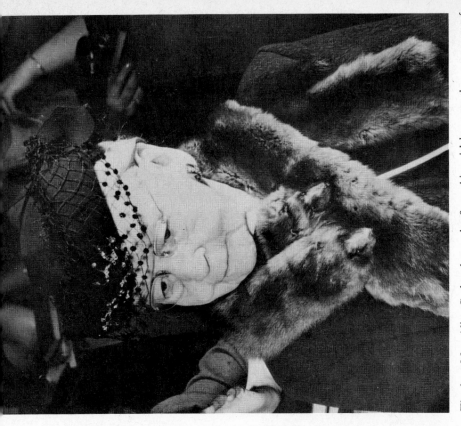

The late Mrs. Alice Crakanthorp, the first white girl born on the west coast of Vancouver Island, on February 26, 1864, in a house near the old Stamp Mill about where Port Alberni's Somass Hotel now stands. Mrs. Crakanthorp died at Vancouver, October 9, 1961. *Vancouver City Archives Photo.*

The late Captain Reece Riley, who knew the coast like the back of his hand.

FIRST WHITE GIRL
BORN ON WEST COAST

OBITUARY: The death occurred at Vancouver on October 9, 1961, of Mrs. Alice Crakanthorp, aged 97.

MRS. CRAKANTHORP was the first white girl born on the west coast of Vancouver Island; on February 26, 1864, in a house near the old Stamp sawmill, about where Port Alberni's Somass Hotel now stands.

In the 1860's, long before the C.P.R. reached the Pacific coast, the only labour available for the few industries which the new Crown colony then boasted — the Alberni mill was one of the first — were men hired in England and brought out in sailing ships, plus a few of the more industrious Indians. Extra men required, especially trained mechanics, they had to look for in the United States. One was John Peabody Patterson, a sawmill mechanic from Portland, Oregon, who got a job at the Stamp mill.

Alice was born to John and Emily Susan Patterson shortly after their arrival at Alberni and lived there until 1873, when at the age of nine the family moved to Burrard Inlet. There was no Vancouver then. Her father became a sort of master mechanic at the Hastings Mill, and was also in charge of loading ships. At twenty-three, Alice married Robert Churchill Crakanthorp, who predeceased her in 1892.

On June 13, 1886, from her home at Moodyville, now part of North Vancouver, Mrs. Crakanthorp (then still Miss Patterson) witnessed the fire which destroyed (all but a few shacks) Vancouver, only sixty-eight days after it had been incorporated as a city. It had previously been known as the Village of Granville (unofficially "Gastown").

256

Mrs. Crakanthorp was the last surviving pupil of the first class of Vancouver's first school, which was at Hastings Mill; attended the first wedding performed by the first minister in the lower mainland, and was a member of the first confirmation class conducted by the first Bishop of New Westminster. She was on hand when the first train pulled into the station at Vancouver, and danced at the opening night ball at the first Hotel Vancouver.

Good health was enjoyed by Mrs. Crakanthorp almost up to the time of her death and reminiscing about her childhood days she liked nothing better:

When I was born, the only white people who lived where Port Alberni now stands were mill employees and their families, about forty all told. A handful of white settlers also farmed on the banks of the Somass River, where Alberni now stands.

I remember those Alberni days, especially the Indians, many of whom were bad. When they got very dangerous the cookhouse bell was rung as a warning for all the white employees to come up from the mill, and the wives and children to gather at the cookhouse. Fearing to return to our homes, we sometimes slept there, but I recall no serious trouble other than threatening demands for food, and payment for the trees. It was the frightening appearance of the Indians which scared us most, especially the women and children newly arrived from England.

SCOW LOAD OF DYNAMITE ADRIFT ON FOGGY NIGHT

And it took Reece Riley to find it.

"ALERTING ALL SHIPS in waters adjacent to the west coast of Vancouver Island to keep a sharp lookout for a derelict scow loaded with dynamite". With frequency channels cleared for the purpose, that terse warning was relayed every half hour by all radio stations between Cape Flattery and Langara; followed by the approximate position of the scow when abandoned and requesting any ships sighting it to report its position to the nearest radio station. The incident occurred twenty-seven years ago.

A Vancouver syndicate for a short while worked a group of gold claims handy to tidewater on Nootka Sound. The cookhouse and power plant was aboard a scow moored at the shoreline adjacent the property. The venture was subsequently abandoned and months later a tug was despatched to take the scow and equipment back to Vancouver. On the scow was 100 boxes of dynamite and the detonating caps which went with it.

All went well until off Long Beach when, shortly after dark, the towline parted. By the time the skipper of the tug realized he had lost his tow, hauled in the broken line and turned the boat around, the scow was probably a mile astern. Owing to the darkness and a thick blanket of fog, which meanwhile had set in, in spite of fruitless searching he was unable to pick it up again. With no radio to report his predicament and realizing the scow was a menace to shipping, he headed for Bamfield, thirty miles way, where the Department of Transport maintains a life-saving station. There was no one aboard the scow and its only light a kerosene lantern lashed to a stanchion.

Within minutes of the tug's arrival at Bamfield, where in addition to the lifeboat, the navy had a minesweeper stationed on life-saving duty, the air waves were cleared and the warning broadcast to all ships and nearby lighthouses to be on the lookout. In response to a joint request of the naval authorities at Esquimalt and the Department of Transport, crews were recalled from their evening shore leave and in no time one of the greatest searches ever undertaken on the West Coast was under way.

A United States Coastguard cutter left Port Angeles, approximately one hundred miles away, to search for the derelict. The minesweeper at Bamfield put to sea. A fisheries patrol vessel in the Nootka area heard the call and immediately headed out, and the Bamfield and Tofino lifeboats were made ready to join in the search. The skipper of the tug phoned through to his agents in Vancouver and, with barely five minutes to spare, a representative of the insurance underwriters caught the last boat to Nanaimo and was in Port Alberni before dawn.

Waiting for the insurance man at Port Alberni was Reece Riley, with his trim little 25-foot speedboat *Maureen* all souped up and ready to go. He knew the waters of the West Coast like the back of his hand and if anyone was to find the abandoned scow, it would be Reece Riley — and it was.

The *Maureen* was off Ucluelet shortly before daybreak, only to discover pea-soup fog enveloping the entire area. Reece felt his way along between reefs and breakers. He knew the approximate position where the scow had been abandoned and with his intimate local knowledge of the tides and currents, figured about how far it would drift. Then, sneaking through the fog to within a few hundred feet of shore, he obtained a fix and headed seaward.

He found the scow lazily riding the swells about five miles off Long Beach; it hadn't drifted very far. About mid-morning the fog commenced to lift and as visibility increased, one by one the other ships engaged in the search showed up, including the cutter from Port Angeles, and all within a five mile radius. Reece Riley slowly cruised around the scow to warn approaching vessels of its danger.

The scow was towed to Ucluelet and its interrupted voyage to Vancouver subsequently resumed. Meanwhile the powder was thrown overboard, which should have been done before leaving Nootka Sound. Not only was it a year old, but the scow's roof leaked, exposing it to the rain. In this state powder is extremely dangerous and perhaps it is as well no vessel collided with the scow in the darkness or fog.

Some fifteen years later, on October 24, 1950, this intrepid sea-faring young man lost his life in these very same waters, but twenty miles further up the coast. Bound from Port Alberni to Quatsino, this time in his new speedboat cruiser *Maureen R*, a trip he had previously made scores of times, some mishap occurred and he was never seen again. He was travelling alone and wreckage found on the outer beaches of Flores Island was the only evidence, but gave no clue as to what happened. By a strange coincidence, the wreckage was found only five miles from "Riley Cove" (Sydney Inlet), a snug little cove named after his father and where Reece had spent much of his young life. Who knows? Reece might might have been making for it.

Reece Riley was born and brought up at Tofino, and when ten years old was running his dad's motorboat. They were powered by kerosene engines in those days, with no spark plugs or self starters. Young Reece was a mechanical genius and could get any old engine to run. Moving to Port Alberni when he grew up, for years he operated a speedboat water taxi and marine ambulance service between Port Alberni and the logging camps on Barkley Sound. He also ferried the pilots between Port Alberni and Cape Beale, where they boarded deep-sea ships inbound for lumber cargoes or were dropped when the vessel was outward bound. At the time of his death he was Harbour Master at Port Alberni.

*   *   *

Reece Riley's father, whose first name also was Reece, was one of Clayoquot Sound's pioneer settlers. He came there from Denver, Colorado, in 1898, and established Tofino's first boat repair shop and marine ways. This part of the country was then just beginning to be opened up and prospectors, mining engineers, timber cruisers and survey parties were arriving by almost every steamer. The activities of these people were mostly at the head of remote inlets. All required water transportation, and launches were scarce. Riley had the *Sweet Briar* and the *Agnes*, stout little vessels destined to play an important role in the Sound's communications for many years to come. These he hired out, along with his services, and for the most part made a snug little cove on Sydney Inlet his base of operations. Located at the northwest tip of Flores Island, the cove was named, by the Hydrographic Board of Canada, Riley Cove, from this fact. When the pilchard industry flourished, 1926-1943, it was the site of one of the west coast of Vancouver Island's twenty-six reduction plants. Today it is uninhabited.

CAPTAIN
GEORGE W. SKINNER

*He survived after three wintry
weeks without food or shelter.*

EARLY IN DECEMBER 1939, the fishpacker *Great Northern V*, out of
Vancouver with a scow in tow for Nootka Sound, lost her rudder
during a raging storm off Estevan Point. Her crew consisted of
Captain George W. Skinner, his son Hugh and Ted Bernard. Other
boats sought shelter so no one witnessed her plight, and having no
radio, she was unable to call for assistance or give her position.
There was no alternative but to cut the scow adrift and for two days
and nights the vessel drifted helplessly before the storm, finally
bringing up on a jagged reef about ten miles west of Cape Cook.

It was here that Bernard lost his life. He was washed overboard
and drowned; father and son clinging to the rigging unable to help.
Within a few hours the pounding sea had smashed the vessel into
matchwood. Fortunately the top of the pilothouse floated free and
to it the two men held and drifted to shore. Drenched to the skin,
with only the clothes they stood in, and wearing hip gumboots,
nearly dead from exhaustion and cold, they were cast up on the most
inhospitable stretch of the entire West Coast. Not a soul, white or
Indian, within thirty miles — either way. They had no food,
matches or blankets. As the elder Skinner had badly injured his leg
and also suffered from a weak heart, his son gathered pieces of
wreckage and erected a crude shelter. This and the trees would at
least break the biting winds and keep off some of the rain.

Unable to walk and feeling certain he would die, the father
pleaded with his son to leave him and seek possible help. But the
boy stayed with him for two days, searching the beaches in hope
of finding some form of food that might be cast up; but in vain. He
made his dad as comfortable as possible with the scant material

261

available and set out in the direction of Quatsino Sound. For five days he walked the rock-strewn shoreline, only making four or five miles a day. His rubber boots were torn to ribbons and his feet cut by the jagged rocks. He slept at times, but only from sheer exhaustion.

Meanwhile a vigorous search was in progress for the overdue fishpacker, which for the first week was conducted in the Estevan-Nootka area. After a fruitless search it was established the boat was no longer afloat. The area was then extended to the beaches for signs of survivors or wreckage.

A Ginger Coote Airways plane taking part in the search with a doctor, police constable and another man aboard, spotted a man on the beach. It was young Skinner and he waved. A landing being impossible owing to the rough seas, the pilot circled and dipped the plane's wings as a signal to let the lad know he had been seen, then headed for Winter Harbour, a small settlement inside the western entrance to Quatsino Sound. There a fisherman offered the services of his boat and within a few hours young Skinner was taken off the beach.

Back at Winter Harbour, Skinner was placed aboard the plane, flown to hospital at Zeballos and later in the same day to a Vancouver hospital where two gangrened toes were amputated. Meanwhile he had told his rescuers of his father's condition and approximately where he had left him five days previously. This information was duly conveyed to the provincial police at Port Alice, in whose area the search was being conducted. The corporal-in-charge proceeded immediately to Quatsino where the services of three trapper-prospectors, all familiar with that part of the coast, were enlisted. The party set out in a salmon troller, but heavy seas were encountered at the entrance to the Sound and it soon became clear that the search would have to be continued on foot. A landing was made and one of the men took the boat back to Quatsino. He would return to a previously arranged rendezvous when the seas moderated. Meanwhile, on days when the weather permitted, planes continued the patrol ready to drop supplies if signalled to do so.

Progress was slow, for each man carried a pack laden with blankets, food and medical supplies. For three days they hacked their way through dense underbrush and finally reached the beach where young Skinner had been picked up. Back-tracking his trail, they continued along the shoreline, detouring where necessary around inaccessible cliffs and ravines, and on January 4th they found Captain Skinner, alive, but reduced to skin and bone. He had lain there for twenty-one days without food and little shelter, and it had rained every day. Close by was a moss-covered rock that the rains had kept well soaked. By reaching out when his strength permitted and squeezing the moss with his hands he had obtained water, and that probably saved his life.

His first words were, "Is Hugh all right?" Assured that he was safe and well seemed to give the father new life. The rescuers soon had a fire going and provided Captain Skinner with warm food and dry clothing. Two of the party were dispatched back to meet the boat at the previously arranged rendezvous. Still the seas were too rough for the troller to come around and they returned a few days later with additional volunteer helpers, for more would be required if Skinner had to be carried out. In the meantime the search plane again appeared in the sky, when guided by smoke signals, the pilot dropped further supplies.

The sea calmed down on the twenty-fourth day. A fishpacker arrived and put its small boat ashore. Skinner was placed on board. Taken to Port Alice hopsital, he lay there for several weeks and was subsequently taken to a hospital in Vancouver. Within six months, father and son were back at sea; Captain Skinner again in command of a fishpacker; Hugh, fishing with his own boat. Captain Skinner died at New Westminster in 1960.

HE KEPT UP
WITH THE TIMES

GEORGE PATRICK SYE, still hale and hearty in spite of his having seen the geese, *kal-ak-a-lah-ma* in his own language, fly south for the past eighty years, is one of the West Coast's best-known Indians. Born and raised in the then primitive environments of his native village, his life is another striking example of how our Indians can completely assimilate the white man's mode of living, if only given the opportunity.

He was born at Kilsemat, an Indian settlement on Vargas Island, near Clayoquot. The sealing schooners called there in the spring to pick up their native hunters. George's father was a hunter and on one trip he took his fourteen-year-old son along. The schooner spent three months in the Bering Sea, where under the tuition of his father, the lad became an expert with the harpoon, an accomplishment he afterwards turned to great profit.

Prior to then he had no education, but a Catholic priest took him in hand and he spent the next four years at Christie Residential Indian School, near Tofino. In fact, he was one of its first pupils. There, in addition to his rudimentary lessons, he learned to play the organ and several other musical instruments. He also played in the school band.

But George was determined to become a great fisherman, sealer and whaler like his father who, with other Indians, he had often seen return from far out in the ocean with their eight-man canoes loaded with seals and halibut. Sometimes they had a big whale in tow, which they had killed, often after a whole day's fight. It therefore was not surprising that canoe-making, which George had already learned from his grandfather, became his pet hobby. Neither was it long before he had not only made several excellent ones, but found himself instructing his fellow pupils in the art.

Some of the few white settlers in these parts possessed either a boat or dory which they had brought in by steamer. These they used for going from place to place and to ferry their freight ashore from the steamer that called every few months. The huge loads they carried impressed George, who soon turned his self-taught skill to building one for himself, for he must have a boat as good as the white man's. There was no sawmill anywhere on that part of the coast and to bring timber in by steamer was costly. But this problem didn't discourage George. With some of his classmates he went by canoe to the outside beaches (Long Beach was one) and salvaged boards that had been cast ashore there from shipwrecks. These they rafted and towed to the school, where a kindly Norwegian pre-empter, a boat-builder himself to whom the priest had appealed on the boys' behalf, assisted them in re-sawing and whittling the boards down to the proper dimensions by hand.

The school also had one of these boats for landing its own freight. Taking this as a model, George went to work with his tools and built one like it, which the Norwegian, who had also given some advice, said was a masterpiece. The lad proudly took it home to show his people, who proclaimed him as their *hyas canim tyee*, meaning "Big Canoe Chief".

Power boats soon made their appearance and before long there were several on the Sound. The kerosene engines that made them go so intrigued George that he was determined to have one himself; not only an engine, but a bigger boat than the one he had just built. Meanwhile, George had left school and not long after he built a 30-foot fishing boat. With the money he had earned fur-sealing, he purchased an engine. This, however, wasn't to be his first and only power boat, for he afterwards built himself several, each one larger and with more power.

Provided they used spears only and did their hunting from canoes, the Indians at that time were permitted to take fur seals off the west coast of Vancouver Island during their spring migration to the Pribiloff Islands. For years this was a profitable industry and thousands of skins taken in these waters during March, April and May were purchased by the fur buyers at Ucluelet, Tofino, Clayo-quot and Nootka. This is when George put to profit the experience gained on that trip to the Bering Sea with his father, and he seldom returned from a day's hunt with less than a dozen skins. For these he was paid from $5 to $10 per skin and the fur buyers regarded him as one of their best seal hunters.

Gas engines were now in general use and the antiquated and hard-to-start kerosene engines were just a memory. In time George became one of the most successful salmon trollers on the West Coast. His last trolling boat, which he still owns, cost him $10,000 to build and equip. But George was just as efficient at net fishing as trolling. In the fall he seined for coho and chum salmon, and in the winter months, for herring. Pilchard fishing commenced in 1925 and knowing George's uncanny reputation for "spotting" fish, one of the largest fishing companies on the coast provided him with a modern 80-foot diesel-powered seine boat. At the close of the four-month fishing season, his was the high boat, landing 3,800 tons for which he and his seven-man crew received $3 per ton divided between them — with an additional bonus for George.

Although the pilchards came in schools by the million, their presence was sometimes hard to detect. Fish boats weren't equipped with echo sounders as they are today and the fishermen had to depend on sight. Only occasionally did the pilchards swim near the surface, when the odd one would flip its tail and make a small splash. George could spot a "flip" a mile away and for that reason was known among the fleet as "Eagle Eye" George.

Apart from his success at locating pilchards, because of his native instincts he usually knew where to find the best spots for fishing herring, salmon, halibut and cod. Therefore, wherever his boat headed, the fleet usually followed. George Sye made *hiyu chickamin* (plenty money) fishing; his income tax often exceeded $500, which he gladly paid.

His wife, Jessie, whom he met while at school and married when barely eighteen, was the daughter of Chief Paul, of the Hesquiats. She also played the organ and excelled at sewing, knitting, crocheting and cooking. Basket-making, an art she learned from her mother, became her main hobby and her work, which included baskets of all sizes and shapes, covered bottles, shells, deer horns and other articles, all decorated with coloured designs of whales, seals, canoes and thunderbirds, were much sought after by tourists travelling on the *Princess Maquinna*.

Perhaps the most frightening experience that ever happened to George and Jessie occurred in their modern home at Kilsemat. This the writer can vouch for, for I lived at nearby Clayoquot at the time. One fine summer's day the Sye family was having lunch, when in through the open window leaped the family dog, yelping its head off. Behind it came a cougar and in a moment the two animals became mixed up among the legs of everyone sitting at the table. The cougar, evidently more scared than the Sye family and losing all interest in the dog, made a quick escape via the back door which fortunately was also open, but not before the table had been upset in the excitement with dishes and food scattered all over the floor. The dog was unharmed.

Both George and Jessie like to tell about their experiences when young, and of the many strange happenings which, according to their parents, occurred either shortly after the first white men came, or long before that. Some of these stories are substantiated in the early history of this coast, but others, although still believed by the older generation Indians, are obviously fables.

The permanent home of George and Jessie Sye is still on Vargas Island, but the summer months they spend at Hot Springs Cove. The Indians have always known that the hot springs are good for their various ailments and George says they give his rheumatic condition considerable relief. He still has his gasboat and fishes on and off, but only catches sufficient to eat and potlatch to the older Indians, some of whom are in their nineties. Both he and Jessie receive the old age pension.

AUTHOR'S NOTE: Jessie Sye died in 1961.

ALL MEN ARE BROTHERS

*Indian and white now prove this
true at scene of many massacres.*

NOT QUITE A CENTURY AGO, the Ahousat Indians massacred the crew
of the trading schooner *Kingfisher*. That was in 1864. It was not
an isolated instance of Indian antipathy to white men and their
customs, and while it cannot be condoned, in the light of events
which went before — and after — is understandable. There was the
Boston trader (Kendrick), seventy-five years before the *Kingfisher's*
misadventure, who traded six decrepit, muzzle-loading guns, some
powder and shot, boat sails, a coil of rope and an American flag,
for a vast tract of land (see page 49). There were others who, after
negotiating over a cask of rum, induced the Indians to fill their
ships with the pelts of sea otter, seals and other valuable furs in
return for a few bolts of calico, some worn clothing, crude tools and
worthless trinkets.

In the case of the *Kingfisher* incident and similar outrages, warships stationed at Esquimalt were dispatched to investigate; their
captains with order to fire on the villages if the Indians showed
defiance and refused to hand over the guilty parties. The missiles
used were no mere slugs; made of solid cast iron, with half an inch
of lead casing, they weighed sixty pounds and to this day are found
in the vicinity of the old villages. One, which came into the possession of the writer, is now in the British Columbia Maritime Museum.
The Ottawa Museum has another.

A few years back, Paul Sam, a counsellor for the Ahousat band,
was asked to speak at the opening of Tofino's new $250,000 hospital.
He told how the Indians had been mercilessly exploited and reminded his listeners how "King George" ships had fired at the houses
of some of his own kin who had been involved in forays against the

traders. But in later years, he said, the attitude of the Indians towards white men had slowly changed. "It took a little time to overcome their natural doubt about the newcomers' good intentions."

He then paid tribute to the early missionaries, the government's education policies and the inspiration behind the building of the new hospital. The Indians, he went on to say, now enjoy practically all the privileges of the white. "If it had not been for the changing attitude demonstrated by the white people, the community of Indians here would not have subscribed $3,000 towards the new hospital. That's what they gave, $3,000."

"Our hearts too can be generous," said Sam, as he gestured towards the hospital which overlooks the water where, in 1811, the trading ship *Tonquin* was plundered and then burned, and Captain Jonathan Thorn and his crew murdered; solely because of the captain's harsh and arbitrary bargaining methods and contempt shown the Indians and their chief. (*Kingfisher* and *Tonquin* stories, see pages 72-74).

MYTHS

*Sasquatch, the Ahoots-oos, Amy
Cadborosaurus and Ogopogo.*

ACCORDING TO George Sye (his story five pages back), some of the
older Indians on the West Coast believe that ape-like aboriginals
corresponding to descriptions of the Sasquatch, the monster which
people swear they have encountered, or at least seen its footprints,
in the hills behind Harrison Lake and other parts of British Columbia, still roam Vancouver Island's mountain ranges.

Known as the Ahoots-oos, they believe them to be descendants of
outlawed members of the Man-ous-aht (Ahousat) tribe, which made
their home on Flores Island. The Reverend A. J. Brabant mentions
in his memoirs the Indians' belief in the existence of the Ahoots-oos,
but himself doubted it. They are said to have lived in caves far up
in the mountains, from which they raided the villages, carried off
young children, stole fish from traps in the rivers and killed lone
Indians when out hunting. Fear of meeting them was so deeply
instilled in the minds of the younger generation, that to this day
one seldom finds a Vancouver Island Indian far from salt water.

The Ahousats are not the only Indians who believe the Ahoots-
oos still exist. In 1930, when the first prospectors went into the
Zeballos hills, they were warned by the Ehattis-ahts (the local band)
that they might meet them. The Haidas also believe that remnants
of a strange-looking race of monsters still roam the mountains of the
Queen Charlotte Islands.

George, who is an authority on Indian lore, further tells us that
hundreds of years ago bad Indians were either killed or chased into
the hills and left there to fare for themselves. Skeletons found in
mountain caves tend to prove this. But while he admits there might
still be the odd one alive, he is quite willing to go along with the
theory believed by most white people: that Sasquatch and the
Ahoots-oos, like Victoria's Amy Cadborosaurus (Caddy) and Lake
Okanagan's Ogopogo, are just myths.

"CADDY"

What people really see.

THE APPARITION so often observed off Cadboro Bay, hence the origin of its name, "Cadborosaurus", or "Caddy" for short, and along Victoria's waterfront, is no sea serpent; although, to the novice, that's what it sometimes looks like.

Three phenomena, common anywhere along our coastline, can and often do present a strong resemblance to some strange denizen of the deep, especially when seen unexpectedly. One is a hair seal or lone sea lion suddenly breaking water and raising its head for a look around, or perhaps to swallow a fish. Another is a weird-shaped water-logged snag floating just under the surface and every so often bobbing up to show its fantastic shape as it drifts along in the swirls of a rip tide. The third and actually more like the real thing, is a group of sea lions on their way to or from their feeding grounds.

Hair seals are quite common in these waters. The head of one suddenly appearing only a few hundred feet away could easily catch the novice off balance and, by its sudden submergence, leave one wondering just what he really had seen. Such a sight starts an immediate reaction in the brain cell controlling one's power of imagination. Half a minute is about the average time a seal keeps its head above water, and it never reappears anywhere near the same spot.

The water-logged snag or tree can look like anything at all and fool almost anyone. It takes a different shape every time it rises to the surface and then disappears again before one is able to get a good look at it. A stub limb can look remarkably like a queer shaped head, or two limbs like two heads, and if the tree trunk happens to be smooth and shiny, there you have the serpent's body.

Now for the sea lions, which are undoubtedly what a great number of people really see and take to be the elusive Caddy. For the greater part of the year sea lions live in small herds or groups on

271

isolated rocks or small islands strategically located where the animals are least liable to be disturbed by man. Actually, each one of these groups is a harem, consisting of from ten to twenty females, all the wives of one bull, usually carrying the scars of battles fought with rival young suitors. Having won their affections the hard way, the master is rewarded by having his women remain faithful throughout the entire season.

It is when one such group happens to be travelling to or from the feeding grounds that the impression of a sea serpent is created. For some reason, they seem to prefer travelling in fast-flowing tidal currents, eddies and rip tides, similiar to those off Clover Point, Trial Island and other favourite spots where "Caddy" is so often reported seen.

The bull always leads, every so often breaking surface to hold his head at least three feet above water and look around as if to see if any strange bachelor bull might be skulking around. Sometimes he opens his mouth as if yawning and shows his teeth, but whether he does or not the big head, high on a thick neck, seen unexpectedly and for only a brief time, could, with the help of a little imagination, be described as that of a camel, horse, the legendary dragon, the mythical sea serpent, or a combination of them all.

So much for the head and neck, but only one head, please. Now for the humps or coils. The females always follow close behind, invariably in line, and for some unexplained reason they never raise their heads out of the water. Maybe they take after their sisters in the harems of the Near East who never show their faces in public. But there appears to be no hesitancy whatever in showing their bodies, and it is these that make the "humps" or "coils" to complete the picture. The fierce looking bewhiskered head of the bull sea lion high out of the water, followed a length or two behind by one or more arched bodies of the females, and all appearing to be part of one animal, admittedly looks like a sea serpent.

Why is it that Caddy is seen only in waters frequented mostly during week-ends by sport fishermen and couples out in rowboats? Or — usually through field glasses — by people walking along Victoria's waterfront pathways? Never from the bridge of a ship plying the regular steamer lanes, by tugboat crews or British Columbia's 5,000 commercial fishermen. Practically every man, woman and child now carries a camera, yet, significantly, we have yet to see a photograph of the sea serpent.

MISFORTUNE AND tragedy overtook a group of youths who twenty-five years ago set off to try their luck at placer mining on the West Coast. One died from injuries after a box of blasting caps exploded in his face and two had to return home through sickness. Of the remainder, three became hopelessly lost in the hills. Two of them were too ill to travel any further, with nothing to eat but a few dried beans. One of the lads managed to find his way out and an air-sea-land rescue party subsequently rescued his chums, bringing one of them out on an improvised stretcher.

Unemployment in the cities was rife at this time (1936) and provincial labour officials were making every effort to find suitable out-of-town employment for single men. In coöperation with the Department of Mines, a plan was evolved whereby groups of selected young men were sent to different mining areas, each in charge of an experienced placer miner. Transportation and equipment were provided, and scrip to purchase supplies sufficient for three months. After that period they were to be left on their own resources. In the meantime any gold recovered was to be retained by the boys themselves.

As rich discoveries had recently been made at Zeballos, one party of ten, their ages ranging from eighteen to twenty years, was sent to that district. They established a camp on Spud Creek, which was known to be rich in alluvial gold and where "colour" could be obtained from the sand in any pool. But the presence of deep ravines and huge boulders forbade successful placer operations, other than with heavy equipment and expensive machinery. All that the boys had were pans, picks and shovels, and a limited amount of lumber for erecting the necessary flumes.

Recovering less than a dollar's worth per day and often none at all, the boys soon became discouraged. One by one they sought other means of employment and the expedition folded up. Some found work in the few small mining camps which were then developing properties in the area. One was an eighteen-year-old Victoria lad. Powder was being used and one day while he was working alone, an unusual explosion was heard by men working a quarter of a mile away. Rushing to the scene they found the lad critically injured; one eye was gone, the other damaged. He was also bleeding badly from wounds in the abdomen. His condition prevented him from being questioned, but it was evident that a box of caps had exploded in his hands.

What a man injured in the hills was up against before there were any hospitals on that part of the coast is typical in what this lad had to suffer before reaching medical aid — and then it was too late. Only by coincidence, a qualified first-aid man (a prospector) was one of those first on the scene and he quickly appraised the nature of the boy's injuries. He then had to be carried five miles over rough trails to tidewater; then taken ten miles by gasboat to Ceepeecee cannery, where a former nurse, the wife of a cannery employee, dressed his injuries as best she could with the scant facilities available. The boat then proceeded to Tofino, seventy-five miles distant and where the nearest doctor resided. The lad died before reaching there.

Prospectors were every day staking claims in this newly-found mining camp and, inspired by their success, three of the lads who had been less fortunate in securing work locally and were now broke, turned to "seeking gold in the hills." Friendly prospectors provided them with provisions, tent, equipment, advice, a rough map and directions where to look. But, as only to be expected, the boys soon became lost and out of grub. To make matters worse two of them became ill from eating unripe berries and were unable to proceed further.

The third boy pitched tent and made his chums as comfortable as possible. Then, with a handful of dry oatmeal in his pocket he set out for help. Coming out at the shoreline, which he followed for the next two days — fortunately in the right direction — he finally reached Zeballos where a search party was immediately organized. That well known bush pilot R. L. "Ginger" Coote, who by chance happened to be stopping overnight, offered his services. He took off at dawn with two miners and the lad who had walked out. By sunrise they spotted them, mainly because the little tent had been pitched in an open clearing. Flying at tree-top level, exceedingly hazardous for a pontoon-equipped plane, food and medical supplies were dropped.

Ginger pin-pointed the spot on his map and immediately upon his return the same men set out by gasboat and landed at the nearest point on the shoreline. After three hours climbing they came across the lost boys. The sicker of the two was carried down the mountain on an improvised stretcher made from the tent, and that evening rescuers and rescued were back at Zeballos.

JOHN GRICE WAS Tofino's first white settler. With Mrs. Grice, he landed there in 1888 before the place had a name. It was named later, after the inlet which the Spanish explorers Galiano and Valdes discovered in 1792.

As shipping master for the sealing schooners, Mr. Grice's principal duty was to hire the Indian hunters and boat steerers. This required him to travel from village to village by canoe, often with an overnight stop at an Indian house. Thus he became familiar with the language and customs of these people. In later years, when Tofino became a settlement, he was appointed postmaster, justice of the peace and coroner. Mr. Grice was born in June 1841 at Gateshead-on-Tyne, Durham, England. He died at Tofino in 1931. Mrs. Grice died the day of her husband's funeral. Both are buried in the Tofino cemetary.

In 1889, Walter T. Dawley and Thomas Stockham, both from Victoria, built a store on a small island adjoining Opitisaht village, trading mostly with the Indians. A few years later they purchased the store and hotel at Clayoquot on Stubbs Island. Clarence Dawley, a brother of W. T., joined the partnership several years later, but confined his activities mostly to mining. The former ownership of the Clayoquot store and the circumstances under which it operated, are referred to elsewhere in these pages. The Dawley brothers lived at Clayoquot for over fifty years. Stockham resided in Victoria.

Had Tofino waited a little longer for a name, it would more than likely have chosen "Arnet," after Jacob Hendrick Arnet, who pre-empted a 200-acre homestead there in 1893 and later became one of its most prominent citizens.

Mr. Arnet was born at Trondhjem, Norway, in 1870. As a lad he fished with his father in the Lofoten Islands and when eighteen left home for Sioux City, Iowa. In those days the majority of migrating Scandinavians headed for the United States to work on the railroads, where the wages were $1 per day. A few years later he came west and went gillnet fishing on the Fraser River.

Jacob Arnet was one of the first men to prospect the possibilities of commercial salmon fishing on the west coast of Vancouver Island. He landed at Tofino, built a log cabin and settled on what is now Long Beach airport. His sweetheart followed him out from Norway and they were married at Victoria shortly afterwards. Later still, his four brothers, Cristopher, August, Sophus and Martin (all now deceased) journeyed out from the Old Country and also settled at Tofino. The two sisters remained behind, but several of their sons followed in their uncles' footsteps. In time they all raised families and soon almost every second man, woman and child in Tofino was either an Arnet or close relation. At one time there were twenty Arnets on the voters list, with politicians vyeing with one another for their vote.

Jacob was the oldest brother. He lived an exceedingly active life and, on later taking up residence in the settlement itself, played a prominent part in every movement for the betterment of the community. As far back as 1895 he headed a delegation to Victoria asking the government to give that part of the West Coast road access to the outside. A road from Alberni to Tofino was built in 1959, but by that time Jacob and his four brothers were dead. Jacob Arnet was the first chairman of the village municipality, re-elected by acclamation from 1932 to 1936. He was also president of the Tofino Hospital Society, chairman of the Board of Trade, and a warden of the Anglican Church. He died in July 1941. Mrs. Arnet died the following year. Throughout her life she was actively interested in the church guild and the hospital women's auxiliary.

Mr. and Mrs. Jacob Arnet left seven children, fourteen grandchildren and many great-grand-children. The six sons are all well-known West Coast fishermen; four served as officers in Fishermen's Naval Reserve during the Second World War.

When Jacob Arnet first engaged in fishing on the West Coast, exceedingly primitive methods were used. His first venture was sockeye fishing at Gold River, at the head of Muchalat Arm, Nootka Sound. There were no canneries then and the fish had to be salted down in barrels. These the Arnets made themselves, hewing the staves out of the woods with a special tool the brothers had brought out from Norway. Hoops for the barrels they shaped out of rough iron, heated on a hand-forge. There were no gasboats and purse-seining was unheard of. They made their own nets and with a drag-seine hauled the fish out onto the beaches, a method long since prohibited by law.

Later, purse-seine fishing was introduced, but also with crude methods. The Arnets made their own webbing and fashioned the purse-rings out of wrought iron. Cork was expensive, so they made their own cedar floats to hold the net up. They fished from a dory, two men rowing, another paying out the net. It was a slow process and hard work, but as the fish were plentiful it mattered little if a few escaped. Nowadays, purse-seining is carried out by large diesel boats carrying six- to eight-man crews, with the vessel's winch doing most of the work, including the hauling in of the purse line and brailing the fish.

It was a big day for Jacob Arnet when he purchased a small power boat. The engine burned kerosene and was upside-down, as were all such engines at that time, but it was a great help in towing the dory as the net was being paid out. It was also useful for fetching supplies from the once-a-month steamer which stopped at Nootka, thirty miles away.

Between fishing seasons Mr. Arnet was busy on his pre-emption; clearing land, logging and building a larger house. He also raised cattle, which grazed on the range back of Long Beach. These he rounded up twice a year, butchering one as required, branding the yearlings and transforming the male calves to oxen. In time many went wild and provided beef for anyone who cared to hunt them. Long after Mr. Arnet abandoned the homestead and went to reside in Tofino settlement the cattle roamed at large, and not until comparatively recently was the last bull shot.

One hundred would be a near guess at the number of direct descendants of Jacob Arnet and his four brothers. Practically all the male members follow the same occupation — fishing.

Anton and John Hansen, both still living at Tofino; John Eik, Jacob Knutsen, Mike Hogan and Tom Wingen (all deceased), from Norway, came shortly after the Arnets. All followed fishing, but Hogan and Wingen later turned to boat-building, at which trade they were experts. Younger generations of Wingens still build boats at Tofino.

Wingen built a sawmill, a unique one at that, on Tofino Inlet in behind Long Beach, but there is little left of it now. Power was generated by a waterwheel which he built himself. Flat stones weighing up to 100 pounds he grooved out by hand and used for bearings in place of steel. The shaft was greased with dogfish oil. A Victoria resident has one of the stone bearings in his basement. It should be in the provincial archives.

Ole Jacobsen, a former sealer and whaler and still living, was another early arrival. He and Eik were head fishermen at Clayoquot cannery, owned by H. C. Brewster, one-time premier of British Columbia. Reece Riley (see page 260) came to Tofino in 1898. Francis C. Garrard arrived in 1904; helped build Lennard Island lighthouse and was its first lightkeeper. Ten years later he was appointed linesman and telegraph operator, a position he held till he retired in 1936. John Chesterman, Virgil Evans, A. Quisenberry and James Sloman, the latter an ex-Royal Marine sergeant-major, also arrived soon after the turn of the century. Chesterman farmed, where the airport now stands (at Long Beach), and later coxswain'd the lifeboat. Chesterman's Beach, a popular recreation area close to the township, was named after him. Quisenberry also farmed. Sloman operated a general store and bought seal skins.

The McLeod clan, from the Orkney Islands, came later, but only Jack and Alec are still living. Between them, the McLeods have almost as many descendants as the Arnets. At this writing, Tofino's oldest resident is George Maltby, ninety-four, who came there in 1890 and took up farming. Prior to that he lived at Long Beach and was then its sole resident.

Ucluelet, also an organized village municipality, is the first settlement reached after driving over the new Alberni-Tofino road. It is situated on the west shore of Ucluelet Inlet and has a population of approximately seven hundred. Its principal industries are also fishing and logging. Another two hundred people live in the immediate area, but beyond the municipal boundary. Sixty years ago, the settlement was on the opposite side of the inlet, at what is now known as Port Albion, the site of a fish reduction plant, where about forty families reside.

Also on this side is the Indian village, mission and church. The original home of the people who reside here now was at Yuclutl, a small open bay a few miles beyond Long Beach. *Yutl* means a good landing place (for canoes), hence the inhabitants of this place were known by other tribes as the *Yuclutl-ahts*, meaning people with a safe landing place. The name Ucluelet was adopted by Captain Richards, H.M.S. *Hecate*, 1861.

The names of Ucluelet's pioneer settlers, twenty in all, who arrived there at different times prior to 1899, are inscribed on a cairn

279

recently erected on the present townsite. The only name missing is that of a man who could rightfully claim to be Ucluelet's first white inhabitant. He could be any one of several who at different times had charge of a fur-trading post which Captain Peter Francis, the owner of several sealing schooners in the 1870's, established at Spring Cove just inside the entrance to the inlet. However, it is known that Captain Francis frequently operated the post himself. He was there in 1874, when Bishop Seghers and Rev. A. J. Brabant made their hectic 250-mile journey — in different stages by canoe and over bush trails — from Kyuquot to Victoria. Captain Spring, another sealing schooner skipper, also used the cove; it was named after him.

Most of Ucluelet's early settlers were attracted by fabulous reports which told of how fine gold could be recovered from the sand at Wreck Bay (now Florencia Bay), four miles to the west. They formed a syndicate and small amounts of gold were actually taken, some reports say as much as $20,000 worth over a period of a few years. But storms demolished their sluice boxes and other workings as fast as they were erected and the project was subsequently abandoned, though for the next fifty years a lone prospector could always be found there. The experiences of one of these prospectors formed the basis of "Florencia Bay," a fiction story which appeared in *Maclean's* magazine a few years back.

Far from being discouraged at the failure of their gold-seeking enterprise, some turned to fishing and logging, both of which industries were then in their infancy. Fishing was all done by canoe. Spring salmon were more plentiful than now and could be taken without leaving the harbour. They fetched 25 cents each (today's price 50 cents per pound), and $2 per day could be made working at Sutton's shingle mill at the head of the inlet. Others took up land. A few left the district, but others married and soon the nucleus of a small community took shape.

William and James Sutton took up a large tract of land in the early 1880's and their shingle and sawmill was then the only one beyond Alberni. Surplus logs they sold to the Alberni mill for $6 per thousand feet, b.m. They also opened Ucluelet's first store. Their holdings, which embraced most of the timber around Kennedy Lake was subsequently disposed of to Seattle Cedar, using the name Sutton Lumber Co. Ltd. in its future operations on the west coast of Vancouver Island. One enterprise was an export shingle mill at Mosquito Harbour, Clayoquot Sound. The Sutton brothers' names appear first on the plaque, though there is doubt about their being Ucluelet's first permanent settlers.

Among other early names is that of George Fraser, a Scottish bachelor and famed horticulturist whose azaleas, heathers, rhododendrons and hybrids of all kinds, which he painstakingly developed himself, were much admired by passengers travelling on the *Princess Maquinna* when that vessel sailed up and down the West Coast.

Another was August Jansen, a Swede, who spent many years in the sealing schooners which called in the spring for their Indian hunters and boat steerers. He later took over the management of Sutton's store. John Kvarno, a Norwegian, settled down to ranching and for years supplied the community with milk at 10 cents a quart, butter 25 cents per pound, eggs 15 cents a dozen and potatoes at $1 a sack. Later he became Ucluelet's first policeman.

A. Herman Lyche, who also farmed, pre-empted the block of land on which the present townsite stands. His wife, a sister of Edwin Lee, another of the early settlers and whose name is also on the plaque, was Ucluelet's first school teacher. Lyche was coxswain of one of the West Coast's first lifeboats, in the days when their only power was oars and sails. The life-saving station was then at Spring Cove but later moved to Tofino. The other is at Bamfield. Ucluelet's Public Health Centre building, opened in 1959, was named in honour of Lyche.

Lee operated a general store and fur-seal buying business until 1939, when he retired and came to live in Victoria. He was also Ucluelet's postmaster and justice of the peace. His father, Thomas Lee, came out from England in the sailing ship *Robert Low* in 1862. He settled in Victoria and for years operated a sixty-acre farm where the Royal Jubilee hospital now stands. The original Lee home which stood at the corner of Fort Street and Lee Avenue (named after him) was torn down only in recent years.

Herbert J. Hillier, another native son of Victoria who was attracted to Ucluelet by the gold fever, arrived there in 1898. His first job was cook at the Wreck Bay mining camp — it paid wages — and when that petered out he worked on the 25-mile road which now connects Ucluelet with Tofino. Wheelbarrows, picks, shovels and crosscut saws was the only equipment used and sufficient funds for the construction (clearing, grading and corduroy only) of barely a mile per year, was all the local politicians could pry out of the treasury in those days. Not till forty years later was the road put through, and it took a war to do it: in 1942, when an operational airfield was established at Long Beach.

The late Mr. and Mrs. Jacob Arnet of Tofino.

The six sturdy fishermen sons of the late Jacob and Mrs. Arnet of Tofino, with their sister, another sailor's wife. Left to right: Alma, Edgar, Harold, Karl, Bjarne, Trygve and Walter. With most of their uncles, sons and cousins also fishermen, the Arnets are one of the largest families engaged in fishing on the British Columbia coast. *Family Album Photos.*

Among Ucluelet's originals were George Fraser, a Scottish botanist (left) and August Jansen, sealer and storekeeper.

Mrs. Mary Karn, aged 94 at the time of her death in 1962, was Ucluelet's oldest pioneer settler. *Family Album Photos.*

Mr. Hillier helped construct the telegraph line along the outside West Coast and for fifty years was linesman and agent. In recognition of his long and faithful service, in 1935 he was awarded the King George V Diamond Jubilee medal. One of his last acts before his death, in 1954, was to cook a goose dinner for Lieutenant-Governor Clarence Wallace. The geese were shot on the Tofino tidal flats behind Long Beach by the governor, who was afterwards entertained at Mr. Hillier's home. One of Ucluelet's most prominent landmarks, the house commanded a full view of the harbour. It was only recently torn down to make way for a modern bungalow in which Mr. Hillier's son George, a bachelor, lives. Two other sons also reside at Ucluelet; a fourth died from wounds received overseas in the First Great War.

William L. Thompson, an Irishman, logged, fished, was telegraph linesman for several years, and later succeeded Lyche as lifeboat skipper. Formerly a seaman, with a master's ticket, he met with an untimely death — or at least is presumed to have. He sailed from Vancouver for the China coast in command of a small freighter. Nothing was ever heard of her again.

George Grant, a Scottish bachelor who wore a kilt and played the bagpipes, after trying his hand at farming, gave that up and was made lightkeeper at Amphitrite Point. He afterwards became Ucluelet's postmaster. Other pioneer settlers whose names appear on the plaque include Dr. Charles McLean, medical officer for the Indian department, James Fraser, James Murphy, Carl Binns, C. McKenzie, John McCarthy, Samuel and John Bragg, F. Margatish and Thomas O'Connor. Younger generations of most of the families still live at Ucluelet.

Around the turn of the century came, among others, Fred Whipp, Wilfred Thornton, Thomas Tugwell, Charles Hughes, Chris Olsen, Walter Saggers, Fritz Bonetti, the Homewood brothers and Chris Fletcher. English-born Mrs. Mary Karn, aged ninety-four at the time of her death in 1962, was Ucluelet's oldest pioneer resident. Her husband was the district's first carpenter and chimney builder.

These are only a few of the men and women who pioneered this part of the West Coast. They were told at the time that the area would soon have road access to the outside. Comparatively young when they settled there first, scarcely half a dozen lived to see one built. Successive governments listened to their representations, and in time a road was built between the two settlements — Tofino and Ucluelet, but still the only means of communication with the outside was by steamer.

Meanwhile the district has grown and the combined population of Tofino, Long Beach and Ucluelet is now approximately 1,600, with at least 15 per cent direct descendants of these same pioneers. Younger generations of the Arnet, Hansen, Eik, Wingen, Fraser and Hillier families alone account for well over 200.

August 22, 1959, was a red letter day for these people, when they were permitted to drive over a new road just built in from Alberni, by way of Sproat and Kennedy Lakes. This was a joint tribute on the part of the provincial government, B.C. Forest Products Ltd. and McMillan, Bloedel and Powell River Co. Ltd., who together built the road — for it was not yet officially opened — to the surviving pioneers who were specially invited guests. Over three hundred persons, in seventy-five cars, made up the caravan. In the past, the journey to Alberni by boat took half-a-day; now one can drive there in two hours.

In September the gates were opened. Forty cars were waiting at the Sproat Lake end and went through immediately. By Monday night, the end of the long Labour Day weekend, over seven hundred cars, carrying an estimated 3,000 passengers, had travelled over the road, both ways. For many, it was their first sight of the Pacific Ocean, for as said elsewhere in these pages, Long Beach is the only place on the British Columbia coast where the shores of the Pacific can be reached by road. In other cars were many who were born on that part of the coast and have since made their homes elsewhere, and with them, children who had yet to see the land of their grandparents and great-grandparents.

The pity is so few of the district's original pioneers lived to see the promised road; but for future generations, the day will go down in history. Its completion marks the turning point in the development of the west coast of Vancouver Island generally.

Typical West Coast fishing vessel. The Ucluelet based *Hillier Queen* landing halibut catch at Victoria. Captain and owner George Hillier (wearing white cap) at right. *Victoria Colonist Photo.*

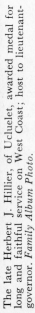

The late Herbert J. Hillier, of Ucluelet, awarded medal for long and faithful service on West Coast; host to lieutenant-governor. *Family Album Photo.*

Frederick Thornberg, his daughter and two sons, photographed aboard the schooner *Libbie* in 1907. He always kept his double-barrel shotgun handy when among the Indians.

Mr. and Mrs. John Grice, the first settlers at Tofino. *Family Album Photo.*

FREDERICK CHRISTIAN THORNBERG was born December 31, 1841, at Stege, on Mooen Island, Denmark. At fifteen he went to sea and on February 22, 1862, after an adventurous voyage around the Horn in the ship *Black Knight* in which he served before the mast, arrived at Esquimalt where, like many seamen did in those days, at the first opportunity he "jumped ship."

This was fortunate for Thornberg. The *Black Knight* had brought out Welsh coal for H.M. ships then stationed at Esquimalt. Loaded with ship's spars — then one of our principal exports — she sailed shortly afterwards and was never heard from again. Spars too long for the hold would be stowed on deck. These might have loosened during bad weather, causing the vessel to become unmanageable. She probably foundered somewhere in the icy waters of the sub-Antarctic.

Thornberg's first voyages were mostly on Danish vessels, which carried coal from Cardiff, Wales, to Constantinople, Alexandria and other eastern Mediterranean ports, and returned with wheat or cotton seed. On one trip his ship capsized and sank when its cargo shifted during a storm, but a passing brig picked up the crew and took them to Malta. He then joined a British ship and later took out his papers as a British subject.

His first job after jumping ship was as a servant to the Honourable David Cameron, first chief justice of Vancouver Island, 1853-1865, after whom Cameron Lake was named and who then lived at Esquimalt. Meanwhile, he married Cecily Harthylia, the daughter of a Songhees sub-chief who was related to the Lummi Island Indians, on the American side. There were three children of this marriage. After several years with Cameron, Thornberg went to the San Juan Islands, then garrisoned by ninety British marines, to visit his wife's relations. While there he took the job of herding a flock of 500 sheep, kept to provide the marines with mutton. While on the Islands, his wife died. Not wishing to become an American citizen, he came back to Victoria when the marines were withdrawn in 1873.

An experienced seaman and, through his marriage to an Indian woman, familiar with the native language, Thornberg's services were much sought after by trading and sealing schooner owners. That's how, in the early 1880's, he came to the west coast of Vancouver Island, as a crew member in Captain Spring's schooner *Favourite*. These were also factors in his being hired to run the Clayoquot trading post. He and the traders at Bamfield, Ucluelet, Nootka and Quatsino, with Rev. A. J. Brabant, the Catholic priest at Hesquiat, were then the only permanent white residents on the entire coast.

Thornberg is frequently mentioned in Brabant's memoirs. In April 1885, he took to himself a second wife, again an Indian woman, named Lucy Harbess. They were married "Indian fashion", but a few months later the ceremony was performed by a priest. This wife died from poisoning in 1901, after eating small mussels. There were five children by this union, four boys and a daughter, but only two are alive today, Andreas Gabriel, in hospital, and Frederick, who still resides at Clayoquot.

In later years, Thornberg had a store of his own at Ahousat. He retired in 1912 and came to live at Victoria, where he died in 1923 at the age of eighty-three. His four sons (of the last marriage) all served in the armed forces during the First World War. How Thornberg conducted his trading post and his experiences with the Indians, the reader will find frequent reference to in previous pages.

CLO-OOSE, that tiny settlement with an Indian name meaning a "safe landing", was the *Princess Maquinna*'s second stop after leaving Victoria. This usually was about 6 a.m., and although her passengers were unable to go ashore as there was no wharf, round-trippers always crowded on deck to watch the inhabitants ferry supplies ashore in a fashion different from that at other ports of call.

The village faces the open ocean, with no protection whatever for the few fishing boats which anchor there during summer months. In bad weather the *Maquinna* passed up the stop altogether and called southbound if by then seas had moderated. This frequently occurred during the winter months and as she only came every ten days, the community often had to go without mail and supplies for several weeks. On one occasion it was late in January before the residents received Christmas supplies.

Unless it was flat calm, which was seldom, the *Maquinna* never dropped anchor. Instead, her captain would ease the ship in as close as possible, then turn her around bow-on to the seas and keep her that way. This was to prevent her from rolling while the canoes were being loaded from open freight doors almost at water level. Pitching didn't matter, but one good roll would not only flood the hold, but smash any canoes alongside. Head on, the canoes would ride the swells with comparative safety if properly handled.

Tourists marvelled at the way such frail craft were manipulated; usually by one old Indian with a short paddle squatting in the stern, and a younger man catching the freight as it was tossed from the ship, an operation which had to be timed with the swells. Occasionally a passenger had to be taken ashore the same way and if it happened to be a woman, camera-armed tourists got a greater thrill.

Watching the heavily-laden canoes go ashore was just as exciting, especially as they neared the beach where, regardless of how smooth the sea appeared to be, the swells always broke. More so when it was really rough and a ducking for someone and wet freight usually resulted.

With Clo-oose, the name of "Dave" Logan and shipwrecks were synonymous. For thirty-five years Dave Logan was its general factotum and there probably never was (on this coast anyway) another men who saw so many marine disasters, gave a valiant hand in rescuing survivors, or helped in the gruesome task of finding and burying the dead.

Mr. Logan was born at Leith, Scotland and, when a boy of four, migrated with his parents to Massachusetts, United States. After leaving school he worked in the iron mines at Illinois and when still in his twenties came to Vancouver Island where he worked in the mines at Wellington. In 1899, a Victoria man hired him to take care of a herd of cattle grazing in the Cheewhat area, half a mile from Clo-oose. People had great faith in the agricultural possibilities of the West Coast at that time and cattle-raising had already been attempted at Tofino, Estevan Point and Nootka. But the country at any of these places was never suited for this or any other kind of farming and it wasn't long before there were no cattle left.

Dave built a house on the beach and afterwards opened a store. Along with his groceries he also brought the mail off the steamer. He later became postmaster and justice of the peace, appointments he held until his death. He was also the linesman and had to patrol a 25-mile section of the single-wire, tree-to-tree telephone line that extended from Victoria to Cape Beale, which had to be kept open at all times in case of shipwrecks.

The stretch of coastline Mr. Logan patrolled — between Carmanah Point and Pachena Point — was the scene of many shipwrecks, all of which are narrated in these pages. Several occurred almost in front of the Logan house. Many of these he personally witnessed and was at the scene within a few hours. And many were the shipwrecked passengers and crew members taken care of in the Logan home.

In November 1918, the fishpacker *Renfrew*, with twenty-six cannery employees aboard, capsized while crossing the Nitinat bar. Thirteen were drowned and, after assisting in rescuing the survivors, Mr. Logan spent the next two days picking up the dead as they washed ashore. On October 26, 1906, the sailing vessel *Skagit* was

287

wrecked at Clo-oose Point; two crew members were drowned and he assisted in saving the other fifteen. The steam schooner *Santa Rita* went ashore on Clo-oose beach on February 14, 1923, but all of her crew managed to reach shore. These were but a few of the wrecks that occurred and in each case the survivors were taken care of by Mr. and Mrs. Logan.

The greatest loss of life occurred when the passenger steamer *Valencia*, inbound from San Francisco to Victoria, was wrecked about twelve miles west of Clo-oose on January 23, 1906. Of the 154 persons on board, 117 perished. Three men reached shore shortly after the ship struck and came to a linesman's cabin. Following the directions by the telephone on the cabin wall, they rang the SOS signal. Mrs. Logan answered and thus the first word of the disaster was received. With several other residents, Dave Logan set out and they were the first land party at the scene. Two rescue ships were already there, but were helpless in the rough seas.

The ship had come to grief at the base of a cliff, too steep for anyone to climb either up or down. By now the tide was high, making it impossible to reach her via the beach. They could see the passengers and crew looking up at them from the deck of the doomed ship but could do nothing to help. The captain fired two rocket lines but both fell short. A third reached them, but parted when they were pulling up a heavier line, and the captain signalled that he had no more lines.

Utterly helpless to aid them in any way, all they could do was stand and look on as the merciless seas took their toll. The ship soon commenced to break up and only thirty-seven were eventually saved. Every woman and child aboard was lost.

Mr. Logan died on March 28, 1938, at the age of seventy-four. He had a big heart and was known up and down the coast for two things in particular, his outstanding generosity and a big voice. As Captain Gillam of the *Maquinna* used to say, "When it was foggy, Clo-oose needed no foghorn, all I had to do was toot the whistle and if I heard Dave Logan bellow out in reply, I knew we were off Clo-oose." Mrs. Logan predeceased him in 1929. They had four children, all born at Clo-oose.

PORT RENFREW

PORT RENFREW was named after Baron Renfrew, Earl of Selkirk, when a post office, with T. Kirkpatrick in charge, was established there in 1896. Two rivers, the San Juan and Gordon (the latter not to be confused with Jordan River) flow into the head of the bay, on the south and north side respectively. As early as 1860 a handful of men recovered gold from the gravel bars of the Gordon, but results were discouraging and when news of the rich Leech River strike — which occurred about that time — reached them, they abandoned their claims and hit the trail for that area.

Attracted by the arable San Juan delta land, thousands of acres in extent, and the promise of a road, the first settlers began to arrive in the mid 1880's, among them: Frank V. Hobbs, Alfred Deakin, Arthur Blakely, Robert Elliott, Frank and Edgar Crampton, E. P. Wiggs, William Emery, William B. Robertson and Charles Blackstaff. Another was John Baird, who shortly afterwards was made customs officer and justice of the peace. By 1900 there were forty embryo farms in the valley, but the land had first to be cleared of heavy bush, a task which required several years of back-breaking work before it could be brought under cultivation.

Years passed and still no road; most of them moved away and the forest stole back what little land they had cleared. Of those who stayed, some found employment on the "Black Prince" and "Corbett" iron and copper showings on Bugaboo Creek, a tributary of the Gordon. The claims had only recently been staked by Alfred Deakin, Julius West and Joe Williams, who in turn disposed of them to the Gordon River Iron Ore Company, an English syndicate headed by the Godman family, several members of whom meanwhile had taken up land in the valley. Steam machinery was installed and development work carried on over a period of years, but the mine never came into production. About this time, John Baird resigned as customs officer to engage in mining. Thomas Baird, a brother, who up till now had been telegraph linesman, took his place and held that position for the next twenty-five years. Others turned to hand-logging when one of the new arrivals, W. H. G. Ellison, a retired Anglican clergyman from the parish of Metchosin, near Victoria, opened a sawmill.

Up till 1900, the only building in the vicinity of the wharf was the post office and telegraph office. There were no roads, only a trail here and there and a one-plank walk to Harris Cove, where, on the door of the Indian chief's house was a sign which read "Chief Peter, The White Man's Guide". Now the settlement boasted a hotel (since burned down) and store, both built and operated by Temple Godman. A wharf came later, but it was 1916 before there were enough children in the district to warrant a school.

The population remained stationary (about fifty) for the next twenty years. Industry lagged and what few farms there were in the valley raised produce sufficient only for local requirements. Then in 1923 Cathels and Sorensen opened up a modern logging camp; others followed and today lumber is Port Renfrew's chief industry, employing about two hundred men. It has also become an important salmon fishing centre, with a fleet of approximately one hundred seine and gillnet boats based there during the summer months. And at this writing, the Bugaboo iron mine, inactive for sixty years, is being developed by the Noranda Mining Co.

Seventy-five years passed before the promised road materialized, when in 1958, Port Renfrew got two, one a continuation of the Victoria-Jordan River road, the other coming in from Shawnigan Lake; not one of the pioneer settlers lived to see them and only a handful of their descendants still reside there. Port Renfrew's population today is about three hundred and fifty.

Port San Juan was a favourite rendezvous for the rum-running schooners during prohibition in the United States. There they received telephone messages from headquarters at Vancouver. It was from this harbour that the *Beryl G.*, in September 1924, sailed before being hi-jacked in the Gulf Islands when Captain William J. Gillis and his seventeen-year-old son were murdered and their bodies thrown overboard. Two men subsequently paid with their lives for this crime.

Port San Juan was surveyed in 1847 by H.M.S. *Pandora*, Lieut.-Commander James Wood. The harbour is exposed to the ocean swells and at this writing industrial interests (fishing, logging and mining) are pressing Ottawa for a breakwater. Gordon River was named after Commander George Thomas Gordon, R.N., H.M. SLOOP *Cormorant*, on this station 1846-1850; San Juan River, from the port.

On January 22, 1949, the Vancouver tug *St. Clair*, ashore a total loss, Port San Juan; two crew members drowned.

MARINE GARDENS OF THE NORTH PACIFIC COAST

Botanical Beach, situated about three miles from Port Renfrew post office and facing the open Pacific, has over the past seventy-five years attracted scientists and biologists from all parts of the continent. Actually there is little beach; the area consists of pools which the action of the sea, over countless ages, has gouged out of the sandstone formation, common on this part of the coast. The pools vary in shape, from bathtub to swimming pool in size, and the crystal-clear water left by the receding tide swarms with marine life, some of which is only found in this area. Sea anemone of every hue, and spiny sea urchins are in abundance. Abalone and different specie of barnacle cling to the rocks, minute forms of crustacea hide under stones on the bottom, and a trapped (by the receding tide) octopus or small cod may be found hiding under the ledges. Rare seaweeds are also found in the locality.

In 1900, the University of Minnesota established on the site the Minnesota Botanical Seaside Station and every summer for the next ten years biological students from that and other universities came to further their studies and gather exhibits. Other groups, both American and Canadian, still come; but now they have to camp out, for the station buildings have long since disappeared and the site is completely overgrown with brush. However, the pools are still there, as full of interesting marine life as ever.

NINETY PER CENT of the salmon taken off the west coast of Vancouver Island are troll-caught, by a fleet of approximately 1,000 Canadian boats operating principally out of Bamfield, Ucluelet, Tofino, Nootka, Kyuquot and Winter Harbour, and almost as many American vessels out of Neah Bay. The total catch by Canadian boats represents fifty per cent of all troll-caught salmon landed in British Columbia.

Most of the Canadian boats are one-man operated and return to port each night, but as the American vessels have to remain at sea for as long as ten days (they carry ice), they usually carry two men. The trollers fish from April to September and as the salmon (mostly springs and coho) are taken from five to twenty-five miles off shore — while still feeding — they are in prime condition. Hence, they fetch the highest price on the fresh fish market. The largest springs mostly find their way to the mild-cure (salted and then smoked) market in the United States. Net fishing is confined to the inlets, where a few small runs of sockeye, humpback and chums occur, but owing to the absence of large spawning rivers like the Fraser, Skeena and Nass, the catch is negligible.

The troller dresses his salmon immediately after it is caught and sells at a fish-buying camp of his own choice. There the fish are iced-down in boxes and shipped to Vancouver or Seattle by packer. Fish buying was spasmodic prior to 1923. Weeks sometimes passed before a buyer showed up. It was useless for the fishermen to go out and find no buyer when he returned, and this frequently happened when fishing was at its best. Often the day's catch had to be given away or thrown overboard.

It was the Nelson Brothers, Ralph, John, Norman and Richard, who pioneered organized buying on the West Coast. Trollers themselves out of Kyuquot, they bought a small packer and carried their own fish. Seattle paid the best price, in fact, almost double that which they had previously received, so they sold their fish there. Salmon carried for other fishermen, they charged on a poundage basis plus a small commission. Ice brought back permitted the boats to fish during the four days required for the packer to make the round trip to Seattle.

Larger packers were soon required and permanent buying camps established, not only at Kyuquot, but at most West Coast centres. Established fishing companies followed the Nelson Brothers' example and from then on permanent buying camps (during the summer months) and fast packers to serve them became the standard method for handling all fish (except herring and pilchards) on the West Coast. Herring and pilchard were delivered to the reduction plants by the seine boats which caught them.

Kyuquot can therefore rightfully claim to be the West Coast's first organized salmon trolling centre, and its inhabitants (normal population about one hundred, with the number tripled in summer) are still dependent on fishing for a livelihood. The settlement, half on floats and half on shore, is located on a small bay on the inside shores of Walters Island. There are two narrow entrances deep enough at high water for fish packers and small tankers. Mail and supplies are brought by launch from the regular West Coast steamer which stops at Chamiss Bay, five miles to the east on Kyuquot Sound. For years there was a whaling station at Cachalot, on Kyuquot Sound.

At one time there were ten canneries on the West Coast; now there are none. With the disappearance of the pilchards and the closing down of the reduction plants (see page 244), the fishing companies found themselves with an excessive number of packers. About the same time, they opened stores at their respective fish-buying camps. Supplies for the stores and canneries were brought in by steamer. Except for ice, the packers returned from Vancouver light. Then to utilize the packers to full capacity, the companies commenced using them for carrying their own freight to both camps and canneries, and also for hauling a considerable part of the canned salmon pack out.

Later still, the companies found it more economical to can their fish at central plants located at industrial centres like Prince Rupert, Vancouver and New Westminster, where shore workers at peak runs were more readily available. The result: one by one the up-coast canneries were done away with and packers brought the salmon to these centrally located plants to be processed.

In 1935, another West Coast fishery folded up, the salting of chum salmon and herring. The fish were caught by Indians and white fishermen, but the plants — there was one or more on nearly every inlet — were owned and operated by Japanese. The product went mostly to China, but when those two countries had a fall-out, the trade ceased and the plants were abandoned.

Loss of freight and passenger traffic resulting from the closing down of the pilchard plants, canneries and salteries, and the fishing companies now packing their own supplies for their fish-buying camps and stores, was largely responsible for the C.P.R. subsequently withdrawing its West Coast steamer service altogether. Waterhouse Steamship Company, which for years operated a fleet of freighters in the same trade, also withdrew.

Herring, as plentiful as ever, are taken by seine boats fishing in the inlets during the winter months. The catch chiefly goes to the Port Albion reduction plant on Ucluelet Inlet, now the only one on the West Coast. Any surplus is taken to plants on the Fraser River. Halibut is also fished off the West Coast, but the grounds are not as productive as those farther to the west. Cod, sole and flounder are taken by trawl.

FORTUNES MADE,
SOME THE HARD WAY

A MILLIONAIRE OWNED a gold mine at Zeballos. Another, at one time practically controlled the West Coast's salmon fisheries. Back in the 1880's an American multi-millionaire purchased "for a song" its choicest stands of cedar forest, and early in this century one bought up one of the most desirable properties on Long Beach where he built a beautiful home and resided for several years. Of the others, none lived on the West Coast. They came in their private yachts about once every year; fished our streams, shot our geese and brant, bought up all the ancient face-masks, tribal head-dresses and other priceless Indian relics (that's where they went instead of to our museums), paid the Indians next to nothing for them, then left.

Meanwhile, enterprising young men of humble origin and brought up on the West Coast's rugged shores, developed the area's natural resources and became millionaires, or at least made modest fortunes. Others sought wider fields and their names can now be found among British Columbia's leading professional and business men.

BROTHERS DARED TO OPERATE WHERE CRITICS FORECAST FAILURE

THIS IS THE STORY of four brothers, two with only elementary school education, who from a small sawmill operated on a "shoe-string" by their father, through sheer determination, enterprise, brawn and cussedness — but always heeding the advice of their parents — built up a successful industrial organization and subsequently retired while still in their early forties and fifties.

Starting from scratch, here are a few of their accomplishments: They owned thousands of acres of valuable timber and operated one of the largest chains of logging camps on the island; owned a fleet of twenty-five vessels of various size and which included fishing boats, fish packers, whalers, tugboats and a log carrier; a cannery and reduction plant, whaling station and a gold mine.

They also owned an airline and their own private amphibious plane for commuting between their different up-coast interests. In addition to the small shingle and sawmill which gave them their first start, they located, built and operated two export mills, one with a capacity of six million feet per month, the other almost as big. Around one of these mills they laid out and built, complete with paved streets, a modern town (Tahsis) which within two years boasted a population of 1,200.

One brother was elected a member of the House of Commons at Ottawa, and another, elected twice to the provincial legislature. Ten years ago they disposed of the greater part of their lumber interests to a multi-million-dollar corporation. Most of their other up-coast interests, including the boats, they also disposed of and although they now live in comparative retirement at Vancouver, their lives are far from inactive for they still own the cannery operation, have since acquired a radio station and the controlling interest in several big base metal mining projects.

William F. Gibson was born at Guelph, Ontario, came to British Columbia in 1896 and first went prospecting in the Lillooet district. He then tried his luck in the Klondike, where two of his sons were born, and afterwards went overseas with the Canadian Forestry Corps. In 1918, he pre-empted 120 acres at Ahousat on the West Coast which was to be the Gibsons' home for the next thirty years. Its population comprised the Gibson family, a government linesman, the principal of a Presbyterian mission school on a nearby reservation and his wife and staff.

Mr. and Mrs. Gibson had four sons, Clarke W., J. Gordon, Jack L. and Earson. There were no daughters. In order to accompany their parents the elder two quit school when in their middle grades and as there was no school at Ahousat, that ended their education. Jack and Earson were left behind in Vancouver to continue their schooling and joined the family soon afterwards.

Mr. Gibson's first venture was a small shingle and sawmill, which for ten years he operated with the assistance of his sons and occasionally employing a few Indians. Logging, mostly trees which grew along the shoreline and preferably those which would fall into the water when felled, was all by hand. A launch to tow the logs to the mill and a steam engine to turn its machinery, was the extent of the operation's equipment. Their first launch was a steam affair with a wood-burning boiler, the next powered by an upside-down kerosene engine. Mr. Gibson also operated a general store and post office, with a fish-buying camp and marine oil station in conjunction. He was also Ahousat's postmaster.

In 1925, pilchard reduction plants were springing up all along the coast. The Gibsons had a suitable site and a plant, operated by them, was built alongside the mill. The boys then laid their peevies and handjacks aside and turned to fishing. Within a short time they acquired a small fleet of seine boats and packers, one of which was the *Otter*, which, before the palatial "Princess" ships arrived on this coast, was the pride of the C.P.R. They traded under the name, W. F. Gibson & Sons Ltd.

Mr. Gibson died in 1927 when they were still struggling to make a success of life and working on borrowed capital. The boys' biggest regret is that their father never lived to enjoy the fruits of his sons' labours and to see the fulfilment of the principles he installed in their young minds. From then on, the mother always presided over their deliberations and much of their success is directly attributable to her wise counsel. Mrs. Julia Gibson is still hale and hearty and at the age of ninety lives in comfortable retirement at Vancouver.

When the pilchards disappeared the boys went back to logging, but on a much larger scale and with modern equipment. They established camps at different points on Nootka Sound, at Chamiss Bay on Kyuquot Sound and at Jeune Landing on Quatsino Sound. By now they had enlarged their fleet and to keep the vessels busy when not towing log booms, they packed fish from the West Coast to Vancouver. The four-masted auxiliary schooner *Malahat*, built at Victoria for the Australian lumber trade and later used as a rum-runner, they purchased and converted into a log carrier. With her, they were the first to carry logs from camps in the Queen Charlotte Islands to Ocean Falls and Powell River; prior to that, all logs were towed across Queen Charlotte Strait in rafts. *Malahat* ended her days in 1944, on the beach in Uchucklesit Inlet, Barkley Sound, where she was towed after being swamped off Cape Beale. It may be a matter of interest to know that *Malahat*'s wheel now serves as a light fixture in "Fort Vancouver", Gordon's vacation residence on the Island of Maui, Hawaii.

Clarke took care of the head office, which meanwhile had been moved to Vancouver. Jack operated the store, post office and fish-buying business at Ahousat. Between them, Gordon and Earson ran the boats and supervised the logging operations. At this time, the mother still resided at Ahousat.

In 1941, they bought out Ginger Coote Airways Ltd., which operated a fleet of aircraft between Vancouver and Zeballos. During the Second World War they held contracts with the government for taking out airplane spruce, and clearing land at the different war-time air bases then being built on the island; meanwhile they continued to operate their own chain of logging camps. After the war they operated a whaling station at Coal Harbour on Quatsino Sound, and later sold it to B.C. Packers Ltd. They also bought a gold mine at Kyuquot, but this was merely a speculation and the only gamble on which they lost money. In 1945, brother Jack was elected M.P. for Comox-Alberni and retained the seat till he resigned in 1953.

Their boldest venture was when they built an export mill at Tahsis, on Nootka Sound. Critics said they were crazy — that ships would never go that far out of their way to load. Not only did they go ahead with the project, but deep-sea freighters began calling there for lumber long before the wharf was completed and had to be loaded from lighters out in the stream. And they have been calling there ever since on an average of one every day.

The first Tahsis mill was built in 1945 and cut 3,000,000 feet per month. When it was destroyed by fire two years later, the Gibsons not only rebuilt it, but trebled its capacity. It employed 300 men. The following year they built a second export mill at Port Alberni. At Tahsis they built a modern town which today has a population of 1,200 and is the largest town on the West Coast beyond the Albernis. Tahsis before the Gibsons went there was virgin forest.

In 1952, the Gibson Brothers disposed of these two mills, together with all their timber interests on the West Coast to the Tahsis Company Ltd., a subsidiary of East Asiatic Company Ltd., a corporation with world-wide ramifications and headed by a Danish prince.

About this time the Gibsons had only recently opened a camp at the head of Muchalat Inlet, also on Nootka Sound. This was later moved by the Tahsis Company bodily across the water and re-established at the mouth of Gold River. Today, Muchalat (the name of its post office) is a modern township with a population of 400; headquarters of the Tahsis Company's logging operations and the terminus of a road recently built across Vancouver Island (through Strathcona Park) from Campbell River. The road was built jointly by Tahsis Company and the Elk River Timber Company Ltd.

Gordon Gibson was later elected M.L.A. for Lillooet, but after one session resigned his seat following a difference of opinion between himself and the government over the granting of forest management licenses. He lost the by-election which subsequently followed, but was elected again in 1960, this time for the North Vancouver constituency.

Meanwhile the brothers had indulged in a new venture and opened Greater Vancouver's fifth commercial radio station, CKLG at North Vancouver. This they operated successfully for five years, then sold out. Their names might well be included in British Columbia's *Who's Who* of successful business men. Each has his own private yacht, Gordon a 100-acre plantation in Hawaii and to avoid any mental or physical reflexing of the energies which brought about their success in up-coast industry, all take an active part in civic affairs, while at the same time enjoying the more congenial social life of the city of Vancouver.

NELSONS HARVESTED
THE SEA

NELSON BROTHERS FISHERIES LTD. had its origin on the west coast of Vancouver Island. Today, it is one of the largest fishing companies in British Columbia; owns and operates a fleet of fifty modern seiners and packers, with canneries and reduction plants at Prince Rupert and on the Fraser River.

The brothers' venture was born of sheer necessity, when as salmon trollers they were among the first to fish out of Kyuquot (see page 293). Prior to that, they had gill-netted on the Fraser and fished halibut out of Prince Rupert. They fished from 20 to 30-foot one-man boats powered by small gas engines; lived in cramped quarters and hauled their lines or nets in by hand. Today's trollers and gillnet boats are from 40 to 50 feet long, with a corresponding beam and powered with diesel engines up to 100 h.p. They are equipped with stabilizers (to prevent rolling), radio telephone, gyro compass, automatic steering, echo sounders, direct engine-room control and power gurdies for hauling in the lines or nets.

After initiating organized fish buying on the West Coast — with its attendant fleet of packers — Nelson Brothers extended their operation to North Island (Langara) at the northern tip of the Queen Charlotte Islands, where another group of fishermen, mostly out of Prince Rupert, had discovered favourable trolling grounds.

The year 1925 saw them heavily involved in the pilchard industry, owning and operating half a dozen reduction plants, all on the West Coast and each with its attendant fleet of seiners, packers and scows. They also entered the cannery business, but this didn't require any great capital outlay, for they already had the boats, and the necessary machinery and equipment was installed adjacent to the reduction plants. When the pilchard industry folded, herring, which are taken during the winter months, were processed into meal and oil. With the result, Nelson Brothers Fisheries Ltd. now has practically an all-year-round operation.

Richard, the youngest brother, whose advice and counsel is frequently sought throughout the industry, is president of the company. He is a director and past president of the Fisheries Association of British Columbia, member of the Fisheries Council of Canada, the International Pacific Halibut Commission and the International North Pacific Fisheries Commission. Norman, who was in charge of production, died in 1961. General management of the company is gradually being taken over by their sons. Of the two elder Nelson brothers, Ralph and John, each now leads a more or less independent life.

GOLD

Prospecting for gold paid off for a group of unemployed fishermen during the "hungry thirties". For several seasons in succession fishermen on the West Coast were finding it hard to make ends meet. Not that salmon fishing was poor, but owing to depressed market conditions they were unable to sell their fish. The pilchard industry, which for the past few seasons had experienced a boom, also slumped.

The picture was black and as conditions in the cities were even worse, many single men decided to try their hand at prospecting. It was known that gold existed in the Zeballos area. Eminent geologists had made favourable reports. The son of one of Quatsino's pioneer settlers made a study of these and afterwards discovered a rich strike. Two Quatsino prospectors (Malmberg and Nordstrom) had recovered gold from the Zeballos river bed, indicating that ore values of considerable consequence would one day be found in the hills. The first gold vein was discovered in 1924 by the same two prospectors from Quatsino. Other properties were staked shortly afterwards and in 1929 the first ore shipment was made; but results were indifferent and activity ceased.

It was in 1931 that the unemployed fishermen hauled their boats out of the water at the head of Zeballos Arm, built log cabins on the beach and spent the time in the hills prospecting. During the winter months they trapped. They were then the area's sole inhabitants.

Soon several properties in different parts of the valley were being developed, but the first to come into production and show worthwhile results was the White Star group of claims, which Andrew Donaldson, the son of one of the original settlers who took up land at Cape Scott on the northern extremity of Vancouver Island in 1890, had staked. Assay returns were high and it proved to be the richest find in the valley up to that time (1932). Donaldson took into partnership his brother John and Mike Francis, a fisherman friend who also hailed from Quatsino, and together they worked the claims. They were joined later by Leslie R. Brown, brother-in-law of the Donaldsons, and his wife, who acted as camp cook.

The property was about six miles from tidewater and for the first few years the only means of communication between the mine and the beach was over bear and elk trails along the river bank. Trees had to be felled to make footbridges over the small streams and gulches, deadfalls crossed, the river waded in two places and ladders scaled up the steeper cliffs. Carrying a pack it was a day's walk either way. Except for hiring an extra man occasionally, for three years they worked the mine alone. They had no machinery; hand drills and powder were their only aids.

The ore had to be back-packed down to the river and loaded into a canoe; down rapids, portaged, canoe and all, around the canyon and finally to the beach. Supplies had to be taken in via the same route, no mean job with heavy items such as steel and the cookstove. It required several days to get one ton of ore from mine to tide-water. On one such trip, Francis was drowned when his canoe capsized. From the beach the ore was conveyed by gasboat to Cee-peecee cannery, ten miles away, where the *Princess Maquinna* called. From there it was shipped to Tacoma.

A total of 47 tons of hand-mined ore was shipped. Returns netted the owners 650 ounces of gold and 175 ounces of silver. In 1937, the brothers leased the property to a Vancouver syndicate (White Star Mine Ltd.) Meanwhile a road had been constructed part way up the valley and machinery was installed. The mine continued to operate and pay dividends. Andrew Donaldson retired and went to live at Vancouver. John went back to fishing. Mike Francis' interests went to his estate. The brother-in-law invested his profits by building Zeballos' first hotel (the Pioneer), sold it soon afterwards and purchased a farm in the Fraser River valley.

Other members of this little band of out-of-work fishermen and reduction plant workers who subsequently profited by their enforced change in occupation include Alfred Bird, Charles Smith, Albert Bloom, Alex MacDonald, Sam Knutsen, Raymond A. Pitre and Herbert Kevis. They were joined later by Norman S. Ray, Swiss-born Andy Morod, and Alec Stewart. Bird, who afterwards owned and worked claims at Bear River on Clayoquot Sound, now lives in retirement at Tofino. Smith returned to his native Nova Scotia, where he took up farming. Bloom committed suicide. The motive behind Bloom taking his own life, the inquest jury never determined. It was known, however, that he never trusted the banks and when found (by this writer who was mining recorder at Zeballos at the time) dead in his cabin with a discharged rifle by his side, his pockets were literally stuffed with one-hundred-dollar bills.

Alex MacDonald made a nice little stake when he discovered — and subsequently sold — the Rey Oro claims. This was the first mine to ship a gold brick, only a small one but it boosted the value of adjoining properties. Sam Knutsen staked the Spud Valley group of claims, which he later sold to millionaire A. B. Trites, sharing the proceeds with his girl friend Irene, who prospected with him. This mine became Zeballos' second biggest producer. Knutsen afterwards returned to his native Norway where he is believed to have lost his life while fighting with the underground against the Nazi occupation forces during World War II.

How Pitre and Kevis, along with J. Frumento and Chester Canning, who joined them later, made their stakes, is told in the next few pages. Morod is the only one of the early prospectors still residing at Zeballos. Ray's home is in Vancouver, but he spends the summer months at Zeballos. How these two men finally "hit the jackpot" is also told farther along.

Notwithstanding these rich discoveries, high assay returns and favourable reports made by mining engineers of repute, lack of road access held up development of most properties for a considerable time; for still provincial mine department officials held to the belief (proved scores of times elsewhere) that owing to structural faults common throughout Vancouver Island's mountain ranges, mineral veins were unpredictable. Neither could the federal government be persuaded to build a wharf. Freight brought in by steamers was still being landed on the beach from lighters, and passengers carried "piggy-back" style ashore (by this writer, who operated the ferry, and his son Mickey). Packhorses were used to carry equipment into the hills.

These difficulties, however, were overcome with the arrival from Ottawa of S. C. Ells, a mining engineer with the Department of Mines and Natural Resources. His report, after examining the different properties, resulted in an arrangement whereby Ottawa would pay seventy-five per cent, and the provincial government the remainder of the cost, and within six months a network of roads were constructed throughout the valley. They were built by Allan W.

Ford, of Parksville. A wharf, small boat landing stages and floats for seaplanes were also built.

Though not a native, Franc. Joubin, who a few years ago discovered vast uranium deposits in Northern Ontario which made him a fortune, as a young geologist fresh from the University of British Columbia, spent several years at Zeballos, incidentally on his honeymoon. Today, he is president of Bralorne Pioneer Mines Ltd., British Columbia's richest gold producer. Jack Crosson, Gordon Ponsford and Vic Davies can also be counted among Zeballos' successful prospectors. Crossan built the first shack where the town now stands. Davies still lives at Zeballos.

AS TO WHO ORIGINALLY discovered Privateer's fabulously rich No. 1 vein was for long a matter of controversy. The son of one of Quatsino's pioneer settlers claimed he did and his claim was substantiated in a government mining engineer's report. But this was disputed by other prospectors who had staked and recorded the claim on which it was subsequently found. The same prospectors (of the fisherman group) were fully aware of the value of the surface showings. Three of them had actually shipped a ton of high-grade ore to the Trail smelter, and received in return an encouraging cheque. But they lacked the necessary capital to prove its depth, which is all important. Nor could they interest any of the big mining companies to finance them, for gold veins which showed high assays had been previously discovered at many places on Vancouver Island but they all petered out when mined. This is due to faults common in the island's geological structure, noted by most geologists.

One mining engineer after another examined the property, but all turned it down. Discouraged, the prospectors finally sold the claims — along with others — to a Victoria man who later formed the Privateer Company; compared to their original asking price, for "a song". Litigation, in which all the above parties were involved, followed. The courts ruled on who was the original discoverer and an out-of-court settlement was subsequently made.

Credit for bringing Privateer into production must go to Raymond A. Pitre, who, with Herb Kevis (both former unemployed fishermen), Jack Frumento of Victoria and C. Canning from Vancouver, had for the past two years been developing a group of adjoining claims (Nootka-Zeballos) owned by a Victoria syndicate. The syndicate provided them with the necessary grubstake, but in lieu of wages they were paid in units (shares in the mine). This property subsequently ceased operations, with the result, its units would normally be worthless. But the syndicate was controlled by the same man who had purchased the Privateer claims and later formed Privateer Mines Ltd. The syndicate's shares (units) were automatically transferred to the new company (Privateer).

Pitre was made mine manager, and with his associates, moved over to Privateer, but with the company short of finances, still accepting units in lieu of wages. A cook was hired for the new camp and his wages were paid mostly in units. Still no road led to the property. However, this was soon overcome when the Pednault brothers, who had just sold out their logging interests at Sooke, made a wise investment and agreed to furnish trucks and other road-building equipment and accept units in lieu of rental and wages.

Soon it was established that the No. 1 vein extended both far up the slope and deep into the ground, and within a few weeks fabulously rich high-grade ore was being hand-mined and shipped in sacks (the exceptionally rich in sealed carbide cans) to Tacoma.

Equally fabulous returns spurred this small group of men on to further efforts. Smelter cheques provided money for steel, powder and other expenses, but not sufficient to pay wages, and the embryo miners continued to draw units.

A Toronto mining company had now become interested in the property. Its engineer recommended that it finance the immediate construction of a mill and the management of the mine be vested in the company till the money was paid back out of production, sharing in the profits at the same time. Overnight, Privateer shares sky-rocketed and units in the original syndicate, which a few months previous had been practically valueless, were now worth $5 each.

The Victoria man who headed the syndicate and who was now president of Privateer Mines Ltd., friends who advanced him the money to make the initial deposit on the claims, Pitre and his three associates, each of whom had by now accumulated (in lieu of wages) thousands of units, and the Pednault brothers, were the principal gainers. Even the cook, whose units represented only a few months work, made enough to establish himself in business (Zeballos' first restaurant).

This occurred in 1936 and during the next two years 9,100 tons of crude ore was shipped to the Tacoma smelter. Between 1938 — the year the mill was built — and 1948, when all the Zeballos mines (there were now five in production) closed down, with Prident, a small property adjoining and which it had in the meantime acquired, Privateer treated 166,313 tons of ore. In all, total ore treated (in the mill) and shipped, returned 168,318 ounces of gold and 68,589 ounces of silver, determined by settlement assay, worth $6½ million.

Pitre, still in his early forties, managed Privateer for two years, then with a moderate fortune, retired and went first to live in Victoria and then Vancouver. But he wasn't to remain inactive for very long, nor were his hard-earned West Coast earnings. He formed a company to manufacture power saws, then coming into general use and finding a ready market. Ten years later, an eastern manufacturing firm bought his patents, plant and equipment outright for $4 million. Meanwhile, Pitre had tried an experiment novel in British Columbia industry, by operating the plant on a coöperative basis; with the result, his share-holding employees participated in its profits and subsequent sale. Machinery and equipment was moved back east. Pitre promptly bought back the buildings for $1 million and formed a new company which manufactures thermolite plastics. He is also president and managing director of Gulf Marina Enterprises Ltd. at Richmond, British Columbia, which is said to be the largest marina in Canada.

Frumento invested his profits in Zeballos real estate, opened a men's furnishing store and later retired. Kevis resumed salmon fishing, but with a modern troller. Canning went back to Vancouver. In all, their years of hard work, living under primitive conditions and at times subsisting on beans and what salmon they caught in the river, finally "paid off".

When news of the success of these men reached the outside, prospectors and mining engineers from all over British Columbia flocked to the head of that remote inlet, hoping to do likewise. Then with visions of "easy money", usually associated with frontier mining camps, hundreds more followed, most of them arriving before a wharf could be built, or even a float for small boats. Because of this, men, women and children, their baggage, canaries and cats, all had to be transferred from the steamer to a flat scow, which in turn was beached in shallow water. Piggy-back style, they were carried ashore.

The fabulous gold rush, which occurred at Zeballos in 1936, was now off to a flying start. The next six months saw over 3,000 claims staked, and in two years' time there were no less than six producing mines in the valley, each with its own mill. And in place of the lone prospector's log cabin on the beach was a town with a population of approximately 1,000, a twenty-bed hospital operated by the Red Cross Society, school, four hotels, stores and the usual establishments found in all frontier mining camps. Smaller communities, two

The late Thomas Baird, a Port Renfrew pioneer settler and for twenty years customs officer there. *Family Album Photo.*

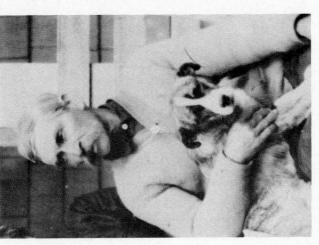

The late David Logan of Clo-oose. *Family Album Photo*

Mrs. Julia Earson Gibson and her four sons: left to right: Earson, Clarke W., J. Gordon, and Jack L. *Photo taken on Mrs. Gibson's ninetieth birthday.*

Tahsis on Nootka Sound, with a population of 1,400, is the largest settlement on the West Coast beyond the Albernis. Town and mill built by the Gibson Brothers; now owned by the Tahsis Company Ltd. The site is where, in 1792, Chief Maquinna entertained Vancouver and Quadra. *Industrial Photographers.*

Richard Nelson, with his brothers, pioneered organized fish-buying on the West Coast. Now heads one of British Columbia's largest fishing companies. *Cameo Studio Photo.*

Zeballos, scene of spectacular gold rush. Between 1938 and 1944, its six mines, including the fabulously-rich Privateer, shipped out gold to the value of $13 million, most if it in bricks. Meanwhile, a mountain of iron ore has been brought into production and shipments are being made to Japan. *Leonard Frank Photo.*

Three of the early prospectors and the first cabin built at Zeballos. Left to right: Mrs. Janet Patmore, Andy Morod and C. H. Smith.

Seven gold bricks, wrapped, labelled and ready for mailing in Zeballos post office. Total value of shipment approximately $150,000.00; postage $240.00.

Looking down double-track, standard gauge surface tramline at Zeballos Iron Mine. Crushing mill at bottom. Concentrates are trucked five miles to tidewater loading facilities. Across river can be seen Privateer (closest) and Spud Valley gold mines. In same valley but hidden from view by forest are three other gold mines: White Star, Prident and Mt. Zeballos. *Leonard Frank (Vancouver) Photo.*

Ivan H. Clarke, storekeeper and postmaster at Hot Springs Cove, who donated a park.

Hot Springs Cove, a haven for fishermen.

of which boasted a school, had also sprung up around each mine.

The principal mines, in order of production, were Privateer, Spud Valley, Mt. Zeballos, Reno (Central Zeballos), White Star and Rey Oro. By 1948, all had closed down, not because the claims had been worked out, but owing to Ottawa having recently pegged the price of gold at $35 an ounce, which made further operation uneconomical. By this time, gold bricks to the value of $11 million and concentrates worth another $2 million (Department of Mines figures) had been shipped. Privateer produced about half.

Manning Lumber Company Ltd. moved in after the mines closed down and for the next ten years lumber was Zeballos' principal industry. Mining operations, however, have since been resumed, but this time it's iron instead of gold. $3 million has been spent on bringing into production a mountain of high grade ore only five miles from tidewater. Wharf, ore bunkers, tramway, crushing mill and houses for the miners have already been built and the first shipment (to Japan) is expected to be made before this appears in print.

The property consists of several groups of claims, discovered and staked between 1936 and 1938 by Felix Letain and added to later by claims staked by Andy Morod and S. Norman Ray. Patience at last paid off for these three prospectors, each of whom, after waiting more than twenty years, now receives a substantial cash payment — sufficient to retire on — plus production royalties.

When Privateer mine poured its first gold brick, the C.P.R. steamer *Princess Norah*, chartered for the purpose, brought from Vancouver and Victoria one hundred and fifty specially invited guests to celebrate the occasion. It was a big day — and night — for Zeballos. The pouring of the same mine's one hundredth brick coincided with the arrival of the steamer *Princess Alice*, which was making a special tour around Vancouver Island with members of the Vancouver Board of Trade and their wives on board. That was another big day and night for Zeballos.

The inside story of Zeballos is spiked with spicy anecdotes, but these the writer is saving for another book. It will tell of feuds — some nearly ending in bloodshed — which existed between the early prospectors, the founding of that frontier mining camp and life among its people.

AUTHOR'S NOTE: On May 24, 1962, the bulk ore carrier *Fukukawa Maru*, of the Kawasaki Line, sailed from Zeballos with 20,700 long tons of iron concentrates for Japan.

SKIPPER HAD FORESIGHT

His enterprise successful.

THIRTY-TWO YEARS AGO, Victoria-born Ivan H. Clarke, the youngest son of a family of eight, at twenty-two years of age held a tugboat master's ticket and was captain of one of the Victoria Tug Company's fleet. In that capacity he made frequent trips up the West Coast and, on one occasion when stormbound — along with about forty fishboats — at Refuge Cove, into the bay came a fishpacker which had been converted into a floating store. Its skipper was doing business at camps on remote inlets and small communities where the regular steamer never called. Bad weather had prevailed for several days and some of the fishermen were nearly out of grub. By nightfall, the sea-going storekeeper had disposed of the greater part of his stock-in-trade. This, Mr. Clarke — who also had previous experience in the wholesale grocery business — figured was a good location for a store and trading post.

Because of the presence of hot springs there and also so not to conflict with another Refuge Cove on the mainland coast, the name of the cove and its post office has since been changed to Hot Springs Cove.

A year later, Clarke was back. The cove wasn't a stopping place for the *Princess Maquinna*, so he hired an Indian to bring him from Ahousat, its nearest port of call. With around $500 worth of groceries and $200 in his wallet, Clarke pitched his tent on the shores of the cove and the following morning the "general store" shingle was posted on the stump of a tree he had cut down to make room for the tent. He also brought along for company two dogs, but a cougar made off with one that night. By noon the first day he had sold half his stock to weather-bound fishermen and curious Indians.

The population of the cove then numbered one person, Clarke himself, plus a few transient Indians. Today, Clarke and Sons' General Store at Hot Springs Cove is one of the largest on the West Coast, yet the Clarke family — Mr. Clarke married after setting up shop and his wife bore him eight children — comprise the cove's entire white population. Its only other inhabitants are ten Indian families who moved there later from Hesquiat.

One might well ask: Where do the store's customers come from? Here is the story.

A month or two later, Clarke built a log cabin and a float. The following year he built, with lumber salvaged from an abandoned copper mine on Sydney Inlet, a store, a house for himself and one for his mother who had come from Victoria to keep house for him.

Then he sent for his fiancée, Miss Mabel Stephens, of Victoria. He met her at Ahousat and they were married aboard the *Princess Maquinna* by Rev. J. Jones, the Presbyterian missionary of the area. Captain E. Gillam gave the bride away.

Years passed and children began to arrive. Soon, four were of school age and something had to be done about providing for their education. Seven was the required number of pupils before a school could be authorized and they were three short. This, however, was soon overcome. A teacher with two children of school age was hired and an Indian family across the bay provided the seventh. Happy at having a store where they could purchase fresh supplies, and with time on their hands in bad weather, fishermen helped out. Space was cleared of brush, an abandoned trapper's cabin moved bodily from where it stood at the mouth of a creek, and in no time the Refuge Cove children had a cosy little classroom, which later was also to serve as a church and meeting place. Bears roamed the countryside and were often seen eating berries near the school. Deer wandered up and down the beach and the children were permitted to keep their dogs in school for fear of them being carried off by cougars — which actually happened.

Not only does the cove afford safe anchorage for vessels in any weather (hence its original name), but it is strategically located in the centre of an extensive salmon fishing area. Clarke extended his enterprise to include fish buying, a facility of which the fishermen were quick to take advantage. It saved them long trips to Tofino or Nootka — twenty miles away in opposite directions — where the nearest camps were located. The big fishing companies followed suit and now every summer several buying camps are moored in the bay. Meanwhile, an oil company established a marine station ashore

311

and made Clarke its agent. A post office was established, the government built a wharf and the cove was now a regular port of call for the West Coast steamer. Clarke also bought furs.

Want of pupils — for the Clarke family (three girls and five boys) are now all grown up — forced the little schoolroom to close its doors, but this is in no way related to the Cove's economy, for other than the Clarke family no white people make their permanent homes there. On the other hand, about two hundred salmon trollers make the Cove their base during eight months of the year. Many move away when peak runs occur in other areas along the coast, but during the greater part of the fishing season they operate out of Hot Spring Cove, where they sell their catch, refuel, purchase supplies and effect minor repairs. It is also the nearest shopping centre for Estevan Point, Hesquiat and several other small communities on this part of the coast, none of which has a store. The springs are also an attraction, not only for fishermen who bathe and do their laundry there, but for visitors who come in their private planes or yachts.

Modern buildings have long since replaced the original store and dwelling houses. Management of the business, which includes a branch store and fish-buying camp recently established at Ahousat, is now taken care of by the sons, with a daughter as head bookkeeper. A few years back, Mr. and Mrs. Clarke donated to the provincial government for park purposes, 35 acres of their 120-acre pre-emption. Known as Maquinna Park and still undeveloped, the trail to the hot springs leads through the park.

THEY PIONEERED
AVIATION ON
THE WEST COAST

BOEING OPEN-COCKPIT, single-engine "pusher" type flying boats were the first aircraft seen on the West Coast. They appeared in the mid-1920's; were used on fisheries patrol and for spotting schools of pilchards. Among the pilots who flew them were Ottawa-born Colonel Donald R. MacLaren, D.S.O., M.C. AND BAR, D.S.C., a World War I air ace with 48 "kills" and six balloons to his credit; now retired and living at Victoria; Earl McLeod, later a group captain with the R.C.A.F. (World War II), and Victoria-born Maurice McGregor.

Commercial flying on the West Coast was pioneered by bush pilots R. L. "Ginger" Coote and "Molly" Small. With their four seater, single-engine, pontoon-equipped "Fairchilds" they brought the first groups of prospectors from the outside into Zeballos. Soon, Ginger Coote Airways Ltd., Canadian Airways Ltd., which afterwards became Canadian Pacific Air Lines Ltd., and Yukon, Southern Airways, all were making daily round flights between the mining camp and Vancouver. In addition, charter flights were being made almost daily by half a dozen independent fliers. Practically every pilot flying out of Vancouver at that time made the run; one was Grant C. McConachie, now president of Canadian Pacific Air Lines Ltd. With the exception of those places where rough seas make regular landings impossible, practically every West Coast settlement now has daily air mail and passenger service.

TRAGEDY RECOUNTED
IN PITIFUL DIARY

IN JULY 1939, two trappers, James H. Ryckman and Lloyd Coombs, both Vancouver men, were flown into Vernon Lake from Zeballos. The following April their remains were brought out. One died of starvation, the other evidently committed suicide. Extracts from a diary found in their cabin recount the tragic last few weeks of their sufferings.

When trappers or prospectors fly into remote lakes they usually set a date to be brought out. On this occasion they told the pilot they would "hitch" a ride if a plane came along, or walk out, either over the hills to Tahsis at the head of Nootka Sound, or down the Nimpkish river on the east coast. Ryckman had trapped at Vernon Lake at the peak of the Zeballos gold rush, when planes frequently ferried prospectors into the lake and returned light. From entries in the diary it was evident he figured it would be the same this year. But in the meantime prospecting in the area ceased and not a plane visited the lake all the time they were there. By then they realized they were too weak to walk out. An entry in the diary of March 16, clearly indicated this and admitted that they had no one but themselves to blame.

Here are a few extracts from the diary:

December 25, Christmas Day: Coon and our last can of corn. So we have to be thankful. Hope we have fish tomorrow.

February 9: Had four small fish heads stewed for breakfast. Two small trout for lunch and a squirrel for supper. If there is a Good Lord in Heaven he has forgotten us poor fellows.

Entries during the next six weeks show how their plight progressively worsened:

Legs so weak had to lay on bunk all day. Nothing to eat till 3 o'clock. Jim gathered bits of coon that were lying outside since Christmas. Boiled them up in baking soda. Was pretty rank but we ate it anyway.

314

We have been eating old yeast cakes, hard on the stomach but they help a little; we have three left and some tea, that's all.

Jim will try fishing tomorrow if he can make it; all I can do is stay here and pray for a plane to come in.

Put on another coon skin to boil; took me two hours to cut the hair off, then only got half of it off.

If we don't get something to eat pretty soon we will be kissing this old world goodbye.

Haven't the strength to get a pail of water from the lake . . . Jim just came in with one trout the size of a minnow. Just ate the coon skin . . . Can't even catch a canary. My legs will hardly keep me up and getting worse.

Our raft has blown away. Just as well for Jim could no longer manage it. That means no more fish.

. . . Got a few cranberries and Jim caught 15 canaries in the cabin. Jim caught a raven in a trap, that will be a meal.

We are slowly starving to death. Caught 20 canaries, only things that keep us alive.

If a plane doesn't come in a few days we are done for.

At this stage both men were apparently stricken with illness, for Ryckman made the entries in the diary from now on:

Lloyd is a lot worse and my legs are swollen to the hips . . . Just salt and four matches left. No strength to get any more wood. Burning moss off the bunks . . . Starvation is the most suffering on earth. Oh God, please send us a plane . . . This is the worst hell either of us has ever gone through. Got some rain water from under drip, that will help.

Coombs now writes up the diary again, and makes these two last entries:

March 16: Jim worse today, nothing but skin and bone . . . If we don't get out in a couple of days dear mother, we have nobody to blame but ourselves. We couldn't hike out when our grub got low on account of the floods. So this is what we get for taking chances on waiting for a plane.

March 17, 1940: Dear Mother. Jim died today at 2 p.m. This might be the last time I'll have the nerve to write. So if I do anything wrong please forgive me. I can't stick it any longer. The Bible is in the bottom of my packsack and I haven't the strength to get it down off the rafters, where we keep it so the mice won't get it. So I can't say a decent prayer for poor old Jim.

That was the last entry in the diary. That night or the following day Coombs apparently took his own life in despair.

April and still no sign of the two men. Fearing they might have met with some mishap, a plane was sent in to investigate. The pilot (Jack Hames) went alone, for his was a small plane with only room for himself and the two men, plus their baggage, and upon tying up his aircraft at the float in front of the cabin he immediately saw that something was wrong. He first noticed two rags tied to long poles on the end of the float, apparently having been placed there to attract the attention of any pilot who might land on the lake. Then, scrawled in large letters on a rough plank, was this poignant message: "SOS, at south end of lake. For God's sake pick us up. Been out of food for two months." The sign had presumably been posted some months before, in case a plane came when they were out fishing (the best fishing is at the south end).

A plane did come, but only because it was sent in specially, and it was three weeks too late. Upon entering the cabin, the pilot found Ryckman's dead body on one bunk and Coombs' remains, with a discharged rifle by his side, on the other. They had been dead about three weeks. On returning to Zeballos he reported his discovery; then flew the local provincial constable (Winegarden) and the coroner in and the bodies were brought out. An inquest was held and the remains subsequently flown to Vancouver for burial.

The hopelessness of their plight was further indicated in two unfinished letters found in the cabin and later read at the inquest. In February, young Coombs wrote his mother and dad:

. . . . this might be my last letter just in case we don't get out of here alive. Every night I pray for you to hear my voice and send a plane. You are entitled to half the furs. This is good-bye. God bless you both. Your loving son, Lloyd.

Dated March 1, Ryckman wrote his son in Vancouver this farewell:

. . . Well Albert, this may be good-bye for ever as we cannot hold out another week. Our food supply was used up long ago. We have been living on fish, squirrels, old coon bones and even an old dead eagle. We caught canaries that flew in the door, had seven today. We hope a plane comes soon. Lloyd is getting sicker and weaker every day. We are starving to death slowly.

From earlier entries in the diary everything appeared to go well for the first few months. Trapping was good, game plentiful and they caught all the trout they could eat. They played cribbage or solitaire at night and appeared quite cheerful. Then the weather broke, the grub ran out and it was too late.

Today, Vernon Lake can be reached via a network of logging roads which extend from tidewater on the east coast of the island to the upper reaches of the Nimpkish River. The lake is one of the river's sources.

"GREATER LOVE
HATH NO MAN"

By an anonymous writer: Victoria Daily Colonist, *June 1, 1958.*

ON MARCH 9, 1939, two surveyors while cruising in the mountainous terrain east of the Alberni Canal, stumbled across the wreckage of an airplane. It was CF-AUX, a pontoon-equipped, single engine Fairchild belonging to Ginger Coote Airways, which had disappeared on May 27 of the previous year, while on a flight from Vancouver to Zeballos. Still in the aircraft were the remains of its pilot, Len Waagen, Mary Nicholson, the wife of the Zeballos postmaster, and two other passengers. Fortunately, no fire had broken out when the crash occurred and the bodies were easily identified.

Mrs. Nicholson was on her way home after personally canvassing Vancouver wholesale merchants for money to build a badly needed hospital at Zeballos, and the fund was several thousand dollars richer for her efforts. A twenty-two-bed hospital was subsequently built and a brass plate at the entrance to the women's ward bears this inscription: "Mary Nicholson Memorial Ward". This was not the first hospital on the west coast of Vancouver Island which Mary Nicholson had helped raise the money to build. A few years earlier, she headed a drive which resulted in the building of Tofino's first hospital, then the only one between Port Alberni and Port Alice, which are separated by 250 miles of rugged coastline. This five-bed institution was destroyed by fire in 1952. A modern twenty-five-bed hospital now stands in its place.

That brass plate on the women's ward at the hospital is in fitting memory of a woman who, perhaps more than anyone else, had so often seen the need of hospitals in these isolated communities. For several years before the Zeballos gold rush, Mary Nicholson was the only woman in that embryo settlement (two others lived in the hills with their prospector husbands), and her cabin at the beach, which she shared with her husband, came to be the accepted place where sick and injured prospectors were taken. There the man was made as comfortable as possible till such time as a launch could be secured to convey him to the nearest first-aid station, which was at Ceepeecee, ten miles away.

Day or night and regardless of the weather, Mary Nicholson usually went along. Open boats were sometimes used. The injured or sick man would be wrapped in blankets and oilskins, but the passengers were often exposed to driving rains and freezing temperatures during the two-hour trip. On one occasion, a box of caps which a young miner was carrying in his hand, exploded. Though one eye was torn out, the other injured and his stomach perforated by metal fragments, he never lost consciousness. First-aid was rendered at the scene of the accident, then the lad was carried over rough bush trails five miles to the beach. There he was nursed by Mrs. Nicholson, who later accompanied him to Ceepeecee. From there a fishboat conveyed him to Tofino, ninety miles away, where the nearest doctor resided, but he died shortly before the boat reached there.

No fewer than three emergency appendectomies and several minor operations were performed on the Nicholson's dining room table; with the room temperature kept at nearly 100° and Mrs. Nicholson sterilizing the instruments on the kitchen stove and passing them, with the swabs, to the doctor. That was at Tofino and before the first hospital was built.

When a nine-year-old Tofino boy received critical head injuries when tobogganing, the doctor ordered his immediate removal to hospital for possible brain surgery. Estevan wireless station contacted the fisheries patrol steamer *Givenchy*, which was then in the vicinity of Nootka. Her captain immediately turned about, picked up the lad, still unconscious, and conveyed him to Port Alberni. Mary Nicholson, who had already nursed the boy, and also the mother who was beside herself with anxiety, for twenty-four hours without sleep, volunteered to accompany the boy. She returned by way of Ucluelet on the mailboat *Victory II* (predecessor of the *Uchucks*). There was no road between Ucluelet and Tofino then; only an abandoned corduroy part way to Long Beach which had been built by the early settlers and who by now had given up their pre-emptions and left. In his Model T Ford, Ed. Lee, the Ucluelet storekeeper's son took Mrs. Nicholson as far as he could. Then she had to walk seven miles over a rough trail through the bush. Wild cattle roamed the area. But she got the scare of her life when a deer fleeing from a cougar — in hot pursuit — almost collided with her. It was almost dark when Mrs. Nicholson came out at the head of Tofino Inlet, where her husband met her with his gasboat.

Twice when the Lennard Island lightkeeper's wife was taken seriously ill, Mary Nicholson braved the rough seas and was landed by the Tofino lifeboat crew on the storm-tossed group of rocks which stand two miles off shore at the entrance to Clayoquot Sound. There she nursed the sick woman and when the weather moderated took her to her own home at Clayoquot. The lighthouse tender would arrive in a few days and take the sick woman to hospital at Port Alberni.

The number of broken collar bones, sprains, cases of fish-poisoning, boils on the neck and other minor ailments which Mary Nicholson treated in her own home before there was a hospital at either of these places, will never be known. In 1924, when Mrs. Nicholson lived at Port Renfrew, a lad was taken seriously ill and fever indicated that he required immediate medical attention. Neither doctor nor nurse was available, and with the *Maquinna* not due for several days, an Indian volunteered to take him to Jordan River, a four-hour trip on the open ocean. The sea was none too calm, but as the boy needed constant attention Mary Nicholson went along. The Jordan River power station had, in the meantime, been alerted by telephone and off-duty operators were there to meet the boat. They waded out breast-deep through the surf, carried the lad ashore and rushed him by car to hospital at Victoria. The westerly wind had increased to gale force by then and Mrs. Nicholson and the lone Indian had a rough journey back to Port Renfrew.

The missing Ginger Coote Airways' aircraft touched off what was then the greatest air-sea search for a missing aircraft ever undertaken in British Columbia. Ten planes, among them two R.C.A.F. Boeing flying boats and two United States Coastguard flying boats, searched the mountains and inlets along the West Coast for ten days, but without success. The missing airplane carried no radio, for this equipment was only then being installed on commercial aircraft. It was seen passing over Port Alberni — and that was the last contact. But as reports were afterwards received that the plane had either been seen or heard on that day at different points along the West Coast, the search was concentrated in the Tofino-Nootka area. However, these reports all proved to be false and not till the search was almost completed was it established that no aircraft of any kind was on the West Coast that particular day.

319

The search planes were based at Zeballos, where the pilots met every night to formulate plans for the following day. A poignant note was introduced, inasmuch as Mrs. Nicholson's whole family took part in the search. Plane movements were coördinated by her husband, Ginger Coote Airways' local agent. Son Mickey operated the base radio-telephone (all search planes were so equipped). Daughter Jean acted as an observer on one of the small planes, while Gretel, another daughter, saw that the crews were provided with sandwiches and thermos flasks of hot coffee. Each plane also carried food, coffee and medical supplies, packed ready to be dropped should the missing aircraft be found. Led by Provincial Constable John Cameron and provided with transportation by local boat owners, volunteer ground parties were also organized to run down numerous reports that an airplane — apparently in trouble — had either been seen or heard on that day somewhere in the hills.

The missing plane also carried a quantity of mail, most of which the Zeballos postmaster was finally able to deliver. And there was some machinery for the gold mines. The crash apparently occurred when the pilot attempted to turn back after being enveloped in fog a few miles beyond Franklin River. Ironically, this area was never searched.

OLD AGE PENSION
CHEQUE NO. 1

To a West Coast man.

WILLIAM HENRY DERBY of Alberni, was the first person in Canada to receive the old age pension. In the fall of 1927, at a modest ceremony held in the office of Mr. A. W. Neill, M.P. for Comox-Alberni, he was presented with cheque No. 1, for $20, the original old age pension amount. Mr. Derby died in February 1938, and his tombstone in the Alberni cemetery bears the inscription "The First Old Age Pensioner in Canada".

The presentation was made by Mr. Neill, who was given that honour by the Prime Minister of Canada who recognized that Mr. Neill, more than any other man, was responsible for parliament introducing social legislation for Canadians in their old age. Also present was Major R. J. Burde, M.C., M.L.A. for Alberni, who had also sponsored legislation favouring old age pensions in the Provincial House. The third interested spectator was A. G. Freeze, government agent at Alberni.

In addition to being asked to present the first cheque, Mr. Neill had previously been requested to nominate some qualified applicant in his constituency, whose pension would be the first one granted. It was therefore only natural for him to nominate William Henry Derby, a fellow townsman and pioneer of the district.

The cheque hasn't been cashed yet, though Mr. Derby duly received the money. Anxious to have a souvenir of the historic occasion, immediately after the presentation Mr. Neill exchanged it for a $20 bill. Then he had the still unendorsed cheque framed. The auditor-general made a bit of a fuss at having the cheque outstanding so long, but letters didn't bother Mr. Neill and the department in time forgot all about it. For years the framed souvenir cheque hung on Mr. Neill's office wall. Then he presented it to Prime Minister St. Laurent. It is now in the Archives at Ottawa. In the British Columbia Provincial Archives are photographs of the cheque and the presentation ceremony.

A. W. NEILL, M.P.

ALLAN WEBSTER NEILL was born in Scotland on October 6, 1868, and as a boy, emigrated to New Zealand where he worked on a station (farm) which sheared 40,000 sheep. In 1891 he came to Canada and took up land in the Alberni valley. With a pack on his back, he walked the wagon road in from Parksville. He cleared an acre and built a shack; but like the other few settlers, found pick and shovel work on the road more profitable.

How Mr. Neill came to enter politics was one of his favourite stories: A fellow workman on the road told him of a political meeting being held that night and suggested they attend. More out of curiosity than anything else, he went. During the nomination period a man on the opposite side of the hall rose and pointed a finger at Mr. Neill. "I nominate that man," he said, not knowing Mr. Neill's name.

The nominee was to oppose the sitting member in the provincial House. It was also the first time the district had been created a separate riding. A few weeks later, Mr. Neill was declared duly elected, and by a comfortable majority. That was in 1898 and he represented the district till 1903, winning three successive elections.

After being elected the first time, he sent to Scotland for his intended bride, but before she arrived he found that he had been disqualified from holding office. He had worked on the government road, but fortunately prior to taking his seat; otherwise he would have been liable to a fine of $500 for every day he had sat in the House. Mr. Neill won the by-election by a larger majority still and so had a happy meeting with the future Mrs. Neill.

After retiring from the provincial House, he was made Indian agent at Alberni and he related that, by coincidence, placed in a tree in front of his house was a dead Indian in a wooden box. The body had been placed there long before his time and out of respect for the Indians' old burial customs, he left it there till the tree had to be cut down to make room for a road.

Mr. Neill was first elected to the Dominion Parliament (Comox-Alberni) in 1921 and at five succeeding elections. He retired from politics in 1945, after representing the different Alberni ridings at Victoria and Ottawa for twenty-nine years. He was a stipendiary magistrate and notary public for more than forty years; was an alderman on Alberni's first city council and also served as mayor. Mr. Neill died at Alberni in 1960, aged ninety-two.

MAN OVERBOARD

An INCIDENT in which John Nelson was involved which occurred while he was returning from a day's trolling out of Kyuquot, is recalled. As he neared harbour, Nelson fell overboard. Meanwhile, with engine still running, the boat continued on its way. Nelson freed himself of his hip-gumboots and managed to reach the safety of some rocks; but the race tide in the channel between him and the shore prevented his swimming further. The tide was flooding and soon the rock would be submerged. Noticing the man's plight, an Indian woman who lived nearby came out in her canoe and rescued Nelson from his precarious perch.

Thoroughly convinced he had lost his boat — and under ordinary circumstances he probably would have — Nelson was taken into the woman's house where he dried his clothing and partook of warm tea. Meanwhile the husband, who had also been out fishing, returned and together they set out to search for the troller. They eventually found her, to their surprise, unharmed and securely tied up alongside the very oil station where Nelson had intended to refuel before entering harbour. Fishermen usually fuel up the night before.

Strange things happen. There are several alternate entrances to Kyuquot basin and because it was shorter Nelson had chosen the one strewn with rocks and submerged reefs, but with deep water between. Miraculously, the troller had steered herself clear of these obstructions, continued on for another two miles and finally went aground on a sandy beach (the only one in the whole area) immediately adjoining the oil station Nelson had been heading for. Observing no sign of life on board and noting the still running engine, the oil man went to investigate and the first thing he did was stop the engine. The tide was rising fast, soon she freed herself and half an hour later the errant troller was safely moored alongside the station.

THE "PORTUGUESE MAN-OF-WAR" is a species of jellyfish known as physalia. It is found all over the world and in parts which it regularly frequents is quite large. The body is round or oval shaped and sometimes twelve inches across. It sits flat on the water, has no under-belly and the translucent tentacles trailing beneath it (by which it feeds) might be anything up to twenty feet long. They excude a poison that causes severe pain and discomfort to human skin and for that reason it is not safe to bathe in waters which they frequent.

The species that appear off our shores is much smaller, usually two or three inches across and its fine tentacles not much longer. The characteristic feature of both the large and small species is its novel means of locomotion. Instead of impelling themselves forward like other jellyfish, using muscle movement or jet-action (the same as the squid and octopus), they are equipped with a sail. This is composed of the same jelly-like substance and is usually about the same height as the body is across. The whole creature is transparent, but has a bluish-purple tint. They are fascinating to watch as they float — in their millions — along the surface of the water and the sun's rays turn each one into a miniature multi-coloured rainbow.

A patch will sometimes cover several square miles of the ocean's surface, and they are cursed by the fishermen who avoid them whenever possible. As they slime the lines and blister their hands, salmon trollers move to other areas when they show up. Purse-seine fishing among them is impossible and if by chance a "set" is made where they are plentiful, they gum-up the huge net and operations have to be called off for the time being. The net has to be taken ashore and blue-stoned, a process used for de-sliming fish nets. This means the boat's crew loses a whole day's fishing and a lot of money when fishing is good.

Insofar as they interfere with fishing, the same applies to all jelly-fish, but the other species seldom appear in huge masses like the Portuguese man-of-war. Fortunately they are seldom found in inside waters; a few sometimes are but the majority are cast up on the outside beaches. Washed ashore by the million (the writer has seen them piled a foot high the entire length of Long Beach), for a time they become nothing but an eyesore and a sticky mess. However, the sun soon dries them up and the nuisance disappears — till another lot arrives. Fortunately, years pass without them showing up.

The appearance of sub-tropical sunfish off the West Coast is also erratic; one summer they may be seen by the hundreds, some as large as four feet across (round), then not even sighted again for several years. Seldom are turtles seen this far north, but in 1934, a monster weighing 1,200 pounds was taken off Nootka by a pilchard fishing boat (weighed at Nootka cannery).

Immense shoals of krill, small shrimp-like crustaceans, also appear off the West Coast, so dense that the ocean is turned a reddish-brown for miles on end; but some summers go by and little shows up. This is commonly known as "whale feed", the principal diet for the humpback and other baleen species of these mammals, but it also provides food for salmon and many other varieties of fish. When pilchard fishing was at its height, some years they failed to appear, but when they did it usually coincided with the presence of these masses of feed. According to our biologists, it is when the summer water temperature is a few degrees above normal, that these strange fish and other forms of marine life — not common on this part of the coast — arrive for brief visits.

A WOODPECKER IN A
PORTHOLE

*Whale breathes down a man's
neck.*

WHAT HAS A GASBOAT to do with a woodpecker three miles out in
the ocean? An eagle providing two men with their supper? Shooting
a cougar just as it was about to kill a doe? A whale literally breathing down a man's neck? Watching live fishballs? These oddities
might interest persons not too familiar with the sea.

Having to contend with fog, storms and tricky tide rips, as well
as always being on the alert for a hidden sandbar or treacherous
reef, is all in the day's work for one who earns his livelihood operating a gasboat up and down the British Columbia coast. However,
seldom a day went by but something of interest would happen to
make one forget these hazards — for the time being at least — and
help while away the monotony, especially when travelling alone.

Apart from the nature of the errand, plus fascinating places and
people, the sea and adjacent shoreline is always full of interest.
Especially when it has to do with nature and more particularly
birds, fish and wild animals. Reference to old diaries recalls several
such incidents that occurred during the course of my travels up
and down the coast. None warranted an entry in the log, because
they concerned neither the operation of the boat nor the business in
hand, but each was a little out of the ordinary.

The incident relating to the woodpecker concerned one of the
smaller species of that bird, which when hard-pressed and within
a "feather" of being caught by a hawk, sought the safety of my
boat. It occurred when taking an Indian department doctor on
one of his periodical visits to up-coast reservations while we were
crossing a three-mile-wide bay with the sea dead calm. Peering out
of the pilot-house window I suddenly sensed something drop out of

the sky like a comet, but taken unawares was unable to identify it. Whatever it was appeared to drop only a few feet from the boat on the port side. Simultaneously, away from the boat flew a small red hawk and we figured this must have been what we saw diving out of the sky. But had the object of its dive been a duck and it escaped by diving just in time?

As was customary, I went below to oil the engine and there, sitting on the edge of my bunk was a little woodpecker, not the least perturbed at the noise of the engine or the oiling-up operation. It had evidently been crossing from one point of land to another and being overtaken by the hawk, spotted the boat (the only one in the vicinity) and dived for it. There was only one porthole on either side and these only six inches in diameter. It must have seen this small hole from high in the sky, dived for it and made it— and with the boat travelling at seven knots. I reached out to stroke it, and away it flew, out the same porthole, and the last we saw of it was making a bee-line for land.

On another trip, when taking a mining engineer to look over some claims and while cruising close to shore, we saw a commotion on the water a little distance ahead. It was a bald-headed eagle struggling with a huge cod. The fish was evidently too heavy to lift but the bird finally managed to drag it ashore. By this time we had slowed down and nosing the bow in close enough, my passenger jumped on the rocks and grabbed the still-struggling cod. In the meantime a mad eagle took off to a handy fir tree in which it had a nest. Its eaglets probably had to wait supper till father caught another fish. This happened to be an overnight trip and thanks to the eagle, in a few hours time we enjoyed fried codfish.

While passing between a group of small islands on another run I observed two animals swimming across the channel about half a mile ahead, one gradually overtaking the other. As the boat drew near, a small doe dragged itself ashore with a cougar only a few yards behind. I promptly shot the cougar, which would have killed the deer if I hadn't come along just in the nick of time.

The "fish balls" which one frequently ran across are interesting objects. They are not the kind the wife makes out of fish left-overs and mashed potatoes, but live ones. This phenomenon consists of thousands of tiny fish packed into a solid mass, perfectly round and up to three or four feet in diameter. They are observed just below the surface of the water and are caused by larger fish, cormorants, loons and other diving birds preying on a school of young herring. Fright and mass hysteria evidently causes them to mill around till

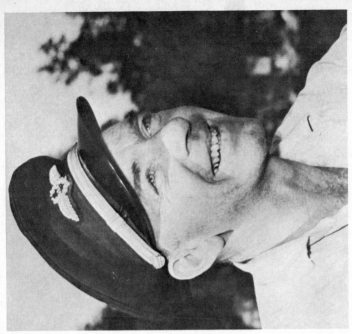

Bush pilot R. L. "Ginger" Coote, who pioneered commercial aviation on the West Coast.

Mary Nicholson. Her memory is held dear.

1,200 pound (weighed at Nootka cannery) turtle caught in fishermen's net off Nootka Island, 1934. (see page 326).

Alfred Bird, the original staker of the Privateer gold claims at Zeballos, now retired and living at Tofino.

"Calling all fishermen." White waters of Kennedy Rapids where Kennedy Lake flows into Tofino Inlet. The lake is only 18 feet above sea level. *B.C. Government Travel Bureau Photo.*

West Coast man receives Old Age Pension Cheque No. 1. Presentation scene and cheque, left to right: W. H. Derby, the recipient; A. W. Neill, m.p.; Major R. J. Burde, m.c., m.l.a., and A. G. Freeze, government agent at Alberni. At that time old age pensions were administered by the Workmen's Compensation Board. *Provincial Archives Photo.*

Governor-General Lord Willingdon's totem at Friendly Cove, Nootka. *B.C. Government Travel Bureau Photo.*

This Douglas fir was a sapling during the reign of King Alfred the Great, about half grown when King John signed the Magna Carta at Runneymede and two-thirds grown when Christopher Columbus reached America. It grew to maturity in the Gold River country at the head of Muchalat Inlet, Nootka Sound, and was the fourth largest of its species found so far (1958) in the forests of British Columbia. *Photo by W. W. Wagner.*

Cougars Beware! Mrs. George Lawson, postmistress at Boat Basin (see page 332).
Photo by John Manning.

Princess Norah, passing Amphitrite Point lighthouse northbound, with Mt. Ozzard in background.

REV. JOHN W. LEIGHTON

ST. COLUMBA'S CHURCH, TOFINO

The author at Zeballos, where he saw first prospectors come in and the last gold brick shipped.

Thirty-five-foot totem presented to author by the Ehatisaht Indians when they made him an honorary chief. For 15 years totem stood in front of Major Nicholson's house at Zeballos and is now in the Campbell River museum. *B.C. Government Travel Bureau Photos.*

they "ball-up" solid. While in this state their numerous enemies attack them from every direction, including seagulls from the air, and in time the entire mass is completely eaten up. So terrified are these tiny little fry that a boat may bump into a "ball" and still they cling together. From the deck of a larger vessel they would never be seen.

Whales are essentially deep-water mammals, and only twice did I sight one in an inlet; each time, however, with an uncomfortably close-up view. First, when a school of blackfish (killer whales) had one at their mercy. Again and again the killers attacked, from all sides and underneath. In its efforts to escape, the monster "blue" repeatedly leapt almost entirely out of the water. Blood which made the sea red spurted from its wounds. After a few rifle shots at close range the killers disappeared, leaving their almost helpless victim hardly able to sound. The second time, instead of witnessing a one-sided battle, I had the unusual — and not too pleasant — experience of a sixty-foot (twenty feet longer than my boat) whale literally "breathing down my neck". Observing the tell-tale spray plumes, caused when the whale exhales through a hole in the top of its head, I cruised a safe few hundred feet from the shoreline. I saw nothing more for about ten minutes, when suddenly it surfaced between boat and the rocks, "spouting" at the same time, so close the fine spray showered me.

Whales are said to suffer from halitosis (bad breath) and the few people who have experienced the novelty of being that close and on the lee side of a whale when it "blows", know the odour from that spray. Simultaneously with it sounding, it hit the water with its huge tail, drenching me with the splash. A whale's tail is set crossways to its body, opposite to that of a fish. This one appeared to be twenty feet wide.

Hundreds of other interesting little "goings-on" occur in or on the sea every day, which few people see or know about. A monster basking shark, too lazy to get out of your way, one often rams broadside-on, with no damage to the boat. In fact, small fisheries department cruisers sometimes have their bows specially fitted with a knife-sharp steel blade to destroy the basking sharks. An hour seldom passes without seeing the playful porpoise, a hair seal or sea lion suddenly raising its head above the surface for a look around. In the summer months one sometimes sees the sunfish, and the surface of the ocean literally covered with that species of jellyfish known as "Portuguese man-of-war", is not an uncommon sight.

LATE IN THE 1920's practically the entire deer population of the West Coast was wiped out owing to a mysterious liver disease. The result: hungry cougars came down from the hills and prowled the widely scattered settlements in search of food — cats, dogs and other domestic animals. Women were scared to leave their homes, and feared for the safety of their children.

As one of a party of four taking the 1930 census, the writer had occasion to visit by gasboat every settlement, cannery and logging camp between Barkley Sound and Cape Cook. Lone trappers and prospectors living at the head of remote inlets also had to be found and counted, and the job took over a month. Almost everywhere the presence of cougars was in evidence: skins stretched out to dry and carcasses rotting on the beach. We hugged the shoreline most of the time, yet not a single deer was sighted. On a similar trip a few years previous, or several years later, scores would have been seen. Normally, Indians, fishermen and isolated settlers relied on them for fresh meat. At one cabin that two prospectors called "home" we were invited to supper and if the appetizing aroma coming from the shack meant anything, we were in for a good meal. Grilling on the open fire were several large juicy steaks which we took for mowach (deer), or perhaps elk, and asked no questions. No meal did we enjoy more throughout the entire trip — cougar steaks!

We learned of no positive threats to human life, but bad scares, loss of pets and exciting encounters with cougars at close quarters appeared to be an everyday experience for these people. Possibly, the closest brush between man and cougar occurred when Mr. Jacob Arnet, chairman of the Tofino municipality, was proceeding across the bay alone in a small gasboat. He sighted what he thought was a dog swimming, and stopped to pick it up. It was a cougar, and as his boat only had a few inches of freeboard the animal had no diffiiculty in seizing the gunwhale and sinking its sharp claws into the soft cedar wood. With the engine crankhandle — the only weapon handy — Mr. Arnet went into action, concentrating his blows on the cougar's head and claws. After a ten-minute battle, with blood streaming from its head and half stunned, the animal finally let go. Tofino's chief magistrate lost no time in re-starting his engine and proceeded on his way. He recalled that this was the first time he could remember not carrying his rifle with him. The tell-tale cougar teeth and claw marks remained in the gunwhale for many years after the incident.

Tofino lost half its dogs, cats and chickens to the marauders. One man, after losing his dog and cat, sent away for a trained cougar hound. It duly arrived and was kept in a large open box on the back verandah. Two nights later, on hearing a commotion outside, the man ran out with a flashlight, only to see a cougar disappearing over his back fence with the hound in its jaws. At Clayoquot, a cougar carried off a big airdale dog playing on the beach with a group of Japanese school children during morning recess. And we have already read (on page 266) how the George Sye family fared when a cougar, while chasing the family dog, jumped through an open window at their Vargas Island home.

Buck fever cost an old beachcomber, living alone, a $20 bounty. One evening, a cougar pressed its face against the cabin window, scarcely two feet away. It was evidently looking for his mongrel dog, curled up as usual back of the stove. The man had his double-barrel shotgun handy, but instead of firing point blank through the window (a new pane of glass would have cost him only fifty cents), made for the back door. His movements alarmed the cougar and it was gone by the time he got outside.

Shortly after placing her baby in its crib on the back porch, the wife of a watchman at a reduction plant saw a cougar jump up on the porch and sniff the sleeping child's face. By banging at the window and screaming at the same time she scared the animal off. Some days later, her husband saw what he thought to be a dog killing his chickens. Armed with a stick he found himself face to face with a cougar in the confines of his chicken yard. It was probably the same cougar. All he could do was land it a few clouts as it jumped over the wire netting fence.

With introduction of a new stock of deer crossing the mountains from the east coast of the island, in time the herds built up again. Cougars still make their presence felt, but not more often than is usual elsewhere.

As to whether or not cougars actually stalk and attack human beings has always been a matter of controversy. Game wardens and professional predatory animal hunters, whose calling brings them so frequently in contact with these animals, also trappers, prospectors and surveyors who spend half their lives in the hills, say no.

An Indian boy at Kyuquot was badly mauled by a cougar and died soon afterwards from his injuries. An investigation held by a game warden flown in the same day, and who incidentally shot the cougar soon after he arrived, disclosed that the animal had not actually attacked the boy. He had disturbed it while eating a freshly killed deer. Under similar circumstances dogs and cats frequently fly at people, biting and clawing them to show their resentment.

Only when cougars become really hungry do encounters with humans occur. Suddenly surprised, or perhaps cornered, the animal naturally puts up a struggle in its efforts to escape and often the resultant mix-up ends in the person involved receiving severe lacerations. Terrifying as the experience might be, with the exception of the Kyuquot boy, so far as is known no loss of life has ever resulted from such incidents, though in isolated cases the victim has required hospital treatment for shock and injuries.

A healthy cougar is far too clever to allow itself to be surprised. Game wardens investigating alleged attacks by cougars invariably find the animal involved to be partially blind and nearly dead from starvation and old age. We are reminded of an incident which occurred near Parksville about thirty years ago, when two school children encountered a cougar as it crossed the road in front of them. Thinking the animal was a dog, they hit it with a bridle. It turned on them, but inflicted only a few scratches. Shot later, it was found to be half blind, almost skin and bone and with only a few teeth left in its head. The cougar is a tremendously strong animal, can bring down a full-grown buck and kill it instantly. They have been known to kill nearly full-grown elk. Against an animal of such strength and armed with those powerful claws and sharp teeth, what chance would an unarmed man have if a cougar really wanted to kill him? Not a chance in the world.

AUTHOR'S NOTE: Top West Coast cougar story (vouched for by the writer) comes from Boat Basin, near Estevan Point, where sixty-two of these predatory animals have fallen to the expert marksmanship of the Rae-Arthur family since they went to live there in 1914. Of this total, forty were shot by the thrice-widowed mother — now Mrs. George Lawson, the last on her 73rd birthday. Her three sons and three daughters accounted for the remainder.

DREAM ISLE CASTLE

A QUESTION practically every passenger travelling up the West Coast for the first time invariably asked when the steamer docked at Tofino. "What is that queer-looking building over there on that island? Is it a lighthouse or a castle?" From the wharf, half a mile away, it could be taken for either.

Actually, it is a plain square three-storied frame building, with a dummy castellated top painted white. The ground floor is one big room about 24 by 24, with the upper stories unfinished inside and reached by ladders. At least that's how it was thirty years ago. To the older residents of Tofino it is known as "Dream Isle" or Tibbs' Island, after the name of the man who once owned it and who built the strange-looking edifice — obviously out of place in such surroundings.

The story as to why Tibbs purchased this three-acre "rock pile", for that's all it is, or why he gave it such a romantic name when he painted "Dream Isle" in six-foot-high white letters on its rocky side facing Tofino, then built the "castle", was for years surrounded in mystery and only became known after tragedy overtook him a few years later. Whether he was a remittance man or not, nobody knew. But though he might have appeared to be somewhat erratic at times, one thing certain is that he was a gentleman, well educated, a good athlete, a powerful swimmer and minded his own business.

Tibbs mysteriously showed up about 1908, when he pre-empted a section at Long Beach and from lumber which he salvaged, built himself a comfortable shack with a commanding view of the ocean. There was only one other settler at Long Beach then and Tibbs made infrequent visits to Tofino for his mail and supplies, which he packed on his back — there was no road. That was his first introduction to the residents of that settlement who came to know him as a friendly but very reticent young man. He subsequently sold his Long Beach property and not long afterwards purchased the island. Why he chose this spot was his own affair, for there was lots of good land to be bought in Tofino at that time. He soon had it cleared, except for one tall spruce tree, which he later topped at fully 100 feet. Then he constructed a small platform at the very top and built an enclosed stairway so that he could climb up without danger to himself or anyone else who wished to accompany him.

It soon transpired that Tibbs was an accomplished cornet player and in the summer evenings he had the habit of sitting on this high platform serenading someone. Everyone for miles around, including the Indians on the nearby reservation, enjoyed the music. But who was this girl-shy young man serenading?

Meanwhile, Tibbs lived in a tent. Then he built the strange-looking edifice, which could best be described as a cross between a castle and a lighthouse, held securely to the rocks by steel guy-ropes. But he only used the ground floor room, beautifully ornamented by artistic designs in plaster work. He installed a few windows in the upper part, but apparently only for effect.

In 1915 Tibbs joined up and went overseas. He returned after the war — where he was wounded twice — and shortly afterwards was appointed keeper of the harbour light buoys which marked the ship channels in the vicinity of Clayoquot and Tofino. These were oil lanterns and required attention and renewal every few days.

It was on one of these these trips to the buoys that tragedy overtook him. While tending one of the lamps he evidently failed to fasten his skiff securely and it drifted away. He probably tried to overtake it but the strong current carried it down channel faster than he could swim. Then he must have headed for the nearest shore and he actually landed on the far end of the Clayoquot sandspit. Between trying to regain his skiff and swimming ashore he must have covered several miles, bucking the tide most of the way.

Being an experienced long-distance swimmer and knowing what to do in an emergency, he apparently shed all his clothing while in the water. This probably enabled him to reach shore, but in the end proved fatal, for at the exact spot where he emerged from the water were several Japanese women — wives of local fishermen — digging clams. Upon seeing a naked man come out of the sea as if from nowhere, instead of throwing some clothes over him, they panicked and fled. At that moment Tibbs collapsed on the beach, apparently overcome by the strain and cold. The women alerted some white settlers, but by the time they arrived at the scene with blankets, Tibbs was dead. Members of the Tofino Legion (then G.W.V.A.) buried him in the local cemetery, which happens to be on an island adjacent to "Dream Isle" and every Remembrance Day place a wreath on his and the graves of other veterans.

In due course a search was made for a will. None was found, but the official administrator's agent unearthed an old writing pad upon which were numerous writings and jottings as of one talking to himself and recording it on paper. On one page, the necessity of making a will was expressed, and also his admiration for two Tofino young ladies of his acquaintance. But who should be made beneficiary?

Once again he was in a quandary, not knowing which one to favour. Probably in the loneliness of his surroundings on that evening, and by the light of his oil lamp he solved the problem by being a sort of a Solomon. He plainly stated that he would leave one young lady the castle house and to the other he would leave the island. The document was unsigned, but the authorities accepted it as his last will and testament.

The girls got the house and the island between them and the serenading from the tree-top was remembered, not forgetting the "Dream Island". Did the girls fall out over their queer legacy? Not a bit. The one who now owned the house sold it to the one owning the island and all who knew Tibbs felt that he would have been perfectly satisfied with the arrangement.

THE BELL OF THE
PRINCESS MAQUINNA

RESIDENTS OF THE West Coast might be interested to know what happened to the *Princess Maquinna*'s bell after that popular ship was withdrawn from service. Its present whereabouts might also interest thousands of other people, who at different times enjoyed the hospitality of her officers and crew during those leisurely seven-day West Coast cruises.

It was presented personally by Captain O. J. Williams, manager of B.C. Coast Steamships, to the Reverend John W. Leighton, formerly in charge of the Anglican Mission with headquarters at Tofino, but who was at that time missionary to the Missions to Seamen at Vancouver. The bell is now in the perpetual care of the mission and is used for the call to worship in the chapel. There it will remain as long as men go down to the sea in ships, to remind those within hearing of its rich tone, of a stout ship which became endeared to the hearts of all who had the privilege of sailing aboard her. Compass and binnacle were given to the Ucluelet Sea Cadets.

WEST COAST
ANGLICAN MISSION

MR. LEIGHTON had more than a passing interest in the *Maquinna*'s bell, for it reminded him also of those pleasant years on the West Coast before taking up his work at Vancouver. His territory extended from Pachena Point lighthouse to Kyuquot and to reach those places and points in between, he frequently travelled on the *Maquinna*. Previous missionaries had also travelled on the *Tees*, which preceded the *Maquinna*. Thus the West Coast steamer was always looked upon as part of the mission. Her arrival at some isolated place with the missionary on board was not only looked forward to by those in need of immediate spiritual counsel, but was appropriate in a parish whose inhabitants mostly earned their livelihood from the sea.

Always prepared for rain — if it wasn't actually raining at the time — and as his means of transportation after leaving the *Maquinna* was often by gasboat or canoe, Mr. Leighton usually found it more convenient to wear his rain hat, oilskins and gumboots, than carry them. The result was when he came on board he looked more like a fisherman than a parson. Many wondered who the rugged pipe-smoking individual was who had just stepped up the gangplank, who hardly before he had time to take the pipe out his mouth, was receiving cordial greetings all round from passengers and crew. But they soon became acquainted with the gentleman when half an hour later they found a conventionally-garbed and jovial clergyman seated at their table in the dining saloon.

Upon his retirement after serving twenty years with the Missions to Seamen at Vancouver, Mr. Leighton's intentions were to live a quiet life in Victoria, where thirty years previously he had been vicar-in-charge of St. Alban's Church, but he was persuaded by the Archbishop to again take up his missionary work on the West Coast.

On settling down, Mr. Leighton observed that the population of the district had more than doubled during his absence. The airport at Long Beach was something new and there were several logging camps, whereas before there were none. The vicarage is now a house instead of a one-room shack and both it and the church have electric light instead of kerosene lamps. No longer does he have to draw water from a well, for the town has since become a village municipality and has its own water supply. The missionary is also provided with a car and there is a good road between Tofino and Ucluelet. Formerly, when the *Maquinna* wasn't handy, he had to travel between these two places part way by gasboat or canoe and the remainder of the distance on foot.

The mission was provided from funds bequeathed by a resident in Portsmouth, England, who stipulated that the church be erected on the most beautiful part of the West Coast. It accordingly stands on a commanding site overlooking the placid waters of Tofino Inlet, with Clayoquot and Opitisaht Indian village across the bay and Lone Cone and Catface Mountain in the distance. The church was built in 1912 and named St. Colomba, after one of the early British missionaries. The Reverend L. A. Todd was its first minister. Fifteen years later a second church was built at Ucluelet and named St. Aidan, one of Columba's contemporaries. Through the courtesy of the Archbishop, the facilities of both churches are made available to the United Church of Canada.

*   *   *   *

This is not the end of the story. Perusal of the previous pages shows it is but a beginning.

Tragedy there will still be, death, birth, and actions both noble and ignoble — the continuing gamut of human behaviour.

But the chronicle of this comparatively small segment of this big world — which probably could have been entitled The West Coast Story — shows in the main valiant men and women, and valiant deeds.

Many of us would do well, as they say, to "take a page from the book," perhaps a few pages.

Altogether apart from historical value, the articles are inspirational.

They are, in all likelihood, slanted at today's and tomorrow's valiant in heart.

GEORGE NICHOLSON

Marine casualties which occurred on the west coast of Vancouver Island and in adjacent waters. Area includes all of Juan de Fuca Strait west of a line drawn from Fisgard lighthouse (Esquimalt Harbour) to Ediz Hook (Port Angeles) and extends to Cape Scott.

It is not generally known, but no government agency, or for that matter any other authority, keeps a specific record of shipwrecks. Compiling the list has therefore necessitated considerable research elsewhere (see acknowledgements at end of list). In a few instances the facts were obtained from actual survivors, those who took part in salvage operations and other first-hand witnesses. Accuracy has been aimed at, but not claimed; hence names are sometimes mis-spelled, given dates open to question and omissions inevitable.

Listed alphabetically: name, type of vessel, place or vicinity and date. For further particulars see printed story.

144   *Glen Fruin*, barque; Barkley Sound, December 8, 1880
61   *Glenorchy*, ship; off Cape Cook, February 1897
122   *Gogovale*, steamer; Bentinck Island, November 2, 1929
61, 261   *Great Northern V*, fishpacker; Brooks Bay, December 1939

121   *Harold*, barque; Race Rocks, September 1918
122   *Harriet E*, fishpacker; Race Rocks, September 1, 1933
125   *Harvey Mills,* ship; off Cape Flattery, December 14, 1886
123   *Hecate*, H.M. SURVEY VESSEL; ashore Cape Flattery, August 19, 1861
179   *Henry Dennis*, schooner; Cape Scott, March 24, 1892
126   *Henry T. Scott*, schooner; in collision Juan de Fuca Strait, November 1922
91   *Hera*, schooner; Clayoquot Sound, November 1899
179   *Hermit*, barque; Cape Scott, March 1892
41   *Highland Light*, barque; Estevan Point, November 1901
124   *Hodgdon*, brig; Juan de Fuca Strait, 1855
122   *Hope*, tug; Bentinck Island, October 17, 1925

121   *Idaho*, steamer; Race Rocks, November 29, 1889
151   *Inlet Queen*, cabin cruiser; Nitinat Bar, April 9, 1912
120   *Iossifoglu*, motorship; Sheringham Point, August 25, 1928
125   *Irene*, barque; entrance Juan de Fuca Strait, December 1886
126   *Ivanhoe,* ship; off Cape Flattery, September 1894
23   *Iwanowna*, barque; Nootka Island, January 1865

122   *James Griffiths*, steamer; Race Rocks, March 3, 1931
61   *Jane Gray*, schooner; off Cape Cook, May 23, 1893
151, 165   *Janet Cowan*, barque; Pachena Point, December 31, 1895
39   *John Bright*, barque; Estevan Point, February 1869
149   *John Marshall*, ship; Bonilla Point, November 10, 1860

126   *Keweenah*, steam collier; entrance Juan de Fuca Strait, December 2, 1894
24   *Kilueve*, schooner; Nootka Island, March 1903
24   *King David*, ship; Nootka Island, December 13, 1905
74   *Kingfisher*, sloop; Matilda Inlet, Ahousat, August 1864
146   *Kodiak*, fishpacker; off Amphitrite Point, January 20, 1959

146   *Lamora*, ship; Barkley Sound, 1904
24   *Laura*, schooner; Nootka Island, January 23, 1892
151, 165   *Laura Pike*, schooner; Pachena Point, March 1891
126   *Leonore*, barque; Cape Flattery, October 4, 1893
61   *Libertad*, barque; Cape Cook, November 6, 1899
146   *Lief E*, schooner; off Cape Beale, August 1920
146   *Lillie*, schooner; Barkley Sound, November 1891
125   *Lillie Grace*, barque; off Cape Flattery, December 1886
124   *Lizzie Boggs*, barque; off Cape Flattery, September 1867
150   *Lizzie Marshall*, barque; Bonilla Point, February 21, 1884
121   *Lookout*, ship; Race Rocks, January 19, 1872
198   *Lord Raglan*, barque; off Cape Flattery, 1853
87   *Lord Weston*, barque; Flores Island, 1854
179   *Louisa Downs*, schooner; Cape Scott, March 1868
24   *Louisiana*, ship converted to barge; Nootka Sound, 1929

179   *Maggie Mac*, schooner; Cape Scott, 1892
87   *Maidie H.*, fishing vessel; off Flores Island, July 1955

343

151	*Vesta*, schooner; Nitinat, December 10, 1897
135	*Victory V* (formerly *Marine Express*) M.V., Alberni Inlet, 1938

124	*W. A. Banks*, barque; near Clallam, November 10, 1856
124	*Washington Libby*, ship; west of Port Angeles, July 23, 1879
150	*Warrimoo*, passenger steamer; Carmanah Point, August 9, 1895
125	*Webfoot*, barque; entrance Juan de Fuca Strait, November 12, 1886
150	*Wempe Bros.*, ship; Carmanah Point, October 28, 1903
122	*Western Ranger*, fishpacker; Race Rocks, September 10, 1951
122	*Western Pilot*, fishpacker; Race Rocks, October 4, 1959
124	*W. H. Meyer*, schooner; west of Port Angeles, May 24, 1872
151	*William*, brig; Pachena Point, 1854
61	*William Foster*, barque; Cape Cook, 1901
149	*William Tell*, ship; Carmanah Point, December 23, 1865
219	*Wm. G. Irwin*, brig; Long Beach, February 1887
150	*Woodrich*, sailing vessel; Clo-oose, 1880's
151, 198	*Woodside*, small steamer; Pachena Point, March 12, 1888

UNIDENTIFIED WRECKS

143	Barkley Sound: trading schooner plundered and burned by Indians about 1880
61	Cape Cook: derelict ashore, November 1899
41	Estevan Point: sailing vessel burned to water's edge drifted ashore three miles to the east; prior to 1870
250	Long Beach: schooner buried in sand, believed to have been there over 150 years ago.
151	Nitinat: iron gunboat wrecked near Tsusiat Falls before 1880
120	Sooke: sunken hull in harbour
216	Sydney Inlet: sailing vessel on bottom at Young's Bay; being investigated by R.C.N. divers

To the list could be added an undetermined number of small craft, mostly one- and two-man fishboats, lost in the same area — some with loss of life. Also, practically every steamer that plied the West Coast, in the government service or trade, for it would be hard to name one that at sometime didn't run aground on a sandbar or hit an uncharted rock, and later freed herself.

ACKNOWLEDGEMENTS IN RESEARCH OF SHIPWRECKS

British Columbia Provincial Archives.
Vancouver City Archives.
Victoria Public Library.
Washington State University Library.
United States Coast Guard.
Puget Sound Maritime Historical Society.
Lewis & Dryden's *Marine History of the Pacific Northwest* (1895)
Captain John T. Walbran's *British Columbia Coast Names* (1909)
Victoria *Daily Colonist* (files dating back to 1858).
Victoria *Daily Times*.
Vancouver *Daily Province* and Vancouver *Sun*.
Seattle *Post Intelligencer* and Seattle *Times*.
Marine Agent, Department of Transport, Victoria, B.C.
Lighthouse keepers, past and present.
Captains and crew, government steamers.
Old Timers on the West Coast.

GENERAL INDEX

*See also index of shipwrecks,
pages 339-344*

345

347

348

349

352

355